Weteriana Methodism

Bicentennial Reflections from
Aotearoa New Zealand

Edited by Peter Lineham

Philip
Garside
Publishing Ltd.

This book is issued by the Wesley Historical Society
as no. 112 of its Proceedings.

Paperback International edition 2024:
ISBN 9781991027863

Also available

New Zealand paperback: ISBN 9781991027856
Paperback print-on-demand USA: ISBN 9798339802532

PDF eBook: ISBN 9781991027870
ePub eBook: ISBN 9781991027887

Philip Garside Publishing Ltd
39 Sydenham Street, Northland,
Wellington 6012
Aotearoa New Zealand

sales@philipgarsidebooks.com
www.philipgarsidebooks.com

Cover painting:
[Artist unknown]: (Detail) Wesleyan mission station at Waingaroa,
New Zealand ; natives assembling for worship. [London]; J. Bannister, [1850s?]
Alexander Turnbull Library ref: A-015-025

Contents

Illustrations and Maps

Illustrations

Maps

Preface

Ian Faulkner

Kia whakatōmuri te haere whakamua
Moving forward into the future ever mindful of what has gone before.

This album publishes some of the papers presented at the Methodism in Aotearoa: Origins and Impact Conference held in 2019. The Methodist Church of New Zealand – Te Haahi Weteriana o Aotearoa, the Wesleyan Methodist Church of New Zealand, the Church of the Nazarene, and the Wesley Historical Society (NZ) collaborated to host an opportunity for these strands of Methodism to examine their roots in Aotearoa, to consider some aspects of what emerged, and to provide an opportunity to predict the future. This record of these presentations has been supplemented with the inclusion of Rowan Tautari's 'Maea te Kupu: Kaeo, he whenua kurahuna – emerging stories of Methodism: Kaeo, land of hidden knowledge'; and further records pertinent to the journey and interactions experienced in this land.

Any record of history has the potential to evoke parallel stories to those included in the publication. Differing memories have been expressed as some of these stories have been reviewed. A response has been: 'the story presented is not my story'. The Society hopes that this volume may bring to life some of these parallel stories. It wishes to encourage those with alternative memories to tell those memories, and allow them to be recorded, so that our mutual journey is recorded in its fullness. This recognises the mutuality and connectedness that are part of creating shared histories.

The Society wishes to express its appreciation to each of the contributors to this volume, and particularly to Emeritus Professor Peter Lineham, who has skillfully drawn together each section, providing readers with an enthralling record of the origins and impact of Methodism in Aotearoa. It creates an inspirational platform for further explorations.

Ian Faulkner
President
Wesley Historical Society (NZ) Inc.

Abbreviations

CMS	Church Missionary Society
DNZB	Dictionary of New Zealand Biography
JKL	John Kinder Theological College Library, Auckland
JRH	Journal of Religious History
MAC	Methodist Church Annual Conference Minutes. These are available at https://www.methodist.org.nz/whakapapa/archives/methodist-history/minutes-of-conference-digital-copies/
MB	Methodist Church of New Zealand Home and Māori Mission Minute Book
MCNZ	Methodist Church in Aotearoa/New Zealand
MCNZA	Methodist Church in Aotearoa New Zealand Archives (Christchurch)
Mitchell	State Library of New South Wales, Sydney.
MMS	Methodist Mission Society
Morley	Morley, William, *The History of Methodism in New Zealand*. Wellington: McKee & Co, 1900.
NLNZ	National Library of New Zealand
NZJH	New Zealand Journal of History
NZMT	New Zealand Methodist Times
Turnbull	Turnbull Library, National Library of New Zealand, Wellington.
WHS (NZ)	Wesley Historical Society New Zealand. Generally each publication has a Proceedings number.
WHS (NZ) Journal	Wesley Historical Society (New Zealand) Journal
WMS	Wesleyan Methodist Missionary Society

Introduction

Peter Lineham

How shall we commemorate the 200th anniversary of the Methodist mission to the Māori of Aotearoa? Previous commemorations, notably of the 100th anniversary in 1922, celebrated it as the beginnings of Methodism in general, although they looked carefully to its Māori beginnings. But it seems appropriate at this time, as Aotearoa New Zealand as a country reflects and debates its desire and its need to decolonise its history, that the church should reflect along the same lines. The Methodist Church today has gone further and deeper along that uncomfortable path than any other denomination. What then, would a decolonised history look like?

In exploring this question, the focus must surely primarily fall upon the Māori people who heard and reacted to the message preached to them, rather than the missionaries who brought the message. It is important to recognise their agency in the process of conversion. Those who became Methodists and who remained Methodist had various options before them. They maintained a curious coexistence with Mihingare (Anglican) converts. Sometimes the choice of faith seems random. Tāmati Wāka Nene for example, was the younger brother of Patuone, and although he was baptised by the Wesleyans, was buried according to Anglican rituals, at Russell. In the Hokianga where Methodism first took root successfully, there were sharp disputes between Wesleyans and those who embraced Catholicism when it arrived. What accounts for the choices they made? Moreover, particularly in the Hokianga but also down the coast, the decision to be a Wesleyan was challenged at various moments by those who embraced the various independent religious movements, including Mormonism, Te Huihuinga, Rātana and Maramatanga. We need to understand each of these options and look at them as deliberate choices, and understand the priorities of those who chose to join and to remain as Methodist.

The greatest significance of this story lies in the new world created by Māori converts and preachers in their own right. To fully explore this story, we need to be cautious of focusing just on the early stages of the story. There was inevitably excitement and conversions in the initial uptake of Christianity. It is time to follow new paths, to explore the longer-term ways in which Methodist faith and the Methodist community interacted with its culture. Papers in this book will enable the reader to do this, although more work remains to be done.

There is also a story about the missionaries. This is better known, although even here, we should note how much better known the story of the CMS missionaries is from that of their Wesleyan counterparts. We should not regard the Wesleyan Mission as simply an alternative route to that of the CMS mission. The supporters and the nature of their support, and the agency of the Wesleyan Mission functioned in quite a different way than that of the CMS. Two papers in this collection do explore aspects of this story, each breaking new historical ground.

The Mission was very much a reflection of the British Methodist vision. Initially there had been some common ground with the early lay missionaries of the CMS, and the recruitment of the London Missionary Society, which was not just Calvinist. But by 1815 Methodism wanted to distinguish itself from both Calvinist non-conformists. The Wesleyan Missionary Society established itself initially in the Pacific where the LMS had struggled, while the links between Marsden and Leigh reminds us that it had a more positive link with the CMS.

The 200th anniversary of the Wesleyan Methodist mission has profoundly stirred Methodists, and was celebrated at a significant conference in the Bay of Islands, but it seems to have passed New Zealand by. No doubt a key reason for this is that the idea of a missionary call is deeply out of fashion in the present age. So indeed is Christianity itself, which is evidently out of tune with the present rediscovery of Aotearoa's indigenous roots. It is useful to reflect on why this is the case, and how the operations of the Wesleyan mission operated within the Māori community, and to compare it with its Anglican and Catholic counterparts. One must recall that after 1854 the Australasian Mission lost its support from the English Methodist church, and so it had to find its own way to sustain itself. That meant a significant decline in recruitment of missionaries, compared to the CMS, although it was in a similar situation to the Catholic Mission.

The accusation of being part of the colonial enterprise can only very loosely be applied to the Methodist mission. They were not part of the established church, and made no pretence to this status. On the other hand, Methodism quickly adapted to the needs of settlers, partly because the missionaries were encouraged to serve the needs of the settlers, and receive support for their roles.

The Methodist mission was a smaller enterprise than the Anglican Mission. As we can see from the appendix with its list of missionaries, prepared by Gary Clover, and developed from the thesis by John Owens, there were seventeen missionary couples from the United Kingdom who were employed in the New Zealand 'field' in that period. In comparison, the CMS had thirty couples in the field in the period to 1840 plus many additional ancillary workers, and significantly those numbers were augmented until 1878 whereas the British Wesleyan mission ceased in 1856.

Relations with the Anglican mission had various ups and downs. The informal Comity Agreement assigned to the Wesleyans a mission that took them down the west coast of the North Island as far south as South Taranaki, while the CMS extended around the island's east coast and as far as Whanganui. There were overlaps and competition in the Manukau and in South Taranaki, but for the most part, they developed in quite separate ways.

The historiography of the mission is much less extensive than the CMS. The Church Missionary Society included in its number well trained and eloquent missionaries like William Williams, whose Christianity among the New Zealanders sits alongside the writings by Yate, Maunsell, Richard Taylor, and their missions were analysed not just in the histories of the Anglican Church but also in theses and studies, notably Bob Glen's edited collection, and most recently Michael Corboys' *Between God and a Hard Place* (2022). There are also magnificent studies of the CMS in which Andrew Porter and Brian Stanley have focused their research. It is noteworthy that because of their links with the British establishment, they were entangled with the Crown, sometimes to their advantage, sometimes not. Recent general studies of the missions to New Zealand have tended to assume the same focus, including Yates and Newman.

The biographies of the Methodist missionaries fit well within the genre of missionary biography. Methodists enjoyed reading the lives of missionaries, and Strachan's 1853 account of Samuel Leigh, somewhat romanticised, was well known (although A.E. Keeling wrote an even more hagiographical account in 1896). Others included Alfred Barrett on John Bumby, and Nathaniel Turner by his son (also a Wesleyan minister) Nathaniel Turner. James Buller lived long enough to write a very extensive account of the missions in 1878. For obvious reasons there was no pious account of the expelled missionary, William White.

The sumptuous history of the Methodist Church in New Zealand published by its General Secretary William Morley in 1900 did include quite a detailed account of the mission, as did a number of Methodist histories, including James Pinfold's 1930 book, and W.J. Williams *Centenary Sketches of New Zealand Methodism* in 1922.

Standing apart from these is the fine little book on Taranaki Methodism published by T.G. Hammond in 1915 (first serialised in the *Hawera Star*) and reprinted in 1940. Hammond was a minister in the church appointed in 1874, and sent to the Māori mission in 1878 because of his facility in Te Reo. From 1915-to his retirement in 1920 he was Superintendent of the Māori missions, and in his retirement he wrote a well-regarded account of the Taranaki tribes.

It was a later General Secretary of the Church, M.A. Rugby Pratt, who did the closest historical work on the missionary origins of the church, most notably his work, *The pioneering days of southern Maoriland* (1932), based on the journals of Rev. James Watkin, which led to his election as a fellow of the Royal Historical Society of London. The Wesley Historical Society (New Zealand Branch) published most of these booklets. He also co-operated with G.H. Scholefield in the 1940 *Dictionary of New Zealand Biography*, and he ardently advocated recognition of the Treaty of Waitangi.

Rev. C.H. Laws, principal of the Trinity College until 1931, was the first president of the Wesley Historical Society from 1930 to 1942. In 1944 and 1945 Laws published accounts of the mission at Whangaroa (1944) and at Hokianga (1945). He intended to write a third brochure on the extension of the mission to Waikato and Taranaki, but this work was never published. In 1940 T.A. Pybus wrote a history of the Wesleyan mission to the Māori of Ōtākou, and in 1942 A.B. Chappell wrote an account of John Skevington's mission work in South Taranaki, and in 1948 Bryan Smith wrote a thesis on Methodist missions in the Waikato. Other theses followed, including Eva Blight on Buller's missionary work, Wesley Chambers using the lens of social psychology and culture contact theory. George Laurenson, superintendent of the Home Mission Department from 1935 and of the Māori Mission Department from 1939 to 1964, wrote extensively on Wesleyan Māori missions, beginning with the little booklet *Methodist-Maori missions yesterday and today* and culminating with his book, *Te Hahi Weteriana. Three Half Centuries of the Methodist Maori Mission 1822-1972*, as part of the 150th sesquicentennial publications of the church. While this is not a work of profound insight, it is enormously helpful for its long perspective. The revolution in the historiography of missions awaited new authors.

The WHS continued to publish studies of Methodist missions in the intervening years, including a study of the Pehiakura mission on the south of the Manukau Harbour written by Clarence Luxton while he was minister at Waiuku. Luxton indeed devoted himself to historical research into both the Solomons mission work of the church, in which he had previously served, and local history.

A profound moment in the research into the Mission came when John Owens chose the topic of the Wesleyan Mission to New Zealand prior to 1840 for his doctoral study. This rich thesis was followed up with a publication covering only the years in which the mission was based at Kaeo before it was driven out in 1827. *Prophets in the Wilderness*, an evocative title, was published by Auckland University Press in 1974. Even before this, Owens had spelt out his interpretation in a lecture given to the 1972 Methodist Conference in Whangarei. Here Owens drew on the themes of his research, analysing the ways in which Māori responded to Methodism, and looking wisely at the missionary options in relation to social change, noting that there was no easy policy to avoid disruption. He explores the notion of the extent of missionary disruption, but noted that the exchange was always two sided. The published booklet is modest in scale but profound in its insight. It was one of several significant contributions Owens made, in which "unexpected impact" was a critical theme.

Gary Clover, the Methodist scholar who has done a significant proportion of the recent work on the Wesleyan missionaries has frequently stated the debt he feels to John Owens' work. It is curious that few other scholars returned to this topic. Wes Chambers was also very active in scholarship, who wrote a substantial work on Samuel Ironside, the pioneer of the Cloudy Bay Mission who like most of the missionaries transitioned into the European church, quite unlike the CMS missionaries.

In 1937, at the suggestion it would seem of Rugby Pratt, the New Zealand church negotiated with the Methodist Missionary Society in London originally hoping to acquire, but then to borrow the originals of the missionaries' correspondence with the home base, and so in 1937 the collection arrived in New Zealand. The originals were retained in New Zealand for the duration of the war, and then returned.[1] Typing these documents proved to be a huge task – there were 1330 records included, and one letter was 80 pages long. Alas, no correspondence from Samuel Leigh remained in the collection. Copies were provided to the Alexander Turnbull Library and the Kinder Library at St John's College. Given the recent work by the University of Otago to transcribe and upload the originals of Marsden's correspondence, a similar project would be possible for the Wesleyan letters, using these transcriptions, especially as the Mitchell Library in Sydney has now placed online the originals. This would do much to make the tools of primary sources available to new scholars. One hope is that very soon they will be made available in this way.

The other voice that becomes significant in Methodist missions is the voice of Māori Methodists. They had played a distinctive role – quite different from Anglican Māori – since the decision was made to retain links with those who moved into Ratana. For many years, the director of Home and Māori missions was held by George Laurenson, who was deeply aware of the Māori Methodist community. Then in 1971 Rua Rakena (Ngāi Tahu and Ngāpuhi) was appointed Associate Superintendent of the Home and Māori Mission. His acute and perceptive if modest book *The Māori Response to the Gospel*, published in 1971 showed a profound perception of the concerns of Māori at the colonial interpretation of Methodism. Interestingly, Owens was aware of Rakena's concerns. In subsequent years, these issues have become stronger within Māori Methodism. The research of Rowan Tautari and Te Aroha Rountree are significant examples of this work, with their sensitivity to iwi, land, and colonial mentalities. Although the Methodist Church has arguably been the most willing to seek ways to address the sense of historical loss, there is still a severe problem. Rakena's writings were in every way farsighted. He wrote: 'Very little in our Māori Mission may pass as an authentic "Māori" response to the Gospel. ... The Mission was paternalistic, the Māori was dependent. .. Hence the Māori membership has for the most part felt incapable of responding on its own account.'[2] Drawing on significant mission studies in New Zealand and world-wide, he raised acute questions, and spoke of "Māori and Pākehā in the Methodist Church Tomorrow", with a radically different approach to gathering, sharing and self-identity.

It is these issues that much contemporary Māori Methodist writers have raised acutely. Rowan Tautari's contribution to the bi-centennial conference was framed around contexts that have not been characteristic of most religious history – the sense of hapu and iwi identity and the issue of land which was provided to the mission on the assumption that it would be used to serve the hapu. This is a rather uncomfortable focus, but is the aspects of the "exchange" which Māori see as expressive of the intentions of the mission. We are delighted this study was with permission made available for this publication. There have been other recent Māori Methodist scholars, among them Arapera Ngaha, Tumuaki for Te taha Māori, a former senior lecturer at the University of Auckland, who served as Vice President of the Church in 2014, and has in a joint publication with Barry Jones, challenged presbyters and lay people to engage with Māori people on Māori terms. She has written extensively on language revitalisation.[3] Te Aroha Rountree, senior lecturer in Moana Studies at Trinity Methodist Theological College has eloquently called for the decolonisation of the history of Aotearoa, and we may look forward to her projected research on Māori interaction with Christianity in Hokianga and the Bay of islands.

It is curious in the light of the meticulous research which has been done on the CMS context in Britain, that much less work has been done until now on analysis of the Wesleyan background among British Methodists. Roshan Allpress has done a great deal to correct this in his chapter in this collection. The financial support of the Methodists was significant. As Allpress indicates, little separated the CMS and WMS missionaries in terms of their financial resources. But he does note that they primarily drew on different networks and received contributions from a much broader base. Allpress also notes the denominationalisation and growing loss of unity of evangelicals in the 1820s, along the lines long ago argued by W.R. Ward.[4] In some ways the WMS continued to remain dependent on Marsden's patronage, since their links were not so extensive. Thus, Leigh's story shows the challenge of the changing world of evangelicalism for the Methodist mission.

Glen O'Brien's paper on Samuel Leigh (complementing the paper he wrote in 2012[5]) explores a man whom he describes as a pioneer but not a builder of Methodism in Australia and New Zealand. In Australia he was seen as a friend of the established church, and his relationship with Marsden proved very useful in New Zealand as well. O'Brien also notes among the later Wesleyan missionaries a very negative approach to Māori traditions, and this he sees as an explanation for their emphasis on civilization. Māori were heathen, and they needed to be freed from a culture which was destructive for them. O'Brien is charitable in his judgement, but Leigh is certainly assessed very differently from in the adulatory early biography.[6]

A constant motif in past research has been the bravery of the English missionaries. Yet until recently very little has been written on the vision and the work and the courage of the first converts. At last they are becoming the focus of extensive research and reflection in all current missions history. One might particularly mention Malcolm Falloon's research on a group of early Anglican converts.[7] A particular focus is increasingly placed on indigenous catechists and colporteurs who were often the pioneer preachers, preceding the missionaries in most instances. Gary Clover's paper on indigenous evangelism is therefore particularly welcome in this collection. It follows the lines of Raeburn Lange's very helpful and trailblazing studies.[8] Clover includes a broader range of participants, noting in particular the role of Rangatira who served as sponsors, domestics and companions of the missionaries. Even before their baptism they are associating closely with missionaries and preparing the way for people to pay attention to their message. Rather than provide a list, Clover notes converts, especially rangatira, and war captives who were enslaved. Some of these including Aperahama Tāonui were later to develop an independent ministry along the lines of traditional tōhunga. Simon Peter Mātanga and Wiremu Nēra were among the most prominent, sometimes such people were appointed assistant missionaries. There were martyrs in this group as well. It feels more difficult to show lists of Wesleyan native assistants, and perhaps this was because they were not required to be recognised by the London office, as were the CMS catechists.

Clover's chronological record of Wesleyan Missionaries of the Hokianga, 1823-1840 briefly lists the English missionaries involved. He also provides in an appendix an invaluable list of Wesleyan Mission stations between 1819 and 1860, which should enable a closer tracing of the missionary impact. It introduces to researchers a range of forgotten European missionary agents, including Rev. Dartnell (a Congregationalist who died the year he arrived in 1835) and a few native agents including Hoani Riu, left in charge of the Orua station. Frederick Miller was a lay catechist, James Hosking a home missionary, George Stannard a lay assistant.

Susan Thompson's study enables us to understand the inner life of the wives of the male missionaries. She surveys the historiography of the wives, such as it is, noting the problem that none except for Eliza White and Mary Anna Bumby left a journal that has survived. Thompson also has explored the correspondence of the missionary women, and from these letters suggests a story of courage and conviction enabled these women to play a major role in sustaining the mission. The gendering of the missionary movement has been a significant trend, in which Cathy Ross's study of a group of CMS missionaries who were wives, mothers and teachers.[9] There are perhaps some differences between the social background of some at least of those featured by Cathy Ross, and those in the scope of Susan Thompson.

A further paper looks at the second generation of the Wesleyan Mission, in the period after 1840. Geoff Troughton has in recent work explored attitudes to war and peace among the churches of New Zealand, and especially those that ministered to the Māori.[10] He sees the era as calamitous for the Wesleyan Māori mission. Troughton refers to James Watkin wanting to be moved to another mission field, and identifies growing tensions with Catholic and CMS missionaries, and the abandonment of an earlier emphasis on peace, for a policy of opposition to the Land Leagues and their hostility to further land sales. The surprising policy adopted by the Wesleyans of siding with the settler government and against their Māori converts at the very time when CMS missionaries were resistant to the policy, is one of the strange paradoxes in Methodist history in Aotearoa. The need for support from the settler church made them so. It was the Wesleyan misfortune, as Troughton notes, to be based in Cloudy Bay and along the west coast of the North Island, where there were so many confrontations in Taranaki and Waikato.

In subsequent years in the nineteenth century William Gittos led work in Northland and T.G. Hammond in Taranaki, but both were very aware that many Māori felt ambivalent about their work.[11] Essentially after the withdrawal of Cort Henry and Annie Schnackenberg from Kawhia in 1864, there was no foreign missionary present in the Waikato and King Country mission stations. On the other hand, the intention was that a group of ordained Māori might lead missionary activity. In the late nineteenth century these included Wiremu Patene (1810-1884), Hoani Waiti Hikitanga (1820-1879) of Ngati Whatua, and his son, Matena Ruta Waiti (1860-1887) and his brother Karawini Waiti (1851-1878) based in the Kaipara, Hamiora Ngaropi (1809-1887), Honi Eketone (1828-1862) based at Kawhia, Hori Te Kuri or Kure (1828-1891) who was based at Taheke in the Hokianga, Heteraka Warihi (1826-1898) based firstly in the Chatham Islands and latterly in the Wairau Valley of Marlborough, Wiremu Te Kote Te Rato (1820-1895) who worked primarily in the South Island, Hauraki Paul (1861-1910) and Piripi Rakena (1858-1934) of Hokianga. Wiremu Warena Pewa (1852-1907) based in Kaeo and then in the Waikato at Te Kopua. In a paper which I specifically wrote to complement the other papers, I seek to establish to my own satisfaction what remained of these missions, and how Methodism fared among the Māori of the former mission areas during the years prior to the great waves of immigration which reshaped the demography of Māori. But, as I argue, there is much iwi-based research which is needed to understand the ways in which Māori Methodism developed its own forms and values.

Māori religiosity in the early twentieth century was reshaped by the ministry of T.W. Ratana. The scholarship of Garth Cant has enhanced our understanding of the distinctive way in which Methodism sought to accommodate this movement. We may notice the distinctive response which Methodism took to Ratana, compared to the Anglican response to Ratana (defined, we may note, by three Pākehā bishops).[12]

Thus these papers shape a story which is both inspiring and disheartening. Perhaps we should note how this legacy has shaped the Wesleyan mission today. Yet to fully tell the story we would need to look carefully at the Twentieth Century Home and Māori Mission Department of Methodism. We would need to understand why it was that Anglicanism took such a dim view of Ratana, and Methodism a more positive one.[13] We would look at the way in which A.J. Seamer extended and cultivated the Māori mission.[14] We might explore the way in which the Waiata choir raised money for that mission.[15] We would look carefully at the Māori missioners who during the twentieth century ministered to out of the way places.

I found it very interesting that in the First and Second World Wars the Methodist Church protested vigorously when all the Māori chaplains appointed to the army were from the Anglican church. Edward Te Tuhi for example, was passed over despite a nomination by the President of the church and an endorsement by William Gittos, 'who is regarded in our church as a kind of Father of the Māori'.[16] Similarly in the Second World War, the 28th Māori Battalion was protected from Methodist chaplains, even though Maharaia Winiata was eager for an appointment.[17] The letterhead from the Māori Section of the Methodist Church included on a side panel the names of Te Tuhi as senior superintendent, and 40 ordained Māori clergy along with 13 deaconesses and two assistants.[18] So the scale of the Methodist work among Maori remained significant, even though it had none of the influence that the Anglican denomination could bring. The locations of these missioners were mostly along the West Coast of the North Island or inland from it. The deaconesses were women of great courage and determination.[19]

Still, it is striking to me that in looking at Methodist statistics, Waitomo and Ōtorohanga and the South Taranaki remain places where Methodism is at its strongest in the 2013 census and in tiny Taharoa, just under 20% of the people in this Māori village describe themselves as Methodist. A preaching station was established here in 1934, and supply preachers were sent to it for many years, until in 1957 Taipua Te Uira was recognised as an honorary home missionary here, and on his death his son Piripi Te Uira held the role until his death in 2000. Although there were no more Methodist services after this, it remained the most Methodist place in New Zealand.[20]

There is a great deal more potential for research, exploring the inner dynamic of the Wesleyan Mission in the setting of the recipient hapu and iwi, and the contributions that Wesleyan Māori have made to the wider life of Māori and the whole community of Aotearoa. We hope that readers will not regard this as the last word, but a stimulus for fresh thinking and writing.

Notes

1 MAC, 1937, 163; MAC, 1938, 156-57; MAC, 1939, 151; MAC, 1940, 170.

2 R. Rakena, *The Māori Response to the Gospel: A Study of Maori-Pakeha Relations in the Methodist Maori Mission from Its Beginnings to the Present Day.* WHS (NZ) Proceedings, 25, nos. 1-4, 5, 1971, 5.

3 See Barry Jones, and Arapera Ngaha. 'All Things New: The Bicultural Journey of the Methodist Church of New Zealand - Te Hahi Weteriana O Aotearoa.' Chap. 5 In *Listening to the People of the Land: Christianity, Colonisation & the Path to Redemption*, edited by J. F. Healy, 113-38. Auckland: Pax Christi, 2019.

4 W.R. Ward, *Religion and Society in England, 1790-1850*, London: B.T. Batsford, 1972.

5 Glen O'Brien, "'Not Radically a Dissenter': Samuel Leigh in the Colony of New South Wales." *Wesley and Methodist Studies*, 4 (2012): 51-70.

6 Alexander Strachan, *Remarkable Incidents in the Life of the Rev. Samuel Leigh, Missionary to the Settlers and Savages of Australia and New Zealand: With a Succinct History of the Origin and Progress of the Missions in Those Colonies.* London: Hamilton, Adams, 1853.

7 Malcolm Falloon, "The Maori Conversion and Four Early Converts." Ph.D. thesis, University of Otago, 2020.

8 Raeburn Lange, "Indigenous Agents of Religious Change in New Zealand, 1830-1860." *JRH*, 24, no. 3 (October 2000): 277-95; Raeburn Lange, "Ordained Ministry in Maori Christianity, 1853-1900." *JRH*, 27, no. 1 (2003): 47-66.

9 Cathy Ross, *Women with a Mission: Rediscovering Missionary Wives in Early New Zealand.* Auckland: Penguin, 2006.

10 Geoffrey Troughton, "Missionaries, Historians and the Peace Tradition in New Zealand." Chap. 12 In *Te Rongopai 1814 'Takoto Te Pai!': Bicentenary Reflections on Christian Beginnings and Developments in Aotearoa New Zealand*, edited by Allan Davidson, Stuart Lange, Peter Lineham and Adrienne Puckey, Auckland: General Synod office of Anglican Church in Aotearoa New Zealand, 2014, 228-245.

11 See T. G. Hammond, *In the Beginning: The History of a Mission*. 2 ed. Auckland: Methodist Literature & Colporteur Society, 1940. Original edition, Hawera: W.A. Parkinson, 1915.

12 See Garth Cant, *The Methodist Response to the Formation of the Ratana Church in 1924-1925*. WHS (NZ) Proceedings, 104, 2018; Garth Cant, "The Methodist and Ratana Connection." *WHS (NZ) Journal*, 100 (2015): 31-42.

13 See Cant, "The Methodist and Ratana Connection." 31-42. Also Cant, *The Methodist Response*. For an older study see H. L. J. Halliday, "The Reverend A.J. Seamer and the Attitudes of the Methodists to the Ratana Movement." Research Essay, University of Auckland, 1966.

14 See Georgia Rae Cervin, "Te Hiima: Reverend A. J. Seamer and His Māori Mission." B.A. Honours, University of Otago, 2011.

15 See Michelle Willyams, "Singing Faith: A History of the Waiata Maori Choir, 1924-1938." MA thesis in History, University of Otago, 2012 and her article, Michelle Walker, "The Methodist Home Mission Party, on Stage in New Zealand, 1924–1934." *Journal of New Zealand Studies*, no. 15 (2013): 77-89.

16 John Dawson, Methodist Church (Wellington) to Hon John Allan 21/7/1915, in Military Chaplains File, New Zealand Army, Archives New Zealand, R22434378.

17 Rev. Maharaia Winiata to Minister of Defence Wellington 9/9/1942 in Military Chaplaincy files, Archives New Zealand R22438911.

18 M. Winiata, Methodist Church of New Zealand Maori Section, Kawhia to Minister of Defence, 14/10/1941 in Military Chaplaincy Files, Archives New Zealand R22438911.

19 See for example D. M. Pointon, *Memoirs of D. M. Pointon (Sister Dorothy) Including Her Work among the Maori People 1939-1953*. Auckland: The author, 1993; Margaret Tennant, "'Sometimes When My Heart Was Sad with Snubs and Coldness ...' Narrative of Maori Mission Work." *History Now: Te Pae Tawhito o te Wa* 7, no. 3 (August 2001): 14-18; Margaret Tennant, "Pakeha Deaconesses and the New Zealand Methodist Mission to Maori, 1893-1940." *JRH*, 23, no. 3 (October 1999): 309-26.

20 I addressed this issue in a paper I gave to the District Synod of Methodism in May 2015.

Section One – The Wesleyan Mission

1 – 'Separating from our best earthly friends':[1] The British and global contexts of Samuel Leigh and the Wesleyan mission to New Zealand

Roshan Allpress

Introduction

In order to understand the origins of the early Wesleyan mission in New Zealand, it is helpful to consider it within three contemporary British and global 'frames'. First among these was an intergenerational evangelical and mercantile 'nexus' in England – a changing set of social connections and institutions that emerged in the mid-eighteenth century and channelled the forces of religious renewal into a wide variety of reforming and conversionary projects, and through which individuals like Samuel Leigh forged careers as missionaries and philanthropists. In arriving and living in Australasia, he and the other Wesleyan missionaries participated in a second frame – that of the transnational networks of the 'British world' that linked its constituent regional systems, including the emerging 'Tasman world' and the wider South Pacific.[2] A third key frame for understanding the mission is the cultural imagination of the evangelical movement in which the 'Methodist self' was formed and embedded within shared narratives.[3] This common imagination, which shaped the tropes and motivations of missionary endeavour, also served to make missionary accounts comprehensible to the supportive British public, and fed back into the wider projects of the evangelical nexus. The purpose of this paper is to show the explanatory power of these wider frames for Leigh's career and the early Wesleyan Missionary Society (WMS), but also to highlight their particularities against a wider backdrop. To do this we are stepping back from the more common historiographical narratives of theological differentiation, missionary means and consequences, to a prior question: how did it become possible for networks of British evangelicals to imagine and inaugurate a Wesleyan mission in New Zealand from May 1819?

The Philanthropists

The roots of the Wesleyan mission's organisational structures lie in the confluence of clerical and mercantile evangelical networks in London's associational culture during the 1750s and 1760s.[4] Two decades on from the Holy Club of the 1730s, 'heart religion' was taking root amidst merchant networks in the City, and these merchants began collaborating, along with those 'serious' clergy who held livings and curacies in greater London, in a small number of philanthropic societies and projects. Their motivation was to use their means to work out the implications of the Gospel in practical love of humanity – becoming known as 'philanthropists'. This collaboration drew together what had hitherto been largely distinct

Establishment and mercantile models of associational organisation – uniting the institution-building tendencies of religious charity[5] with the entrepreneurial energies of merchant committees.[6] The spread of this new model of organisation – with its distinctive volunteer committee culture and active management of society agents borrowed from the practices of joint-stock companies – was critical for the development of later evangelical activism. It allowed persistent missional focus and experimentation as to methods – making possible the development of new modes of Christian philanthropy and mission. Coordinating the committees of these new model associations was a small nexus of philanthropists – largely comprising Russia Company merchants and merchant bankers who were Evangelical converts or supporters, or members of dissenting communities. These sat on multiple boards, were highly connected, and functioned as a kind of social hub for the transfer of new ideas and practices between organisations. Managing shipping routes, correspondence networks and credit relationships, particularly across northern Europe and the Atlantic, this nexus of evangelical philanthropists became an important conduit in the spread of religious literature, and in the movement and support of individual missionaries.

An example of how this nexus served to promote Anglophone missionary initiatives was that of the *English Trustees of the Indian Charity School*.[7] Founded in 1754 by Eleazar Wheelock in Connecticut to educate indigenous North American missionaries, the School's supporting English Trust was established in 1767 by John Thornton – an Evangelical Russia Company merchant living in the village of Clapham, who was an integral member of the evangelical nexus in London and a longstanding patron and financial supporter of John Wesley and other Methodist preachers.[8] In forming the committee, Thornton gathered nine Trustees – six of whom were partners in banking concerns, the remaining three being pious merchants. Among them were Lord Dartmouth, a friend of John Wesley; Samuel Roffey, with strong dissenting family connections; and Robert Keen, a supporter of the Countess of Huntingdon. These men leveraged their personal and professional networks to facilitate the raising of funds to support the missionary School, setting up innovative remittance flows through nascent credit networks involving twelve selected banks, that anticipated the auxiliary societies of the nineteenth century. While the relationship with Wheelock broke down and the School itself failed as an ongoing missionary endeavour, the experience continued to shape subsequent evangelical projects. The banking partners that had collaborated in fundraising continued to collaborate – appearing in subscription and committee lists together as backers and facilitators of a wide variety of evangelical projects into the 1790s, continuing the earlier nexus of evangelical philanthropists. Thornton and other trustees continued as patrons and financial supporters of individual missionaries on the North American frontier, and the story of the attempt and the structural innovations in philanthropic and missionary fundraising can be seen in diaries and letters informing subsequent generations of evangelicals.

Benefits to the Wesleyans

One consequence more directly related to Samuel Leigh and the WMS, of this new collaboration between evangelical bankers was the support provided to David Bogue's Academy in Gosport by George Welch of *Welch, Rogers and Co*, one of the banks involved in the Indian Charity School fundraising, in collaboration with John Thornton.[9] Samuel Leigh spent two years at this Congregationalist school at Gosport before applying as a Wesleyan missionary. Welch and Thornton appear to have taken a joint interest following their initial collaboration in furthering the training and careers of a number of evangelical ministers during the 1770s and 1780s, including co-funding other dissenting academies and tutors.[10] Walter Lawry too benefited indirectly from this developing pattern of financial support, during his studies at an informal academy in Cornwall.[11] These patterns of ministerial patronage and the creation of new career pathways for young evangelicals were essential in a climate during the last decades of the eighteenth century where any young 'notorious Methodist'[12] was unlikely to be able to gain a living in the Church of England, and in which opportunities for irregular and itinerant ministry were increasingly curtailed.[13] Richard Johnson and Samuel Marsden, Church of England chaplains in New South Wales, were both beneficiaries of this patronage. Marsden in particular owed every step of his journey – from relative poverty on the outskirts of Leeds, to discovery by Miles Atkinson of the Elland Society, study under Joseph Milner at Hull Grammar School, admission and financial support at Magdalene College, Cambridge, selection as chaplain to Botany Bay, and subsequent financial and political protection – to direct patronage by the Thornton family and their associates.[14] Remarkably then, nearly all the primary local protagonists behind the Wesleyan mission to New Zealand had benefited directly or at one step removed from a small group of patrons who participated in the evangelical nexus in the 1770s and 1780s.

New Models of Mission

The late 1780s and 1790s, as Britain's imperial situation stabilised following the end of the American war, was a period of significant experimentation in which the philanthropic organisational model developed by merchant evangelicals was turned with intensity to the task of conversionary missions. Thomas Coke's *Plan of the Society for the Establishment of Missions among the Heathens* (1784) framed a simple call to action and proposed a society organised along simple lines, unsurprisingly akin to the pattern of Wesley's societies – the entire proposal amounting to less than two printed pages.[15] David Brown and Charles Grant's *A Proposal for Establishing a Protestant Mission in Bengal and Behar* (1787) leveraged their connections to the evangelical nexus in London in presenting a much longer case and plan that adopted the fuller organisational structure now common across philanthropic societies, and while unsuccessful in gaining political support for its primary aim, put in place what Henry Morris has called the relational and institutional "bed-rock" on which later mission societies were built.[16] The next significant project was the Sierra Leone Company (SLC), which formed as merchants within the evangelical nexus sought to turn their professional expertise to additional Gospel ends – combining abolitionist, poor relief and missionary aims in a commercial colony in 1792. The SLC adapted mercantile administrative systems to the management of this project, requiring detailed accounts and journals to be returned, and sustaining an active correspondence between the central committee and their agents on the ground. Inspired by the Bengal *Proposal* and by William Carey's *Enquiry*, the Baptist Missionary Society was formed in the same year, and the interdenominational London Missionary Society (LMS) in 1795.

Notably however, these two societies lacked significant commercial expertise on their committees, and while they had success in the raising of funds in England and in recruiting and commissioning missionaries, they struggled significantly with the complexities of adequately supporting their missionaries in the field. In India, for example, Carey was able to gain employment in indigo plantations and later the College of Fort William to sustain the mission, while in Otaheite, the LMS mission suffered sequential disasters, partly due to the vulnerability and inadequacy of their supporting infrastructure. More apposite to the development of missions best practice was the formation in 1799 of the Church Missionary Society (CMS) – led by a committee that included a significant number of merchants, including proprietors and directors of the SLC. The CMS adopted the organisational structure that had been developed and passed down intergenerationally through the nexus of evangelical merchant directors. Using its relationships with Britain's colonial governance, banking and shipping sectors, and the lessons learned from the successive failures of Sierra Leone, the CMS began developing an infrastructure for the support of small permanent settlements of missionaries. By the 1810s, a nationwide network of CMS auxiliary and branch societies provided relatively stable finances, built directly off the country banking networks of its directors that had developed from the twelve banks that had come together in support of the Indian Charity School. In addition, the patronage networks of evangelical merchants provided a steady stream of well-trained candidates, and the desk-based system of correspondence provided a model for managing the logistical and administrative challenges of mission settlements.

The Formation of the WMS

It was in this context that the WMS was formally instituted. Its constitution echoed John Wesley's call to mission and referenced Thomas Coke's *Plan*,[17] but the structure that it adopted between its beginnings in 1813 and approval by the Methodist Conference in 1818 directly mirrored that of the CMS,[18] adapted to align auxiliary and branch societies to the existing circuits and districts. The Committee of the Society included key individuals who were immersed in the wider evangelical philanthropic nexus, and who reflected a wide variety of ministry, commercial and other professional vocations. Thomas Thompson, the Treasurer, had started his professional life as a clerk in the Wilberforce family partnership in Hull, later serving in the bank of Wilberforce, Smith and Co, and by 1787 had become a full partner, retaining links to the families of the Clapham Sect until his death in 1828. Christopher Sundius, a Swedish migrant to England rose to prominence in the British Navy and was appointed to the Admiralty in 1800 through the patronage of Anglican Evangelical 'blue lights'.[19] In addition to his leadership in Methodist circles, Sundius had been involved on wider evangelical committees – serving on the LMS, the British and Foreign Bible Society and the Religious Tract Society.[20] However, reflecting both the denominational specificity of the new society and a shift in the sociability of the evangelical nexus, there is a noticeable lack of contemporaneous connectedness of the WMS committee members. That is, in contrast to the high overlaps in society boards even a decade earlier, very few of them were simultaneously active on the boards of other societies.

Structural parallels aside, there were notable differences in the funding composition of the WMS. Reflecting Methodism's humbler social base, of the £18 434 income reported by the WMS in its first *Annual Report* (1818), the vast majority came from "Sums under 20s" or "Public collections", with only £736 – less than four percent – deriving from individual donations of more than five pounds. The CMS had actively worked with established country banking networks and local civic and ecclesiastical leadership to build its auxiliary structures, whereas the WMS leveraged a combination of District and Circuit structures, the richly diverse world of religious associations, and informal personal networks. Those key figures who did anchor giving with large donations did so primarily in their personal capacities – institutional donations were light. In Stockport near Manchester, the two largest singular donations were from members of the Heald and Philips families of bankers, and in Yorkshire, Thomas Thompson was by far the largest single donor in the Hull Circuit, contributing fifteen guineas. Anglican Evangelical names and other religious celebrities appear strategically in the list of donors, with over £100 given by members of the Clapham Sect, including William Wilberforce and Zachary Macaulay. This grassroots fundraising, encouraged by influential donors, was effective in rapidly building an income base – in 1818 nearly three-quarters of the income of the CMS, which had more than a decade head start. In contrast to the wider financial pressures faced by the Wesleyan Conference in this period,[21] the success of fundraising for missions highlighted the continued associational vitality and evangelical fervour in the movement.

The WMS and the Wesleyan Church

As the Wesleyan movement reorganised, as W.R. Ward succinctly noted, from "a Society" into "a Church", the WMS became an increasingly integrated arm of the denomination. This was accompanied by a wider inflection point in evangelical societies between the mid-1810s and late 1820s whereby the singular nexus of philanthropic and evangelical societies that had begun to form during the 1750s was fragmenting – caused by the explosive growth of societies and a generational change among the directorship. The loss of social connection between elites fed into the much-debated loss of interdenominational unity and trust amongst evangelicals during the 1830s, leading to increasing competitiveness between missionary societies in London circles. Leigh and the New Zealand mission should be regarded as somewhat liminal in this process of fragmentation – in part because their formation and education had occurred in an earlier period, and in part because their geographical isolation provided some insulation from the cultural and social shifts occurring in Britain. They operated under administrative oversight that more closely paralleled that exercised by the CMS than other missionary projects – a degree of detailed accountability that would come to chafe as the mission progressed. However, it is critical in reading the progress of the mission to recognise that at the London end at least, channels for interdenominational and inter-organisational cooperation had become more formal and narrow. Collaboration between, for example, Jabez Bunting, Secretary of the WMS, and Dandeson Coates, Secretary of the CMS, in opposing New Zealand settlement in the late 1830s, was warm but formal. The WMS could lobby politicians against the New Zealand Company, but relied on the social circles of the CMS for key information on political realities.[22] In contrast, the reality that the Wesleyans' friends and allies in the Australasian region (such as Marsden) were also products of an earlier period of high trust and common sociability between evangelicals, facilitated continued cooperation and mutual regard in the New Zealand context well into the 1830s and 1840s – until the deaths of the older missionaries and the arrival of new settlers translated the new cultural and denominational realities. It is to the effects of the geographical context of the mission, beyond this cultural delay, that we must now turn.

The WMS and the Pacific

It is an historiographical commonplace to note that Britain's trade and territorial second empire was not monolithic, but was comprised of interlocking regional systems, managed by a diverse set of entities from the Colonial Office to the East India Company. The blockades of British shipping in European waters during the American war had exposed weaknesses in Britain's strategic shipping routes – particularly the Baltic sources of spar lumber and iron for naval production that were under the purview of the Russia Company. The belief that the next naval war with France would likely be fought over trade access to China and India and the presence of sources of suitable naval lumber in the greater Tasman region led to consultations with leading Russia Company merchants about the possibility of creating a permanent British presence in the South Pacific. This also solved the additional problem of what to do with London's overflowing prisons now that transportation to North America was no longer an option. As noted, evangelical conversion had made significant inroads into the merchant communities of the Russia Company, and so it was to the Thornton family and members of the evangelical nexus that Pitt's cabinet turned for advice.[23] In consulting on how a strategic colony might be set up in Botany Bay, they extracted the concession that chaplains would be provided to the new colony, and so it was that John Thornton personally selected Richard Johnson and later Samuel Marsden to join the settlement that would become New South Wales. Given this foundational input into the design of the colonial society by evangelicals, and with Marsden's additional personal ties to politically-influential evangelicals in London and Yorkshire, the small coterie of evangelicals in Sydney were well positioned to wield significant influence in the region. The complications of Marsden's attempts to manage the interpersonal politics of participation in this regional system are well documented, but three features that emerged as critical were his attempts to balance involvement in the changing civic life of the colony with clerical independence, his ability to mobilise support at the imperial metropole, and his mediation of relationships between non-Anglican evangelicals, such as his work as corresponding agent for the LMS.[24]

In contrast, Samuel Leigh's interactions reflect the different positioning of the WMS to the imperial and colonial states. The somewhat clumsy means by which Leigh's official standing as a teacher in the NSW colony was negotiated after he had already sailed reflects the lack of direct inroads the WMS enjoyed to the corridors of power, and some misunderstandings about how to best conduct business with government.[25] Similarly, his first interactions with Governor Macquarie, and the subsequent need for reassuring correspondence from the London committee regarding his position in relationship to the colonial authorities and Establishment expose the lack of local information and relational connections.[26] Nevertheless, Leigh and his ministry found a welcome among the vibrant associational culture of the colony, especially among those who embraced both heart religion and the Established Church. In this respect, Leigh's collaboration with Marsden, and his ministry and philanthropic activities aligned much more with the pattern seen in the United Kingdom prior to the 1790s, with clearly negotiated complementarities between the Anglican chaplains and Wesleyan societies, rather than the creation of separate parallel structures. Here Marsden's own displacement from the changing patterns of evangelicalism fostered interdenominational collegiality in ways that were becoming less common in the United Kingdom.

The Wesleyans' distinctive place within the British regional system of Australasia continued to play out in subtle practical ways. As a great number of Royal and East India Company naval officers were Anglican Evangelicals, letters from Marsden and CMS missionaries were frequently prioritised – in critical instances, such as the Philo Free scandal, arriving in London before official correspondence. There is no evidence that Wesleyan missionaries received similar preference – they seem to have been primarily reliant on commercial shipping, later supplemented by the ships of the CMS. As the British presence in the region grew, Wesleyan ministry showed a predilection towards itinerant circuits that could be conducted on horseback or by coastal and river craft, and reflecting the wider demographic appeal of the movement, was more centred on the colonial settler population than those with imperial career paths. Wesleyan ministers and laypeople played an active part in the growing set of evangelical and philanthropic societies – local and auxiliary – forming a kind of evangelical nexus in miniature, but any initiative that interacted with the local British government was carefully mediated through Church of England ministers. Similarly, Methodists in the region were not significant participants in the informational networks that fuelled Evangelical humanitarianism from the 1820s. The Parliamentary Select Committee Report on Aborigines, for example, did not reference 'intelligence' from Wesleyan sources in its accounts of the Australasian region.[27]

Nevertheless, though the regional dynamics were critical to the practical outworkings of the mission, Leigh and his colleagues consciously existed within a global and growing evangelical public culture. Mid-eighteenth-century narratives of mission – such as those of David Brainerd, Moravian and Halle missionaries, and John Wesley – had focused on the trope of the missionary journey. Filled with 'good Samaritan' encounters, these narratives emphasised the individual nature of the missions project. By the early-nineteenth century, missions societies were consciously seeking to draw British audiences into the narrative of missions – using ethnographic information to create an imaginative bridge by which audiences came to understand the humanitarian impact of missions.

The Significance of Samuel Leigh

Leigh contributed significantly and enthusiastically to this project. His preaching notes, used in his itinerating around New South Wales, as well as on return to England, show adherence to a rigid structure designed to make the need for missionaries intelligible to an audience enculturated to think in terms of conversion. Leigh's notes show a standard narrative template, built from a conversionary imagination, that first laid out the origins of the particular people under discussion, their current state and 'progress' or history that had led them to this state, followed by four or five examples of depravity, then the change observed upon encountering the missionaries, and finally comments on their future prospects. This template was just as readily applied to British settlers in New South Wales as to Tongans or Māori.[28] The desired effect was both to stir support by illustrating the need for the mission, and to engage the listener in sympathetic identification as one too who knew the realities of sin, repentance and redemption. Until the last two decades of the eighteenth century, missionary narratives had largely been embedded within autobiographies and travel accounts, but as the growth of missionary and other evangelical magazines paralleled the expansion in missionary societies, it became a standard requirement for personal journals and letters to be returned to the London committees alongside financial accounts and inventories, to be edited and republished across multiple channels in order to encourage interest in and support for the projects. Thus, we find reported a lurid account of cannibalism first delivered by Leigh to the Methodist conference in Liverpool in 1820 republished in the *London Magazine* under "scientific intelligence", the *Imperial* as a "shocking instance of cannibalism in New Zealand", and as an "anecdote from New Zealand" in the *Evangelical Magazine*.[29] As the Wesleyan Mission Society wrote in its report of 1820, in sharing these "habitations of cruelty", they desired that those in England might become permanently connected to the improvement of distant peoples:

> should the work which has been begun by Missionary Societies be properly supported, and receive the blessing of God… another people, for ages separated from the human family [will] … be brought within its pale, and receive its oracles, its God, and its Saviour.[30]

As Leigh prepared to return from Australia to England, sixteen fellow Methodists signed an address, later approved by the quarterly board, honouring him for his work among them.[31] The associational nature of this farewell was fitting, for it reflected the longer threads of support by which Leigh's presence in NSW and the Wesleyan mission to New Zealand had been made possible. By the end of the 1820s the intergenerational nexus of British evangelical philanthropy out of which the societies, practices and culture that allowed missions such as Leigh's to exist had largely broken down – replaced with a much more geographically and denominationally fractured set of religious and humanitarian projects. Replete with formal tropes of gratefulness for Leigh's Gospel work among them, the document is poignant for its acknowledgement of the grief arising from the parting that Leigh's departure represented – "separating from our best earthly friends".

Notes

1 'Address of thanks presented to Rev. Samuel Leigh on departure for England, 31 December 1828 from congregation and friends', Mitchell Library, AL5.

2 Philippa Mein Smith, Peter Hempenstall & Shaun Goldfinch, *Remaking the Tasman World.* Christchurch: Canterbury University Press, 2008.

3 David Hempton, *The Church in the Long Eighteenth Century.* London, IB Tauris, 2011, 164. David Hempton, 'The people called Methodists: Transitions in Britain and North America', in *The Oxford Handbook of Methodist Studies,* edited by William J. Abraham and James E. Kirby, Oxford: Oxford University Press, 2009, 67–84.

4 See Roshan Allpress, 'Making Philanthropists: Entrepreneurs, Evangelicals and the Growth of Philanthropy in the British World, 1756–1840', DPhil thesis, University of Oxford, 2015.

5 Exemplified by such projects as the *Foundling Hospital* or the *Society for the Propagation of the Gospel in Foreign Parts.*

6 Contemporary examples of which included the *Committee for Clothing French Prisoners of War* (1760) and the *Committee appointed for relieving the Poor Germans,* (1764).

7 'Minute Book of the English Trust of the Indian Charity School', Royal Bank of Scotland Archive, *Pole, Thornton, Free, Down & Scott Papers*, PT/1/21.

8 Milton M. Klein, *An Amazing Grace: John Thornton and the Clapham Sect.* New Orleans: University Press of the South, 2004.

9 See David Bogue and James Bennett, *History of Dissenters from the Revolution in 1688, to the year 1808*, IV, London: the Authors, 1812, 280–281.

10 See discussion in Deryck W. Lovegrove, *Established Church, Sectarian People: Itinerancy and the Transformation of English Dissent, 1780–1830*, Cambridge: Cambridge University Press, 1988, 88–104.

11 William Pennington Burgess, *Memoirs of the Rev. Joseph Burgess,* London: John Mason, 1842. E.W. Hames, 'Walter Lawry and the Wesleyan Mission in the South Seas', WHS (NZ) Proceedings, 23, no. 4. (1967).

12 Thomas Bere, *The controversy between Mrs Hannah More and the Curate of Blagdon relative to the Conduct of her Teacher of the Sunday School in that Parish.* London, 1801, p. 7. See Anne Stott See Anne Stott, "Hannah More and the Blagdon Controversy, 1799–1802", *Journal of Ecclesiastical History,* 51 no.2 (2000): 319–346.

13 Gareth Atkins, *Converting Britannia: Evangelicals and British Public Life, 1770–1840.* Woodbridge: Boydell Press, 2019, 33–38, 54–61.

14 A.T. Yarwood, *Samuel Marsden: The Great Survivor.* Wellington: A.H & A.W. Reed, 1977, 10–21.

15 Thomas Coke, *A Plan of the Society for the Establishment of Missions among the Heathens,* [no publication details] 1784. See also, Kenneth Hylson-Smith, *Evangelicals in the Church of England, 1734-1984.* Edinburgh: T&T Clark, 1988, 17–21; R. Jeffrey Hiatt, 'John Wesley's Approach to Mission', *The Asbury Journal,* 68 no.1 (2013): 108–124.

16 Henry Morris, *The Life of Charles Grant.* London: John Murray, 1904, 108.

17 Coke, *Plan of the Society for the Establishment of Missions,* vii.

18 Part of the wider solidification of Methodism's denominational infrastructure and decoupling from Anglican institutions.

19 See Donald M. Lewis (ed.) *Dictionary of Evangelical Biography, 1730–1860,* Oxford: Blackwell, 1995, 2, 1073. See also Richard Blake, *Evangelicals in the Royal Navy, 1775-1815: Blue Lights and Psalm-Singers.* Woodbridge: Boydell & Brewer, 2008.

20 Sundius represented a small group of wealthy Methodist merchants, frequently with European connections, that included George Wolff, Danish Consul, who was one of the larger donors to the WMS. Peder Borgen, 'George Wolff (1736–1828)', *Methodist History*, 40 no.1 (October 2001): 17–28.

21 W.R. Ward, *The Early Correspondence of Jabez Bunting 1820–1829.* London: Royal Historical Society, 1972, 15.

22 W.R. Ward, *The Early Correspondence of Jabez Bunting 1830–1858*, Oxford: Oxford University Press, 1976, 206–207.

23 Alan Frost, *Botany Bay and the First Fleet: The Real Story*, Melbourne: Black, 2019, 174–5.

24 Peter G. Bolt & Malcolm Falloon (eds.), *Freedom to Libel? Samuel Marsden v Philo Free: Australia's First Libel Case.* Epping: Bolt Publishing, 2017, 57–78, 218–228.

25 Alexander Strachan, *The Life of the Rev. Samuel Leigh.* London: Hamilton Adams, 1870, 25–27.

26 Glen O'Brien, '"Not Radically a Dissenter": Samuel Leigh in the Colony of New South Wales.' *Wesley and Methodist Studies*, 4 (2012): 51–69, especially 63–65.

27 *Report of the Parliamentary Select Committee on Aboriginal Tribes*, 1837.

28 'Rev. Samuel Leigh Notebook', Mitchell Library, B378.

29 *London Magazine,* 2 (1820): 691; *Imperial Magazine*, 3 (1821): 27–28; *Evangelical Magazine*, 29 (1821): 127–128.

30 *The First Report of the General Wesleyan Methodist Missionary Society,* London, 1818, p. liii.

31 'Address of thanks', Mitchell Library, AL5.

2 – Samuel and Catherine Leigh in Australia and New Zealand

Glen O'Brien

Introduction

Samuel and Catherine Leigh may justly be remembered as pioneers of Wesleyan Methodism in Aotearoa/New Zealand. They made a small but significant contribution to the religious history of both Australia and New Zealand and should be celebrated as authentic pioneers of what is today the Uniting Church in Australia, the Methodist Church of New Zealand / Te Hahi Weteriana o Aotearoa, with its commitment to a bicultural journey, as well as churches in the Wesleyan-Holiness tradition. This paper seeks a fresh examination of the Leighs' work not as an exercise in hagiography but in order, at least partly, to explore the nature of commemoration in settler societies tempted to reconstruct memory in ways that avert the national gaze from the impact of dispossession on indigenous cultures.

Australian and New Zealand Methodism are linked by Leigh (1785-1852) as he was the first Wesleyan Methodist missionary to arrive in both places. He visited Samuel Marsden's mission at the Bay of Islands in 1819 and then, in 1822 established the first Wesleyan mission, Wesleydale in Whangaroa, in the Māori community accused of the Boyd massacre in December 1809. Leigh belonged to a period when Methodism had close ties to the Church of England, and the fact that he was 'not radically a Dissenter' was one cause of conflict with his fellow missionaries. The wave of the future for nineteenth-century Methodism would be as a strong, independent, body of Dissenters. This chapter will examine Leigh's relationships with his co-workers and argue that, as a man who belonged more naturally to an earlier period of Methodist development, he may be remembered as a pioneer, but not as a builder, of Methodism in Australia and New Zealand.

Samuel Leigh arrived in New South Wales on 10 August 1815 in response to a request from class meetings led by John Hosking and Edward Eagar, to begin what would turn out to be a gruelling ministry with little earthly reward.[1] Born in Milton, Staffordshire, Leigh was first a lay preacher with the Independent Church at Hanley. Finding the Calvinism in those circles distasteful, he joined the Wesleyans at Portsmouth and was soon appointed to the Shaftesbury Circuit. Following a missionary call, he was preparing to remove to Montreal, Canada when the Wesleyan Missionary Committee decided he should instead be appointed to New South Wales. Like most early nineteenth-century Methodist preachers, Leigh had very limited education. His manuscripts from his days at Dr. David Bogue's Congregational Seminary at Gosport show little by way of advanced intellect.[2] What he lacked in native intelligence he made up for in a strict application of Methodist polity, a vigorous approach to discipline that led to some loss of members soon after his arrival.[3]

Leigh's work cannot be described as a resounding success, but he did establish the requisite Methodist discipline that provided a foundation for subsequent growth, something the earlier lay preachers had not been able to do. Birtwhistle rather optimistically sees the home Church's appointment of Leigh in response to the need in NSW as a 'splendid appointment.' He is said to have encountered only 'initial difficulties with the Governor,' but Leigh's 'difficulties' with Lachlan Macquarie were the least of his problems.[4]

Leigh and Governor Lachlan Macquarie

Leigh received a less than enthusiastic welcome from lay preacher, and converted ex-convict, Edward Eagar. When Leigh introduced himself as a Wesleyan missionary, Eagar replied, 'Indeed! I am sorry to inform you that it is now doubtful whether the Governor will allow you to remain in the country in that capacity.'[5] Staying overnight in the Eagar household, Leigh felt so despondent that he retired to his room after supper, overwhelmed by the uncertainty of his prospects. The next day he presented himself to Governor Lachlan Macquarie, accompanied by Eagar, and it seemed that the latter's fears were not unfounded, when the Governor informed Leigh, 'I regret you have come here as a missionary, and feel sorry, and cannot give you any encouragement in that capacity.'[6] The Governor informed Leigh that he had 'missed his way' by not presenting proper letters of introduction from British government officials. The authorization papers Leigh had brought with him were of no use in this 'strange country' to which he had come. Cautious about sectarian conflicts erupting in the colony, Macquarie referred to a recent rebellion 'aggravated by the bitter hostility of both papists and Protestants,'[7] perhaps a reference to the Irish convict rebellion at Castle Hill in March 1804. 'I had rather you had come from any other Society than the Methodist. I profess to be a member of the Church of England and wish all to be of the same profession and therefore cannot encourage any parties.' Leigh then assured Macquarie of his own churchmanship and of his desire to remain himself closely attached to the Church of England.[8]

Macquarie offered Leigh a position in the government, through which he was assured he would grow much more rich and comfortable than by going about preaching. Leigh turned down the offer, insisting that he had come to the colony as a Wesleyan missionary and could act in no other capacity while he remained there.[9] Before the interview was over, however, Macquarie had given qualified approval to Leigh's itinerancy so long as he stuck to his own Wesleyan flock and expected no government funds. The Surveyor General's Office was instructed to provide Leigh with free passage throughout the colony.[10] The Governor seems to have admired Leigh's character, but requested that in future 'only regular and pious clergymen of the Church of England and not sectaries' should be sent to 'the new and rising colony.'[11]

Macquarie's initial scepticism toward the arrival of a Methodist preacher need not be read too negatively. It more than likely arose out of his conscientious sense of responsibility. According to his biographer John Ritchie, the Governor saw himself as a benevolent landlord; he saw all of the citizens of the colony, from the lowest to the highest estate, including the Aborigines, as his personal responsibility.[12] According to John Hirst the reason that Macquarie is so well remembered today is because 'he treated a ramshackle colony of 5000 people as if it were or could be a significant place.'[13] The sudden arrival of a new religious sect imported from the home country had the potential to destabilise this development project.

Leigh and the Anglican Clergy

In requesting a minister, the Wesleyan class leaders had made it clear that they did not want anyone who was 'radically a Dissenter,' but rather, one who could work with the Anglican chaplains, and not act independently of the Church of England.[14] Thomas Bowden expressed a desire that whoever was sent should follow 'the primitive way of Methodism, not in hostility against the church, but rather in unison with it, not so much as to make a party distinct from the church as to save souls in it.'[15] They appear then to have been 'Church Methodists' rather than 'Chapel Methodists,' not thinking of themselves primarily as Dissenters but as allied closely with the Established Church.[16] Eagar himself had on occasion read the Anglican service on behalf of the Rev. Richard Cartwright, one of the colonial chaplains.

Leigh turned out to be just the man they wanted, and he quickly established good relations with the Anglican clergy and made it his business to cooperate fully with them, ensuring that Methodist activity would in no way interfere with the routines of Anglicanism. Leigh wrote home to the Wesleyan Missionary Society on 2 March 1816, assuring its members that the Anglican clergy were entirely friendly toward him.[17] Samuel Marsden who had himself been influenced by Yorkshire Methodism in his youth, donated land to the Methodists for a chapel in Windsor whose foundation stone was laid on 13 September 1818.[18] Leigh was invited to Newcastle to preach by the local Evangelical Anglican chaplain William Cowper.

Not all colonial Methodists shared Leigh's enthusiasm for the Anglican formularies and, as we shall see, this would become the locus of much of the conflict between Leigh and his colleagues. Leigh saw the Methodist mission as ancillary to the Church of England, but others did not seem to share that opinion. In reality, Methodists functioned more often as an alternative to Anglican worship than a supplement to it. Leigh held services at 9 a.m. and 7 p.m. so as not to clash with church hours, but in 1821 the missionaries established an 11 a.m. service in Sydney and held Communion services there as well as at Parramatta and Windsor. Benjamin Carvosso may have been the chief belligerent in the bitter dispute that ensued.[19] He made it clear that 'scarcely an individual of those who attend our morning worship was accustomed to attend the Established Church at the disputed hour,'[20] a practice that flew in the face of Leigh's preferences.

These events led to the earlier close relations between Wesleyans and the Church of England being disrupted so that after the 1820s the two churches had little to do with other after and when they did, they were not always friendly encounters.[21] In any case, identification with the Church of England, if it had continued, may well have been a hindrance to Methodist growth, as the population was largely emancipist in sentiment and felt disenfranchised by Anglican exclusivity.[22]

Leigh and His Fellow Workers

Leigh's ministry as a circuit rider took him on a regular 240 km circuit covering Parramatta, Liverpool, Windsor, Richmond, Castlereagh, and the Hawkesbury River district. Spending ten days in Sydney, frequenting the Rocks areas with its evident human need, then ten or eleven days traveling his circuit, Leigh sought to establish a cause in the tried and true Methodist pattern. It soon became apparent that there was more work in the colony of New South Wales than a single Methodist preacher could handle and in 1817 Leigh began to request the Committee to forward a co-worker. The Cornishman Walter Lawry arrived on the convict ship *Castlereagh*, on which he had served as chaplain, in May 1818.

The two got on famously at first but stresses in their relationship soon became apparent. Wright and Clancy give the following character portraits:

> Leigh was a humourless, intense, single-minded man, quite prepared to kill himself in the fulfillment of his mission; Lawry was warm, even emotional, found it difficult to remain serious in company for long and, while willing to work hard, placed rather more importance on his home comforts than did Leigh.[23]

According to Bollen, Leigh's manner was 'heavy like his frame.'[24] It probably did not help that Lawry decided that he should 'faithfully and affectionately' apprise Leigh of the 'most glaring deficiencies and inconsistencies' he discovered in him.[25] Nor would it have been taken kindly by Leigh that Lawry successfully won the hand of Mary Hassall, a young woman whom Leigh had earlier failed to court successfully. In the estimate of the preachers who would join them on the field in 1821, the two men were 'naturally unfitted for agreement in all the affairs of life.'[26] Leigh was twenty-nine or thirty, Lawry twenty-three upon arriving in NSW. Most of the twenty-five who followed them up to 1840 were under thirty, reflecting the youthfulness of Methodist missionary work.[27] Young, sometimes hot-headed men without the wisdom and restraint of age can often fail to see eye to eye and be unwilling to compromise. In 1819 Lawry expressed his concern about the deteriorating relationship between Leigh and himself. 'Mr. Leigh, with whom I wish the most intimate union, is of such a curious and eccentric manner that I find it most difficult to labour in unison with him. His preaching talent appears to be all dwindled away. He is a most miserable speaker.'[28]

The Committee reinforced its earlier insistence that the utmost deference be shown to the Anglican clergy and both the Committee and Leigh wrote to the colonial chaplains supporting them over against their fellow Methodists who seemed deliberately to be working against the clergy. A situation soon developed in which Leigh, the colonial Anglican chaplains, and the Missionary Committee in London on the one side were arrayed against every Methodist preacher in NSW on the other. There were many accusations flung in both direction and much behind-closed-door plotting and scheming.[29] The Missionary Committee sided with Leigh and the Anglican clergy on all the matters that came before them. They issued rebukes and warnings to each of the missionaries, threatening to withdraw them from the field if they persisted in their actions. The towns were to be left to the Established Church; the Methodist preachers were to confine themselves to the scattered population in the bush.[30] Any refusal to obey this directive would be considered a dereliction of duty.[31] Leigh's original plan should be followed, the work of the Anglican clergy was not to be interfered with, services were not to be held in church hours, and all controversial sermons should be avoided.

The arrival of the Rev. George Erskine to serve as Superintendent and later District Chairman, on 4 November 1822, only further isolated the already besieged Leigh. The conflict between Leigh and his fellow preachers, Erskine considered 'an exceedingly unpleasant affair.'[32] For Erskine, the Wesleyan Methodist Church needed to show little deference to the Established Church. It was its own ecclesial body with its own doctrine and discipline. To be stationed at so far a distance from England required the granting of 'a discretionary power to act in accordance with local circumstances, and to have liberty to embrace with prudence every opening of usefulness.'[33] In this missional pragmatism he was at one with the other preachers, pointing toward the self-sustaining and independent future of nineteenth-century Wesleyan Methodism, leaving Leigh looking backward to the previous century. But Erskine too was not a well man and he lacked the drive and energy to offer strong leadership.

The Wesleyan Mission in New Zealand

It was out of concern for Leigh's health that Samuel Marsden invited Leigh to travel to New Zealand at Marsden's expense and scout out the possibility of establishing a mission there, hoping that the change would do him good. The first Christian mission in New Zealand had been established by Marsden in the Bay of Islands in 1814 and Leigh made his first trip there in 1819. Once Walter Lawry had arrived and settled in, Leigh felt free to accept Marsden's invitation to visit the Bay of Islands and encourage the lay settlers there. Leigh's trips to New Zealand and to England were a source of continual irritation to his colleagues, who felt they had to defer to the authority of one who was not as intimately acquainted as they with conditions on the field.[34]

Leigh's understanding of the Māori people would have been shaped by Samuel Marsden's positive views first developed after interaction with those visiting Sydney. Their reputation as fierce cannibals was widely known, but Marsden was of the opinion that massacres had been retaliation for instances of European injustice and cruelty.[35] Leigh did not confine himself to the settlers but visited six surrounding Māori villages and, after gaining the people's assent to receive Christian instruction, he formed them into a circuit. He drew a preaching plan, attaching the names of the lay settlers who evidently had up to this point done very little to reach out to the indigenous people. Lord's Day services were held every Sunday. The second Sunday after his arrival he entered a nearby Māori village lined at the entrance by twelve severed tattooed heads stuck on poles on the assumption that Leigh would want to purchase them.[36] The sale of such heads was strongly opposed by Marsden.[37]

Leigh travelled to London in 1820 and toured the circuits promoting the work in Australia and New Zealand. He also married Catherine Clewes, and requested the Missionary Committee to supply at least three additional preachers for New South Wales.[38] He was given permission to raise money for a Wesleyan mission to New Zealand, though the missionary committee balked at forwarding any direct funds while the New South Wales mission was £10,000 in debt.[39] Leigh returned to New Zealand arriving in the Bay of Islands on 22 February 1822.[40] During his deputational trip to England, Leigh had befriended the visiting Māori warrior Hongi Hika, who had been much impressed by the musketry and military discipline of the troops of King George. Now returned to New Zealand, Hongi sought to settle scores with his traditional enemies, determined 'to sweep [them] from the earth.'[41] The warrior declared that since Leigh and other missionaries stood in the way of the local people obtaining muskets and gunpowder, 'we New Zealanders hate both your worship and your God. In our very hearts we hate them. They are not like ours. We only worship in sacred places, where no food has been cooked or eaten. You worship anywhere!' After Hongi Hika had gathered a thousand warriors the loan of the mission's boat was requested. Leigh consented to this but when greater demands were made, he resisted and was shown the point of a spear. At this point he tore open his shirt and rushed upon the spearman saying he would receive the spear before surrendering any more property. At this point Hongi intervened and told his over-zealous warrior that he was being unreasonable before banishing him to the bush.[42] Hongi's war raged for five years spreading through the northern part of the country and as far south as the Waikato and Rotorua. Leigh had at first intended to establish a mission to the Thames River (Waihou River) and Mercury Bay, but after Hongi had declared that he would carry his war into these districts, he settled instead on Kaeo near Whangaroa harbour, 56 kilometres north-west of the Bay of Islands.

Whangaroa was the home of the Māori who had been accused of the *Boyd* massacre of December 1809 in which up to 70 Europeans had been killed and eaten in a dispute over the ill treatment of Māori on board. Te Pahi, a Māori chief well known in Sydney, and another young chief refused to do manual labour *en route* from Sydney on the basis that they were chiefs and such work was beneath them. Thompson thought they were lying and had them whipped. Upon arrival in Whangaroa, Te Ara reported his ill treatment to his father and a retribution party resulted.[43] This incident made the choice of location a difficult one for the missionaries. The burnt hulk of the *Boyd* had been found at that time with only four survivors including a young mother, an infant and a toddler. Alexander Berry, who was in charge of cargo on the ship *City of Edinburgh*, laid the blame for the incident at the feet of Te Pahi, though he was innocent of the charges and a victim of Berry's dislike. Samuel Marsden had taken a great interest in this matter and, through his investigations, aimed to clear Te Pahi's name, fixing blame instead on Te Puhi and his brother Te Ara (known as 'George') and his sons, who had been treated poorly by the Boyd's Captain Thompson. Marsden built on his investigations to argue for the prosecution of ships captains who treated Māori with brutality and petitioned the British government to establish and protect the rule of law in New Zealand.[44] Te Ara was still present in 1823 when Leigh arrived and he showed him the wreck of the *Boyd*, giving his version of events, which substantially matched Marsden's account.

Leigh was not at first welcomed by the tribe at Whangaroa who charged upon him ferociously, Te Ara doing nothing to prevent them. He made a narrow escape by distributing fish hooks, but returned later on the 6 June accompanied by his wife Catherine, the Rev. J. Butler and laymen Shepherd and Hall. Sailing into the harbour past the imposing

300 foot *pa* they were greeted in a friendly manner, the earlier gift of fish hooks being remembered. The first Christian service held in that part of New Zealand took place on 8 June with Leigh preaching from 1 Samuel 7:12, 'Hitherto hath the Lord helped us.' Seven miles upriver, in the picturesque valley that was the home of Te Ara and his brother Te Puhi, they established 'Wesleydale.' Anticipating that the country would be colonised by Great Britain, Leigh secured the land on which the mission station stood, paying twice what the local people demanded in 'spades, hoes, blankets, and pairs of trousers,' and securing five acres of property. When the validity of such transactions were later tested by the British government, and many rendered invalid because inequitable, the arrangement at Wesleydale was deemed to have been just.[45] The Māori people were introduced to European crop production raising wheat, fruit, and vegetables and the mission would eventually develop into quite a thriving enterprise.

Catherine Leigh appears to have been a resourceful and spirited woman. She learned the Māori language and introduced the local women to needle and thread. On one occasion, faced with a band of attacking warriors who had knocked her husband to the ground and demanded a high quality garment to settle some earlier score, she rushed to her cottage and removed her bedspread, offering it to a grateful assailant who wore it with pride. Later that day she physically restrained a warrior who was attempting to open a cask of pork.[46] Alarmed at the high rate of infanticide among the Māori women, Catherine conceived a plan to dress every infant in highly prized European clothes promising to visit each child to watch over its growth and development. In this manner she was convinced that she had saved 'scores of lives.'[47]

On 6 August 1823, two new Wesleyan missionaries Nathaniel Turner and John Hobbs arrived at Wesleydale and were warmly welcomed. On the 15 August the government ship Snapper carried Samuel Marsden, along with Turner's wife and children, into the harbour, much to the delight of both missionaries and the local people. Marsden led the Sunday services on 17 August including the administration of the sacraments. Marsden was convinced that Leigh's health had deteriorated to the point where he should immediately return to Sydney. Reluctant to leave, he was persuaded only when Te Puhi told him that if he went to New South Wales, promising to return after he had recovered, that he would give up war and stay at home and plant *kumara*. They sailed on 19 August for the Bay of Islands but the *Brompton* was shipwrecked and they took refuge on a deserted Pacific island for three days and nights before being rescued by a passing vessel. As exciting a missionary narrative as this is, it should be noted that it all took place in the space of two or three months (though Leigh spent a total of about 16 months in New Zealand, mostly in the Bay of Islands).[48] Nathaniel Turner and John Hobbs continued to lead the mission, but Hongi's forces attacked Whangaroa in January 1827 and Wesleydale was abandoned. Catherine Leigh died in Sydney on 15 May 1831, in the midst of an epidemic. Leigh finally retired from the field and returned to England the following year, broken in spirit and in health. Remarrying in 1842 he continued for a time in circuit work, until finally suffering a stroke while addressing a Missionary Meeting in 1851 and dying the following year.

Both Anglicans and Wesleyans subsequently saw considerable success in Northland so that by 1840 half the Māori people of the Bay of Islands had converted to Christianity.[49]

The Māori believed in the spiritual powers of nature (atua), the spiritual authority of individuals within the community (mana), the concept of the special sacredness of holy things (tapu), and that codes of behaviour (tikanga) existed to regulate communities.[50] Therefore it was not a huge jump for them to add to this religious cosmology, belief in one God, whom they named Te Atua. Some have even perceived evidence for belief in a supreme deity, Io, in pre-Christian-contact Māori belief. According to Michael King, however,

> The major points of Christian belief that would contrast with tikanga Māori were the notions that natural man was a fallen creature needing to be redeemed by Christ's suffering and death; and that every human life - whether of rangatira [chief], commoner or slave - was of equal value in the eyes of Te Atua and those who acknowledged Him.[51]

CMS missionaries, led by Henry Williams, spoke to a group of thirty or forty Māori from Tauranga in July 1825 and asked them how many gods were among them. One of the group whispered to another that he should reply, 'One,' but when asked the name and location of this god, the man demurred. The missionaries then urged the Māori people to follow the example of the Tahitians and adopt the Christian religion.[52] As late as 1922 the Rev W.J. Williams in his *Centenary Sketches of New Zealand Methodism* wrote in a manner that reflected quite a low view of the Māori people, 'Anything more unlovely than the character and disposition of the Natives who at that time lived on [the shores of Whangaroa Harbour] it is impossible for the human mind to picture.'[53]

In Māori mythology, the term *Te Reinga* (from the noun meaning 'a place of leaping') is used to refer both to the place of departed spirits and to the locality of the North Cape the area to which the *wairua* (soul or spirit) travels.[54] Missionaries taught that those who did not believe the teachings of the Bible would be 'the devil's servants here and…his slaves in the Rainga [sic].' In conversation with the Tauranga 'chief' Rangi, who was from Whangarei but living at that time in the Bay of Islands, CMS missionaries enquired into the state of the dying man.

> Sometimes when sitting alone, I feel my heart gloomy or dark; and think that the God of the White people is not our God, and that the Rainga [sic] is the only place which we have to go to: then my heart feels enlightened, and again becomes gladdened with the thought of going to heaven…I think of the love of Christ, and ask him to wash this bad heart, and take away this native heart and give me a new heart.[55]

To these missionaries, the designation 'Christian' was more or less equivalent to 'European.' They told Rangi, 'The people who believe in Jesus Christ are called by one name after him, which is, Christian. We, who are here now, are called so; that is Europeans: but those who do not believe are call Heathens: the New Zealanders are Heathens…'[56] Te Rangi died on Thursday, 15 September, 1825, but not before confessing faith in Jesus Christ, being baptised on the previous day and entrusting the care of his children to the missionaries. The missionaries regarded his 'stedfastness [sic]…on the verge of the grave, and his firm resistance of all the Native Superstitions' as sufficient grounds for baptism. In addition to his Māori name he took the name 'Christian' energetically repeating his new name several times during the ceremony. Though he expressed a desire that his body be delivered over to the missionaries, presumably so that it could receive a Christian burial, the local people took the body away in a canoe and would not reveal to the missionaries what burial customs would be observed. There may be some sour grapes in the missionaries telling the local people that 'their disposing of the body was of no consequence as to his salvation; for his body was all corruption, but his soul was in heaven.'[57]

Though the conversion of Te Rangi is not a Methodist conversion narrative, it shares a common evangelical culture and theology of baptism. The insistence on a conscious understanding as a prerequisite for adult baptism, the concern to see signs of repentance and joy in believing, eagerness to testify, and readiness to 'die well,' with the certainty of salvation were common to Methodists, Congregationalists, and other evangelicals of the period. The recollection of Te Rangi's conversion played a part in the conversion of the first Wesleyan convert, Hika Tawa, whose baptism in January 1831, as well as that of the second Wesleyan convert, Hae Hae in February 1832, shared similar traits.[58] Falloon rejects the claims of those who see such conversions as the result of missionaries playing upon the fear of hell. He argues that Te Rangi saw the missionaries as the source of new and valuable spiritual knowledge and recognised the spiritual authority of missionaries like Williams and of the Bible as a source of divine truth. The attractiveness of heaven as a resting place for Māori, was a greater motivation than any fear of eternal punishment, the idea of which seems not to have been taken very seriously. This expectation of heaven was confirmed in Te Rangi's experience of prayer which brought him an inward change of heart.[59]

Keith Sinclair, not known for his high regard for religion in New Zealand life, took a dim view of the missionaries' approach to indigenous beliefs.

> It is probable that many aspects of Māori religion have been forgotten by the Māoris and were never accurately written down or even understood by Europeans. Few of the early missionaries, who made a determined onslaught upon heathenism, were concerned to record for posterity what they were so busy destroying.[60]

Generally speaking, Wesleyans shared with other Protestants of the period a sense of European cultural superiority. There were, however, some exceptions to this approach. Wesleyan missionary Thomas Buddle (1812-1883), first principal of the Wesleyan Native Institution established at Grafton in 1845, and editor of the Māori newspaper *Te Haeata* from 1859-1862 gained a considerable wealth of knowledge regarding Māori language, customs, and mythology.[61] William Morley, writing in 1900, looked back favourably on the educational ministry of the early missionary work as having enabled missionaries 'to become acquainted with the mental powers and habits of their people…and, by communicating knowledge, sap the foundations of their superstitious practices. Moreover, the facts thus placed before [the Māori] gave them fresh food for thought, directed that thought into healthier channels, and so tended to raise and purify their minds.'[62] Morley thought of Māori culture as something to be supplanted by a civilising process that went hand in hand with Christianisation.[63] The education of Māori ministers (though they were not considered ministers in their own right, but merely 'assistants') was best carried out, according to Morley, 'away from the demoralising influence of the native kaingas [villages]'.[64] In a context such as this little interest was likely to be expressed toward the religious beliefs of the Indigenous people.

The attitude toward the declining Māori population and culture reflected in W.H. Daniel's *History of Methodism* (1879) is typical of the 'social Darwinist' view of the time. 'The Māoris are a rapidly declining race. Like the aborigines of Tasmania and Australia, they seemed destined to melt away before the Anglo-Saxon.'[65] One Māori view of the situation was similar: 'The white man's rat has killed the native rat. The fly which came with the Englishman has driven our fly away. The clover which he has sown in our fields is killing the ferns which covered our hills, and the Māori will disappear before the Pakeha [white man].'[66]

The New Zealand Wars raged between 1860 and 1870 as largely Protestant settlers appropriating large tracts of traditional Māori lands met fierce resistance from a people with a proud warrior culture.[67] During this time many Māori converts renounced the Christian faith. Susan J. Thompson states that 'of all the churches involved in Māori work, Methodism suffered most damage as a result of the wars' with fighting beginning in Taranaki 'a Wesleyan stronghold' and the spread of hostilities to the Waikato and King Country forced Wesleyan missionary personnel to withdraw from those areas. When missionaries sided with settlers during the conflict many Māori defected and returned to their traditional beliefs, leaving Wesleyan churches seriously depleted by the 1870s.[68] Some adopted a new hybrid religion of their own, blending elements of traditional Māori religion with Jewish and Christian customs.[69] After the New Zealand Wars the importance of strengthening the autonomy of Māori culture and language became of central importance, leaving the paternalistic views of some Wesleyans to appear all the more archaic.

A very negative view of the traditional religious beliefs of the peoples of the Southern World was typical of Methodist missionaries. The Australian Aborigine was thought to have had no religion at all but to have the potential to be raised from a primitive state through the civilising influences of the Gospel. The Māori were thought to have a more complex set of beliefs, but this perception was flawed, since Aborigines had in their own way just as sophisticated a set of beliefs. With some notable exceptions it was thought best to keep Māori converts away from the debilitating effects of their traditional religious culture. This attitude of rejection is understandable given the conviction of nineteenth century Methodists that the Gospel of Jesus Christ was the only hope for the 'heathen' world. Even if their work must inevitably be seen as part of a colonising process, missionaries did not engage in the civilizing project for its own sake. Believing that people were lost without Christ they tried to bring them the good news of salvation. Largely they acted out of love and compassion, and this may be said without denying the detrimental effect that missionary work often had on indigenous cultures.

The role of missionaries in Australasia and the Pacific, as elsewhere, has been presented in both positive and negative ways. They have been seen either as perpetrators of cultural genocide or as benevolent and enlightened humanitarians. Though examples of both types of missionary may be found, the truth is found somewhere in between these extremes.[70] Many missionaries had a paternalistic view of indigenous people as 'children' of a 'degraded and depraved race',[71] and as 'the ultimate example of Ham's curse'.[72] At the same time, humanitarian missionary efforts were respected by indigenous people who often admired the missionaries' 'raw courage' and who benefited from the application of European medicines to treat endemic health problems.[73] Henry Reynolds, writing about the Australian colonies in the 1830s and 40s reminds us that it was often missionaries and clergy who spoke up for Aboriginal welfare 'when so many fellow colonists looked on with indifference or were keen to see the indigenous people and their legal rights trodden under foot in the onrush of colonial progress'.[74] They 'may not have changed many minds, significantly altered colonial behaviour or moderated the violence out on the vast frontiers but they clearly troubled many consciences and raised questions which didn't easily go away'.[75] Samuel Marsden stands as perhaps the finest example of this advocacy for the rights of indigenous New Zealanders, and Marsden was perhaps Samuel Leigh's most significant mentor.

It also does a disservice to the peoples of the Southern World to portray them merely as passive victims of cultural genocide as though they had no self-determination. Rather, they often actively and creatively negotiated the new situation that presented itself to them in order to ensure their ongoing survival and flourishing. Embracing Christianity and creating unique expressions of the faith in terms of their own traditional culture was one such strategy.[76]

Falloon confirms this in the case of New Zealand, by demonstrating how Māori converts were attracted to the new message of Christianity as an alternative way of living in light of the changed circumstances brought upon them by European contact. So enthusiastic was the response that by 1852 up to 90% of the Māori population had converted to Christianity.[77] Traditional Māori society was transformed not simply because of displacement by European colonisation but as the result of 'the emergence of a distinctly Māori expression of Christianity'.[78]

Thankfully a more positive view of traditional religious beliefs is discernible in a second stage of missionary encounter with indigenous Australians and New Zealanders beginning in the twentieth century. This greater openness toward traditional cultures occurred partly because of the need for settler societies and the traditional custodians of the land to arrive at an understanding of their shared past in order to move toward national reconciliation.

Conclusion

Samuel Leigh may justly be remembered as a pioneer of Wesleyan Methodism in both Australia and Aotearoa/New Zealand. He assiduously followed the tried and true Methodist pattern of classes, circuits, and frontier preaching, working closely with the Church of England clergy. He bought an organisational discipline that was absent from the work of the earlier lay preachers. Though his time in New Zealand was brief, along with his wife Catherine, Leigh showed great courage in facing the challenge of hostile Māori warriors in wild, inhospitable country. No doubt they shared the assumption of European superiority that was typical of the era. Yet they attempted to learn the Māori language and exhibited genuine compassion toward them. Their shock at what they considered the 'savagery' of such practices as cannibalism and infanticide was a driven by a humanitarian concern and their conviction about the dignity and value of persons made in the image of God.

The constant bickering between Leigh and his colleagues over the nature of Methodism's relationship to the Church of England was a major contributing factor in the lack of success in NSW. Leigh was a hard worker, but he worked *too* hard, so hard that his health broke down, and he was warned by the Missionary Committee against killing himself with too much hard work. Owens suggests that Leigh was not only stressed but showed signs of mental illness. His colleagues accused him of being 'mentally unbalanced; and although colleagues are not always charitable in their judgments, it is hard to believe they were wrong [about Leigh].'[79] Robert Howe, editor of the Sydney Gazette, considered Leigh 'diseased in the mind,' though it is hard to know how seriously to take Howe's opinion.[80] In any case he was not a team player, he lacked tact and administrative skill and he systematically worked against his own closest colleagues in a situation of extreme physical isolation where unity was an all the more valuable commodity.

The fact that Leigh was 'not radically a Dissenter,' a quality admired by the lay preachers who first requested a missionary, kept him tied to an earlier phase of Methodist development. Walter Lawry, Benjamin Carvosso, and George Erskine were the wave of the future with their vision of Methodism as a strong, independent Dissenting body, holding its own distinctive doctrines and discipline, albeit with Anglican origins. Leigh was a man who belonged more naturally to the eighteenth-century status of Methodism as closely aligned to the Church of England, and thus was a constant drag to their progressivism. He may for these reasons be remembered as a pioneer but not as a builder of Australasian Methodism. Notwithstanding this natural conservatism, the more fully developed structures of late nineteenth-century Methodism, would not have been possible without the pioneering efforts of our Wesleyan ancestors Samuel and Catherine Leigh, whose memory we honour today.

Notes

1   Early correspondence with the MMS in London, Minutes, and Leigh's journal are available on microfilm, MMS Archives, London, IDC Microform Publishers, 1991, H-2720 – H-2721. Much valuable early correspondence is also available on microfilm in the Missionary Papers of the Bonwick Transcripts in the Mitchell Library, though these should be approached with some degree of caution as the original correspondence has been corrupted. The basic facts about Leigh and early Methodism in NSW are well covered in the secondary literature. See Glen O'Brien, 'Methodism in the Australian Colonies, 1811-1855,' in *Methodism in Australia: A History*. Edited by Glen O'Brien and Hilary Carey, Farnham, Surrey and Burlington, Vermont: Ashgate, 2015, 15-27; Don Wright and Eric G. Clancy, *The Methodists: A History of Methodism in New South Wales* Sydney: Allen and Unwin, 1993, 3-32; Lengthy quotations from the primary sources are available in Gloster S. Udy, *Spark of Grace: The Story of the Methodist Church in Parramatta and the Surrounding Region.* Parramatta: Epworth Press, 1977. This paper draws extensively on Glen O'Brien, '"Not Radically a Dissenter": Samuel Leigh in the Colony of New South Wales,' *Wesley and Methodist Studies*, 4 (2012): 51-69.

2   J.M.R. Owens, 'The Wesleyan Missionaries to New Zealand before 1840,' *JRH*, 7, no. 4 (December 1973): 326. Details on Bogue's seminary can be found in W. N. Gunson, 'Evangelical Missionaries in the South Seas, 1797-1860,' PhD thesis, Australian National University, 1959, 60-62.

3   J. D. Bollen, 'A Time of Small Things: The Methodist Mission in New South Wales, 1815-1836.' *JRH*, 7 no. 3 (June 1973): 234. Leigh was determined to establish and maintain 'every part of the discipline of Methodism' believing it to be 'God's discipline.' Leigh to WMS Committee, December 1817 [the day does not appear on the original], Bonwick Transcripts, Missionary Papers, 2:306, Box 50.

4   Birtwhistle, 'Methodist Missions,' in *A History of the Methodist Church in Great Britain* London: Epworth Press, 1983, 37.

5   Alexander Strachan, *Remarkable Incidents in the Life of the Rev. Samuel Leigh: Missionary to the Settlers and Savages of Australia and New Zealand with a Succinct History of the Origin and Progress of the Missions in those Colonies.* London: Hamilton, Adams, 1853, 34-35.

6   Strachan, *Remarkable Incidents*, 35.

7   Strachan, *Remarkable Incidents*, 36.

8   Samuel Leigh to WMS, 6 March 1816, Bonwick Transcripts, Missionary 2: 213-14, Box 50.

9   Strachan, *Remarkable Incidents*, 35.

10 Strachan, *Remarkable Incidents*, 36.

11 Michael Hogan, *The Sectarian Strand: Religion in Australian History.* Melbourne: Penguin, 1987, 31.

12 John Ritchie, *Lachlan Macquarie.* Melbourne: Melbourne University Press, 1986. Ritchie focuses on the Governor's character. Malcolm Ellis' earlier work gives greater attention to Macquarie's administration of the colony. Malcolm H. Ellis, *Lachlan Macquarie: His Life, Adventures and Times.* Sydney: Dymock's, 1947.

13 John Hirst, 'Lachlan Macquarie,' in *The Oxford Companion to Australian History*, edited by Graeme Davison, John Hirst, and Stuart Macintyre. Melbourne: Oxford University Press, 2001, 408.

14 Thomas Bowden to WMS, 20 July 1812; Bowden and Hosking to WWS, n.d. see James Colwell, *The Illustrated History of Methodism.* Sydney: William Brooks & Co., 1904, 36-39.

15 Thomas Bowden, 30 July 1812, cited in Udy, 'Spark of Grace,' 17.

16 Detailed discussion of the nature of the relationship between Methodism, the Established Church, and the Dissenting churches is found in John Munsey Turner, *Conflict and Reconciliation: Studies in Methodism and Ecumenism in England, 1740-1982*. London: Epworth, 1985.

17 Samuel Leigh to WMS, 2 March 1816, cited in Wright and Clancy, 'The Methodists,' 4. The same sentiment is expressed again in Leigh to Adam Clarke, 14 Oct 1817, Bonwick Transcripts, Missionary Papers 2:202, Box 50.

18 For good biographies of Marsden, see A. T. Yarwood, *Samuel Marsden: The Great Survivor*. Melbourne: Melbourne University Press, 1996 and Andrew Sharp, *The World, The Flesh and the Devil: The Life and Opinions of Samuel Marsden in England and the Antipodes, 1765-1838*. Auckland: Auckland University Press, 2016.

19 R. B. Walker, 'The Growth and Typology of the Wesleyan Methodist Church in New South Wales, 1812-1901.' *JRH*, 6 no. 4 (December 1971): 332.

20 Benjamin Carvosso, District Minutes, 2 October 1822, cited in Bollen, 'A Time of Small Things,' 242.

21 Walker, 'Growth and Typology,' 346.

22 The ranks of early Methodist leadership included many emancipists including Edward Eagar, John Ennis, Lancelot Iredale and Thomas Street. Walker, 'Growth and Typology,' 332.

23 Wright and Clancy, *The Methodists*, 6.

24 Bollen, 'A Time of Small Things,' 234.

25 Wright and Clancy, *The Methodists*, 6.

26 Benjamin Carvosso, Ralph Mansfield and William Walker, letter to WMS, cited in Udy, *Spark of Grace*, 58-9.

27 Bollen, 'A Time of Small Things,' 228.

28 Walter Lawry to WMS, 11 August 1819, cited in Udy, *Spark of Grace*, 43.

29 For a detailed discussion of this dispute see Udy, *Spark of Grace*, 43-61.

30 Committee Minute Book, 3 July 1822 cited in Wright and Clancy, *The Methodists*, 10-11.

31 Udy, *Spark of Grace*, 52-53.

32 George Erskine to R. Watson, 19 Nov 1822, Bonwick Transcripts, Missionary Papers, 4:1200, Box 52.

33 George Erskine to R. Watson, 19 Nov 1822, Bonwick Transcripts, Missionary Papers, 4:1201, Box 52.

34 During Lawry's three years in the colony, Leigh was present for only two short periods totalling nine months. Udy, *Spark of Grace*, 44-45.

35 Strachan, *Remarkable Incidents*, 79. For a recent collection of essays on Marsden's establishment of the Church Missionary Society in New Zealand, see Peter G. Bolt and David B. Pettett, eds. *Launching Marsden's Mission: The Beginnings of the Church Missionary Society in New Zealand, Viewed from New South Wales*. London: The Latimer Trust, 2014.

36 Strachan, *Remarkable Incidents*, 86.

37 See reference in Bolt and Pettett.

38 Samuel Leigh to WMMS, 22 June 1820, Bonwick Transcripts, Missionary 3:676, Box 51.

39 Strachan, *Remarkable Incidents*, 96-101.

40 For a helpful general discussion of the earliest Wesleyan missionaries to New Zealand see J.M.R. Owens, 'The Wesleyan Missionaries to New Zealand,' 324-41.

41 Strachan, *Remarkable Incidents*, 126-27.

42 Strachan, *Remarkable Incidents*, 127.

43 Te Ara's version of the events is recounted in Strachan, *Remarkable Incidents*, 132-33.

44 Peter Bolt, 'The Boyd Set-Back to Marsden's Mission: The View from New South Wales,' in *Launching Marsden's Mission*, 61-78.

45 Strachan, *Remarkable Incidents*, 147.

46 Strachan, *Remarkable Incidents*, 153-54.

47 Strachan, *Remarkable Incidents*, 158.

48 I am grateful to Allan Davidson for pointing this out.

49 Keith Sinclair, *A History of New Zealand*. New edition, Auckland: Penguin 2000, 43.

50 A fascinating 19th century discussion of *mana* can be found in chapter 15 of Frederick Edward Maning's, *Old New Zealand: Being Incidents of Native Customs and Character in the Old Times by A Pakeha Māori*. London: Smith, Elder and Co., 1863. See also Allan K. Davidson, *Aotearoa New Zealand: Defining Moments in the Gospel-Culture Encounter*. Geneva: WCC Publications, 1996, for a good, though brief, survey of Maori responses to Christianity.

51 Michael King, *The Penguin History of New Zealand*. Auckland: Penguin, 2003, 139-40.

52 'Death of Christian Rhangi [sic], a New-Zealand Chief, who died September 15, 1825, the day after his baptism,' *Primitive Methodist Magazine*, 7 no. 9 (September 1826): 316. It is unclear whether Te Rangi was his given name or whether this was an honorific derived from *rangatira*, the Maori word for 'chief.' The *ariki* was the paramount chief at the head of the tribe. *Rangi* was also the name of a god who along with *Papa* had produced a pantheon of lesser gods. Sinclair, 21-22. Though this account is given in a Primitive Methodist magazine it is drawing on an earlier CMS account without providing the provenance. Primitive Methodism did not arrive in New Zealand until 1844. For a recent exploration of the conversion of Karaitiana (Christian) Te Rangi, see Malcolm Falloon, 'The Maori Conversion and Four Early Converts,' PhD thesis, University of Otago, 2020, 163-199. See also, Malcolm Falloon, "Christian Rangi: 'A Brand Plucked from the Burning'?" in *Te Rongopai 1814 'Takoto Te Pai!': Bicentenary Reflections on Christian Beginnings and Developments in Aotearoa New Zealand*, edited by Allan Davidson, et al. Auckland: General Synod Office, 2014.

53 W.J. Williams, *Centenary Sketches of New Zealand Methodism*. Christchurch: Lyttleton Times Co., 1922, 12.

54 https://www.maoridictionary.co.nz/ accessed 4 February 2022.

55 'Death of Christian Rhangi,' 317.

56 'Death of Christian Rhangi,' 317.

57 The author of the account is not given but those present are named as 'Messrs. Davies, C. Davis, Fairburn, and myself.' William Puckey served as interpreter during the baptismal rite. 'Death of Christian Rhangi,' 320-21.

58 Owens, 'The Wesleyan Mission to New Zealand 1819–1840,' PhD thesis, Victoria University of Wellington, 1969, 395–96, cited in Falloon, 'The Maori Conversion,' 194-95.

59 Falloon, 'The Maori Conversion,' 196-98.

60 Sinclair, 21-22.

61 Y. L. Sutherland, 'Te Reo o te Perehi: Messages to Maori in the Wesleyan Newspaper *Te Haeata* 1859-62,' MA thesis, University of Auckland, 1999.

62 Morley, 109.

63 James Belich, *Making Peoples: A History of the New Zealanders from Polynesian Settlement to the End of the Nineteenth Century.* Auckland: Allan Lane, 1996, 124-127. For a good discussion of missionaries in New Zealand see Michael King, *The Penguin History of New Zealand.* Auckland: Penguin, 2003, ch. 10, 'God and Guns,' 131-50. For other valuable insights into settler-Maori relations see Keith Sinclair, *A History of New Zealand.* Auckland: Penguin, 2000. especially 'Part One: Maori and Settlers, 1642-1870.'

64 Morley, 47.

65 W. H. Daniels, *The Illustrated History of Methodism in Great Britain, America, and Australia.* Sydney and Melbourne: George Coffey, 1879, 792.

66 Daniels, 792.

67 Once called the 'Maori Wars' it is now recognised that this one-sided designation places blame on only one party to the conflict. Wars are always conducted between two opposing sides.

68 Susan J. Thompon, *Knowledge and Vital Piety: Education for Methodist Ministry in New Zealand from the 1840s.* Auckland: WHS (NZ) Proceedings, 90 & 91, 2012, 35. Maori attendance in Wesleyan churches dropped steeply from 7,590 in 1855 to 2,434 in 1874. The number of Maori chapels also declined during the same period. Eric W. Hames, *Out of the Common Way, The European Church in the Colonial Era 1840-1913.* WHS (NZ) Proceedings, 27, nos. 3 & 4, 1972, 51-52.

69 King, *Penguin History of New Zealand*, 147-48.

70 Richard Broome, *Aboriginal Australians.* Sydney: Allan and Unwin, 2001, 108.

71 Broome, *Aboriginal Australians*, 108.

72 Harris, *One Blood*, 31.

73 Broome, *Aboriginal Australians*, 105-107.

74 Henry Reynolds, *This Whispering in Our Hearts.* St. Leonards NSW: Allan and Unwin, 1998, 22.

75 Reynolds, *This Whispering in Our Hearts*, 13.

76 Broome, *Aboriginal Victorians: a History since 1800.* Sydney: Allen & Unwin, 2005, 127.

77 Falloon, 'The Maori Conversion,' 270.

78 Falloon, 'The Maori Conversion,' 270-71.

79 Owens, 'Wesleyan Missionaries to New Zealand,' 340.

80 Robert Howe to WMS Committee, 20 Feb 1824, Bonwick Transcripts, Missionary Papers, 5:1391, Box 53.

Section Two – Interactions in Aotearoa

3 – Indigenous Evangelism – with a Wesleyan focus

Gary Clover

Introduction: a Diffusion of Christian Influence

'History tends to be written by the victors'.[1] This has largely been true of New Zealand history writing of Māori subjects. Until the mid-twentieth century, for example, general histories, and histories of Māori embracing of Christianity, tended to express the 'fatal impact' culture change theories of colonial-era historians who sought to 'smooth the pillow of a dying Māori race'. However, from the late 1950s, histories of New Zealand's missions and Māori conversion and evangelism have become the domain of mainly Pākeha (European) academics writing from non-missionary secular perspectives derived from the insights of anthropology and sociology.[2]

This paper, instead, draws upon the more culturally balanced frameworks of former Massey University historian, Dr John Owens's 1969 PhD thesis's alternative metaphor of a 'contest of ideas' between Māori and missionaries,[3] and upon Dr Vincent O'Malley's 2014 metaphor of the 'beach' as the 'middle ground' where trade goods and ideas were exchanged on the basis of cultural equality.[4] In my book, *Collision, Compromise and Conversion during the Wesleyan Hokianga Mission, 1827-1855*,[5] I argue, similarly, that during the early colonial era Māori were more in control of their own destiny than they have generally been given credit. Chiefly patrons, certainly initially, often had great influence over where mission stations and European missionaries were placed, and very intelligently, rationally, and from a position of cultural and military strength, decided what Christian doctrines, rituals and values were adopted into Māori society and culture. So by 1840, especially in the North, much of Māori society, was generally 'Christianised' to some extent by a 'diffusion of Christian influence' – to use Surgeon Major Arthur S. Thomson's remarkably perceptive phrase of 1859.[6] Initially for most Māori, this 'diffusion' was somewhat less than a transformative 'conversion' to a totally new system of Christian beliefs and way of life, and rather more of an overlay of aspects of English Missionary Christianity that, as they were added to traditional Māori customs and belief systems, were 'Māorified' or 'indigenised' in the process.

At first, experiential 'conversion' in the manner the missionaries sought was seen to be limited. There was little of the Rev John Waterhouse, the Wesleyans' South Seas Superintendent's, 'experimental and practical' religion.[7] Nevertheless, an amazing degree of transformation of Māori society, culture, and spirituality did eventually occur. In fact, with a culture steeped in the rhetorical arts of the cut and thrust of paepae debate, and through many spiritual parallels or 'seeds of the Gospel' between Missionary Christianity and Māori traditional ethnic religion, in some ways Māori were extraordinarily well prepared for receiving the missionaries' Christianity once the communication barrier was overcome. One such 'seed' was the prophetic foresight which disposed some in Hokianga to expect the arrival of a teacher 'who had no wife' which the unmarried Bishop Pompallier in 1838 was seen to fulfil.[8] And there were fundamental similarities shared between the world views of both missionaries and Māori. Both held no distinction between the 'sacred' and the profane.[9] Both lived their lives feeling they were directed or controlled by wider supernatural forces; the missionaries by God's providential oversight set within the 'Great Chain of Being', and Māori by a fate or destiny defined by the tribal customary sanctions of tapu (sacredness, danger, apartness), utu (reciprocity, balance), and muru (justice, pay-back).[10]

By 1842, just twenty years after the start of the Mission, a census carried out by the Crown's 'Protector of Aborigines', George Clarke, reported that some 64,000 Maori out of a total population of about 109,000, or close to 60%, were 'Christian', in that they followed missionary leadership and embraced certain Christian doctrines, liturgies, and spiritual practices. Of these, some 16,000 or 15%, were classed as Wesleyans.[11] It is in this religious environment of spiritual experimentation and adaptation that the phenomenon of Wesleyan 'indigenous evangelism' took place.

Drawing principally upon written missionary sources - today almost the only resource now available - this paper will illustrate my thesis in three parts. Firstly, I name and outline the principal personalities in the band of Wesleyan Māori evangelists who arose from the missionaries' endeavour. Then I highlight a good many of the Wesleyan Māori evangelistic initiatives that occurred throughout much of Āotearoa from the 1830s to the late 1850s which helped to bring about the cultural and religious transformation of Māori society. Thirdly, by enlarging upon the three words by which I encapsulate the process of this religious transformation, *Trade*, *Transmission*, and *Transformation*, I consider the environment in which arose the culture and spiritual change wrought by indigenous Māori evangelism.

Early in the twenty first century, mission scholars such as Dr Raeburn Lange and Dr Nathan Matthews in New Zealand, and in Great Britain the Rev Canon-Emeritus Dr Timothy Yates,[12] proposed a need to shift focus from a past historical emphasis on the English missionaries to a focus more on the Māori evangelists who in the missionaries' system became the mission teachers, class leaders, local preachers, catechists, and, Wesleyan Conference appointed Māori 'minita' or 'Assistant Ministers', who embedded aspects of the missionaries' Christianity into traditional Maori society and culture. Hence, Lange in 2000 concluded that:

> ... in the dissemination of new religious ideas, and the insertion of Christianity into Māori culture, Māori initiatives were no less significant than the much chronicled deeds of the missionaries from Britain and Europe.[13]

And Yates quotes E.R. Simmonds, the biographer of Bishop Pompallier:

> ... [the] change of heart and mind that created a Catholic church in New Zealand was essentially the work of Māori to Māori.[14]

Significant Wesleyan Māori Evangelists, Hokianga-Rakiura

A large number of Wesleyan indigenous evangelists spread the Wesleyan message throughout early colonial New Zealand.[15] The Rev Robert Young, the English Conference's investigator of the Wesleyan South Pacific missions, in 1853 reported that the Wesleyans listed 322 'local preachers' and five 'catechists' in their employ.[16] They, up to around 1860, contributed, perhaps, most to the transmission of Wesleyan religious ideas and concepts into Māori society and culture. The following narrative names, and is an account of some of the exploits of the most notable of the Wesleyan indigenous evangelists who spread the Gospel throughout New Zealand. It is no exaggeration to say that in many regions south of Hokianga they paved the way for Christianity and for the Wesleyan mission to expand to the far south of the South Island, often well advance of any European missionary to these regions.

Beginning at Māngungu in Hokianga, by around 1840 the number of prominent Wesleyan Māori class leaders and preachers included: Hoani Ri (John Leigh) Tutu, Mohi (Moses) Rewa, and Rihari Watoni (Richard Watson) Patuone (a son of the great chief), Haimona Pita (Simon Peter) Mātangi, Wiremu Pātene (William Barton) and Āperahama (Abraham) Tāonui (eldest son of Makoare (Macquarie) Te Tāonui, high chief of the Pōpotō hapū at Utakura); also two 1837 martyrs Matiu (Matthew) and Rihimona (Richmond), and a group of younger Wesleyan Ngāpuhi chiefs, who volunteered valuable service to the mission as class leaders, monitors and 'Native teachers' (or in Māori, 'kaiwhakaako'). Most were only paid in kind with gifts of food and clothing, although from 1845 'Wesleyan teachers' were granted £5 per annum.[17] So full of mana did these mission-established roles become, that John Hobbs in October 1843 recorded that, one 'Local Preacher', Hoani Waitere (John Whiteley), was assuming 'more importance than the chiefs themselves'.[18]

Of the early Hokianga Wesleyan 'converts' named, Hori Mori (George Morley) Kōtia, Hoani Ri (John Leigh) Tutu, Timoti (Timothy) Ōtene and Hohepa (Joseph) Ōtene Titokowaru (from South Taranaki, the Wesleyans' first stipended 'Assistant Minister'), were readily identified as slaves. Early on, there were at first, four notable death bed baptisms – those of Hika Tawa in January 1831, Hori Mori Kōtia in December 1832, Moses Hae Hae in February 1835, and William King Moetara, at Pākanae in December 1838. Through William White's efforts to encourage tribal economic and commercial development, some leading Hokianga chiefs such as Tamati Waka (Thomas Walker) Nene, Āperahama Tāonui, Mohi (Moses) Tāwhai, and Arama Karaka (Adam Clark) Pī, were key Wesleyan mission friends who became firm 'Mihanere' supporters of William White, even after his dismissal in 1836.[19] But the great majority of 'converts' at first tended to be young or minor chiefs who greatly increased their mana by their involvement with the Mission. Observed John Whiteley of the often considerable authority of a 'Native teacher':

> … if his attainments have raised him to that office, the most respectful deference
> is paid to his Authority and his word is law.[20]

Nevertheless, many traditional, pre-eminent, chiefs of Ngāpuhi, particularly Nene, Patuone and Te Tāonui, noticeably delayed identifying with the Wesleyans through baptism for a number of years. Nene was not baptised until at least mid-1839. Patuone, instead, joined the Church Mission in January 1840. And Te Tāonui delayed until May 1841.[21] One notable exception was Haimona Pita (Simon Peter) Mātangi who was among ten mostly younger chiefs of senior lines who White baptised together on 23 December 1833 at Māngungu. A cousin of the former paramount chief Muriwai, Mātangi was already aged about fifty. Described by William White as 'celebrated as a Warrior, murderer and cannibal', after November 1834 at Kāwhia, Mātangi translated for William Woon, newly arrived from Tonga. Whiteley noted that as a class teacher he was 'universally respected by the people … although he was formerly dreaded by them as one of their worst enemies'.[22] Other Hokianga chiefs contributed to the early success of the Wesleyans' expansion to the Waikato coast. They included Hoani Ri Tutu, Noah, Ngaro, and others from the Māngungu region like Matangi's son Hamuera (Samuel). But it was to Mātangi that Whiteley at Te Ahuahu reserved his most fulsome praise: 'Simon Peter who had suffered a most dangerous sickness was a great help'.[23]

In time, Nene too began to display a complete about turn from his old warrior ways. Beginning from the time he lost his entire family to disease, in William Woon's phrase, he began to 'declare for Christianity', and following his baptism, in 1840 he journeyed back to the people he had decimated during the inter-tribal wars to seek to bring peace and to declare the 'Gospel of peace'. In May 1840 Nene gave this testimony to Superintendent Waterhouse:

> Before the Mission came, we went to all parts of the land to kill and devour our countrymen. My hand was against everyman, and every man's hand was against me. I delighted in the blood of others, and never went forth but to scatter, tear, and slay; but since I heard of Jesus Christ and his Gospel, I have desired to publish peace, and gone to different parts of the land, to persuade the people to turn to God.[24]

At Tangiteroria, northern Kaipara, following numerous representations by Te Uri-o-hau paramount chief Tirarau, in April 1836 James Wallis established a mission station. Though Tirarau never fully accepted Christianity, other important chiefs such as Te Āwha Parore of Te Roroa, through his journeys to Whāngarei, Kaihu, Pouto and Otamatea, and many 'Native teachers', including Wiremu Tipene, Tomati Toia, Āperahama Tukupunga, and Paora (Paul) Tūhaere from Auckland, did much to teach the Gospel to the people of Kaipara. Indeed, at James Buller's 'fifth annual meeting' of the Kaipara Circuit in 1851, eleven Kaipara chiefs in turn addressed the assembly. Each advocated in favour of Māori Christians funding mission work in Fiji, resulting in the meeting raising £13.[25]

At the Manukau Harbour Te Rangi-taahua Ngāmuka, a young Ngāti Tamaoho chief from Pehiakura on the Āwhitu Peninsula, spent two years as a 'Native' teacher at the Māngungu mission before, according to James Wallis, at Whaingaroa on October 18 1835, William White baptised 'two chiefs of considerable rank and influence'. One of these was Te Rangi-taahua who was named Epiha Putini (Jabez Bunting), the other was Honi Pihama (John Beecham), both named after two of the Wesleyan Society's secretaries in London.[26] In 1837 Putini returned to his pā at Pehiakura. In the absence of any available English missionary, he became a teacher and preacher to his people. When approached by Bishop Selwyn to receive Anglican baptism and join the Church Missionary Society (CMS), Putini replied:

> 'No, I will adhere to my own people; I have waited a long time for a missionary and shall wait till I get one. … How many times was Jesus Christ baptised, once or more than once?', asked the chief. 'Only once', was [the bishop's] answer. 'Then one will do for me … as I wish to imitate his example as closely as possible.'[27]

On the Waikato coast, at Kāwhia Simon Peter Mātangi, Hori Mori, and Wiremu Pātene, were the first evangelists, arriving with William Woon from Māngungu early in November 1834. With Woon, newly arrived from Tonga, and not yet proficient in te reo Māori, Mātangi undertook most of the preaching responsibility. When Wallis began the Whaingaroa (Raglan) mission at Waiomu, Te Horea, on the northern side of the harbour entrance in April 1835, the Ngāti Māhanga high chief Wiremu Nera (William Naylor) Te Awaitaia, already influenced by Christianity, and Paora (Paul) Muriwhenua, became great friends of the Mission. Te Awaitaia defended the mission from neighbouring hostile tribes, early built a 500-seat chapel for the mission, liberated Taranaki slaves, and in 1840 unsuccessfully tried to mediate peace between Taupo and South Taranaki tribes.[28] Hāmiora (Samuel) Honeybee Ngāropi the first Wesleyan convert at Te Horea and their first ordained 'Native minister', was another key evangelist at Whaingaroa.[29]

In Taranaki the key pioneering Wesleyan evangelist was Wiremu Nēra (William Naylor) Ngātai (also known as Wi Parirau), a returned slave released from the Hokianga about 1836. The missionaries credited him with converting the whole Taranaki coast before any English missionary arrived.[30] In 1841 Hoani Ri Tutu was an important 'assistant missionary' to Charles Creed at Ngāmotu. In South Taranaki significant Maori mission assistants and class leaders included Jabez Waterhouse a seventeen-year-old class leader and 'best born' high chief at Waimate pā, Rihari Watoni (Richard Watson) from before 1840 a class leader and local preacher also of Waimate, and Thomas Rayner at Orokowhai. Watoni was baptised by John Whiteley at Kāwhia but died in January 1843. Richard Watson Ngawaka Tauroa, an early Wesleyan teacher at Pātea, was a faithful Wesleyan chief of Pākākohe. He died in 1888.[31] Hare Tipene (Charles Stephenson) Kāroro, a class leader at Tihoi, so impressed Whiteley in July 1842 that he reported there was, 'something so much like simple old-fashioned Methodism about this leader and his people that I was really at home with them.'[32] In June 1847 Woon revealed how greatly he relied on 'native agency' to work his mission when he submitted to the London Secretaries the following list of the Waimate Circuit's 10 preaching places and their Wesleyan teachers who needed bells for their chapels:

Ihupuku:	Thomas Ririmu	The Orokowhai:	Thomas Rayner
Patea:	Timothy	Pukeoha:	Solomon
Taumaha:	Matthew	Puketi:	Brown
Ohangai:	Bartholomew	Mawhitiwhiti:	Jacob
Turangarere:	Enoch	Okaiawa:	Thomas

Another teacher at Ōhāngai was a young Māori woman, Anne Turner, a returned slave from Whaingaroa who had been 'converted' by James Wallis.[33]

Four more Wesleyan martyrs, Te Pūtakarua, Te Awaroa, Te Mātoe and Te Hau Māringi, from South Taranaki's Ngāti Ruanui tribe, were killed for their faith by Whānganui Māori in two separate incidents between 1836 and 1839. In fact, a former prominent local Whānganui local historian, Athol Kirk, believes that South Taranaki Wesleyan evangelists introduced the Gospel to Whānganui Māori months before did Wiremu Te Tauri, the CMS evangelist across the river at Putiki, usually credited with being Whānganui's first evangelist.[34] On an early visit in 1836, Wiremu Neira Ngātai converted Māre, the Ngā Rauru chief at Te Ahi-tuatini pā (near today's Whānganui Hospital). Also in 1836 the first two of the four martyrs influenced two mid-Whānganui River chiefs from Operiki, Nōpera and Tahana-rehua, to seek New Testaments from Whenuakura River Māori (today near Marton), where before they returned with their precious New Testaments, Nōpera and Tahana-rehua were 'converted' and 'baptised' at Mātangi pā by Henere (Henry) its chief. Henere's 'baptismal' ritual may have been similar to the 'kokiro' ritual in December 1839 Henry Williams observed Ngātai carrying out on his converts. Williams described it as being 'very much according to native custom' but 'an abominable perversion of baptism', as Ngātai washed the heads of his converts with water warmed in a cooking pot which Williams reckoned represented as much a customary release from tapu as a cleansing from sin.[35]

On 27 September 1845 *The New Zealander* newspaper in Auckland published in full the testimony of Wereta, a young associate of John Skevington at Heretoa in South Taranaki, and one of the first scholars at the 'Wesleyan Native Institution' in Auckland. Wereta's testimony contains all the elements of the classic English conversion experience: a sense of sinfulness and need to seek Christ's grace and forgiveness, a time of spiritual crisis involving a period of calling out for God's mercy, and a point of acceptance and peace leading to an ethical change of behaviour and vocation when '... I rested upon him, and I felt His spirit bearing witness with mine, that I was a child of God. Then I became anxious for the salvation of my friends.' Indeed, shortly before his death at the Wesleyan Native Institution in March 1846, Wereta, writing to his relatives back at Heretoa that he was about to die, urged them 'to maintain the fire of the Holy Ghost in their hearts ...'[36]

At Te Āro pā, Port Nicholson, in 1839, until a European missionary could be sent, John Bumby and John Hobbs left four Māngungu 'native' teachers, Minarapa Te Rangi-hatu-ake, (another) Hori Mori, Paora (Paul), and Hemi (James) Parai[37] to minister to Wellington Māori. Minarapa had volunteered to accompany Bumby and Hobbs to begin a Wesleyan mission at Port Nicholson and was left at Te Āro pā in charge. Other teachers were, Mohi (Moses) Ngāponga, and Te Teira Whatakore who worked alongside two CMS Māori teachers, Reihana (Richard Davis) Te Kamo or Te Karoro, and Tamihana (Thomas) Rauparahā, son of the celebrated Ngāti Toa chief Te Rauparahā. In 1842 when Minarapa's Taranaki relatives called for him to return to them, he appointed a fellow Te Ati Awa teacher, Wi Upo or Ipu Rangiwahia, who had arrived with Henry Williams on the *Columbine* in November 1839, to act as lay preacher in his stead.[38]

Across Cook Strait, at Cloudy Bay, the Wesleyan missionary, Samuel Ironside, arrived in December 1840 to find that Wiriamu (Williams), a Māori teacher from the Bay of Islands, had preceded him. Earlier, in June 1839, the Wesleyans John Hobbs and John Bumby had found 'literate' Māori teachers from Kāwhia already instructing the people for Sabbath worship in Queen Charlotte Sound, Tory Channel and at Cloudy Bay. When the *Tory*, the New Zealand Company's survey ship, moored nearby, Wiriamu assembled the Māori Christians on board for worship.[39] To cover his vast Top-of-the-South mission field from Motueka to Cloudy Bay, Ironside made good use of CMS taught Ngāti Toa evangelists from Kāpiti who were already evangelising the Cook Strait district. He appointed the CMS-trained young chief from Kāpiti, Rāwiri Kingi (David King) Puaha, a close relative of Te Rauparahā and Rangihaeta, as a 'Native' catechist, and is said to have used some thirty Māori teachers to preach, teach, and give pastoral care around his vast domain. These included: Hoani Koinaki at Queen Charlotte Sound, who gave Ironside payment for the missionary's 'pukapuka tapu' 'greater than if the books had been sold.' Pirimona, Pirihira, Josaia, Hori Patara (George Buttle) Hori Paratene (George Broughton), Rāwiri Pihana at Pelorus Sound and Rāwiri Waitere the pioneer teacher converted by John Whiteley at Kāwhia around 1836. One, Naohu (Noa), prepared forty candidates for Ironside to baptise on d'Urville Island in July 1842, including the first Ironside baptised, 'the dying Toheroa, who confessed Jesus as the sinners' friend.'[40]

On Banks Peninsula at Koukourarata, Port Levy, there appears the rather mysterious figure of Taawao, the first, in 1839, to preach the Gospel at the little Kai (or Ngai) Tāhu settlement. Variously referred to as 'Taawao', 'Tāwai', 'Towai', and 'Tawaonui-a-Tane' (Son of Taawaonui), a tradition has it that a Wesleyan convert from Ngāpuhi taught Taawao his Christianity at Māwhera (today's Greymouth). In June 1840 James Watkin began a Wesleyan mission at Waikouaiti (North Otago). There he evidently baptised Taawao on 27 September 1843, with the baptismal name, Rāwiri Kingi (David King). With Hōhepa Korehi, who likely came from Cloudy Bay, Watkin appointed both as Wesleyan teachers at Koukourarata (Port Levy), from where they evangelised Kai Tahu communities around Banks Peninsula and North Canterbury.[41]

Taawao's legacy is the stream of high-ranking southern Kai Tahu chiefly leaders, preachers and teachers, who were important interpreters of the faith to their people and carried on the Wesleyan cause through the nineteenth century in the Otago and South Canterbury regions long after the Ōtakou Wesleyan Mission ceased. Such men included, Rāwiri (David) Te Maire from Ārowhenua, near Temuka, South Canterbury (who lived until 1899). In February 1843 he was the first young Kai Tahu chief James Watkin baptised. He was followed on 18 June by Iwikau or Horomona (Solomon) Pōhio, 'a man of high rank' from Ruapuke Island in Foveaux Strait, who on his own initiative ventured to Waikouaiti shortly after Watkin arrived to learn about Christianity. (He died in 1880).[42] In the 1870s both men were spokesmen and aides of the Ārowhenua prophetic leader, Hipa Te Maiharoa, and his messianic movement known as 'Kaingarara'.[43] Hoani Wetere (John Wesley) Kōrako and Tari Wetere (Charles Wesley) Te Kahu, both of Ōtakou, on Otago Peninsula, and also baptised in June 1843, became leaders and teachers in the Catlins area. The most prominent of other chiefs baptised in July 1843 was Matiaha (Matthias)

Tiramorehu who became the foremost teacher at Moeraki. Also baptised in July 1843 were Anaru (Andrew) Takairaki of Rakiura (Stewart Island), and Rāwiri Waitiri (David White) Mamaru, who was appointed a class leader at his kaika (kainga, village). Other Maori teachers Watkin trained included, Kurukuru who drowned soon after in a tragic flax gathering trip, and Watkin's first convert Māhaka who on being baptised in December 1842 took the name Hemi Watekini (James Watkin).[44]

Trade, Transmission, Transformation and Cross-over Points

It is to be noticed that one era and place, namely, the missionaries' first four years at 'Wesleydale', their mission station at the head of the Whāngaroa Harbour, has not been included in the above narrative of Wesleyan 'indigenous evangelism'. This is because, despite a considerable exchange of ideas and debates, especially between the lay catechist James Stack, and various chiefly conversationalists, the missionaries for much of the time were at odds with their erstwhile Ngāti Uru 'patrons', the elderly chief Te Puhi and his two sons, Ngāhuruhuru and 'George' Te Aara. They were unable to maintain a mission school. And they could not within the mission station retain 'mission Māori' residents to begin to train them in the rudiments of literacy and Christianity, agricultural husbandry and cultivation, or pit sawing of kauri logs. Hence, during 'the Whāngaroa episode', writes John Owens, it seemed that 'the missionary ideas were completely resisted and no converts were made ...'[45] This reality the missionaries were forced to face in their earliest years at both Whāngaroa and Māngungu, leads us, therefore, to examine the cultural and social environment of the Māori world in which came about the eventual cultural and religious change which led to the phenomenon of Wesleyan 'indigenous evangelism'.

Of the three basic chronological decades or stages that illustrate this process, firstly, there was the decade of *Trade*, 1820-1830, dominated by each tribe's willingness to accept the missionaries in their midst primarily as a source of trade goods. This was the first years of missionary endeavour, before they had any grasp of the nature of the society they sought to convert, or much of the language to communicate their ideas, and when Māori debated, assessed, ridiculed, and generally dismissed Christian ideas and rituals.

Murray B. Gittos, the biographer of William White, from 1830-1836 the Wesleyans' Mission Superintendent, in his rather archaic prose, articulated well the cultural and economic exchange the Hokianga chiefs had in mind and the dilemma the missionaries faced:

> ... The Maori mind was not closed to new ideas if some advantage could be seen in them. ... Ideas that did not fly directly in the face of Maori beliefs were worthy of being tried out. Sunday observance was an example. ... But ideas that did conflict were not conceded. ... [Some] claimed that all [the missionary] gave them was karakia (prayers), which [they] thought nothing of and did not want. What [they] did want was muskets and powder and tomahawks, etc., and if the missionaries loved [them] they should give ... more of these things.[46]

As in 1814 the chiefs Te Pahi and Ruatara at Rangihoua invited, and paved the way for, Samuel Marsden to begin a CMS mission in the Bay of Islands, so in 1823 the 'indigenous agency' of Ngāi Tāwake chief Hongi Hika, a leading patron of both missionary societies', played a substantial role in determining where the Wesleyan Mission began. A station at 'Hododo' (perhaps Ōruru, inland of Doubtless Bay) was recommended to Samuel Leigh by Hongi (because his sister lived there). Leigh's intention had been to settle at Mercury Bay, Coromandel Peninsula, but Hongi told Leigh, 'he must give up that design, as it was [Hongi's] purpose to kill all the people in those parts.'[47] Indeed, Wesleydale was established at Whāngaroa because Hongi's raid of the previous year had denuded the population of the missionaries' next preferred site at Whāngarei. Then it was through the interventions of several leading Hokianga chiefs, Patuone, Muriwai, Wiremu Kingi (William King) Moetara, and Mōhi (Moses) Tāwhai, that over the next decade all the Wesleyans' Hokianga stations (at Te Toke, Māngungu, 'Newark' Pākanae, and Te Poinga (in the lower Waimā Valley) were established.

Ten months after Wesleydale's sacking on 10 January 1827, on 30 October 1827, at the invitation of Patuone, a leading Ngāti Hao chief on the Waihou arm of the southern inland Hokianga Harbour, the Wesleyans recommenced their Mission in Hokianga. As they had fled from Wesleydale Patuone had placed his cloak of protection over the fleeing missionaries.[48] But trade - to establish a trading post and a supply of muskets to rival those of Hongi - not religion - was more what Patuone had in mind in inviting them. Likewise, Muriwai, of Te Māhurehure, the paramount chief of the inland southern Hokianga, stated to the lay missionary James Stack, later that year, he 'would favour having a missionary living with him, as "he liked the articles we give in barter".'[49] Trade was clearly also on the minds of other chiefs along the Waihou arm. James Stack was told on one occasion, 'we dealt too hardly in our bartering[;] that if we would price our blankets lower they would believe what we said on Religion.'[50]

In fact, missionary activity in the Hokianga began in the context of considerable European contact and trade, both before and during the life of the mission.[51] Hokianga chiefs engaged in a lively and vigorous exchange of religious views with nearby European kauri traders and sawyers, ship-builders and settlers, as well as with the Wesleyans. From the start the chiefs were developing their own incipient Māori theology as they engaged with Stack's attempts to engage them in his evangelism. Fifty years later, the early Hokianga Pākeha-Māori settler, Jacky Marmon, gave this candid assessment of the early Wesleyan-Māori engagement:

> The Wesleyan missionaries bought a nice place on the Hokianga, at Mangungu, and lived there. The natives took very little notice of them; they used to go and trade for blankets, spades, or anything they had, for which they used to pay in potatoes. Mr Stack … would wander about among them, and when he saw a few sitting together would talk about their souls. … They would say they believed what they were told on purpose to get into favour with the missionaries, or to get something out of them that they wanted, and then have a good laugh behind the parson's back for his being such a fool as to believe what they had said. …[52]

On the other hand, it is probable that some chiefs really did find Stack's 'strange ideas' intriguing. Stack found, on 15 June 1828, they talked past each other from two very different world views, in Owens's terms the 'literary' and the 'pragmatic',[53] where the missionaries assumed a special validity and authority from the literary qualities of the printed word of the Bible. But Māori understood their religion only in the terms which had meaning for them - 'practical experience'. Māori belief about the invisible world was based on their experience of dreams. They believed in 'ātua' because they 'could see and hear them, even if the missionaries could not', Owens wrote.[54] In June 1828 Stack reported that during a conversation, Muriwai and Te Taonui

> … wished to know where our knowledge of the state of separate spirits was derived and because we had not seen the fires of hell with our bodily eyes laughed at our belief of it all. …

> Muri-wai [sic] said our idea was absurd to suppose the man's spirit was wholly absent from the body as long as any portion of him remained behind. What food do they eat in the world of spirrits [sic] said Te Taonoui. To which being answered that they had not the same bodily organs and appetites which we have in our present state he replied. "How do they see then? How do they hear? What are they employed about? If a brave man dies and goes to the place of which you are speaking will he be able to exercise his valour if there are no places to besiege, must he become dull and inactive? Ah you are a set of old women … Are there no guns in the pō [dark abyss?] No people to be fought with?" I then talked to them on the resurrection when the following remarks were made … "How many persons have already been raised from the dead? Did you see them?" Being answered in the negative they laughed heartily saying "Oh *indeed* you only heard of it from someone else." I then spoke to them on the judgement but was equally unsuccessful in overcoming their levity.[55]

The same month, Captain Clark, the Deptford shipyard manager at nearby Hōreke, who spoke Māori, reported to Stack a discussion in which Te Tāonui asked Clark,

> '[D]o you think you can persuade me that the body of the man whose thigh bone is round his neck yonder, a piece of him is in my belly, another part of him at the East Cape[,] and another part somewhere else will ever be reunited?' …[56]

The following years, 1830-1840, may be defined as the second decade of the conversion process: *Transmission*. They were years when large-scale printing and distribution of the translated scriptures occurred and literate Māori evangelists began to promote and spread 'Te Rongo pai', the 'Gospel of Peace', among their own communities.

By 1830, the missionaries were on the eve of the first signs of a turning to Christianity. Gittos again aptly summed up the situation the missionaries faced. The missionaries experience generally was still 'the same as at Wesleydale: trade, yes; religion, no', but under the 'cordial' Patuone's protection their treatment was 'more cordial' and they were more willing to enter into religious discussions. However, more than blankets, learning to read and write was what Māori now most valued. And access to reading material in te reo Māori, Gittos argues, was what 'ultimately paved the way for the real break-through in conversions, for it enabled religion to be taught by native teachers and congregations to read the scriptures for themselves'.[57]

A first sign of progress at Māngungu occurred in January 1828. Hongi, a son of Te Puhi, the leading Ngāti Uru chief at Whāngaroa, had now became a mission 'domestick' and with Hika Tawa, a long-standing missionary companion, resided with the missionaries. A young woman slave, a daughter of Te Puhi (probably Mōtio), became its first 'female servant'. Others soon followed. They enabled the missionaries to begin a small school to teach in te reo Māori, reading and writing and numbers; also to teach the women domestic arts and to have the men assist John Hobbs at the mission's sawyer's pit sawing and planking timber for the Māngungu building projects.[58] Two months later in March, Kāri, a young chief who had been to Tahiti and there experienced the London Missionary Society's (LMS) mission, returned to his people on Mōtiti Island in the middle of the Hokianga Harbour and told his whanau of Christianity in Tāhiti. For a time, he created some interest in Stack's attempts to evangelise. But, Stack recorded, the people found the doctrine of the resurrection to be 'an idle tale'. They seemed 'more eager for our clothes than for our religion'.[59]

Early in 1830, a more substantial breakthrough occurred, as Church Mission Māori spread Christianity from the Bay of Islands. On 8 February William and Eliza White at Kerikeri witnessed the baptism of Rāwiri (David) Taiwhanga, a chief from near Kaikohe and a companion of Hongi Hika. He had learnt European agricultural skills from six months with Samuel Marsden at Parramatta and with John Butler at Kerikeri where he became overseer of Butler's Kerikeri farm, arguably New Zealand's first commercial Māori dairy farmer. When Taiwhanga visited Hokianga in September 1830 he spread a message of support for Christianity. His testimony was important in promoting interest, so that after his visit Nene declared, 'when the Bay of Islanders believe, I and my brother will believe too'.[60]

The death-bed baptisms of Hika Tawa in January 1831, and in February 1832 of Mōhi (Moses) Hae Hae, an important Mangamuka chief from the northern side of the harbour, had significant evangelistic implications also, as these events were closely observed. On 16 January 1831, Hika Tawa became the Wesleyans' first baptised 'convert'. He had been with the missionaries throughout their Wesleydale trials at Whāngaroa, fled with them to Sydney, and then returned with them as their sole 'domestic' when they again started in Hokianga. Hae Hae died on 7 February 1832, two days after his baptism.[61] Hae Hae's baptism and 'Christian' death, as that of a chief of some mana, was of particular importance in bringing many Mangamuka Māori under Wesleyan influence.

Another influential talking point was that two young Wesleyan protégés from Whāngaroa were baptised about this time in Tonga. 'Shukey', or 'Huki', had travelled to England with White in 1826. On Huki's return he joined the Tongan Wesleyan missionaries as a lay helper. But he died shortly after his baptism 'in a state of hope'. The second, 'Tungahe', had spent time in New South Wales with Leigh and Marsden.[62]

A further important breakthrough about this time, was that Church Missionary Society printed scriptures began to appear in the Hokianga creating an enthusiasm for translated scriptures as Mission Māori learnt to read the missionaries' literature for themselves and to develop their own understandings of Christian doctrine. A small 117-page booklet William Yate in Sydney in 1830 had translated and printed for the CMS mission, began to be found at Māngungu. White heard of several 'natives' who worked two months to obtain this little book. Wesleyan Māori now travelled about telling other Māori that what these strange 'mihingere' had been saying was '*true*'. It was written in their Book 'which all who knew the secret would understand.'[63] By 1835 some 'native' teachers began to uphold the authority and truth of the Bible as being superior to their Māori customary lore.[64]

More baptisms followed, at first one or two a year, then after December 1833, in a flood. Each was an important instrument of evangelism. One chief baptised was the elderly Pōpotō chief, Mātangi, a relative of Patuone, baptised as Simon Peter (Haimona Pita). In March 1834, Edward Markham (a grandson of an Archbishop of York) independently observed how effective was Mātangi's preaching in influencing Hokianga Māori to embrace Christianity. Markham described how,

> ... I could have fancied myself among the Covenanters ... Thirty Tatooed earnest Faces, reading and singing by the Fire with their Muskets across their Breasts, and then an old man [most likely Mātangi] gave them an Exhortation ... He recapitulated the Heads of Mr White's sermon leaning on the Butt end of his Musket with a blanket on; as he got animated his figure appeared to great advantage. ... There was nothing to be gained to these men, No Worldly distinctions, Vain praises or Pomp. They laid down and slept where they had prayed with their Arms in their hands, quite a Bivouac.[65]

Following a sermon by a 'native preacher' (again possibly Mātangi), the following Sunday Nene and Kaweka Warekani (another influential chief from Mangamuka) declared themselves 'in favour of Christianity'.[66] By November 1837, Nene, himself, began to take a stand for Christianity. The mission's printer, William Woon, recorded:

> Good attendance at the native services yesterday, and in the evening Thos. Walker gave a powerful address to the people at the close of the service and stated that God had taken his wife and children – that he was now an orphan – but he had only now begun to be in earnest about his soul. A very affecting time![67]

Meanwhile, raupo chapels at Huatau and Paremata, and at Mangataipa near Mangamuka were built, entirely by Māori initiative. Mission pupils practised their writing by inscribing scriptures into the sand on beaches, as well as on their classroom slates. Others carved verses into trees or along bush paths.[68]

Undoubtedly, social and cultural changes also influenced this turning to the Gospel. They included: musket warfare between tribes, new European diseases, new crops and industry, which necessitated leaving hilltop pā for less healthy swampy lowland flax and timber gathering, wearing blankets at all times in all weathers as a permanent garment, a lack of sanitation, a tragic increase in sterility and infant mortality and the passing of the older generation of warrior chiefs. Yet up to 1840 and into the colonial era, there is still evidence of much continuity and endurance of traditional tribal institutions, authority, and practices in the face of the rapid social change of the time. As Raeburn Lange explains,

> What is clear is that the [Christian] teachers did take over at least some aspects of the role of religious experts in the traditional order. ... Much of the existing

Maori approach to the supernatural could be taken into the new religion ...[The Christian teachers'] religious leadership did not represent a clean break from the assumptions and practices of the traditional religious specialists.[69]

Hence this writer senses that the Rev George Laurenson,the long-standing former Methodist Māori Mission Superintendent, in his 1972 history of the Methodist Māori Mission, overstates the degree to which Māori embracing of Christianity had shaken Māori society's older sanctions and structures when he stated that, 'all the older restraints had collapsed. The laws of Tapu and Mana had been deeply shaken by the new forces of European weapons against which the "Karakia Maori" was powerless'.[70] Rather, most Hokianga Māori at this time turned to embrace 'Missionary Christianity' for reasons that were positive and from their own initiative, rather than because they had lost faith in their old ways. So, Belich argues that up to the 1830s European trade and technology did not convert Māori. But it did change them. In John Owens' terms, the social context cannot be ignored. It did not provide the initial impetus for conversion. But it helped make a turning to Christianity possible.[71]

Brief mention has already been made of some of the spiritual 'crossover points' or 'mythic parallels' between traditional ethnic Māori spirituality and Christianity: in their non-distinction between the sacred and the secular; similarities between the social constraints of tapu, utu and muru and the Christian belief in providence and 'the Great Chain of Being'; also the similarities to be found in their respective creation stories. Bill Dacker, a recent historian of Otago Kai Tahu, writes similarly that Māori and missionary

> spoke the same symbolic language in some fundamental ways. Similarities include the whakapapa or genealogy of the Old Testament, and concepts of darkness and light that begin and pervade the bible [sic]. The idea that death or disaster results from sin parallels the Maori idea that disaster is the result of transgression of a tapu.[72]

Other 'Praeparatio Evangelica', or 'seeds of the Gospel', which to Wesleyans may be seen to be examples of God's 'prevenient grace' working ahead of the missionaries, can be seen in karakia – whether used as a traditional incantation, or used as a grace before a meal and then to remove the tapu linked with food afterward – or in similarities between 'whanaungatanga' 'kaitiakitanga' and arohatanga, and Christian grace, gentleness, peacefulness and hospitality. Also between kōkiri or tohi, and baptism; cannibalism and Holy Communion; and in the experience of prophetic dreams which in both cultures were a way to give access to the mysterious numinous, and were often associated with seemingly supernatural 'power encounters'. Also in the wahi tapu (sacred places) of each culture - for Māori mountain tops, for example Rangihoua and Whiria mountains in the Far North, and churches for the missionaries. In Io, who for some Māori came to be seen as an ultimate supreme Ātua, equivalent to Yahweh; and in being able to appropriate Hine as a Māori type of Mary,[73] Tiki as a type of Adam, and Maui who died trying to save humanity from death as a type of the Creator Christ. The idea of 'redemptive sacrifice' was not unknown in pre-Christian Māori theology either. Peace and reconciliation, for instance, could require that 'one man from the offending party was killed as utu.'[74]

Moreover, in spite of the missionaries' disputatious relationships, Canon Yates suggests that over time many 'Mission Maori' living within the mission compound did come to see an attractiveness in the missionaries' style of Christian living which led some into observing Christian prayer and a strict Sabbath keeping.[75] Likewise, the American social anthropologist, H.G. Barnett, in 1953 argued that the lure of 'advocate characteristics' such as 'prestige, popularity and benefit' as perceived from the stimulation of 'innovation' or 'novelty', can be a basis of culture change.[76] Enthusiasm, excitement and novelty, leading to an embracing of the 'new', was certainly to the fore when the Wesleyans' little 'Columbian' printing press arrived at Māngungu early in 1836. When Woon began to operate the press, there was no shortage of fascinated young chiefs who 'crowded day and night into the little printing office' to work the press, while Woon set the type and checked the proofs. Eliza White reported that 'we cannot keep the natives out – they are highly delighted with it'. Among the eager printers Woon later identified were Nikorima (Nicholas), Āperahama Tautoru Te Tāonui, and Hemi Karana (James Garland), who was later to draw a notable sketch of how in the Hauraki Gulf in June 1840 John Bumby drowned (among the first Māori drawing to be recorded).[77]

And there were what missiologists calls 'power encounters', where the spiritual power of the Christian God was tested. For example, before battles some Christian Māori recited Christian prayers and used the Bible as a talisman to ward off bullets. During fighting warriors of 'Pai Marire' raised their hands while shouting out 'Hau Hau Pai Marire!'[78]

The decades 1840 and beyond were certainly years of significant degrees of *Transformation*, when throughout the land, aspects of Christianity, ranging from Sabbath observance to establishing Christian pacifist villages, greatly transformed the spiritual, ethical and structural basis of Māori society, culture and spirituality.

By 1840, the missionaries saw enormous changes in Māori attitudes towards themselves and towards Missionary Christianity. Murray Gittos, with some perception, again astutely described some of the range of Māori motives and attitudes:

> The hunger for European trade and technology was still rampant although some now wondered if the price paid in the mortality rate from European diseases and in alcohol-loosened tribal bonds was not too high. Some saw the missionaries as providers of trade, technology, medicine, peace and support against European excesses; others [saw them] as corrupters of traditional values, as hypocrites who pretended to offer material advancement but actually did very little to close the enormous gap of wealth between the mission native and the missionary. Some opposed the missionaries because they resided with a rival tribe, giving the rival a material advantage over tribes that had no missionary. Some were determined to stand firm in their native beliefs and defy the European god to do his worst; some wanted the new god on their side; others wanted to nationalise the Christian god and give the saviour a Maori face. Some were ready to give up their lands for a musket and blanket needed now. Others saw the folly of this. It was a time of ferment.[79]

Mission Field Phenomena: Missiologists' Categories

Gittos here astutely hints at the many different collective tribal economic, cultural and spiritual responses to the arrival of Christianity, and some of the individual Māori evangelistic initiatives. In turn, this writer builds upon a 'phenomenological' model of 'cultural analysis' to categorise mission field phenomena that two New Zealand-born missiologists, the Rev Dr Harold Turner and James Irwin, observed in Africa and South Asia.[80] Turner, like Irwin sought to classify the various collective and individualistic mission- field Māori responses and initiatives towards and away from missionary leadership observable in Āotearoa from 1830 onwards. He identifies three main categories that represent movements toward missionary leadership and oversight. While Irwin identified four categories of movements away from missionary leadership, one of which included 'nativistic', or 'resistance, movements' (which earlier historians classified as types of syncretistic 'adjustment' or 'cargo cults'). All seven categories represent to varying degrees a transformation of Māori spiritualty to include, at least a veneer of, or 'diffusion' of, Christian influence within traditional Māori customary spirituality and culture. Some were more orthodox and missionary approved; others were more syncretistic and opposed missionary oversight. We focus first on the three which represent movements toward missionary oversight and leadership.

There were, firstly, what Irwin called *sodality conversions* of often individual, detribalised Māori. Many lived within the mission compound at Māngungu, isolated from their whanau and hapū as redeemed slaves or domestic servants or students. Hika Tawa was one. Another was Hori Mori (George Morley) Kōtia. In a letter, dated 25 July 1835, to the WMS Committee in London John Hobbs gave a very fulsome eulogy praising Mori's 'conversion' and influence upon the life of the mission which is very illustrative of the ethical transformation 'sodality conversion' could bring about in some converts' lives:

> Kotia was older than most of our domestics ... and he was anything but a favourite with us; ... [full of] the duplicity, dishonesty, and licentiousness of the New-Zealanders, ... [then] his heart was smitten; ... For more than two years his conduct was truly exemplary. From the stiff-necked, dishonest, deceitful, impertinent New-Zealand slave, he became humble, teachable, obliging, and trustworthy, and a sincere follower of the Lord Jesus Christ.[81]

Edward Markham described how Simon Peter Mātangi's conversion also drastically transformed his life:

> [Mātangi] at last ... came to read and write, and cipher: "he had several Wives, he had not seen or spoken to his first Wife for years"; but, as a measure of his newly-gained religious fervour, ... he returned to the "Beastly Old Hag", ... a thoroughly changed Man and like Saul baptised [and whose] conversion is well attested.[82]

At Kāwhia in November 1834, when told of non-Christian Waikato tribes' intentions to murder him, Mātangi responded, 'And what is my life compared with the life of their souls that I should hesitate.'[83]

And in April 1835, at an assembly of 1,000 at Māngungu, three Wesleyan converts, the chiefs Noah, Ngaro and Mātangi addressed the crowd, extolling the 'advantages of the Christian religion' and the end of war. White used the occasion to urge the assembled congregation 'to turn to God.' Noted Yates:

> … the effectiveness of Māori speaking to Maori in the cause of the mission appeared to have one identifiable and welcome result: various chiefs pledged themselves (after running to and fro in Māori rhetorical style) to "cease from war".
> … Simon Peter then preached in Woon's hearing to another chief an exhortation "that included the approved missionary references to the fall of man, the love of God, and the gift of Christ: on Woon's account, the chief's attention was "riveted".[84]

Testimonies translated for the NSW Mission Superintendent the Rev Joseph Orton during his mid-1833 visit to Māngungu, also indicated a growing spiritual transformation among Hokianga Māori. One, compared himself to 'a man on a journey and needing food; for his spiritual journey he had food of "the word of God and the means of grace which when he grew faint and weary were exceedingly sweet and refreshing to his soul."'[85]

At the mission service on Sunday 17 May 1840 the important Wesleyan high chiefs of the Waihou River, Waimā, and Mangamuka areas, Patuone and Tamati Waka Nene, Wiremu Pātene, and Mohi Tāwhai, all testified to Wesleyan South Pacific Mission Superintendent the Rev John Waterhouse of their transformation.[86] Wiremu Pātene's testimony is of particular interest as it illustrates the phenomenon often noted in mission fields around the world of the 'two hearts' inner conflict within the mind of the neophyte convert over whether to convert or remain loyal to one's traditional indigenous spirituality:

> I have long been a worshipper of God; but my heart has been divided in two parts; with one part I loved God, with the other the world. I know that this is not right, and I desire to give my whole heart to God. I know this is the only way for my heart to be light. When I think about God, the Holy Spirit brings joy into my soul; [now] my prayer to God is, that I may be fully his. This is the end of my speech.[87]

Similarly, the Waimā Wesleyan chief, Mōhi Tāwhai, testified to a reconciled, changed heart and belief in Christ's salvation after some two years of inner emotional turmoil.[88] While Patuone declared to Waterhouse, 'I am filled with indignation at our former habits and customs. The word of God has been made known, and this has made the change.'[89]

Secondly, there were what might be called '*People movements*', collective tribal-wide following of chiefs in embracing aspects of the missionaries' Christian worship, liturgy and values. In late 1834, John Whiteley reported that 'whole tribes seemed to be coming over'[90] to the mission cause, as all around Hokianga tribes were building chapels, assembling for 'Sabbath' worship, and seeking missionary instruction to learn to read and write.

Similar to people movements, but called '*Going Mihanere*' by the Auckland historian Kathleen Shawcross,[91] and of a more secular nature, were also chief-led collective tribal turnings to associate with the missionaries for their economic and commercial advantage, and political guidance. Around Hokianga a major form of '*Going Mihanere*' was the backing that his 'Mihanere' chiefs Nene, Tāwhai, Ngaro, and Wiremu Pātene gave to William White to mentor them in their kauri logging and milling enterprises. The chiefs entrusted large tracts of their tribal lands to White to protect them from European sawyers' exploitation, and to promote their tribes' economic and commercial development in the new kauri milling economy. But initially they were hesitant to identify with the missionaries' religion through baptism. The backing of these chiefs, however, meant that by early April 1835 White was able to claim that Hokianga's '... Principal chiefs were in favour of Christianity ...'[92]

The other side of the coin to the more orthodox indigenous evangelism of missionary-friendly 'Native teachers' were a number of more unorthodox faiths or *resistance movements* which were led by Māori religious leaders. Many were Wesleyan or Church-trained 'Native teachers'. Regarded as 'heretical' by missionaries, and by most historians as primarily 'syncretistic new religions' which combined customary traditional Māori and Christian rituals and doctrines, Bronwyn Elsmore, divided them into three types: *The Early Reactions'* *1830-1850*; in the 1850s *'The Decade of the Healers'*; and *'The Prophetic Period'* *1860-1900*.

'The Early Reactions' period was 'the great baptism period' when Māori gave up many of their practices that did not equate with Christianity, embraced the Christian community, or identified with Old Testament Jewish history as a way to 'regain the corporate protection previously provided by tribal alliances', so 'gaining even stronger social solidarity through membership of an even greater association.'[93] This aligns with Catholic historian E.R. Simmonds's insight on why some Māori embraced Catholicism:

> The chosen people of the Old Testament could provide a fresh *whakapapa* (ancestry) 'larger than the Māori race' and 'in Christ they could find the hero ancestor of the New tribe of Christians and could find their own identity in that tribe ... and find that wholeness which was given by the religions of old. ...'[94]

'The Decade of the Healers' or 'Wahi Tapu' movements of the 1850s, Elsmore described as an era of a growing disillusionment with the missionaries and their 'Ātuanui'. Their adherents believed that diseases were this Ātua's retribution for Māori breaking the tapu of their sacred 'wahi tapu'. But on the whole, these faiths, she wrote, were 'mainly Christian-oriented with individual healers advocating belief in the Atuanui as a requisite for health', while 'the old ways were deliberately discontinued in favour of Christian practices.'[95] Thirdly, Elsmore identified *'The Prophetic Period' 1860-1900*, when a new type of leader emerged who 'combined the motivation of dissatisfaction and injustice [over land confiscations] with religious backing and fervour' as 'agents of metaphysical or religious-ethical revelation.'[96]

Te Ātua Wera or Papahurihia (fl. 1834-1875), was a Te Hikutū prophet whose Nākahi (serpent) faith was first encountered in 1834. As Elsmore highlighted, he appropriated Christian and Jewish doctrines and rituals from the Bible, suggesting that 'these are all ideas which can be seen to have some appeal to Maori of the period, in that they not only added something to already existing Maori beliefs but, perhaps more importantly, did not oppose or contradict any of them.'[97] So Belich could artfully state that Te Ātua Wera's unorthodoxy 'usually stayed just below the threshold at which European missionaries cried heretic', while missionary-approved Māori Christian evangelists stayed 'just above'.[98] However, in 2016 a Massey University PhD graduate, Dr Judith Ward, argued that rather than founding a new proto-Christian 'syncretistic' religion, Te Ātua Wera was actually operating completely in a way that was consistent with the behaviour of tōhunga matakite (specialists in religion) at the time, that is, as a traditional priest of Māori ritual and religion who appropriated to his pantheon of Māori ātua aspects of Christian doctrine and practices.[99] Ward thus strengthens Raeburn Lange's and this writer's contention that 'continuity', more than 'disruption' or 'cultural dislocation', characterised Māori society at this time of the great early nineteenth century turning to Missionary Christianity.

Irwin, in turn, classified and named these new religious movements according to the chronological order of their foundation, calling them: *Nativistic Faith* (his example, Te Ātua Wera's 'Nākahi' faith); *Syncretist Faith* (the 'Pai Marire' or 'Hau Hau' movement founded in Taranaki by the prophet Te Ua Haumene, who flourished 1863-1874); *Hebraist Religion* (of the Tairawhiti prophet Te Kōoti Arikirangi te Turuki and his 'Ringatu Church', founded in 1868); and *Independent Church* (T.W. Ratana's indigenous Church of the twentieth century).[100] All may be seen as *'resistance movements'*, or 'adjustment cults' by which Māori religious leaders expressed independence from missionary-led Christianity. Nevertheless, all borrowed freely from the Christian Bible, and from Christianity's doctrines and practices.

In Hokianga in 1834, the 'Nākahi' faith whose worship centred around the serpent of Genesis chapter three, was one of Irwin's 'Nativistic Faiths'.[101] Another who the Wesleyans saw as being in religious opposition to their Mission at the same time, was Āperahama Tāonui an early baptised and prominent Wesleyan teacher. Both men were tōhunga trained in the ancient whare wānanga learnings of their people. Both were perhaps influenced by the missionaries own Messianic expectations, announcing their own apocalyptic visions of the Second Coming, and claiming to be mouth-pieces of 'The Spirit', while John Hobbs 'was himself prone to receiving prophetic dreams.'[102] Of Āperahama, Elsmore, suggested that his vision of 'Christ' may be seen in a much more positive light than the missionaries gave it, even as 'a triumph for the mission' rather than for the 'Devil!'. For she suggested he was reflecting the missionaries own messianic expectations and making the 'foreign atua much more familiar' to Māori.[103] One outcome of this episode was that it sparked Āperahama's father, Makaore Te Tāonui, to take an interest in exploring Christianity. Similarly, with their traditional enemies all Wesleyan, Te Hikutū expressed their resistance by embracing Catholicism as a 'denomination of dissent' – to use Belich's phrase.[104] And a Te Hikutū prophecy which foretold that 'an unmarried teacher would come who had no wife',[105] helped pave the way for their warm welcome to Bishop Pompallier and Marist Catholicism after 1838.

Elsewhere, and later into the nineteenth century, especially in North and South Taranaki, but also down to South Canterbury and Otago, the Wesleyan missionaries encountered a number of other Māori resistance or messianic movements which fit quite easily either into Elsmore's category of 'Wahi Tapu' faiths or into Irwin's categories of 'Syncretist' movements. To Belich, in them there is a sense that many of these 'prophetic movements were biblical but not Christian'.[106] Or in Elsmore's words, they were 'not a rejection of the Christian religion itself, but a discarding of the outward forms of Christian worship.'[107]

The first of two Taranaki 'Wahi Tapu' faiths was the 'Tikanga Hou' Movement ('The New Rule), which around September 1845 emerged at Wārea near Cape Egmont. Both Church and Wesleyan missionaries derogatively called it the 'Warea Delusion'. Its leader, Hakaraia (Zechariah) Hākopa Niko, a CMS 'Native teacher', 'removed the Bible, sin, the Sabbath, hell, and the devil', but still maintained that his religion was 'Christian'.[108] Another, called 'Kai Ngarara' (or Eat Lizard), in the early 1850s arose in the vacuum of the Wesleyans' waning influence as a response to the waves of disease of the era. It was led by a Wesleyan teacher at Weriweri, 'Tamati (Thomas) Te Ito Ngamoke, who titled himself 'a brother of Christ' and a new and powerful deity who removed tapu.[109]

After 1860 the Taranaki troubles saw the rise of a new pattern of resistance movements which shaped many of those which followed. The most prominent of these was the 'Pai Marire' (Good and Peaceful) movement led by Te Ua Haumene who had been baptised by John Whiteley at Kāwhia as Horopāpera (Zerubbabel) Tuwhakararo. It fits well into Irwin's category of 'Syncretist Faith'. For Belich writes of 'Pai Marire' as a:

> new Maori religion of many variants, which converted European Christianity as much as it was converted by it. There were elements of syncretism, the merging of the old and new, … developing non-European interpretations of Christianity, non-Christian interpretations of the Bible, and new elements that were neither traditional, nor Christian nor biblical.[110]

Similar was the faith of Hōhepa Ōtene Titokowaru who was a chief and tōhunga of his Ngā Ruahine iwi in South Taranaki. Enslaved in the late 1820s, at Māngungu he was baptised in February 1834 and became a Wesleyan 'Native teacher', then in 1857-59 a Conference-appointed 'Assistant Minister' at Manukau Harbour. In 1864 he fought in the Taranaki War at Sentry Hill where he lost an eye.[111] About this time Titokowaru adopted the rituals of the 'Pai Marire' movement. Being recognised as a priest and prophet in the ancient tradition of the tōhunga, from 1867 he returned to the worship of 'Maru', the ancient Taranaki ātua of Ngā Ruahine who accompanied Turi on the Āotea canoe from Hawaiki. After proclaiming 'the year of the lamb' (or year of peace) as a time of preparation for war, Titokowaru invoked Uenuku and Tu, the deities of war, to seek justice and the return of his people's confiscated land. Yet his faith still invoked Te Ua's Pai Marire chants of the Trinity of Christianity.[112]

Another syncretistic messianic movement with Wesleyan connections, known as 'Kaingarara', was centred at Ārowhenua in South Canterbury. It was led by its prophet, Hipa Te Maiharoa or 'Patu-whenua', a high chief of Waitaha ancestry and a member of the 'Church of England' whose movement combined elements of the traditional Kai Tāhu 'rangatira-tōhuka' (chief-tōhunga) with those of Moses in the Bible and rituals from Te Ua Haumene's Pai Marire faith.[113] Notably, Rāwiri Te Maire from Ārowhenua, and Horomona Pōhio from Ruapuke Island, were both influential 'Native teachers' of James Watkin at Waikouaiti. But both men had become spokesmen and aides to Te Maiharoa when in 1877 he led an occupation of disputed land at Ōmārama in the Mackenzie Country. By contrast, the teachings of Tohu Kākahi and Te Whiti o Rongomai, the prophetic leaders at Parihaka, and their civil disobedience to colonial land policy in Taranaki, drew heavily on the Christian scriptures, especially Jesus' Sermon on the Mount, but fit less well into

Irwin's category of a 'syncretistic faith'. Both men had been 'Native teachers' under the North German missionary Johann Friedrich Riemenschneider who was employed by the Wesleyans at Wārea until 1866.[114]

Conclusion: A Māorified Christianity

By 1840, like many chiefs, Nene and Patuone, had become acutely aware of the need for a renewal of many of their traditional tribal values and for new cultural structures to meet the challenges of the huge changes being wrought by the invasion of English settlers and the onset of Crown Government. These challenges had already led to an intense engagement between traditional Māori cultural and religious beliefs and the missionaries' Christian faith. In the process, writes Dr Lyndsay Head, lecturer in the University of Canterbury Maori Department, the 'northern chiefs felt that a choice of futures had to be made'.[115] Though many Māori after 1840 rejected the missionaries, they did not abandon Christianity. Instead, in Christianity, many found a way to engage with the European 'modernity' of the age. In the faith of the imperial superpower of the day, many found a renewed sense of personal dignity, social belonging and political empowerment. As Head further explains:

> Christianity has an ambiguous reputation: it was the face of empire; it gave structure and meaning to the impulse to modernity that had produced Māori assent to the Treaty of Waitangi in 1840 ... [yet] it provided the moral authority for armed resistance to the state. ... No one expected Māori to develop a Christian politics of their own, whose pillars were: te Whakapono, te Aroha, and te Ture (faith, love, and the Law of God).[116]

In the early colonial era Māori were very much actors in their own history. They were well versed in the art of debate, ridicule, scorn, and learning through question and answer. When confronted by the missionaries' evangelising, and their violating of tapu and Māori rules of hospitality and reciprocity, in the process, Māori, in turn, were masters at countering with their own scorn and ridicule. So in 'the contest of ideas', the missionaries, to their chagrin, found that many Māori proved to be more than equal combatants. But their evangelising of the Wesleyan's brand of austere, evangelical 'Missionary Christianity' from mid-1830 to the mid-1850s, in the main, was not the result of a late adolescent spiritual crisis and personal cathartic emotional release from the duelling of 'two hearts' which the missionaries looked for from their 'converts'. Although many individual instances of English evangelical conversion did occur. It was, rather, a part of a much broader 'conversion to modernity', whereby a veneer of missionary leadership and orthodox Christian rituals and doctrines was fused with traditional, indigenous, ethnic Māori religion to create a new 'indigenised' Christianity. For in the process of being adopted, Missionary Christianity was adapted and 'Māorified' by Māori 'indigenous agency', the Māori Christian teachers, preachers, class leaders, catechists, and assistant missionaries, who took the Gospel to their own people. By such means both European missionaries and Māori evangelists together irrevocably shifted the spiritual and religious foundation of Māori society, so that, as earlier referenced, Raeburn Lange rightly concludes that 'in the dissemination of new religious ideas, and the insertion of Christianity into Māori culture ... Māori initiatives were no less significant than the much chronicled deeds of the missionaries from Britain and Europe.[117]

Notes

1 https://history.stackexchange.com/questions/5597/is-history-always-written-by-the-victors (Accessed 15 April 2019). Supposedly attributed to Winston Churchill.

2 Examples include: Harrison M. Wright, *New Zealand 1769-1840: Early Years of Western Contact.* Cambridge, Mass.: Harvard University Press, 1959; Keith Sinclair, *A History of New Zealand.* Harmondsworth: Penguin Books, 1959; rev. ed., 1969; Alan Ward, *A Show of Justice: Racial 'Amalgamation' in Nineteenth Century New Zealand.* Canberra: Australian National University Press, 'Corrected edn.', Auckland: Auckland & Oxford University Presses, 1995.

3 John Morley Roberts Owens, 'The Wesleyan Mission to New Zealand, 1819-1840', PhD thesis in History, Victoria University of Wellington, 1969. (Hereinafter 'Wesleyan Mission')

4 Vincent O'Malley, *The Meeting Place: Māori and Pākeha Encounters, 1642-1840.* Auckland: Auckland University Press, 2012.

5 Gary A.M. Clover, *Collision, Compromise and Conversion, 1827-1855: A Critical Study of Hokianga Māori, Missionary, and Kauri Merchant Interactions.* (hereinafter *CCC*), Nelson: The Author, 2018.

6 Arthur S. Thomson, *The Story of New Zealand: Past and Present, Savage and Civilized.* London: John Murray, 1859; reprinted, New York, Praeger Scholarly Reprint, 1970, 314-15.

7 Rev Jabez Waterhouse, Hobart to WMS, 8 September 1840, MS, 'Tasmania II, 1837-57', MMS, WMS archives, now in The School of Oriental and African Studies, London University; Owens, 'Wesleyan Mission', 672; Clover, *CCC*, 358.

8 Pope Paul VI, *Evangelization of the World*, Encyclical, Vatican City, 1976, para.53; Gary A.M. Clover, '"Going Mihinare", "Experimental Religion" and Maori Embracing of Missionary Christianity: A Re-Assessment.' in *Christian Brethren Research Fellowship Journal*, 121, (April 1990): 50-51; Jean Irvine, *Historic Hokianga: An Introductory Guide.* Rāwene: The Author, 1965, 49; Clover: *CCC*, 49-50.

9 Bronwyn Elsmore, *Like them that Dream: the Maori and the Old Testament.* Tauranga: Moana Press, 1985, 16.

10 Anne Salmond, *Between Worlds: Early Exchanges Between Maori and Europeans 1773-1815.* Auckland: Viking/Penguin Books, 1997, 401-404.

11 Native Protector Clarke's 1843 Census, by adherents' 'profession' of faith, similarly assessed Church Missionary Society (CMS) support at 42,700 or 39%; 'Maori' [i.e., Marist?] at 5,000 (4.5%); 'Pagans' at 45,759 (42%), making the total of Māori Christians 63,700 or approximately 58.5%; Malcolm Falloon, 'Maori Conversion to Christianity; Population Statistics, 1830-1859.' in Sophia Sinclair, ed., *Our History: Aotearoa, The Story of Mission in Aotearoa through the Lens of the New Zealand Church Missionary Society.* [Christchurch]: New Zealand Church Missionary Society, 2014, 26; Clover, *CCC*, 348.

12 Raeburn Lange, 'Indigenous Agents of Religious Change in New Zealand 1830-1860.' *JRH*, 24, no.3, (October 2000): 279-95; Nathan Matthews, 'Kaikatikihama: "Our Most Precious Resource.",' in *Mana Māori and Christianity.* Wellington: Huia, 2012, 141-57; Timothy Yates, *The Conversion of the Māori: Years of Religious and Social Change, 1814-1842.* Grand Rapids, Michigan: William Eerdmans Publishing, 2013, 108-115.

13 Lange, 'Indigenous Agents', 287-88. For more in-depth coverage, see also, Raeburn Lange, *Island Ministers: Indigenous Leadership in Nineteenth Century Pacific Islands Christianity.* Christchurch: Macmillan Brown Centre for Pacific Studies, University of Canterbury and Canberra: Pandanus Books, Research School of Pacific and Asian Studies, Australian National University, 2005, c.8, 149-79.

14 E.R. Simmonds, *Pompallier: Prince of Bishops*. Auckland: CPC Publishing, 1984, 36-37; Yates, *Conversion*, 109.

15 Gary A.M. Clover, 'Heroes of the Faith: Early Wesleyan Māori Teachers and Conversion' in *WHS (NZ) Journal*, 99 (2014): 18-33.

16 Lange, 'Indigenous Agents', 287; Yates, *Conversion*, 110-11; Clover, 'Heroes of the Faith', 23.

17 Lange, *Island Ministers*, 160; Clover, *CCC*, 374-5; Gary A. Clover, 'More Heroes of the Faith: the Two Methodist Maori missionaries martyred near Mangataipa in the Hokianga in 1837', *WHS (NZ) Journal*, 93 (2011): 5-11.

18 John Hobbs, Letter to WMS, 30 October 1843, WMS 'Letters to Secretaries, 1817-1867' [typescript of New Zealand Wesleyan Mission correspondence & District Minutes held in bound volumes in the John Kinder Library (JKL); Clover, 'Heroes of the Faith', 20.

19 Clover, *CCC*, 375.

20 Lange, 'Indigenous Agents', 287; *CCC*, 374.

21 Clover, *CCC*, especially. 255-56, 299-302. Nene's peace journey to the Thames & Waikato is referred to at 311.

22 Clover *CCC*, 174; Lange, *Island Ministers*, 153; &, Owens, 'Wesleyan Mission', 492-93, 532, 465, 570. For White's description of the chiefs baptised on 23 December 1833 see Clover, *CCC*, 195-96.

23 Clover, *CCC*, 199, Owens, 'Wesleyan Mission', 568.

24 Clover, *CCC*, 299, 311.

25 Morley, 129-131; George I. Laurenson, *Te Hahi Weteriana: Three Half Centuries of the Methodist Maori Mission 1822-1972*, Auckland: WHS (NZ) Proceedings, 27, nos.1 & 2, 1972, 57.

26 Morley, 103-4, 124, & 204; Clarence T.J. Luxton, *Methodist Beginnings in the Manukau: the Story of the Pehiakura Mission 1834-1862*, WHS (NZ) Proceedings, 17, no.4, 1960, esp. 8-19.

27 Morley, 95; *CCC*, 321.

28 Morley, 86, 124; Gary Scott, 'Te Awa-i-taia, Wiremu Nera', *DNZB*, I, Wellington: Allen & Unwin & Department of Internal Affairs, 1990, 441-2, 'Te Ara - the Encyclopedia of New Zealand', https://teara.govt.nz/en/biographies/1n9/ngatai-wiremu-nera (accessed 9 September 2019).

29 Morley, 134-5; Lyn Williams, 'The Dead tell Tales', *Waikato Times*, 5 January 2015. See *New Zealand Genealogist*, 47 no 359 (June 2016): 98-99.

30 Ian Church, 'Wiremu Nera Ngatai', Ian Church. 'Ngātai, Wiremu Nēra', *DNZB*, I, 1990 Te Ara - the Encyclopedia of New Zealand, https://teara.govt.nz/en/biographies/1n9/ngatai-wiremu-nera (accessed 29 March 2023); Thomas G. Hammond, *In the Beginning; The History of a Mission*, 2 edn., Auckland: Epworth, 1940, 14–24; Gary A. Clover, 'Rescuing from Obscurity; a Life of the Reverend John Skevington, 1815-1845.' *WHS (NZ) Journal*, 89, (2009): 22-24; also, Clover, *CCC*, 375.

31 Ian Church, *Heartland of Aotea: Maori and European in South Taranaki Before the Taranaki Wars*, Hawera: The Author, 1992, 21, 25-27; Ian Church. 'Taurua, Ngāwaka', *DNZB*, I, 1990, Te Ara - the Encyclopedia of New Zealand, https://teara.govt.nz/en/biographies/1t20/taurua-ngawaka (accessed 29 March 2023); Gary A.M. Clover, *William Woon 1803-1858: Wesleyan Printer in Tonga and New Zealand*, Auckland, WHS (NZ) Proceedings, 97, 2014, 63-64; Clover, 'Rescuing from Obscurity', 33.

32 John Whiteley, 'Report of the Wesleyan Southern District Meeting', September 1842 (WMS 'Letters to secretaries, 1817-1867', JKL); Clover, 'Rescuing from Obscurity', 33, 38.

33 T.G. Hammond, *In the Beginning*, 70; Church, 'Heartland', 82; Clover, *Woon*, 69.

34 Athol Kirk, 'Christian Martyrs recalled', in, Wanganui Historical Society *Historical Record*, 17, no.2, (November 1986): 8-10; Gary Clover, 'Te Putakarua, Te Awaroa, Te Matoe, and Te Hau Maringi; Why Methodists should know and commemorate them', *WHS (NZ) Journal*, 92 (2010): 10-13; Athol Kirk, 'Tour of Methodist Historic Places, Sunday 16th October [1988], 1.30pm', pamphlet compiled for tour; Clover, 'Early Wesleyan Māori Teachers', *WHS (NZ) Journal*, 99 (2010): 21; T.W. Downes, *Old Whanganui*, Hawera: W.A. Parkinson, 1915, 170-71. On Wiremu Te Tauri see, Lange, *Island Ministers*, 151.

35 Clover, *CCC*, 31; Lawrence M. Rogers, ed, *The Early Journals of Henry Williams*, Christchurch: Pegasus Press, 1962, 463-64; Lange, *Island Ministers*, 158.

36 *The New Zealander*, 27 September 1845, 2, cited in Clover, 'Heroes of the Faith'. 28-30; &, Clover, Skevington, '*Rescuing from Obscurity*', *WHS (NZ) Journal*, 89 (2009): Appendix Two, 40-41

37 Renatus Kempthorne, *Maori Christianity in Te Waipounamu: A History*, Christchurch: Te Hui Amorangi o Te Waipounamu, 2000, 24-25, 27-28.

38 Wi Upo's full name was *Wi Omere Te Ipu Rangiwahia*, Clover, 'More Heroes of the Faith: Minarapa Te Rangi-hatu-ake and Te Aro Pa 1839-1841', *WHS (NZ) Journal*, 95 (2008): 39; *Island Ministers*, 154.

39 Wesley A. Chambers, *Samuel Ironside in New Zealand 1839-1858*, Auckland: Ray Richards with WHS (NZ), 1982, 116-127; Yates, *Conversion*, 111-12.

40 Kempthorne, *Maori Christianity*, 24-25, 27-28.

41 Paul Wynyard Fairclough, *Early History of Missions in Otago*, [Dunedin]: New Zealand Bible & Tract Society, 1902, cited by T.A. Pybus, *Maori and Missionary: Early Christian Missions in the South Island of New Zealand*, Wellington: A.H. & A.W. Reed, 1954, 67-68; W.A. Taylor, *Lore and History of the South Island Maori*, Christchurch: Bascands Ltd, [1951, 1952], c.14, 'Maori Associations of Banks Peninsula', p.124. See also Lange, *Island Ministers*, 151; Gary Clover, 'Another Hero of the Faith; Taawao, First Missionary to Banks Peninsula', in *WHS (NZ) Journal*, 96 (2013): 29-31.

42 R. Lange, *Island Ministers*, 151; Clover, 'Taawao', 29-31.

43 Bill Dacker, *Te Mamae me Te Aroha, the Pain and the Love: A History of Kai Tahu Whanui in Otago, 1844- 1944*, Dunedin: University of Otago Press & Dunedin City Council, 1994, Side Note, 15, 29-41; Clover, 'Taawao', 29-31; Lange, '*Indigenous Agents*', 282; Lange, *Island Ministers*, 151. See also Te Maire Tau. 'Pōhio, Horomona', *DNZB*, I, 1990, 342-43, Te Ara - the Encyclopedia of New Zealand, https://teara.govt.nz/en/biographies/1p16/pohio-horomona (accessed 29 March 2023); Harry C. Evison. 'Tiramōrehu, Matiaha', *DNZB*, I, 1990. Te Ara - the Encyclopedia of New Zealand, https://teara.govt.nz/en/biographies/1t100/tiramorehu-matiaha (accessed 29 March 2023).

44 Pybus, 66, 155-59; Dacker, 16-17, 68; Lange, *Island Ministers*, 53; Clover, 'Taawao', 30; Kempthorne, *Maori Christianity*, cc.4, 5, 6, 55-89.

45 J.M.R. Owens, *Prophets in the Wilderness: the Wesleyan Mission to New Zealand 1819-27*, Auckland: Auckland University Press/Oxford University Press, 1974, 116-147; C.H. Laws, *The Methodist Mission to New Zealand: Toil and Adversity at Whangaroa*, WHS (NZ) Proceedings, 1 & 2, 1944, 20; Clover, *CCC*, 71-78.

46 Murray B. Gittos, *Mana at Mangungu: a Biography of William White 1794-1875, Wesleyan Missionary at Whangaroa and Hokianga 1823-1836*. Auckland: The Author, 1982, 10-11.

47 *The Missionary Register* 1823 (Church Missionary Society), 351; Paul Moon, *A Savage Country: the Untold Story of New Zealand in the 1820s*, Auckland: Penguin, 2012, 74; Clover, *CCC*, 58.

48 Charles H. Laws, *The Methodist Mission to New Zealand; First Years at Hokianga, 1827-1836*, WHS (NZ) Proceedings, 4, nos.2 & 3, 1943, 22; Owens, *Prophets in the Wilderness*, 97-99, 109.

49 Tola M.I. Williment, *John Hobbs 1800-1883: Wesleyan Missionary to the Ngapuhi Tribe of Northern New Zealand*. Wellington: Government Printer, 1985, 79-80; Clover, *CCC*, 93.

50 James Stack, Journal, 29 June 1829, cited in Stack, to WMS, 30 September 1830, MMS, 'N.Z. I, 1819-1834'; Owens, 'Wesleyan Mission', 345; Clover, *CCC*, 113.

51 Owens, Wesleyan Mission, 277; Clover, *CCC*, c.3, 37-55, 85.

52 John Marmon, *Auckland Weekly News*, 13 November 1880; Jack Lee, *An Unholy Trinity: Three Hokianga Characters*, Russell: Northland Historical Society Publications Society, 1990, 33; Clover, *CCC*, 70-71.

53 Owens, 'Wesleyan Mission', 310.

54 Owens, 'Wesleyan Mission', 309; Clover, *CCC*, 101-102.

55 Stack, Journal, 11 June 1828 (MMS); Owens, 'Wesleyan Mission', 309-10; Clover, *CCC*, 70-71.

56 Owens, 'Wesleyan Mission', 310; *CCC*, 102.

57 Gittos, 42; Clover, *CCC*, 132-33.

58 Williment, *John Hobbs*, 85; Clover, *CCC*, 111-12.

59 Stack, Journal extracts, 24 March, 1 April 1828, in Hobbs to WMS, 27 March & 25 May 1828 (MMS); Owens, 'Wesleyan Mission', 308; Clover, ccc, 101.

60 Owens, Wesleyan Mission, 288; William White, 9 September 1830, in, 'Journal 16 May 1823-21 September 1835' (JKL), 389-92; Williment, *Hobbs*, 96; Clover, *CCC*, 134.

61 William White, Journal, 10 & 16 January 1831 & 9 July 1832 (JKL); Eliza White, Journal, 5 February 1832 (JKL); White, Hobbs & Stack, letter to WMS, 17 February 1831 (JKL); Owens, 'Wesleyan Mission', 395-96, 434-35; Clover, *CCC*, 137-39 & 148-49.

62 Owens, 'Wesleyan Mission', 396; Clover, *CCC*, 139-40.

63 White, letter, 9 September 1830, (MMS), [JKL], Owens, 'Wesleyan Mission', p.389; Clover, *CCC*, 134.

64 Eliza White, Journal, 16-25 October 1835 [JKL]; Owens, 'Wesleyan Mission', p.587; Clover, *CCC*, 200.

65 Edward Markham, *New Zealand or Recollections of it*, ed. E.H. McCormick, Wellington: Government Printer, 1963, 47; Owens, Wesleyan Mission, 511; Gittos, *Mana*, 72; Clover, *CCC*, 184.

66 William Woon, Journal extract, 25 August 1834, in Woon to WMS secretaries, 3 September 1834 in Letters to Secretaries (copy in JKL); Owens, 'Wesleyan Mission', 523; Clover, *CCC*, 194.

67 Woon Journal, 6 November 1837, cited in letter to WMS secretaries, 24 November 1837 (Letters to Secretaries in JKL). Underlining in original. Also, Owens, 'Wesleyan Mission', 626; Williment, *John Hobbs*, 124-25; Clover, *CCC*, 255-6.

68 Rev Joseph Orton, Journal, 16, 19, & 26 June 1833, Mitchell Library; Owens, 'Wesleyan Mission', 468-69; White, Journal, 25 December 1832 (JKL), Gittos, *Mana*, 63; Owens, 'Wesleyan Mission', 45; Clover, *CCC*, 152-54, 165-66.

69 R. Lange, *Island Ministers*, 158; Clover, CCC, 364-67.

70 George I. Laurenson, *Te Hahi Weteriana*, 25-26; Clover, *CCC*, 136.

71 James Belich, *Making Peoples: A History of New Zealanders, from Polynesian Settlements to the End of the Nineteenth Century*, Auckland: Penguin, 1990, 213; J.M.R. Owens, 'New Zealand before

Annexation', in *The Oxford History of New Zealand,* Second Edition, ed. Geoffrey W. Rice, Auckland: Oxford University Press, 1992, 38; Clover, *CCC,* 364-65.

72 Dacker, *Te Mamae me Te Aroha,* 14-17; Clover, 'Taawao', 25-27.

73 Belich, *Making Peoples,* 219; Clover, 'Going Mihinare', 50-51.

74 Dacker, 16-17; Clover, 'Heroes of the Faith', 23-25; Clover, *CCC,* 365-66.

75 Yates, *Conversion,* 123; Clover, 'Going Mihinare', 50; Clover, *CCC,* 365-66.

76 H.G. Barnett, *Innovation: the basis of cultural change,* New York: McGraw Hill, 1953, 140.

77 Eliza White, Journal, 9 &13 November 1836, & Woon to WMS, 28 May 1840 (JKL), Owens, 'Wesleyan Mission', 587-8; Clover, *CCC,* 209-10.

78 Bronwyn Elsmore, *Mana from Heaven: A Century of Maori Prophets in New Zealand,* Tauranga: Moana Press, 1989, 200; Clover, *CCC,* 366-67; Clover, 'Going Mihinare', 50-51.

79 Gittos, *Mana at Mangungu,* 68; Clover, *CCC,* 59.

80 Harold W. Turner used a phenomenological approach to new religious movements in primal society. See Harold Turner, 'The Gospel's Mission to Culture in New Zealand', [1992], https://www.latimer. org.nz/wp-content/uploads/Harold-Turner-The-Gospels-Mission-to-Culture-in-New-Zealand.pdf (accessed 11 October 2021); James Irwin, *An Introduction to Māori Religion: its Character before European Contact and its Survival in Contemporary Māori and New Zealand Culture,* [Adelaide], Australian Association for the Study of Religions, 1984, Special Studies in Religions, no. 4.

81 Hobbs to WMS, 25 July 1835, 'Letters' (JKL); Alfred Barrett, *The Life of The Rev John Hewgill Bumby; With a Brief History of the Commencement and Progress of the Wesleyan Mission in New Zealand,* 2 edition, London: John Mason, 1853, 'New Zealand – His Destination', 105-107; Clover, *CCC,* 171-73.

82 Edward Markham, 47; Yates, *Conversion,* 126; Clover, *CCC,* 175.

83 White, Journal, 5 February 1835 (MMS, 'N.Z. II, 1835-1840'); Owens, 'Wesleyan Mission', 553; Clover, *CCC,* 195.

84 Yates, *Conversion,* 62. This cites Woon's observations of March 1834; Clover, *CCC,* 373.

85 Orton, Journal, 15 June 1833 [JKL]; Owens, 'Wesleyan Mission', 467; Clover, *CCC,* 165.

86 Testimonies from, Rev John Waterhouse, Journal, Sunday, 17 May 1840, 16, in *Wesleyan Methodist Magazine,* LXIV, (January 1841): 81-84, Wesley Chambers, MS 118, Box 22, MCNZA; Nene's testimony, 5; Yates, *Conversion,* 117; Clover, *CCC,* 299-300.

87 Raoul Allier, *La Psychologie de la Conversion ches les Peuples non-civilisées,* Paris: Payot, 1925; Yates, *Conversion,* 117; Waterhouse, Journal extracts, 1840, [JKL], Clover, *CCC,* 299-300.

88 Waterhouse Journal, in, Chambers 'MS 118, Box 22' 16; Clover, *CCC,* 299.

89 Waterhouse Journal, 25-26; Clover, *CCC,* 300.

90 John Whiteley, letter to WMS, 12 November 1834, (MMS), 'N.Z. I, 1919-1834', [JKL], Owens, 'Wesleyan Mission', 543; Clover, *CCC,* 191.

91 Kathleen Shawcross, 'The Maoris of the Bay of Islands, 1769-1840: a Study of Changing Maori Responses to European Contact', MA thesis in History, University of Auckland, 1967, 357-58; Clover, 'Going Mihinare', 50-52.

92 White, Journal, 4 April 1835 (JKL); Owens, Wesleyan Mission, 557; Clover, *CCC,* 197.

93 Elsmore, *Mana from Heaven,* [iv-v], 21-22.

94 Simmonds, *Pompallier,* 12-15.

95 Elsmore, *Mana from Heaven*, c.14, 'The 1850s: The Decade of the Healers', 95-106, esp, 99.

96 Elsmore, *Mana from Heaven*, c.24, '1860-1900: The Prophetic Period', 160-190, esp, 175-77.

97 For example, *Mana from Heaven*, c.4, 'The Papahurihia Movement', 37-48. Also, Judith Binney, 'Papahurihia: Some Thoughts on Interpretation.' *Journal of the Polynesian Society*, 93, no.4, 345-98. Te Ātua Wera died 3 November 1875, Death-bed portrait, in, 'Northland Pilgrimage 1972', Box 'Northland 1065, Mangungu Mission + Waimea Oak', MCNZA; Clover, *CCC*, 228.

98 Belich, *Making Peoples*, 222-23.

99 Judith Ward, 'The Invention of Papahurihia', PhD thesis in History, Massey University, 2016, 'Abstract', p.iii, https://mro.massey.ac.nz/server/api/core/bitstreams/124854c9-5b7c-4652-b4dd-b111c5cae5ff/content (accessed 11 May 2022).

100 Irwin, *Introduction to Māori Religion*, passim. What Irwin calls 'Nativistic Faith' Clover describes as 'Neo-ethnic faith'.

101 Elsmore, *Mana from Heaven*, c.4, 'The Papahurihia Movement', 37-48, esp. 37-41.

102 Elsmore, *Mana from Heaven*, Endnote 13, 55.

103 Elsmore, *Mana from Heaven*, c.5, 'Aperahama Taonui', 49-55, esp.52.

104 Belich, 219-20.

105 Jean Irvine, *Historic Hokianga: An Introductory Guide*, Rāwene: The Author, 1965, 47.

106 Belich, 221.

107 Elsmore, *Mana from Heaven*, c.11, 'The Tikanga Hou Movement', 79.

108 ibid, 76-85; Church, *Heartland of Aotea*, 127; Belich, 221.

109 Elsmore, *Mana from Heaven*, c.19, 'The Wahi Tapu and Kaingarara Response', 127-40, esp. 131-35.

110 Belich, 223.

111 Elsmore, *Mana from Heaven*, c.28, 'Titokowaru and His Hauhau', 222-23.

112 ibid, 223.

113 Elsmore, *Mana from Heaven*, c.11, 77; Belich, 222.

114 *Mana from Heaven*, c.31, 'The Arowhenua Movement', 257. Also, Dacker, *Te Mamae me Aroha*, 29-41; Clover, 'Taawao', 29-31; Lange, 'Indigenous Agents', 282; &, Lange, *Island Ministers*, 151; also Te Maire Tau, 'Pohio, Horomona 1815-1880', in *DNZB*, first published in 1990. Te Ara - the Encyclopedia of New Zealand, https://teara.govt.nz/en/biographies/1p16/pohio-horomona (accessed 28 August 2024). 1, 1990, 342-43.

115 Lyndsay Head, 'The Pursuit of Modernity in Māori Society: the Conceptual Bases of Citizenship in the Early Colonial Period', in Andrew Sharp and Paul McHugh eds, *Histories, Power, and Loss*, Wellington: Bridget Williams Books, 2001, 97-121; Yates, *Conversion*, 122-23.

116 Lyndsay Head, 'Wiremu Tamihana and the Mana of Christianity', 58-60, &, Tony Ballantyne, 'Christianity, Colonization and Cross-Cultural Communication', 23-57, both in *Christianity, Modernity and Culture*, edited by John Stenhouse, Adelaide: ATF Press, 2005, 58-86; Clover, *CCC*, 13.

117 Lange, Indigenous Agents, 280, 283; Yates, *Conversion*, 109; Clover, *CCC*, 376.

4 – 'Prepared for Life or Death in the Discharge of our Duty': Pakeha Missionaries and their Wives

Susan Thompson

If it is the case that modern-day Methodists do not talk much about our Pākehā missionary ancestors, how much more is that so for their wives? Over the years these women have been mostly rendered invisible; their stories lost to the mists of history.

The aim of this paper is to give an overview of the work that has been done to this point to tell the women's stories; reflecting on why this area of history has been so neglected and pointing to some possible directions for future research in this area. I hope this historiographical approach will prompt further conversation particularly about source material and be a useful foundation for future work.

A Neglected Topic

Writing about the wives of the first Pākehā Wesleyan missionaries to Aotearoa-New Zealand, Paul Moon noted that references to them in early records tended to be brief and incidental.[1] A quick look at Donald Phillipps' index to William Morley's 1901 *The History of Methodism in New Zealand* confirms this suggestion. Morley gave most of the wives no more than a passing mention. He did include photographs of a number of the women but most of these photographs show them in old age as 'grim Victorian grandmothers, tight lipped and buttoned up'. The reality of course was that most arrived in New Zealand in their twenties.[2]

The impression of women being made invisible is reinforced by a search of the Methodist newspaper. Most missionary wives received tributes when they died but they were rarely given their first names and the stories tended to focus on the work of their husbands. In the words of Kathryn Rountree, the women themselves remained 'shadowy background figures toiling silently and invisibly for the glory of God and the comfort of their husbands and children'.[3] They were eulogised in such flowery language that it's hard to get a sense of them as individuals. Mary Ann Wallis, for example, was described as a 'perfect Christian lady', whatever that is.[4]

The first writer to pay any real attention to the wives of the missionaries was the Methodist deaconess and writer Rita Snowden. Her book *The Ladies of Wesleydale* was an attempt to fill the gap in knowledge about missionary women and was based on a lecture given in 1956, the year she became the first woman to be elected Vice-President of the Methodist Conference. Using missionary records held in Auckland, Sydney and London, Snowden wrote a vivid detailed narrative of the experiences of Catherine Leigh and Anne Turner. While frustrated by a lack of source material from the women themselves, she wrote from a woman's perspective and managed to convey the strength and spirit of both women.

After that pioneering work, little seems to have been written about the wives until the early 1970s. George Laurenson's 1972 history marking the 150th anniversary of the Māori Mission, *Te Hahi Weteriana*, concentrated on the male missionaries although he did note that the story of the womenfolk 'deserves a larger volume than has yet appeared'.[5] Laurenson gave important glimpses of the women's lives, noting their courage and patience as they shared the hardships of their husbands. He observed that they spent long periods alone far from 'congenial female companionship or skilled medical attention especially during childbirth' and that this took an inevitable toll on their health and spirit.[6]

The early 1970s was also notable for the scholarship of John Owens. In his 1973 article printed in the *Journal of Religious History* Owens delved more deeply into the backgrounds of the male missionaries and some of their wives. Owens believed that the influence of wives as teachers, organisers and shapers of a domestic ethos was considerable but also argued that their family duties limited their direct missionary role. He prepared the first comprehensive list of the wives who had arrived in New Zealand by May 1840, although a lack of information meant he wasn't able to give first names to Mrs Creed, Buttle or Warren.[7]

It was not until 1987 that the first sustained study was made of the history of women in the Methodist Church of New Zealand. Ruth Fry's ground-breaking book *Out of the Silence* devoted two chapters to women in the missionary period and for the first time began to identify and draw upon their surviving writings.[8] Like Laurenson, she noted their courage and loneliness and the way they reached out to each other in friendship and support. She also made some early comments about the relationships between Pākehā and Māori women, noting areas of reserve and misunderstanding but also times of shared feeling.[9]

Fry's work was followed by another long gap in the telling of the stories of the Wesleyan wives. Nearly thirty years passed before the historian Paul Moon offered his reappraisal of the role of missionary wives in a 2015 article in the theological journal *Stimulus*. Moon affirmed the vital contribution made by women suggesting that missionary couples functioned as a single unit although each partner had different roles. He also explored the complex ways issues of gender, ethnicity and religion intersected in the representation of European and Māori women. While portrayed as the weaker sex, missionary wives were at the same time regarded as morally superior to Māori women and were given the task of raising them up to 'civilisation'. As Moon noted, assumptions of European superiority 'curdled' relations between Māori and Pākehā.[10]

Told in fits and starts, the stories of Wesleyan missionary wives have been largely overlooked by historians. They certainly have not had the kind of attention that has been paid to women belonging to the Church Missionary Society (CMS). In the first volume of the *New Zealand Dictionary of Biography* published in 1990, for example, women make up nine of the fifty-nine Anglican entries and one of the twelve Wesleyan entries.[11] CMS women have also been the main subject of two academic theses including a very fine in-depth study by Cathy Ross of the lives of four CMS wives published in 2006.[12]

This kind of neglect reflects a general tendency in the writing of history for women to be placed at the margins. Often seen as appendages to men, women have been confined to the roles of wives, mothers and daughters and their experiences subsumed under those of men.[13] One result of this privileging of male experience was that women's own writings and reflections are few and far between. In her entry on Eliza White in *The Book of New Zealand Women*, Sandra Coney observed that women were unlikely to have the sense of significance which leads to a decision to record one's life in a diary. Even if they did do so, descendants were less likely to preserve what their female ancestors had written.[14]

Diaries

The lack of surviving writings by women is a major cause in the invisibility of the wives of the Pākehā Wesleyan missionaries and a major difficulty in telling their stories. Where some CMS women were prolific writers of letters and diaries, women belonging to the Wesleyan tradition do not yet appear to have been so productive. Eliza White, wife of the missionary William White, was a key exception in keeping a diary from the time she left England in 1829 to 1836, just before her husband's dismissal from mission employment. Held in the Kinder Library, White's diaries were transcribed by Frances Porter in 2004 but have not yet been published. They are a mine of information about the daily life of the early mission, Eliza's work teaching and instructing young Māori women, her relationships with other wives and her grief at the death of three of her children. She chose not to mention the scandals surrounding William.[15]

Ruth Fry called White's diary the 'only substantial source material giving a woman's viewpoint' on the early Methodist mission in New Zealand.[16] Fortunately this is not completely the case. Mary Anna Bumby, who came to New Zealand with her missionary brother John in 1840 and is known as the first person to bring honeybees to this country, also kept a journal. Held in the Turnbull Library, it has not yet been transcribed. It is a shorter and more introspective document than White's and its early sections are dominated by Mary Anna's grief over John's early death and her decision to marry the Wesleyan missionary Gideon Smales. Yet it offers a valuable perspective on the challenges facing young single women in the missionary period.[17]

The only other diary that I'm aware of was kept by Sarah Ironside, wife of the missionary Samuel Ironside who came to New Zealand in 1839. Unfortunately, this diary has disappeared. All that remains of it are brief extracts printed after her death in a series of articles Samuel wrote for the Methodist newspaper in 1891.[18] Reading these left me wanting to know more about the woman who in the 1840s brightened her home by painting each wall a different colour, who along with Samuel drank a dozen bottles of 'choice French wines' for the sake of her health and who sat up to all hours of the night transcribing the scriptures for Samuel's converts.[19] There was more to the Ironsides than met the eye.

Correspondence

Another important source of material giving insights into the lives and experiences of Wesleyan wives is letters the women wrote to each other and to family back in England.

Cathy Ross noted that, more than anything else, the relationships missionary women had with their correspondents sustained and nurtured them in their time in New Zealand. Letters were eagerly awaited as they provided news, friendship, advice and encouragement. They 'were places to find comfort and intimacy and delight in small things'.[20] 'Among themselves', observed Ross, the women could be 'totally honest, open and vulnerable'.[21]

Letters written by the Wesleyan wives are scattered across a number of collections. The Kinder Library has a handful of delightful letters written in the 1830s by Eliza White to Jane Hobbs in Tonga. Their friendship remained strong even though their husbands were at odds and Eliza was able to open up to Jane about her unhappiness at the charges being made against William.[22]

The Turnbull Library has letters written by Jane Buttle, wife of the missionary George Buttle, to family members in England in the 1840s and 1850s. One of the saddest of these was sent to her mother in 1856 informing her of her latest pregnancy. 'We must not murmur', Jane wrote in a slightly anxious tone. 'We are in the Lord's hands, he gives life and he will give strength'. Jane's forebodings were fulfilled and she died in 1857 possibly in childbirth.[23]

Jane's sister Mehetabel Newman came to New Zealand in 1846 and lived with Jane and George at the Te Kopua mission station in Waipa. She wrote letters to England for nearly forty years and a large collection of these is also held at the Alexander Turnbull Library. Some of her correspondence has been transcribed and printed in Frances Porter and Charlotte Macdonald's wonderful book 'My Hand Will Write What My Heart Dictates'.[24] I am not aware that her letters have ever been closely studied but, as Ruth Fry noted, they illustrate the experience of an unmarried woman in middle-class colonial society. Mehetabel became the subject of family criticism when she remained at Te Kopua after Jane's death. She and George eventually married in 1874.[25]

A number of individual letters also survive written by missionary wives such as Jane Woon and Catherine Riemenschneider and it's likely that there are more to be discovered in other libraries and collections. Any suggestions will be gratefully received.

Scrapbooks

One other interesting source of material opening a window into the inner worlds of the wives is the scrapbook or album kept by a number of the women. Such volumes were popular in the Victorian period and albums belonging to Mary Aldred, Eliza White and Mary Anna Bumby have been located. They contain a mixture of autographs, spiritual quotations, visiting cards, photos and sketches often contributed by the missionaries and their wives.

Mary Aldred's scrapbook, for example, covered the period from 1843 to the early 1860s. Pasted in its pages were all sorts of drawings and images, writings and other ephemera. It was signed by a number of Wesleyan missionaries including Thomas Buddle who was displaying his early knowledge of the Māori language.[26] The album belonging to Eliza White was begun in 1837 and kept until 1870. It contains a lovely pencil sketch of the mission station at Mangungu.[27] Mary Anna Bumby's album, kept between 1839 and

1860, is particularly interesting as its pages include messages of comfort written by the missionary wives Jane Woon and Eliza White after the death of her brother John. Eliza was not averse to tweaking scripture to suit the situation, writing, 'Jesus said unto her, I am the resurrection and the life'.[28]

In one sense these albums might be thought of as curiosities or spiritual craft projects. But they were put together with love and care and the fact that they survived the rigours of the pioneer setting suggests that they were seen as precious by their owners. A study of all three albums might offer new insights into their owners' personalities, their friendships and social connections, the sources of their emotional and spiritual nourishment, their joys, struggles and hopes. Women's history is often an exercise in reading between the lines.

It may be that telling the stories of the wives of Pākehā Wesleyan missionaries will require further readings of this nature. Historians live in hope of discovering vanished diaries, previously unknown caches of letters or hidden albums of never-before seen photos. It's always possible that materials of this kind relating to the Wesleyan wives will one day be found. The Kinder librarian Judith Bright has suggested that letters sent to relatives in England may yet survive in family papers which have been deposited in English libraries or museums.

However, if such material remains elusive future researchers may have no choice but to turn to the diaries, letters and records of the male missionaries which have survived in large numbers. Reading this material for references to the Wesleyan wives is hard work but such writings can be useful sources of information. They are limited because the glimpses they offer are always mediated by a male perspective and the actions, responses and attitudes of the women they refer to sometimes need to be inferred. Yet they do give clues to roles and relationships, activities and beliefs, ways of thinking and being. It was the male missionary Nathaniel Turner, for example, who in 1824 wonderfully described his wife Anne as 'just such a partner as my soul desireth and such as I needed for a station like this'.[29]

Conclusion

There is much work to be done to make more visible the lives and experiences of the wives of the first Pākehā Wesleyan missionaries to Aotearoa-New Zealand. Like other groups who have been relegated to the margins of history, their stories need to be told so 'we can begin to imagine a more inclusive past'.[30] As we engage in this task, part of the wider work of assessing and reassessing the impact of Methodism in Aotearoa, one thing becomes clear.

The role played by such women was by no means passive or perfunctory. When in 1821 news reached Samuel and Catherine Leigh of escalating violence in New Zealand which might have delayed their mission, it was Catherine who stated that nothing she had heard had shaken her confidence in God. Until the mission began, she said, 'I shall not be happy another day …. We are prepared for death or life in the discharge of our duty'.[31] Whatever else we discover about them, the wives of the Wesleyan missionaries were women of determination and devotion, of strength and of spirit. Their stories deserve to be told.

Notes

1 Paul Moon, 'Wesleyan Wives: The Role of Women in the Wesleyan Mission to New Zealand in the 1820s', *Stimulus*, 22, no.2 (July 2015): 27.

2 J.M.R. Owens, *The Wesleyan Missionaries to New Zealand Before 1840*, WHS (NZ) Proceedings, 38 1982: 17. [originally published in *JRH*, 7, no. 4 (1973).]

3 K. Rountree. 'Re-Making the Maori Female Body: Marianne Williams's Mission in the Bay of Islands'. *Journal of Pacific History*, 35, no. 1 (2000), quoted in Moon, 'Wesleyan wives', 24.

4 'Mrs Wallis', *The New Zealand Methodist*, 11 March 1893, 4.

5 George I. Laurenson, *Te Hahi Weteriana: Three Half Centuries of the Methodist Maori Missions 1822-1972*, WHS (NZ) Proceedings, 27, nos.1-2 (1972), 12.

6 *Ibid.*, 27-28.

7 Owens, *The Wesleyan Missionaries*, 16-18. 20-21.

8 Ruth Fry, *Out of the Silence: Methodist Women of Aotearoa 1822-1985*, Christchurch: Methodist Publishing, 1987. Fry consulted the diaries of both Eliza White and Mary Anna Bumby.

9 Fry, *Out of the Silence*, 40-41.

10 Moon, 'Wesleyan Wives', 23, 25 and 26.

11 *DNZB*, I, edited by W.H. Oliver, Wellington: Allen & Unwin/Department of Internal Affairs, 1990, 622-23.

12 Cathy Ross, *Women with a Mission*, Penguin Books, Auckland, 2006.

13 *Ibid.*, 12.

14 Sandra Coney, 'Eliza White', *The Book of New Zealand Women: Ko Kui Ma Te Kaupapa*, edited by Charlotte Macdonald, Merimeri Penfold & Bridget Williams, Wellington: Bridget William Books, 1991, 722-23.

15 Eliza White Diaries, 1829-1836, JKL, MET 011/1/1-4.

16 Fry, *Out of the Silence*, 23.

17 Mary Anna Smales Journal 1838-1842 in John H. Bumby and Smales Family Papers 1832-1860, Turnbull Library, MS-Copy-Micro-0490.

18 Extracts from Sarah Ironside's Journal in Samuel Ironside Scrapbook, MCA, ChCh, MS 215.

19 Samuel Ironside, 'Missionary Reminiscences in New Zealand', Samuel Ironside Scrapbook, MCNZA, MS 215.

20 Frances Porter and Charlotte Macdonald, ed., *'My Hand will write what my Heart dictates': The Unsettled Lives of Women in Nineteenth Century New Zealand s revealed to Sisters, Family and Friends.* Auckland: Auckland University Press & Bridget Williams Books, 1996, p. 12, quoted in Ross, *Women with a Mission*, 18.

21 Ross, *Women with a Mission*, 21.

22 E. White to Mrs Hobbs, 17 October 1834, JKL, MET 003/1/3; E. White to Mrs Hobbs, n.d., JKL, MET 003/4/1; and E. White to Mrs Hobbs, n.d., JKL, MET 003/4/6.

23 Jane Buttle Letters in Newman-Buttle Family Papers 1831-85, Turnbull Library, MS Papers-0402-12; 0402-17 and 2507-12.

24 Mehetabel Newman Letters in *Ibid*.

25 Ruth Fry. 'Newman, Mehetabel', *DNZB*, I, 1990. Te Ara - the Encyclopedia of New Zealand, https://teara.govt.nz/en/biographies/1n3/newman-mehetabel (accessed 1 April 2023)

26 Mary Aldred Scrapbook, MCNZA, MS 258.

27 Eliza White Album 1837-1870, JKL, MET 011/1/5.

28 Mary Anna Smales Album 1839-1860 in John H. Bumby and Smales Family Papers 1832-1860, Turnbull Library, MS Micro 0490.

29 Quoted in Fry, *Out of the Silence*, 21.

30 Ross, *Women with a Mission*, 19.

31 Quoted in Moon, "Wesleyan Wives", 28.

5 – Treaty to Tribulation: Methodism, 1840–1870

Geoffrey Troughton

Introduction

In Aotearoa, 1840 stands out as an obvious watershed. New Zealanders justifiably acknowledge the year as utterly pivotal in the nation's history. Its profound importance for religious history must also be recognised, notably in the shaping of the missions and of New Zealand Christianity more generally. This chapter examines the development of Methodism during the tumultuous years from the signing of the Treaty through to the end of 1860s. This was a period of expansion but also of calamity for the Wesleyan mission as much of its ministry crumbled in the wake of tensions between settlers, the Crown, and Māori communities, which erupted spectacularly in the wars of 1860–72. The chapter provides an overview of key developments during these years, focusing mainly on Wesleyan missionary efforts.

Wesleyans and the Treaty of Waitangi

Like their Church Missionary Society (CMS) peers, Wesleyan missionaries showed little enthusiasm for British annexation of New Zealand prior to 1840. They pushed at times for specific interventions to address particular problems, but the overall sentiment opposed largescale European settlement and colonisation. It was presumed that this would be bad for Māori, and also for the missions.

This perspective was on clear display at the Select Committee of the House of Commons on Aborigines (British Settlement), instituted in the mid-1830s as the fruit of evangelical humanitarian lobbying. Wesleyan Methodist Missionary Society (WMS), London Missionary Society (LMS), and CMS representatives testified unequivocally that – missionaries excepted – contact between Europeans and native peoples produced uniformly disastrous results. John Beecham, the WMS Chairman, conceded that colonisation conducted on 'truly Christian principles' might have benefits. But he also had profound reservations, expressing a 'very strong opinion as to the evil of the principle on which our present system of colonization is based.'[1]

Aware of such opposition, the New Zealand Association attempted to cast its colonisation plans in high-minded terms, as:

> a deliberate and methodical scheme for leading a savage people to embrace the religion, language, laws, and social habits of an advanced country, – for serving in the highest degree, instead of gradually exterminating, the aborigines of the country to be settled…. This … is not a plan of mere colonization: it has for

its object to civilize as well as to colonize: … to preserve the New Zealand race from extermination.[2]

The missions were unpersuaded. Yet, when it became clear in 1839 that colonisation of New Zealand was inevitable, they quickly adopted a pragmatic approach.

Gary Clover has recently highlighted that there is a Wesleyan Treaty story as well as a CMS one.[3] We know for example that James Buller had contact with Hobson while the Treaty was being drafted.[4] Two junior WMS missionaries were also present at the deliberations at Waitangi: John Warren and Samuel Ironside, the latter of whom was a signatory and the official witness for the Wesleyans. There is no evidence, however, of Warren or Ironside exerting any great influence on proceedings. By contrast, two rangatira with close Wesleyan connections did have influence. Tāmati Wāka Nene's pro-Treaty speech is widely regarded as *the* critical intervention that swung sentiment in favour of signing. He was assisted in his arguments by Patuone, his elder brother. By 1840, Patuone had fallen out with the Wesleyans and was aligned with the CMS, but he had been the key figure in the establishment of the Hokianga mission and retained significant connections with it.

Notwithstanding the importance of Waitangi, it was actually at Māngungu on 12 February 1840 that the single largest number of signatures to the Treaty were obtained. Hobson faced sharp opposition at that gathering. He also benefited from strong WMS support, especially from John Hobbs, and support continued at subsequent signings. John Whiteley and James Wallis, for example, spent several months procuring signatures on Hobson's behalf further south.[5] Hobson expressed appreciation for this in a letter to John Bumby, the young leader of the WMS in New Zealand, in which he acknowledged 'the [active], zealous, and able assistance' rendered during 'negotiation with the Native Chiefs at Hokianga, and Manukau, when I was in treaty for the cession to Her Majesty of the Sovereignty of these Islands'.[6]

Māori had their own reasons for signing the Treaty, and as others have argued, their assent reflected their own priorities and understandings of what was at stake. They did so cognizant of missionary support, both for the Treaty itself and for the wider project of establishing Crown authority.[7] That wider project was critical, and one that Hobson also addressed in his short letter to Bumby, where he thanked the Wesleyans for their commitment to him personally, as well as to his larger 'Mission, to promote the benevolent designs of Her Majesty'. Indeed, their large investment meant that the WMS had a deep stake in 'the maintenance of the Treaty of Waitangi, in its full integrity'.[8] This was Beecham's assessment in 1848 as disputes raged over Earl Grey's famous and controversial despatch of 23 December 1846. By then it was already evident that Wesleyans were becoming haunted by their 'prominent part in the settlement of the Treaty', as Beecham himself described it.[9]

Growth in the Early 1840s

All of that came a little later as debates about land and authority came to the fore. The immediate context of the early 1840s was tumultuous, but it was also a period of great promise and reconfiguration. On the positive side, there was significant expansion in the 1840s as the Wesleyans' sphere of influence widened. Bumby and Hobbs had engaged in a scoping tour in mid-1839 that took them to Port Nicholson, Wairau, Queen Charlotte Sound, Kapiti, and Taranaki.[10] These fields all developed in the early 1840s, and became vibrant centres of activity, serving in various configurations both settler and Māori communities. Significant expansion in these regions led to the New Zealand District being split into Northern and Southern Divisions.[11]

Reports and correspondence of the period suggested flourishing Māori interest in Christianity. Māori engagement with the Bible provided one significant barometer. In this respect, the outlook was optimistic, with the insatiable demand for text of the 1830s continuing in the following decade. In 1841, Samuel Ironside claimed:

> Such is the demand for Testaments, that I could dispose of hundreds without expense to the Mission. For instance a man came from Queen Charlotte's Sound, a week or two ago with a large pig, worth a pound at Port Nicholson. He said 'I don't want money, I don't want garments, I want food for my soul, I want a Testament'.[12]

"'Give me a Hymn Book, give me a Testament" is the universal cry', wrote James Watkin, a little later, reporting back on his itinerant tour through the South Island in 1843.[13] This plea was replicated in numerous missionary reports related to the new southern stations.

Most of the northern missions also had cause for optimism. In 1845, Walter Lawry reported that Māori in Auckland were gathering to read the Bible and pray twice a day.[14] In the Waikato, the Waipā mission expanded under George Buttle and then Alexander Reid, developing into a significant farming operation. The Hokianga mission, on the other hand, weakened as Northland's fortunes waned with the growth of Auckland.

The net effect was a remarkable breadth of engagement and influence. In 1848, Beecham described the extent of the WMS's work: twelve principal stations in the North Island, and two in the South, each with 'operations extending over a considerable District' servicing 89 chapels and 112 other buildings for worship; 3,700 accredited Church-Members or Communicants, with 6,212 scholars attending week-day and Sabbath schools; these institutions were superintended by eighteen ordained missionaries, assisted by thirteen other 'subordinate paid Agents', and 630 'Christian Natives who render their services gratuitously as Teachers in the Mission-Schools, or in conducting occasional Religious Services among their countrymen'.[15] The Native Institution for training Māori ministers was also established in Auckland in 1845, and the Three Kings School (Native Institution) in 1848.

Challenges and Tensions

It was not all plain sailing, of course, and the new stations experienced challenges. The Port Nicholson mission began in turmoil with disputes over the WMS's Te Aro purchase, which the New Zealand Company claimed, brazenly, as its own. The Company's tactics created tensions around the region, including the Wairau Incident of 1843; 22 settlers and four Māori died in this confrontation, which ultimately put paid to the Cloudy Bay mission.

The Waikouaiti station was established among whalers, settlers, and Kāi Tahu following requests from the Ōtākou chiefs Karetai and Taiaroa.[16] James and Hannah Watkin took up this challenge, after 6 years in Tonga and a shorter residence in Sydney, arriving with their five children on 16 May 1840. The results were impressive: in four years, there were more than 250 baptisms, and 39 couples were married – recognising that regularising relationships through marriage was a major preoccupation at the time.[17]

Yet the standout feature in James Watkin's papers is not success but despair and strain. Watkin's first letter, from June 1840, noted that he would be 700 miles from Hokianga and 300 miles from the closest other station. 'I trust I have not lost the spirit of sacrifice, I trust I shall not.'[18] Three months later, he wrote again:

> One very unworthy to claim such relationship, again addresses you from the remote corner in which he is isolated from the Christian world and from Brethren, where he is attempting to labour with a heart never light, but often heavy.... I wish that I was anywhere but here; and I think that the Committee if they saw my misery would in pity remove me to a more distant field and send another here more likely to be useful.[19]

Watkin lamented over his personal failings and weaknesses, fretted about his children's needs for proper education, and bemoaned the 'awful depravity' that surrounded him. These, he claimed, 'conspire to sink me into the dust, and to make my days and nights miserable.'

He wrote again the following year: 'From the ends of the earth with my heart overwhelmed within me, I again address you, not that I have anything that is interesting to communicate, but it is my duty to write, and at the present time I feel impelled to do so by the very strong desire I have to be removed from New Zealand.'[20] And in February 1842:

> I sometimes fear that my Letters have miscarried, and that my humble but earnest petition has not reached its destination. I therefore venture to repeat it. It is that I may be removed from New Zealand, at least from this part of it.... I have neither the strength nor inclination for New Zealand Missionary work. Long journeys and voyages I am not in circumstances to undertake.... I have no heart to study this language and I fear my proficiency in it is wretched.

He then requested three more missionaries to service Moeraki, Ōtākou, Port Levy, and Ruapuke, where local Māori interest was strong, before signing off: 'Your Affectionate unhappy Son and Servant, James Watkin.'[21] Poor Watkin. His correspondence is painful to read. Yet his request to move was subsequently accepted, and by 1844 he was in Wellington. In some senses, it was out of the frying pan and into the fire.

Watkin's case was extreme, but it highlighted the sense of dislocation, isolation, and vulnerability that remained a factor in this period.[22] There were other challenges, some of them severe. The death by drowning of Bumby on 26 June 1840 was particularly shocking. His waka overturned between Motutapu Island and Tiritiri Matangi Island, in an incident that also saw eleven Māori travelling companions and one young Tongan man die. Colleagues were left in despair: 'We are now walking in darkness and have no light', wrote William Woon just weeks after tragedy.[23]

Competition between the various missions sharpened. With the advent of Catholic mission in 1838, anxiety about 'papists' became a factor. In 1840, Woon complained about the growing influence of the 'emissaries of the Church of Rome' whilst also attributing Catholicism's appeal to native ignorance and material inducements – the 'distribution of presents, such as red blankets, shirts, Jackets, &c., and the 'Punch and Judy' exhibition at mass &c. by the Reverend Episcopas'.[24] More New Testaments and teachers such as Mohi Tāwhai from Waimā were needed to expose 'the nakedness of the Babylonish Whore'.

It was Woon who also described an extraordinary sermon, delivered to 1,000 guests, at the wedding of Wiremu Patēne and Marara Hira. Woon preached from John 2, the famous passage on 'the wedding at Cana', explaining that 'this ordinance was divine in its origin, and instituted by Heaven for the happiness of all God's rational creatures'. He then condemned 'the Popish declaration propagated by the Romanists in New Zealand as in other places 'forbidding to marry, and to abstain from meats,' &c. &c.... After the errors of Popery were thus exposed ... I married them'.[25] Woon's severity illustrates the intense competition that rose when the missions were in close proximity. In places like the Hokianga, the 'enemies of the cross of Christ' were highly visible, and therefore a greater threat, so tensions often ran high. Protecting one's patch became important, and this partly explains Whiteley's insistence that Māori prohibit land sales to 'papists' as one condition of ministry.[26]

Relationships between the CMS and WMS also experienced strain, particularly when the CMS moved into the West Coast of the North Island – for example, at Ōtaki – though by-and-large the missions there worked well enough together. In Nelson, Whiteley noted the presence of 'United Christians' of all denominations joining together in the absence of a stated ministry, and happily contributed to it.[27] Bishop Selwyn's arrival in 1842 tested harmony, however. The Wesleyans had a reputation in CMS eyes, and evidently among Māori, as being the less strict mission in the Waikato because they were relatively quick to baptise, and were considered less demanding of would-be converts.[28] Selwyn reignited these debates, angering WMS missionaries who received reports that CMS missionaries were requiring Māori who had been baptised by Wesleyans to undergo rebaptism. They objected, petitioning Selwyn, and urging him to stop authorizing such baptisms and casting doubt on Wesleyan orders.[29] A degree of rivalry continued, however. Watkin complained about 'high church' Anglican influences being sent into his region through native teachers and others, sowing bigotry and division. He claimed that Anglicans were accusing Methodists of being new and young—precisely the criticisms that Roman Catholics were making of Anglicans.[30]

Questions of Land and Peace

Questions of land and peace were perhaps the two most consequential, contested, and fractious ones in mid-nineteenth century New Zealand. They were deeply connected to questions of authority. It was in the nexus of disputes over land ownership and authority that visions of peace were tested, and ultimately the Wesleyan ministry among Māori foundered.

In recent years, there has been a growing body of research exploring Christian peace activism in New Zealand, including missionary peacemaking.[31] It is clear that WMS missionaries regarded themselves as agents of a 'gospel of peace', committed to inculcating a gospel of spiritual salvation, and also of peace as an ethical imperative. Missionary references to the 'gospel of peace' actually incorporated a wide range of meanings, including spiritual and social peace, and a variety of other meanings. The phrase was even deployed as a sectarian moniker, differentiating Protestant from Catholic Christianity.[32] Yet it also included a distinct ethical emphasis that opposed violence, utu (understood in a restricted sense as retribution, or violent retaliation), and warfare.

We have numerous accounts of Wesleyan missionaries teaching renunciation of these, and seeking to act as peace-brokers in various contexts – from local arguments and skirmishes through to bigger conflicts like the Northern War. More importantly, Wesleyan Māori such as the influential leader of Ngāti Māhanga, Te Awaitaia (baptised as Wiremu Nēra), clearly embraced this rendering of Christianity, acting independently as mediators and explicitly pursuing peace in the name of Christ. Ironside reported encountering Christian Māori who had travelled to Taranaki from the Waikato, determined to accompany 'their heathen neighbours and thus as far as possible restrain them' from violence.[33] Charles Creed reported meeting Māori in Taranaki and Waikato who claimed to have turned from warfare to peace and reconciliation on account of their Christianity.[34]

As late as 1850, Riwha Tītokowaru was preaching peace in explicitly Christian terms: 'Give over war. Do not say I am laying down the law, it is Christ who is doing so.'[35] Tītokowaru's story had various phases. Yet his serious engagement with an ethics of peace, tied to serious engagement with the Bible, was a striking and critical dimension. Indeed, this was a feature shared with other leaders from the region including Te Ua Haumēne and Te Whiti O Rongomai who also had significant Wesleyan connections. It is reasonable to see the cultivation of these outlooks, at least in part, as the fruit of Methodist piety – of commitments forged in the reading of scripture, worship, and the formation of eschatological imagination.[36] In terms of the latter, Buller's interpretation of the use of musket barrels to strike bells, ushering in the Sabbath, is notable: he took the practise as symbolic of the triumph of the Gospel of Peace, and the fulfilment of Isaiah's eschatological vision of a world in which swords would be turned into ploughshares.[37]

The Bible became an important resource and symbol in this, and Māori parsed out a disjunction between the Bible and warfare in various ways. Wiremu Nēra, for example, juxtaposed his people's previous delight 'in killing and devouring one another' with their contemporary devotion to the New Testament, cultivating lands, and living in peace. His explanation for the change was a simple one: 'We found the book to be the truth'. Whiteley argued that the Bible provided Māori with a symbol, argument, and motive for peace – not only within Māori society, but also in contestation with European settlers. Thus, Rawiri Kingi confronted a group of settlers, holding out his Testament and remonstrating with them saying: 'See, see! This is my weapon – the white man's book! You sent us this book, and it tells us not to fight. You have got other weapons, weapons of blood: use them not;

fight not, or my heathen relatives will fight too: remember your book; remember your book!'[38]

Land was central to the key political conflicts of the period including the war in Taranaki from 1860, and subsequently in the Waikato and beyond. In their thinking about land issues, Wesleyan missionaries' perspectives shifted over time. This had profound consequences for their application of the peace gospel, and for the mission itself.

After 1840, land purchases became increasingly contentious. So, too, did missionary land-holdings. On this score, the Wesleyan record was straightforward: by contrast with the CMS, the WMS forbade their missionaries to own land. Two did: 'William White, who was expelled from the mission for other reasons; and Nathaniel Turner, who purchased some land from a European and disposed of it quickly when he realised it was a sensitive issue.'[39] In terms of their own purchases, then, there was little scope for criticism.

WMS missionaries were also vigorous defenders of Māori land rights in the early 1840s. When Earl Grey's 1846 despatch sought to introduce a 'waste lands' doctrine, senior Methodists rejected it. The policy would have categorised as 'waste land' any land not registered as 'native lands' by Government-appointed officers. Such land would have become the property of the Crown – including land claimed by Māori but not actually used and occupied by them 'by means of labour expended thereon.' Walter Lawry condemned this doctrine as a 'direct violation of the Treaty of Waitangi'. He claimed that, 'there is not an inch of the island unclaimed by a native owner,' and warned of the consequences of not respecting this.[40]

Over a relatively short period of time, the strength of these convictions evidently waned. In 1857, Whiteley expressed his private and confidential view of the land question to C.W. Richmond. His analysis was blunt:

> I think it would greatly benefit the Natives if they would sell every acre they possess and then each one for himself repurchase and hold by Crown Grant so much only as they individually require. I think it should be the primary object of the General Government to extinguish the Native title as soon as practicable.

Despite the contested and complex nature of land claims, he recommended accepting all offers to sell, leaving any disputes to work themselves out over time. Furthermore, he argued: 'I would have the natives paid as low a price as possible for these claims – the lower the better for themselves – but even if high prices had to be given the money would soon return into the hands of the Europeans and thus the Colony be benefitted.'[41]

Soon after, Thomas Buddle argued publicly that possession of large tracts of land had not been good for Māori. He then spurned the prospect that 'extensive tracts of country' might be left to 'remain waste in their hands', posing a distinctly rhetorical question: 'does Divine Providence intend these vast tracts of country to remain a wilderness, or are these parts of the earth, like other parts, to be subdued and made to yield food for man and beast?'[42] By 1866, George Buttle was reflecting on the unfavourable situation at Waipā, attributing the problems of the age to the 'worldliness' of Māori there. 'Land', he opined, was 'their great bane' and likely to become the source of serious future conflict. He diagnosed the heart of the problem as a 'steady but absurd resistance of all fair proposals to relieve them of so great an evil as the large but to them useless tracts of land to which they lay claim.'[43]

The obvious question here is what on earth had happened, not only to earlier opposition to the 'waste lands' policy, but more generally to a Wesleyan missionary 'peace gospel'? For principled opposition to warfare also seemed to fade in the face of conflict initiated by the colonial state.

Theologising Colonisation

A number of factors were at play. At one level, Wesleyan support for land sales and changes to customary tenure were inspired by a hope that ministry to Māori would be made simpler logistically if their living arrangements were consolidated into one locality – and, indeed, a belief that such a development would be more generally desirable for Māori. Whiteley was also aware of the divisiveness caused by land disputes in Taranaki and hoped that individualisation of title might resolve this.[44] But underlying these arguments were decisive shifts in thinking: on the one hand to more thoroughgoing theologies of dominion, and submission to the state, and on the other hand to an embrace of colonisation. The shifts were in fact related, and may be regarded as a theologising of colonisation.

In the early 1850s, Māori resistance to increasing European settlement and demand for land led to development of so-called Land Leagues. Kīngitanga also emerged as a formal movement in the late 1850s, shaped by concerns about land loss and the erosion of chiefly authority. Despite Kīngitanga's strong Christian connections, WMS missionaries became increasingly opposed to it. Cort Schnackenberg interpreted alignment with the Māori King as disloyalty to the British Crown, and to the missions.[45] Buddle became increasingly convinced that the movement challenged British sovereignty and law, and that this threatened Māori progress in civilisation.[46]

When war eventually erupted in Taranaki in March 1860, Whiteley explicitly urged Wiremu Kīngi Te Rangitāke to surrender, rationalising this advice on the Romans 13 principle of submission to governing authorities.[47] Throughout the war, he urged Māori opponents to give up fighting the government, 'submit to the authorities and withdraw their opposition to land sales'.[48] No wonder settler politicians like J. C. Richmond lavished praise in Parliament on 'the Wesleyan clergy to a man', hailing their example as 'good citizens and loyal subjects'.[49] To the extent that there remained a vision for social peace, the primary vehicle for this was now through British law and submission to the powers that be. War might be regrettable, but it was necessary in the absence of such submission.

If that sounds like a defence of colonisation, it was. In his retrospective, *Forty Years in New Zealand*, published in 1878, James Buller expressed pride in Wesleyan opposition to Earl Grey's 1846 despatch—which he dubbed 'the obnoxious instruction'. He also argued, however, that there had indeed been waste lands; that it would have served Māori interests to sell them 'by fair purchase'; but that opportunities to ensure this had been squandered: 'They had, and still have, far more than they can use. As far as I can see, without the co-operation of the sons of Japhet, those descendants of Shem could not fulfil the Divine command to "replenish the earth and subdue it." Buller dismissed those who objected to purchases made at nominal prices leading to profits for the purchasers—since land without improvements was 'valueless', 'waste, howling wilderness', and profit enabled improvement. 'Read in the light of facts', he said, 'the colonization of New Zealand was essential to the development of its latent resources. If colonized, it was necessary to obtain territory: on what consideration was of no consequence, provided the original claimants were pleased, and enough soil was retained for their occupation, use, and profit.'[50] This was an extraordinary assessment coming from a WMS missionary who had been with Hobson in the lead-up to the Treaty.

War and the Methodist Ministry

This shift in outlook seems particularly strange, given that it was not entirely shared by Anglican colleagues. Numerous so-called 'church party leaders' and CMS missionaries maintained a critical but sympathetic attitude to the Kīngitanga for some time.[51] And when war erupted in Taranaki, this group opposed the government's aggression as unjust and immoral. They were left fuming at their Wesleyan counterparts, whom they charged, in Mary Anne Martin's words, with 'toadying to a man ... to the government'.[52] Oddly, Wesleyans were now behaving as a state religion might, submitting with little evident reserve to the government and baptizing its agenda.

From a contemporary vantage point, it is remarkable to read Williams' *Centenary Sketches of New Zealand Methodism*, and see how little space it gives to the wars of the 1860s. Williams' narrative emphasised the growth of the settler church, and expressed little sympathy or understanding of the implications for Māori.[53] His narrative seems impossibly jaundiced now. Yet Williams' brief account does allude to a tension that lies at the heart of the Wesleyan change in perspective. That tension was a structural one: Wesleyan missionaries, on the whole, found themselves ministering – or attempting to minister – to both Māori and settler communities alike.

Ministry to settlers put them in closer contact with settler aspirations. The continuing growth in settler numbers, their obvious needs, and the opportunity to influence the shape of the emerging settlements all represented compellingly attractive openings for ministry. The formation of an Australasian Wesleyan Methodist Connexion, with two New Zealand districts, sharpened a conviction that there existed an 'intimate connection ... between colonial progress and prosperity and the spread of Scriptural Christianity'.[54] Yet the needs and aspirations of settler and Māori communities were obviously not well aligned. Settler pressure was substantial, and in practice, settler priorities began to predominate; 'civilizing' narratives were re-formed and deployed in ways that tied Māori improvement to their accommodation of settler demands.

In the context of wartime, continuing ministry to 'both sides' became challenging and deeply fraught, even within the context of regular parish and circuit ministry. How much more so when attempting to minister to colonial and imperial troops as well, as some attempted to do? These included Alexander Reid, who was prevailed upon to leave the Waipā station in May 1863; he then made his way north to Auckland, and ultimately ended up being employed among the soldiers during the Waikato War.[55] As Government troops moved south from Auckland into the Waikato,[56] they were accompanied at various points by Thomas Buddle, James Wallis, and John Rishworth.[57] Rishworth hoped to exercise a broad ministry, but this presented obvious difficulties. He articulated his troubles in his journal in 1864: 'my heart was overwhelmed … I feel an earnest longing to be useful to my fellow man whether black or white but my sphere of labour is most difficult and peculiar but God can open my way so that in this untoward district his word shall prevail.'[58] There were risks in pursuing this approach. The killing of Whiteley at Pukearuhe Redoubt in February 1869 was very likely not premeditated, but it clearly demonstrated the hazards and perils that attended such ministry.[59]

Two other factors were important, and help to explain the shift in Methodist position. The first relates to the political conservatism that numerous commentators note emerged from the turmoil of the 1790s and early 1800s among British Wesleyans. Growing conservatism has been interpreted as a response to pressure on the one hand from the British government, notably in the famous Sidmouth Bills of 1811, and on the other hand from political radicals.[60] As a consequence, Wesleyan 'loyalty' to the Crown became a point of acute sensitivity. This sensitivity had an enduring impact. Arguably, it was transported to the colonial setting, and institutionalised with considerable intensity. Methodist leaders became prone to grand expressions of political loyalty, often to a greater extreme than other religious groups in New Zealand. Their minority status and character as a tight society contributed to this position.

Another factor relates simply to institutional geography. In the 1830s, the WMS and CMS agreed to operate in different parts of the country under a comity agreement. As it happened, the WMS's designated sphere took in precisely the places where the most contentious land purchases occurred, and where conflicts erupted, such as Wairau, Wellington, and the West Coast of the North Island including Taranaki. Whereas the larger CMS body was more dispersed around the country, WMS ministry was concentrated in areas of high volatility, where the imposition of British law and norms promised – in their view – the only feasible pathway to stability and peace.

Conclusion

For New Zealand Methodism, the three decades from 1840 were marked by substantial change. Growth, expansion, conflict, and reconfiguration were all evident during this period. At the end of the 1860s, Methodism was actually on the cusp of a period of tremendous growth, fuelled by the Vogel immigrants, and the opening up of new regions for settlement.[61] Settler Methodism profited particularly in this environment, so much that by the end of the nineteenth century it was arguably at the peak of its influence. Nimble organization, support for lay ministry, and promotion of heart-felt, high-commitment faith enabled it to adapt and grow. At the start of the 1860s, there had been vastly more Māori than European members. Within ten years that situation had completely reversed. In the turmoil of the period, the most substantial and enduring change was the transition of the Wesleyan mission into a settler colonial church.

Notes

1 *Report from the Select Committee on Aborigines (British Settlements) Together with the Minutes of Evidence, Appendix and Index*. London: House of Commons, 1836, 515.

2 *He Whakaputanga me te Tiriti | The Declaration and the Treaty: The Report on Stage 1 of the Te Paparahi o te Raki Inquiry (WAI 1040)*. Lower Hutt: Waitangi Tribunal, 2014, 6.2.3, 300.

3 Gary Clover, 'The Māngungu Treaty Signing, 12 February 1840, and its Importance,' *WHS (NZ) Journal,* 105 (2018): 25–49.

4 J. M. R. Owens, 'Missionaries and the Treaty of Waitangi,' *WHS (NZ) Journal,* 49 (1986): 27.

5 Claudia Orange, *The Treaty of Waitangi*, second edition, Wellington: Bridget Williams Books, 2013, c. 4.

6 Lieutenant Governor William Hobson to John Hewgill Bumby, 29 May 1840, Government House Russell, MS 282, PPHR Box 53 (MCNZA).

7 Hobbs is said to have conversed at length with Nene prior to the Waitangi signings about the benefits of British intervention. See Clover, 'The Māngungu Treaty Signing'.

8 John Beecham to Earl Grey, 23 February 1848, in *New Zealand Correspondence between the Wesleyan Missionary Committee and the Right Honourable Earl Grey, Her Majesty's Principal Secretary of State for the Colonial Department, on the Apprehended Infringement of the Treaty of Waitangi*. London: Wesleyan Missionary Society, 1848, 4.

9 John Beecham to Earl Grey, 23 February 1848, *New Zealand Correspondence*, 5.

10 G. I. Laurenson, *Te Hāhi Weteriana: Three Half Centuries of the Methodist Māori Mission, 1822–1972*. WHS (NZ) *Proceedings*, 27, nos. 1-2, 1972, 55.

11 A. L. Olsson, *Methodism in Wellington: Methodism in Wellington 1839 to 1989: A Chronological Outline of the Growth and Development of the Methodist Church in the Wellington District*. Wellington: Wellington District Synod of the Methodist Church of New Zealand, 1989, 12.

12 Samuel Ironside, 3 May 1841, MS39, Box 3, Folder 15, MCNZA.

13 James Watkin Journal, 10 June 1843, MS39, Box 4, Folder 17, MCNZA.

14 Peter Lineham, 'This is My Weapon: Maori Response to the Maori Bible,' in *Mission and Moko: The Church Missionary Society in New Zealand, 1814–1882*. Christchurch: Latimer Fellowship, 1993, 178.

15 John Beecham to Earl Grey, 23 February 1848, *New Zealand Correspondence*, 4.

16 Mary-Anne Woodfield, 'Sowing the Gospel of Peace: Missionary James Watkin at Karitāne and Wellington, 1840–1855,' MA thesis in History, Victoria University of Wellington, 2016, 25. Waikouaiti is now known as Karitāne.

17 See Angela Wanhalla, "The Natives Uncivilize Me': Missionaries and Interracial Intimacy in Early New Zealand,' in *Missionaries, Indigenous People and Cultural Exchange*, edited by Patricia Grimshaw and Andrew May, Eastbourne: Sussex Academic Press, 2010, 26–34; Angela Wanhalla, *Matters of the Heart: A History of Interracial Marriage in New Zealand*. Auckland: Auckland University Press, 2013.

18 James Watkin to the Secretaries, 18 June 1840, MS39, Box 3, Folder 14, MCNZA.

19 James Watkin to the Secretaries, 15 September 1840, MS39, Box 3, Folder 14, MCNZA.

20 James Watkin to the Secretaries, 8 May 1841, MS39, Box 3, Folder 15, MCNZA.

21 James Watkin to the Secretaries, 5 February 1842, MS39, Box 4, Folder 16, MCNZA.

22 A plan in 1840 illustrated that it was never imagined that a station would contain more than 2 missionaries at any one site (other than Hokianga), and often at a significant remove. See J. H. Bumby to the Secretaries, 12 May 1840, MS39, Box 3, Folder 14, MCNZA. The plan for mission distribution was: Mangungu (Bumby, Woon, Creed), Waima (Warren), Neward (Hobbs), Wangaroa (Smales), Kaipara (Buller), Waingaroa (Wallis, Buddle), Kawia (Whiteley, Turton), Taranaki (Ironside), Kapiti (Buttle), Port Nicholson (Aldred), Otago (Watkin).

23 William Woon Journal, 24 July 1840, extract in William Woon to the Secretaries, 31 July 1840, MS39, Box 3, Folder 14, MCNZA.

24 William Woon to the Secretaries, 23 June 1840, MS39, Box 3, Folder 14, MCNZA.

25 William Woon to the Secretaries, 23 June 1840.

26 John Whiteley to the Secretaries, 10 March 1840, MS39, Box 3, Folder 14, MCNZA.

27 John Whiteley to the Secretaries, 14 June 1842, MS39, Box 4, Folder 16, MCNZA.

28 K. R. Howe, 'The Maori Response to Christianity in the Thames-Waikato Area, 1833–1840.' *New Zealand Journal of History,* 7, no. 1 (1973): 39.

29 Graham Brazendale, *John Whiteley: Land Sovereignty and the Land Wars of the 19th Century.* WHS (NZ) Proceedings, 64, 1996, 11.

30 James Watkin Journal, 25 May 1843.

31 For my own contributions, see Geoffrey Troughton, ed., *Pacifying Missions: Christianity, Violence, and Empire in the Nineteenth Century,* Studies in Christian Mission, 58, Leiden: Brill, 2023; Geoffrey Troughton, 'Scripture, Piety and the Practice of Peace in Nineteenth-Century New Zealand Mission.' *Studies in World Christianity* 25, no. 2 (2019), 128-144; Geoffrey Troughton and Philip Fountain, eds., *Pursuing Peace in Godzone: Christianity and the Peace Tradition in New Zealand.* Wellington: Victoria University Press, 2018; Geoffrey Troughton, ed., *Saints and Stirrers: Christianity, Conflict, and Peacemaking in New Zealand, 1814–1945.* Wellington: Victoria University Press, 2017, Geoffrey Troughton, 'Missionaries, Historians and the Peace Tradition in New Zealand,' in *Te Rongopai 1814, 'Takoto te pai!': Bicentenary Reflections on Christian Beginnings and Developments in Aotearoa New Zealand,* edited by Allan K. Davidson, Stuart Lange, Peter Lineham and Adrienne Puckey, Auckland: General Synod of the Anglican Church in Aotearoa New Zealand and Polynesia, 2014, 228–245.

32 Thomas Buddle to the Secretaries, 2 March 1842, MS39, Box 4, Folder 16, MCNZA. This letter provides an account of the establishment of mission site at Waipā, including contestation over alleged building on a tapu site; and discussions with a taua, which they persuade to turn back, before discovering that the taua involved the same people who had been threatening to burn down their house – 'they were the same party that had been threatening to burn down my house professors of the Religion not of the Gospel of Peace but of the Pope.'

33 Samuel Ironside Diary, 13 June 1840, MS39, Box 3, Folder 14, MCNZA.

34 Charles Creed to the Secretaries, 25 January 1842, MS39, Box 4, Folder 16, MCNZA.

35 James Belich, *I Shall Not Die: Titokowaru's War, 1868–1869.* second edition, Wellington, Bridget Williams Books, 2015, 5.

36 See Troughton, 'Scripture, Piety and the Practice of Peace.'

37 James Buller to the Secretaries, 11 February 1840, MS39, Box 3, Folder 14, MA; also Charles Creed to the Secretaries, 30 August 1841, MS39, Box 3, Folder 15, MCNZA.

38 See extract quoted in *The Methodist Magazine,* August 1844, 689–698.

39 Owens, 'Missionaries and the Treaty', 26.

40 *The Colonial Intelligencer or Aborigines Friend*, 2, no. 1 (1849): 47–48, cited in John Stenhouse, 'Church and State in New Zealand, 1835–1870.' in *Church and State in Old and New Worlds*, edited by Hilary M. Carey and John Gascoigne, Leiden: Brill, 2010, 242.

41 J. Whiteley to C. W. Richmond, New Plymouth, 17 August 1857, in *The Richmond-Atkinson Papers*, edited by Guy H. Scholefield, Wellington: R. E. Owen, Government Printer, 1960, 1, 292.

42 Thomas Buddle, *The Maori King Movement in New Zealand, with a Full Report of the Native Meetings held at Waikato, April and May 1860*. Auckland: The New Zealander Office, 1860, 21-22.

43 Waipa Circuit Report 1866, Wesleyan Conference Circuit and School Reports, 1851–1870, Box 162, Folder 1, CON-210, MCNZA.

44 Brazendale, *John Whiteley*, 31.

45 Kaipara Circuit School Report 1862, Box 162, Folder 3, CON-210, MCNZA.

46 Brazendale, *John Whiteley*, 37.

47 *Wellington Independent*, 27 March 1860.

48 Brazendale, *John Whiteley*, 35.

49 *New Zealand Parliamentary Debates*, vol. C [1858-1860] 580 (25 September 1860), cited in Stenhouse, 'Church and State in New Zealand', 252.

50 James Buller, *Forty Years in New Zealand: Including a Personal Narrative, An Account of Maoridom, and of the Christianization and Colonization of the Country*. London: Hodder and Stoughton, 1878, 405-406.

51 Grant Phillipson, 'The Thirteenth Apostle: Bishop Selwyn and the Transplantation of Anglicanism in New Zealand, 1841–1868,' PhD thesis in History, University of Otago, 1992, 343–345.

52 Cited in Stenhouse, 'Church and State in New Zealand', 253.

53 W. J. Williams, *Centenary Sketches of New Zealand Methodism*. Christchurch: Lyttelton Times Co., 1922, 141–142.

54 'Wesleyan Missionary Meeting.' *New Zealander*, 9 December 1854, 3.

55 Frank G. Glen, *Methodism in Auckland During the Maori Wars, 1860-1864*.WHS (NZ) Proceedings, 16, nos. 1-2, 1957, 13.

56 Extension of war into the Waikato in 1863-1864 is now widely accepted as both premeditated and unjust. In Vincent O'Malley's assessment, Governor Grey spent the better part of eighteen months from 1861 talking of 'peace while openly preparing for war'. Vincent O'Malley, *The New Zealand Wars | Ngā Pakanga o Aotearoa*. Wellington: Bridget Williams Books, 2019, 103. Colonial and Imperial troops built the Great South Road from Auckland down to the Waikato River, completing this in March 1863, before a series of accusations and ultimatums culminated in open conflict beginning on 17 July 1863. For an alternative interpretation, see Simon Abbott, 'How Governor George Grey failed to bring Peace, 1861–1863,' MA thesis in History, Massey University, 2020.

57 H. R. Vyle, *A Hundred Years of Methodist Witness in Hamilton: St Paul's Church, London Street*. WHS (NZ) Proceedings, 20, no. 4, 1964, 3.

58 John Rishworth Journal, 8 May 1864, Rev. J. S. Rishworth Journal, 1864–67, MS19, MCNZA.

59 Brazendale, *John Whiteley*, 39–40.

60 See David Hempton, *Methodism and Politics in British Society 1750–1850.* London: Hutchinson, 1984, esp. 85–110; also, on the Sidmouth Bills, Maldwyn Edwards, *After Wesley: A Study of the Social and Political Influence of Methodism in the Middle Period (1791–1849).* London: Epworth Press, 75–82.

61 For an interpretation of this growth, and subsequent decline, see Peter J. Lineham, *New Zealanders and the Methodist Evangel: An Interpretation of the Policies and Performance of the Methodist Church of New Zealand.* WHS (NZ) Proceedings, 42, 1983.

Section Three: Te Hahi Weteriana

6 – Maea te Kupu: Kaeo, he whenua kurahuna – emerging stories of Methodism: Kaeo, land of hidden knowledge

Rowan Tautari

Mihi

"Toitū te kupu, toitū te mana, toitū te whenua".

He mihi tēnei ki a Ranginui e tu iho nei ki a Papatūānuku e takoto nei. Ka huri ngā mihi ki a koutou te hunga kua riro ki tua o te arai, okioki mai ra. Ka hoki mai ki a tātou ki te hunga ora tēnā tātou katoa.

Ko nga mihi nui ki te kaituhi i whakapau ai ōna pukenga kōrero kia whai take ai tēnei kaupapa i tēnei te rua rau tau o te Hāhi Weteriana o Aotearoa. E mihi ana ki te wairua me te tapu o ngā kōrero kurahuna i roto i tēnei kohinga kōrero. Nāu ra mātou i hāpai i manaaki i ngā rangahau mō tēnei kaupapa whānui. Ko te tūmanako, mā roto i te rangahau ka hua ake he whakaaroaro anō hei whāinga mō te reanga i muri i a mātou. Nā reira e te tuahine Rowan he aroha nui tēnei ki a koe.

Maea te kupu, he whenua kurahuna shares origin threads and themes to an evolving *Kaeo whenua story*. Not one dominant reality, but a divergence of many. The stories and histories of the Kaeo whenua are as a rendering of parables, multi-layered and meant to be told so we might hear the hidden voices and share of the sacred knowledge they tell. In our history making spanning 200 years new insights of knowledge emerge, challenging us to reconcile our own understandings of sacred lands, people, and awaken us to fresh pathways forward.

Our Papatūānuku past reveals much about her treatment and re-identification by the Church for purposes of a Wesleyan Mission. The hidden narratives of Māori encounter Western conceptions of knowledge *Kaeo as settler colonial imaginary* highlights where *Kaeo exclusions and inclusions* intersect in our lives as a cross-cultural story of relationships. With each generation contextualised understandings of whenua have influenced the arbitrary relationship between Māori and Tauiwi in church and society. The gains have come not without negotiation, contestation and struggle. In caring for climate justice for future generations, restoration of ecologies of natural habitats, and heritage values, our sacred lands are sites of deep wisdom. Borrowing from our past and our shared heritage raises further reflections on a future of Kaeo whenua reimagined and inclusive of the diversity present in our church.

What remains is the permanence of Kaeo as whenua kurahuna valued as it was last century, and now two centuries later. The themes stir within us a deep reflection of our attitudes and beliefs to land and people, and the ongoing relationship of tangata whenua and Tauiwi embodied in the church. Maea te kupu he whenua kurahuna contributes significantly to understanding the forces at play in the evolving *Kaeo as yearning story*, and as a body of knowledge for all who draw affiliation to our Methodist roots in Aotearoa/New Zealand. What emerges is a gleaning of the past, before, after and for the future.

Whenu (strands) of the kōrari (flax plant) come in complimentary pairs, bringing the balance in mahi raranga (weaving). As each whenu is laid the kairaranga (weaver) seeks to maintain a horizonal ara (the pathway) and the weaving unfolds. In some designs of the poutama (staircase of knowledge) the whakatū motif dictates that the weaving move vertically. The ara disappears, in faith the kairaranga continues weaving upwards and across. The ara returns when the gradient of the step is achieved. Patterns of this nature invite us to move into the unknown without fear, and with faith prompting us to move where the wairua leads us. We are challenged to take heed of the voiceless of our past, the voiceless in our midst, and for future generations are encouraged to seek innovative, constructive and transformative ways to move us forward. Conscious always, although not obvious to all, that which is hidden is never forgotten.

Rev. Akinihi Keita Hotere

He Kupu Timatatanga

"The Treaty of Waitangi is the covenant establishing our nation on the basis of a power- sharing relationship, and will guide how we undertake mission."[1]

This is a contextual study about the origins of the Methodist Church in Aotearoa/New Zealand. Origins refer to beginnings, specifically 'the point at which something begins or rises from which it derives.[2] In this story, origins are linked to themes. A theme is a recurring idea, a broad message with an underlying meaning. Themes reflect broad shifts in time. They are not always evident in the beginning. They may become more apparent with time, hence the title, maea te kupu (emerging words). Themes may be obvious to some but not to others. The expression whenua kurahuna, invites reflection of Kaeo not only as a physical place and a literal site, but as a symbol with multiple reference points depending on one's location.

While this document can be described as a story or a series of stories, it is also offered as an outline to guide a reconsideration of origins, and to generate discussion about what a bicultural history might look like in 2022. The themes discussed in this story have been extrapolated from Methodist Church of New Zealand (MCNZ) archives, land story questions, Conference papers, and the Church's mission statement. They reflect the Church's historic and ongoing role as an agent of transformation and change. The story is also shaped by scholarship that sits outside the Church, by revisionist history, as well as postcolonial and Kaupapa-Māori theory. Finally, it reflects the broader Aotearoa/New Zealand context that has always influenced the Church, including the natural environment.

While this story makes reference to tangata whenua of Whangaroa it does not claim to tell their stories. Kōrero tuku iho (oral tradition) is best told by those who, through whakapapa and appropriate training, have the right to do so. In saying so it does make general observations. Published and unpublished accounts, including evidence submitted to the Waitangi Tribunal hint at a complex world involving rangatira, hapū, decisions made, actions taken, collaborations formed amidst constant negotiation, and a deepening awareness of the world beyond. The reasons why tangata whenua chose to engage with Wesleyan missionaries have been explored by many historians. Apart from noting the existence of personal commitments and expectations between Māori (including clergy) and the Church, that appear as fragments in personal papers and offer a counterpoint to general theories, this story does not seek to relitigate or join those debates.

Structure

The themes in this study span two centuries of Methodism in Aotearoa and are loosely divided into three time periods, 1822, 1922, and 2022. While each time period is allocated two themes, these are not restricted to a particular time or location. For example, the theme of Kaeo as whenua precedes 1822, extends beyond 2022, transcends Western concepts of time, and applies to all whenua in Aotearoa. The themes also overlap in terms of their subject matter. For example, there is a constant interplay between Kaeo as exclusion and inclusion, and between Kaeo as remembrance and yearning.

Kaeo as whenua focusses attention on a Māori ontological relationship to land. This relationship is mediated by Papatūānuku (earth, creation). While much has been written about Papatūānuku in academic scholarship, the normativity of Papatūānuku to Māori is overlooked in Church histories and until recently by the Church.[3] This theme also provides a wider cultural context for understanding the influence of tikanga in shaping Māori relationships including with each other, with the missionaries and with te taiao (environment). This theme explains why the first transaction of land between Māori and the Church was predicated on tikanga.

Kaeo as settler colonial imaginary concerns the perceptions of the non-Western world by Western observers, beginning with accounts of Māori by missionaries. Church origin stories based on missionary accounts depicted Māori through a deficit lens based on stereotypes held about indigenous people. Despite the apparent health and well-being of Māori, they were described as heathen, uncivilised, filthy, depraved, bestial, and savages with badly behaved children. This theme makes explicit the colonial logic that underpinned the purchase of land at Kaeo for the Wesleyan mission. One in which land was remade as property and missions marked as sites of civilisation. That Māori did not see themselves or their surroundings in this way was irrelevant.

Kaeo as exclusion explores the invisibility of those who do not appear in the origin stories of the Church. This includes women, largely perceived as adjuncts to men, yet as a group were and are diverse. There are other silences in the Kaeo story. Categorisations that involved children and people with disabilities. Heteronormative discourses that assume uniformity and conformity and block cultural diversity, invisibilising sexual orientation and other gender identities. Hegemonic narratives that subjugate the environment, privilege human exceptionalism and enable other-than-human whanaunga (kin) including rivers, mountains, forests, wetlands, trees, birds and fish to be treated as an inexhaustible resource.

Kaeo as inclusion seeks to expand our definition of origin stories beyond linear readings of missionary journals and archival records. It also suggests alternative methods from which to construct Methodist history as a counterpoint to the written word. Material objects can embody and reveal other ways of knowing and being. The dominance of te reo in Aotearoa in 1822, and its ongoing expression in Māori spaces via whaikōrero, wānanga and waiata suggest other ways to define origins. This opens the door for a wider decolonial discussion of origins in 2022 through the lens of Māori women and girls.

Kaeo as remembrance explores what is remembered and why. The act of remembering is recorded in the names of Methodist dead and in the honouring of their deeds. Kaeo mission as a site of remembrance symbolises the beginning of this tradition; the names listed on the cairn, the Kaeo Memorial Church, the cemetery recording the names of early settlers. As the Church's acts of remembrance necessitate engagement with public history and overlap with touristic consumption and local remembrance, public and private spaces collide. Acts of remembrance sit uneasily alongside acts of forgetting. Understanding why some things are remembered and others are not is revealing of these tensions.

Kaeo as yearning draws on the historic role of yearning in shaping the present, and its present role in shaping the future. It explores the aspirations of Māori who saw opportunity in developing relationships with the missionaries, with the technologies that they brought, and the world that they had come from, who were enriched by some engagements and impoverished by others. The yearning to possess, appropriate, erase and recategorise is explored in the Kaeo as settler colonial imaginary theme. However, this theme looks beyond what was envisaged two centuries ago to the Church's bicultural journey and beyond. Yearnings to belong, to be included, to find purpose and relevance, and to be in relationality with all creation. Perhaps it is in this space of shared yearnings, pathways of mutual and relational responsibility emerge.

In adopting a thematic approach this study considers origins by applying whakapapa as methodology. Whakapapa is inclusive of relationships, past and present. Guided by Church documents this study makes connections between Church origins and three critical issues that challenge the Church and nation today. The first issue concerns Te Tiriti o Waitangi which is articulated by the Church in its bicultural journey. The second issue concerns climate justice which has roots in the transformation of the landscape of Aotearoa from whenua to property. The third issue concerns the Abuse in Care Royal Commission of Inquiry and specifically, abuse in faith-based care. One may consider this approach overtly presentist yet all three issues interlock and reveal systemic and historic inequities within Aotearoa/New Zealand. Their existence calls us to question power and privilege and their links to what we choose to remember, including what we define as origins.

This story acknowledges the intersections of colonialism, racism and patriarchy, their roots in the origins of the state, and in the history of Methodism in Aotearoa. In doing so it seeks to approach the origins of Kaeo differently. Not as a chronology of famed clergy valorising deeds that reflect linear, traditional church hierarchies, but as a series of points that are emergent, that provide opportunity from which to accommodate divergences and contradictions, expanding our collective view of what constitutes the Church and its history.

Wāhanga 1: Kaeo, 1822

Theme 1: Kaeo as Whenua

> 'It is important to appreciate that Māori understanding of land differs from that of Pākehā, not only in terms of collective ownership – something held within the tribe and handed on from generation to generation, not a commodity to be bought and sold – but also that, for Māori, land has spiritual value from which they draw strength.'[4]

This theme is a prologue to the establishment of Kaeo mission. It acknowledges the wairua (spirit) and mauri (life force) of whenua, and their nurturing of human existence and endeavour.

Prior to the creation of tangata (people), there was whenua. The ancestors of Māori left Hawaiki and crossed Te Moana Nui a Kiwa (Pacific Ocean) to Aotearoa, but they did not come alone. They brought mātauranga (knowledge) with them. This knowledge emerged from Oceania and was shaped by thousands of years of accumulated experience and observation. It included wayfinding, the ways of the ocean, weather patterns, the movement of the stars. It was a complete system of how to live. Knowledge transfer was porous, embodied and performative. It was experimental and responsive. It was expressed in te reo Māori, in kōrero tuku iho (oral tradition), waiata (song), whaikōrero (oratory), whakapapa (genealogy), whakairo (carving), raranga (weaving) and held in numerous other repositories.

The concept of whenua comes from Te Orokohanga, the creation story, and begins with Te Kore (darkness, potential). Te Kore reflects the various states of becoming, which is also the development of knowledge, from darkest night to dawn, to Te Ao Marama (the world of light). In this cosmos, which reflects the shape of a koru (spiral) as opposed to a linear progression, Papatūānuku and Ranginui (earth and sky), formed from Te Kore, hold seemingly incompatible atua (natural forces personified) together in a state of balance. This is a cosmological whakapapa in which everything has a place and is in a process of becoming. Whenua, as land and placenta, was the life support system of te ao Māori. Whenua is linked to humanity, to whānau (birth, extended family), hapū (pregnancy, kinship group), iwi (bones, extended kinship group), and ūkaipō (mother). Through complex life cycles, some known and many unknown, whenua supplied their needs.

Māori relationships with whenua were mediated through tikanga. Tikanga as a system of practices enabled people to live their lives with ethical and mutual responsibility, in accordance with what was tika (lawful, just). Tikanga framed relationships with whenua within a space that existed outside of Gregorian time, in a knowledge system that incorporated maramataka (Māori lunar calendar). Honed by constant returnings and rememberings, this was a generative space that required creativity, connection and focus.

While colonisation introduced a legal system and economic conditions that altered the natural landscape and restructured Māori ways of life, Te Orokohanga evidences an alternative reality that emerges within whenua and exists beyond and irrespective of the colonial project. While much has been written about Papatūānuku in academic scholarship, Methodist histories have overlooked Māori understandings of whenua. This can be traced to the missionaries who associated Māori beliefs and values with heathen practices. This created a binary where Māori were considered uncivilised and the missionaries civilised. Yet for Māori to accept Christianity, they needed to participate as themselves, as Māori.

With the arrival of the missionaries, Māori interest in the world beyond te ao Māori, in the material objects that were seen and tested, in the knowledge associated with this world and its potential benefits, grew. In the report, He Whakaputanga me te Tiriti, the Waitangi Tribunal discussed Māori – non-Māori relationships in the Bay of Islands and Hokianga, between 1769 and 1840.[5] What seems clear during this period is that rangatira were not interested in the wholesale change to their beliefs, values, and practices. Instead, they wanted to enhance their world, to improve their collective quality of life and the standing of their hapū within it. While open to other knowledge, their desire to learn did not constitute a cession of authority or a renouncement of themselves as Māori.

Locating Kaeo mission within this context, Whangaroa rangatira had travelled overseas by 1823 and had exposure to a different world. However, their knowledge of this world remained limited. By 1840, many more transactions had taken place between Māori and land speculators. Very little written information survives as to the detail of what was agreed to. Between 1841-1844, these transactions were investigated by a commission that focused on documents written in English and the evidence of one party rather than what was discussed and agreed to by both. There is more information on this in the next section.

Given the early date of the Kaeo transaction, it seems unlikely that Māori would have overridden tikanga, the only law they understood, and consented to an exchange of property that effectively alienated them from their whenua in perpetuity for 'two blankets, three red cloaks and fifteen axes.'[6] Accepting that the first transaction of land between Māori and the Church was (for Māori) predicated on tikanga, warrants a reconsideration of its implications. Recent work undertaken by the Church on whenua and climate justice reintroduces Māori concepts of whenua into Methodist spaces and focusses attention on Papatūānuku as an alternative way to visualise and be in relation to earth.

Theme 2: Kaeo as Settler Colonial Imaginary

> 'Hardly anywhere on the face of the earth could there be found a need more terrible and clamorous than that of the Natives of New Zealand. Hence the Missionaries came, saw and conquered.'[7]

This theme draws on a field of study called settler colonialism to theorise the contradictions and inconsistencies between colonisation as a force for good and indigenous ways of being, in essence between whenua and property. The term "imaginary" refers to a common set of values, laws, practices, institutions and conventions used to interpret the unknown and make sense of the inexplicable. In 1823, Kaeo mission was named and claimed by Wesleyan missionaries. They depicted an inferior and savage people who were required to learn the external trappings of civilisation in order to be saved. In their descriptions of te ao Māori (Māori world), a settler colonial imaginary at odds with how Māori perceived themselves was deployed.

Converted into a site of civilisation, like many other early missions Kaeo became the vanguard of Empire, Dominion, British rule, and the Crown. Following the signing of Te Tiriti o Waitangi, church and state assumed a transfer of authority from Māori to the Crown had taken place. This understanding is made explicit in Church histories. That Māori consistently regarded this as a myth did not weaken its power to be projected into the future. Throughout the Te Paparahi o te Raki (Northland) Inquiry hearings, many claimants, including from Whangaroa hapū, denied that sovereignty was ceded by their tūpuna. In 2014, the Waitangi Tribunal concluded that Ngāpuhi did not cede sovereignty.[8] The history of Kaeo mission reflects this contradiction one where opposing views overlay shared space and co-exist in tension.

Kaeo mission can be viewed from multiple perspectives that are either valid or not depending on their framing. As a tuku whenua (customary means of allocating land). As an exchange of goodwill that signalled the beginning of an enduring relationship based on Christian beliefs and values. As a site that marked the introduction of Methodism. As a display of power by two parties of sovereignty and mana (authority, control). As a moment in which whenua was converted into property. As a precursor to the Church's bicultural journey. As a marker of the future direction of the Church. Kaeo speaks of all these moments and its significance to the church is never static.

What is apparent in terms of church history, is that from the very first encounter concerning a transaction of land, Kaeo as shared space was splintered. This theme explores how that happened and asks with the benefit of hindsight whether a sale occurred in 1823.

> 'A suitable selection of land was purchased at Kaeo, at the entrance to a beautiful valley of that name, seven miles up the river from the harbour. In connection with that first purchase of land by the Wesleyan Church in New Zealand – a property which the Church still retains – it should be stated that the validity of the purchase has never been successfully disputed.'[9]

The story begins in 1989, when, in response to the bicultural journey, a land story policy was developed by the Church. This policy paved the way for a more bicultural assessment of the Church's history of land acquisition to take place.

The splintering of Kaeo begins with a contradiction, between a conversation that took place and the meaning later ascribed to it. What is known is that encounters between Church Missionary Society (CMS) and Wesleyan Missionary Society (WMS) church men took place in Australia and then Aotearoa. Encounters between rangatira and the same missionaries also occurred. Then on 16 August 1823, a deed of purchase confirms that a sale took place. What is not well known is whether Māori, unlikely to speak or read formal English, understood the land purchase deed, and considered themselves party to a sale.

The Waitangi Tribunal provides an explanation for such a discrepancy. Without repeating their arguments, they state that prior to 1830, Māori had little understanding of English land tenure and operated in accordance with tikanga (Māori law). In the Tribunal's opinion, context was important.[10] Māori would have granted use rights in exchange for a reciprocal, mutually beneficial relationship.

There are other inconsistencies concerning Kaeo mission including explanations concerning the raid that occurred in 1827. Muru (raid, to take ritual compensation) were undertaken for perceived offences to restore fairness and balance. It was a practice designed to resolve rather than cause conflict. Missionary accounts of what happened reflect genuine alarm and anxiety. The existence of a muru suggests the authority and tenure claimed by the missionaries was provisional.

Did the raid arise because of disagreements between rangatira that were unrelated to the missionaries? Could Māori have been disappointed in the missionaries for not fulfilling some purpose expected of them, but unknown to the missionaries? Were local Māori understandings of non-Māori shaped by events surrounding the Boyd in 1809? Is there some other explanation that was missed by missionaries, intent on saving souls rather than understanding tikanga? While kōrero tuku iho (oral tradition) may provide insights, without a comprehensive understanding of the local context, we can only speculate.

After the mission ended in 1827, several years elapsed. Then between 1841-1844, an Old Land Claims Commission was set up to inquire into numerous claims (more than 1000 old land claims) made by non-Māori concerning pre-1840 land transactions. Successive generations of Māori have considered this a controversial inquiry that resulted in the alienation of thousands of acres of land in the Bay of Islands, Kaipara, and Auckland. Areas of land considered valid sales by the commission were typically doubled in size. Under this scheme, the Church was granted 100 acres of land at Kaeo, double the area described in the deed of purchase.

After Kaeo was disbanded a Wesleyan mission was established at Te Mangungu, Hokianga in 1828. Kaeo land lay in abeyance for several years. Having realised a need to train Māori to minister to Māori, in 1844, a school was established at Grafton in Auckland for Māori youth. This was moved to Three Kings in 1848, before being moved to its present site at Paerata, in 1924. Over the years, many students came from Te Tai Tokerau (Northland).

It was not until 1869 that Kaeo mission was used again when a church building was erected. This reflected an internal shift in the Church towards supporting the needs of settlers, who nationwide were beginning to outnumber Māori. Meanwhile, Māori continued to live in separate communities that were either encircled by settlers or pushed to the margins.

While the Church continued to support Māori communities in late nineteenth century Te Tai Tokerau, this was undertaken by Māori ministers and much later, deaconesses, both Māori and Pakeha. When the 1869 church building outgrew its purpose, it was replaced by another church and parsonage in 1886. The site of the current memorial church is located on land donated by a local, long-serving Methodist family and lies outside the mission property.

For many years the remainder of Kaeo mission was leased or used for farming and the proceeds managed by Whangaroa circuit. Between the 1950s and 1970s most of the land was subdivided and sold. With the establishment of Taha Māori in 1973, the Tumuaki took on shared oversight of the property. What remains of Kaeo mission is currently administered by Te Taha Māori Property Trust.

There are many property-related records concerning Kaeo mission, the church buildings, administrative trusts, the local parish and circuit. Collectively these documents provide a timeline of decisions made and actions taken. Less is known about the Māori Methodist community, a church that was built in the early 1900s, and relationships to ancestral whenua including Kaeo mission. Some of this history can be deduced from education records, from attendance at Wesley College, at Kurahuna School of Domestic Science and Hygiene for Māori girls, and training in the ministry at Trinity College. The records reflect a system that privileged legal and administrative practices and structures and ultimately upheld the view of the missionaries, described in this context, as the settler colonial imaginary.

Wāhanga 2: Kaeo, 1922

Theme 3: Kaeo as Exclusion

> 'Before long, the log-raupo hut that had so imperfectly sheltered Mr and Mrs Leigh, gave way to a comfortable wooden building, the frame of which had been brought from Sydney. The ground was well fenced and well tilled and the Mission Station at Wesleydale, as it was called, stood out in the midst of a moral and physical waste as an advanced post of civilisation.'[11]

This section explores invisibility and silences. It emerges in response to the overwhelming number of accounts that focus on the observations of missionaries and clergy who tended to be men. While a lack of records makes it difficult to fill in the blanks about other people, it attempts to surface this issue by reflecting on the materiality of a simple fence and its relation to people rendered invisible.

This includes Māori as whānau, hapū, iwi. While the profile of women in the Church has increased significantly across all spaces, it includes women whose marginalisation at various points within Church history restricted participation. It includes children whose silences can be read in the scarcity of personal records concerning schooling and children's homes. The absence of records and/or poor record-keeping was noted by the Abuse in

Care Royal Commission of Inquiry as a cause of distress and trauma for those whose voices were ignored.

People with disabilities are also hidden from view as are those who are not British, who did not identify with the missionaries or the culture they brought with them. It includes people who are diverse in other ways whether by way of sexual orientation or in the naming of gender. People who experience cultural, ethnic, social, geographic and economic marginalisation. It can also mean a combination of all the above.

Records shape how we remember the past. While the Methodist Church has created an archive of value, records tend to focus on administration and property matters, meeting minutes, building repairs, and expenses. This is not to say that documents that hint at the existence of other stories, or experiences, do not exist. However, such content may have survived more by accident than by design.

Until the 1970s, official histories of the Church tended to be written by men who were clergy, or appointed by clergy. Well-researched and well-intended, reflecting the way history was written in New Zealand at the time, these documents provide information in painstaking detail. However, they do not convey the voices of those who occupied marginal spaces.

Acknowledging that to some extent matters of inequity have been or are being addressed by the Church, the issue of a scarcity of records concerning the silenced remains. When sweeping statements have been made about an entire population, as was the case with Māori, should we respond to the absence and provide an alternative? Is it necessary to plug early accounts and histories with gap fillers? Or should we use our time differently and allow those stories to stand in their context and consider other ways to tell ours?

Reflecting on this methodological dilemma, the image of fences comes to mind, their ubiquity and perplexity. Whether they are protective or offensive barriers depends on context and one's position. Before the missionaries came to Kaeo, Māori already had fences. Tūwatawata used to fortify pā, takitaki comprised upright posts used in palisades or to protect gardens and food stores from wind and birds, taiapa were constructed horizontally. They were relatively simple structures as there were few terrestrial animals. Rather than rely on external structures Māori applied tikanga and whakapapa to order and maintain relationships to whenua, to identify who belonged where.

It is difficult to visualise the Kaeo mission without fences. Paintings and sketches seem to stress the allotment of space. To the missionaries the division of land was synonymous with Englishness. Fences were associated with domesticity, gardens, homely buildings. Visually they conveyed a sense of safety and peace. It was important that these spaces were brought under their control. In their sketches, trees have been cut down, and the land cleared and ploughed. Gardens and fruit trees have replaced the forest. Letters describe the tidy appearance of the mission. There is genuine pride in these achievements, in the labour undertaken to tame the land and bring it under human control.

Fences demarcated wilderness and waste land from domesticated space, whenua from property. They demarcated who was in and who was out, who mattered and who did not. Within the mission fence, Papatūānuku and other diverse expressions of living earth, other-than-human whanaunga (kin), native plants, birds, mountains, trees, rivers and stones were silenced, depicted as insentient or inanimate. Separating humans from nature, fences reinforce invisible hierarchies, subject-object binaries, the power to define, to represent and enforce new realities, to create imagined borders, and foreclose creative responses to alterity.

Fences tell stories. They speak of salvation offered by the missionaries and colonialism, of purchase deeds and survey lines on a map. To step through the mission gate was to leave civilisation and enter a barbaric world. For the missionaries, barriers were important yet the raid in 1827 revealed the tenuous nature of their existence and destroyed the illusion of stability. Fences were taken down and destroyed. Goods removed and valued possessions plundered. Fences reveal silences in the record, what took place and what did not, who was present and who was absent, what was removed and what was left behind. Most of all fences speak of the loneliness of empty spaces, of separation from the land, and the opposite, of renewal and continuity. In considering invisibility and silence, the metaphor of a mission fence provides a useful starting point from which to explore exclusion.

Theme 4: Kaeo as Inclusion

'The fugitives consisted of the Rev. Nathaniel Turner and Mrs Turner, with three children, the youngest only five weeks' old, Miss Davis, a visitor from Kern Kern, Rev. John Hobbs, Luke Wade, an English servant, and his wife, who was in a very delicate state of health, five Native boys and two Native girls.'[12]

This theme examines the experience of Māori women and girls. In 1827, a raid on Kaeo mission causes the missionaries to flee some twenty miles overland to Kerikeri. Two Maori girls join the journey and are mentioned in passing. Like the five Māori boys, they remain nameless. We do not know their ages, whether they were children or young adults. In this story their identities and the details of their lives are irrelevant.

Stories of Kaeo mission focus on the efforts of missionaries to preach the Gospel, convince Māori of the unsuitability of their ways, and educate them in English ways of civilisation regarded as the best measure of one's proximity to a Christian God. Such was the value placed on outward expressions of English beliefs and values, it was not considered appropriate or feasible that Māori would respond to the Gospel in their own way, as Māori.

While they were keenly interested in the world beyond Aotearoa, and the potential opportunities that it offered to prosper, Māori were less convinced of the need to alter practices they had maintained for a millennium, for example, communal living. Their refusal to do what they were told was problematic for the missionaries who associated such behaviour with a stubborn mindset rather than a choice based on logic.

The ostracisation of Māori women by missionaries is well documented. Considered depraved and vile, they were expected to discipline their bodies, minds, and spirits by emulating the superior behaviour and morals of missionary wives. In 2021, evidence presented at the Waitangi Tribunal Mana Wahine inquiry described the assault on Māori women through the undermining of whānau and hapū structures.[13] It was asserted that despite many women being rangatira, and most women having rights to whenua, missionaries and early settlers expressed a preference for dealing with men. This practice of separating individuals from whānau resonates with the treatment of Māori children who were separated from their whānau at mission schools.

In the case of children, salvation was to be achieved through the education and schooling of young minds. While schools would eventually become a powerful mechanism for separating Māori children from their language and culture, at Kaeo missionaries were disappointed in the intermittent attendance by children who were, according to them disorderly, unreliable and filthy. Despite the purported unreliable behaviour they were still considered more malleable than the adults with the girls showing particular promise in needlework.[14]

In considering visibility and inclusion perhaps the materiality of needlework and raranga (weaving) can be deployed to draw attention to the liminal space that is neither complete exclusion or total inclusion.

Patchwork is a process of needlework whereby strips of fabric are sewn together to form a quilt. In many cultures, the quilt has come to be a symbol of stability and family. In Aotearoa/New Zealand they are linked to coloniality and women's work. While performing a functional purpose, quilts tell stories through the layering of imagery, colour, and texture. The woven banner displayed at Conference provides an example.

In pre- and post-colonial times, Māori women also made functional items of clothing, kete, nets, and mats. Such items were ubiquitous at all kainga (village). Despite being ordinary, everyday objects they were embodied with spiritual meaning and mātauranga (knowledge). This mātauranga was associated with the whakapapa (genealogy) of weaving materials like harakeke (flax) and linked to Te Orokohanga (creation story). Whenua, referred to in the first theme of this study, is embodied in the materiality of raranga.

At Kaeo mission, two worlds collide in a knowledge exchange that takes place between women and girls through the medium of needlework. This is not a balanced exchange. There are presumptions of superiority, of civilising as a subject. Certainly, there are misunderstandings. However, it is an encounter, an engagement, in which difference is confronted. In this exchange of cultures, perhaps analogies, allegories and metaphors were employed on both sides to sew and weave new understandings together. A story of origins through the practice of sewing and raranga, offers a bricolage of impressions, images, and words that reveal female spaces, expanding the origins of Methodism at Kaeo beyond the male gaze.

While the stories of Māori women in the missions are inaccurate and inappropriate in framing them as fallen women, in looking for other stories about Māori women in the Church it is interesting to note how little has been written about the work of the deaconesses in Maori communities in the early to mid-twentieth century. In 1893, Conference agreed to a Methodist Deaconess Order to support religious and social ministry to Māori women and children. The records reveal an impressive amount of work undertaken.

It was not until 1921 that the work of the deaconesses in Te Tai Tokerau (Northland) began in earnest. A review of their files shows a depth of experience and contact with Māori women in whānau settings. In some instances, deaconesses developed relationships with whānau that transcended generations. Māori women also trained in the order and were stationed in Te Tai Tokerau and around Aotearoa/New Zealand. Allocated cars to support them to undertake their role, they became well-known and respected figures in the communities they served.

While the deaconess order intersects with Kaeo on many levels, their work in the field remains under reported. It could be that they undertook a similar role to that of missionary wives, as agents of assimilation, but this would be simplistic. Using the resources of the Church to support Māori whānau in isolated, rural communities, their work anticipated the Church's bicultural journey decades later.

Returning to the two girls who departed Kaeo with the missionaries and remain nameless, a contradiction is exposed. The story of their salvation is mediated by the missionary gaze and a particular cultural frame of reference that renders them invisible. While they are not credited with any greatness, we can assume that they offered to journey with the missionaries as a gesture of kindness. Unlike the missionaries, they lived on both sides of the fence and navigated two worlds. Whatever their fate, their presence and absence in this story reveals the complicated place of Māori women in the Church. As helpers undertaking their own spiritual journeys, included, but kept at a distance, leaders amongst their whānau and hapū, working in the background in the service of the Church.

Wāhanga 3: Kaeo, 2022

Theme 5: Kaeo as Remembrance

> 'With the last stroke of twelve at midnight, the Book of the First Century will be closed and sealed, only to be opened again in that Day when all the Books will be opened. Of every entry in the Book of the First Century of New Zealand Methodism, the Recording Angel will say, "What I have written, I have written."'[15]

Remembrance can be viewed in many ways, yet its basic purpose is to serve the ideals of continuity and connection. Church histories traditionally begin with stories about the missionaries who follow a historical trajectory that frames them as forefathers and founders of a nation. For the Methodist Church of New Zealand, their presence at Kaeo mission marks the beginning of this tradition.

Acts of remembering are recorded in the annual announcements of Methodist dead and the honouring of their deeds, in the existence of Kaeo Memorial Church, in the names listed on the cairn in 1922, and in the cemetery naming early settlers. At times symbolic, remembrance merges with pilgrimage and the broad outlines of Church history. At other times it merges with touristic consumption and public history. As a site of power, Kaeo resonates with a deep emotional charge and demonstrates the ongoing power of place. Yet it would be a mistake to assume that Kaeo is remembered in the same way by everyone. Acts of remembrance sit uneasily alongside acts of forgetting.

Local remembrance is complex. In the context of Church history, the lived experience of local people including tangata whenua can be overlooked. The lifespan of Kaeo mission was short. Within six years the missionaries had abandoned the area and settled at Te Mangungu. In practical terms, it is the presence of local Methodists, Māori and Pakeha, who have kept a Methodist presence alive at Kaeo. While their stories are entwined with the Church, they are also personal and intersect with family history, kōrero tuku iho, and whakapapa. The presence of residents who are not Methodist adds to the richness of these local stories that are not necessarily easily understood by or relatable to outsiders.

Understanding why some things are remembered and others are not is just as revealing of the present as it is of the past. The presence of whenua evokes ways of remembering at odds with the single trajectory approach that begins with the missionaries and ends with a subdivision. It suggests a need to create discourses other than the Church's settler colonial heritage. While addressing the detail may surface previously unknown facts that do not sit easily alongside established orthodoxies, in its bicultural journey, confronting the past has been explored and taken seriously by the Church, for the past 40 years.

While this journey continues, other interconnected issues of global and national magnitude are at the forefront of consideration by the Church. This can be confronting however, re-evaluating our remembrance of the past may lead us to discover a Church history replete with unknown stories of other forms of leadership, resilience, and kindness. Perhaps this is what the Kaeo cairn ultimately speaks of, stories scattered like stones, waiting to be gathered, circumventing and drawing us back to the whenua.

Rather than seeing our history as something to be contained, closed, and sealed in a Book of the Century, perhaps we could consider a history that unfurls like the ponga (silver fern) frond. in a state of perpetual regeneration and growth, conveying beauty and strength, held together by whakapapa and connection, always returning to its origins which are simultaneously points of departure.

Theme 6: Kaeo as Yearning

'The condition of the residue of the Maori race, whose appalling need first drew Missionaries to New Zealand, is such to-day as to call for a more vigorous and advanced policy on the part of the Churches than is at present pursued...Any readjustment of Church relationships that would secure a more consecrated and intensified effort to secure moral and religious welfare of those dusky Children of the Dawn, would be in the way of justifying, in the handsomest way possible the European occupation of New Zealand.'[16]

In this theme Kaeo as yearning is a liminal space that looks forward to the past while turning back to the future. That reinscribes the ponga frond as generative pattern that enables continuity and renewal. Te Orokohanga (Māori creation story) explains how Papatūānuku and Ranginui were once bound together by their shared aroha. Their ensuing separation created freedom and space for their children but left a perpetual yearning for wholeness. Yearning is posited as aspirational, as a search for belonging, roots, and unity. As something that is given different expressions depending on one's context.

The missionaries came to Aotearoa with a deep-seated yearning. To preach the Gospel and impart their understanding of how to lead a good life. This reflected their response to the Gospel. Māori saw a world beyond Aotearoa filled with promise and opportunity and yearned to be a part of it. To participate in this world education was vital and they sent their children to learn this knowledge entrusting them to the care of the missionaries. When their expectations were not met, they challenged the missionaries and their authority.

If yearning drives actions and decisions, history shows the results rarely match expectations. In 1922, a century after the arrival of the missionaries, Māori are impoverished and survival is their priority. The detail of how this happened is well established yet none of this history is referred to in the Church's centenary sketches account in 1923. The yearning to preach the Gospel has merged with a yearning to possess, appropriate, erase and recategorise. To forget the promise of earlier relationships forged on shared soil. Instead, it focuses on settler colonial stories of church progress and growth.

Kaeo mission can be viewed from multiple angles. One aspect that makes it fascinating is that it reflects so many strands prevalent in New Zealand history. Those strands are also underpinned by yearnings, hidden motivations that lie beneath the surface, behind certain actions. It could be said therefore that yearning is common to all. On this basis, Kaeo stories can provide guidance to anyone who yearns to exist in a respectful relationship with whenua, to share Christian beliefs and values, to mark sites with meaning, to observe the covenant of Te Tiriti o Waitangi, to collectively decide the future direction of the Church. This is an inclusive space.

Pacific immigration to Aotearoa began a thousand years ago when Māori first arrived in Aotearoa. The Church has had a unique history with the Pacific through Wesley College, the training of clergy and in parish life. Yet despite this history, there is little mention until the final chapter of the centenary sketches account in 1923.

> "...raised by Missionary devotion from savagery to civilisation, New Zealand lies to-day in the midst of Southern Seas as a predestined centre of Missionary effort that is to sweep within its compass other groups in the Pacific, in which heathen savagery is still rampant."[17]

Perhaps it is time for a reorienting of sacred geographies and histories to show the true diversity that exists in the Church not only of today but historically as well. In raranga many strands are combined to make a kete. Is it time to expand our kete of Kaeo mission stories, to enable it to hold multiple encounters and perspectives simultaneously? The story is never one-sided or straightforward, there is no beginning or end, instead, we are always looking to find our way to the centre, yearning to belong, to be included, to find purpose and relevance in relationality with all creation. As mentioned at the beginning of this study, in this space of shared yearning, of listening to the stories of others and accepting them without the need to silence, pathways of mutual and relational responsibility can emerge.

Conclusion

This study began with a simple request from Te Taha Māori Property Trust, in 2018. To write he kōrero papatupu whenua (land story) for Kaeo mission. A search through the archive revealed many permutations and gaps in the story. As time passed research began to surface concerning the entwined and separate histories of Taha Māori and Tauiwi. Te Taha Māori Property Trust asked that this land story be prepared in time for Conference 2022. Multiple strands of Church history began to emerge revealing alignments and discrepancies with Kaeo mission. It soon became clear that a chronological account was not adequate to tell a story that is as much about exclusion as it is about inclusion.

I wish to acknowledge Te Taha Māori Property Trust for requesting this study and in particular Jo Smith, former Methodist Archivist, for her invaluable assistance and Rev. Dr Arapera Ngaha for supporting the entire process. I also wish to thank Rev Keita Akinihi Hotere for her contribution to the Mihi in this chapter. That said, all mistakes, errors and omissions are my own.

Aku mihi ki a koutou katoa.
Ahakoa he iti, he pounamu

Notes

1 Mission Statement, Methodist Church of New Zealand.

2 https://www.google.com/search?q=origins+meaning.

3 Whenua Papatupu policy (proposed), Methodist Church of New Zealand.

4 *Our Land Story and Guidelines for taking Action on Land and responding to the Waitangi Tribunal*, Bricks and Mortar, 1991.

5 He Whakaputanga me te Tiriti – The Declaration and the Treaty: Stage 1 of the Te Paparahi o te Raki Inquiry (Wai 1040), Waitangi Tribunal, 2014.

6 Copy of Deed of Purchase of the Wesleyan Mission Station at Kaeo, 1823, MCNZA: MS-288, Personal Papers Historical Records Collection.

7 W. J. Williams, *Centenary Sketches of New Zealand Methodism*, Christchurch: Lyttleton Times Co., 1923, 8.

8 He Whakaputanga me te Tiriti – The Declaration and the Treaty: Stage 1 of the Te Paparahi o te Raki Inquiry (Wai 1040), Waitangi Tribunal, 2014.

9 W. J. Williams, *Centenary Sketches*, 18.

10 Muriwhenua Land Report (Wai 45), Waitangi Tribunal, 1997, 74-75.

11 W. J. Williams, *Centenary Sketches*, 21.

12 W. J. Williams, *Centenary Sketches*, 24.

13 The Waitangi Tribunal Mana Wāhine Kaupapa Inquiry (Wai 2700) is ongoing.

14 Owens J.M.R, *Prophets in the Wilderness: the Wesleyan Mission to New Zealand 1819-27*, Auckland: Auckland University Press & Oxford University Press, 1974, 52.

15 W. J. Williams, *Centenary Sketches*, 212.

16 W. J. Williams, *Centenary Sketches*, 213.

17 W. J. Williams, *Centenary Sketches*, 213.

The New Zealand Chiefs in Wesley's House, 1863.

Commemorating the 1863 visit to England by a Maori group led by Nelson-based William Jenkins, a Wesleyan lay preacher employed as a catechist, 1843-1850 (not defrocked as some claim), and thereafter a native interpreter; this painting was commissioned for the fortieth anniversary of the Wesleyan mission in New Zealand, although few of the Māori were Wesleyan.

William Jenkins is right centre and also on the left, standing, Kihirini te Tuahu (Tuhourangi Lake Tarawera), and Hirini Tipene Pakia (Ngāpuhi), a distant relation of Hongi Hika. In front of them, Miss Jobson and her father Rev Dr F.J. Jobson (Secretary of the WMS), Harieta Te Iringa Pakia (wife of Hirini) and Aramu Hall an English "warm supporter of missions".

The group on the left is dominated in the centre by Wiremu Te Wana Pou (Ngāpuhi, 1834-1872), son of one of Hongi's generals. Below and to the left are three figures, Paratane Te Manu (Ngāpuhi) left to Kamariera te Hautakiri Wharepapa (Ngāpuhi, 1822-1920), and left to Hapimana Ngapiro (Te Ati Awa).

The two standing figures are Hāre Pōmare (Ngāti Manu) whose wife is below him, and Horomona te Atua (Ngāpuhi, so possibly a Wesleyan), and slightly behind, Takarei Ngawaka (Tuwharatoa), grandson of Te Heuheu.

The group in the lower left are (left to right), Huria Ngahuia (Ngāti Whanaunga) from the Coromandel, Hariata Tutapuiti (Ngāpuhi), wife of Hare Parata, and Reihana Taukawau (Ngāpuhi).

James Smetham (1821-1889). Oil on canvas: 1025 x 1835mm.

(Hocken Collections – Uare Taoka o Hākena, University of Otago – Ōtākou Whakaihu Waka, 13,395)
[See p.197 Jenkins, William]

The New Zealand Chiefs in Wesley's House, 1863.
[See details previous page]

The Native Village of Ki-ho New Zealand. With the original. Mission House of M' White/one of the Wesleyan. Missionary's.} 1833

The Native Village of Ki-ho New Zealand with the original mission house of W White one of the Wesleyan missionaries 1833 by Thomas Laslett. (detail) Laslett was carpenter on the *HMS Buffalo*. White's mission house surprisingly survived the sack of the mission station in 1827 and was lived in by local Māori.
(Alexander Turnbull Library, Wellington. MS-Papers-8349-1-17). [See pp 38, 58, 105, 106, 205]

Wesleydale Mission Station, Kaeo, Whangaroa, Northland. c.1825, by Nathaniel Turner.
Turner arrived at the Whangaroa station in August 1823, just before Samuel Leigh departed.
(Alexander Turnbull Library, Wellington. B-121-023). [See pp 38, 58, 105, 106, 205]

Dedication of the Cairn at Wesleydale, Kaeo, 8 March 1922. Group of ministers addressing crowd at unveiling. The memorial cairn was erected by Māori Methodists under the direction of A.J. Seamer, using stones from the Whangaroa harbour. The unchiselled stones, commemorate the centennial of the mission at Kaeo. A large contingent of Methodist ministers and members attended.
Rev Paru/Tapua Patuone (Ngāti Hao, Hokianga), home missionary for Whangaroa 1922-1923, sits on the top of the Cairn.
He was a descendent of the great Rangatira Eruera Maihi Patuone.
(Kei Muri Māpara/Methodist Church of New Zealand Archives Christchurch. P-101, 1040-2). [See p. 109]

Dedication of the Cairn at Wesleydale, Kaeo, 1922. Rev Robert Tahupōtiki Haddon (senior Māori minister, from Ngāti Ruanui, Hokianga) is speaking to about 800 Māori present at the event. The contingent of 230 people travelled by ship from Auckland to Whangaroa, then walked up from the harbour to the cairn, and subsequently laid the foundation for the Kaeo memorial church.
(Kei Muri Māpara/Methodist Church of New Zealand Archives Christchurch. P-94, 1040-2).
[See p. 109]

Mangungu mission station 1850s. Probably drawn by Emma, daughter of John Hobbs.
The second mission station at the head of the Hokianga Harbour commenced in 1828.
Fences were intended to delineate the space where Māori needed permission to enter.
(Alexander Turnbull Library, Wellington. PUBL-0205-001). [See pp 59, 206 Hokianga]

Mangungu mission station 6 January 1858, drawn by Sarah Orriss. Photograph by Susan Thompson.
A front view of the same station with a clearer image of the various buildings.
(Eliza White Album 1837-1870, Kinder Library, MET 011/1/5 item 8195) [See pp 59, 206 Hokianga]

Reverend Samuel and Sarah Ironside.
Sarah Ironside née Eades (1818-1890)
married Samuel (1814-1883)
on 24 August 1838. (detail)
(Alexander Turnbull Library, Wellington.
1/2-049303-F, taken from Morley).
[See pp 57, 79, 190]

Jane Hobbs nee Brogriffe or Broggreff (1799-
1883) married John Hobbs, 14 August 1827
in Sydney, and had nine children.
(Kinder Library) [See pp 80, 190].

Eliza White née Leigh (1809-1883).
Married William White on 30 June 1829 at
Bluntisham Huntingdonshire, who had returned
to England to find a wife. Four children, only one
survived. She stood by her husband to the end.
(Eliza White Album 1837-1870, Kinder Library,
Methodist Collection 11/1/5 Album 8195).
[See pp 79, 196]

Drawing by Thomas Buddle showing the Te Kopua Wesleyan Mission Station at the base of Pirongia on the bank of the Waipa River. Native Chapel, (left), and the
Rev Thomas Buddle's raupo house, (right). Buddle established the mission station in 1841. (detail)
(Auckland Libraries Heritage Images Collection). [See pp 80, 156, 214]

Missionary distributing bibles to Taranaki Māori in 1842. Working Men's Educational Union printed 1850s. The missionary is probably John Skevington at Heratoa, Waimate South.
(Alexander Turnbull Library, Wellington. 1/2-049303-F). [See pp 55, 153, 216]

WESLEYAN MISSION STATION AT WAINGAROA, NEW ZEALAND.
NATIVES ASSEMBLING FOR WORSHIP.

PRINTED IN COLOURS BY J. BANNISTER
SOUTHAMPTON STREET PENTONVILLE

Wesleyan Mission Station, Waingaroa [Raglan] natives assembling for worship.
Drawn by J. Bannister ca.1850s. This is Te Hōrea on the north side of the harbour, James and Mary
Ann Wallis's first mission station, built in 1835. (detail)
(Alexander Turnbull Library, Wellington. A-015-025). [See pp 54, 156, 212]

Samuel Leigh, the first Wesleyan
missionary in New Zealand.
Engraved by G. Stodard from a painting by
J. Jackson, London, 1863. (detail)
(Alexander Turnbull Library, Wellington.
PUBL-0157-front).
[See pp 29, 30, 44]

Hone Mohi Tawhai (Ngāpuhi, 1834-1894) rangatira, land court assessor and MP, photographed by W.B. Gibbs, circa 1880. He was from Waimā, the main Hokianga station of the WMS. His (baptismal) name means John Moses.
(Alexander Turnbull Library, Wellington. PA2-0771). [See pp 53, 66, 88, 200]

Horomona Pōhio (Ngāi Tahu, Ngāti Māmoe and Waitaha, 1815-1880), a Wesleyan catechist at Ruapake Island, Foveaux Strait. Baptised by John Watkin, he later became a follower of Te Maihāroa, the prophet. (H. J. Gill photograph, Box-001-054, Hocken Collections – Uare Taoka o Hākena, University of Otago – Ōtākou Whakaihu Waka)
[See pp 57, 69, 199]

Tamati Waka Nene (Ngāti Hao, died 1872) Hokianga rangatira. A key supporter of the signing of the Treaty of Waitangi, he adhered to the Wesleyan faith from about 1835. Robert Way (1872-1947).
(Hocken Collections – Uare Taoka o Hākena, University of Otago – Ōtākou Whakaihu Waka, 24,062) [See pp 11, 53, 54, 198]

Wiremu Nēra Te Awa-i-taia, (Ngāti Māhanga, d 1866), rangatira, converted in 1834 through William White, sponsor of the Kāwhia station, supporter of land sales, hostile to Kingitanga.
(Hamilton City Libraries, HCL_11510).
[See pp 55, 200]

The Māori Mission Party, 1908.
Back row (left to right): Rev. Robert Tahupotiki Haddon Ngāti Hao, 1866-1936), Rev. Hapeta Rari Renata (Nga Puhi, Te Aupori, 1866-1955), Rev. Hone Marena Hare (Ngapuhi, 1857-1937), Rev Koroneho (Neho) Hemi Papakakura (Ngāti Pou, 1881-1956), Mr W. Koripi.
Front row: Rev. Thomas G. Hammond (1846-1926), Rev. Hauraki Paul= Hauraki Paora Kawharu (Ngāti Whatua, 1861-1910), Rev. William Gittos (1829-1916), Rev. Piripi Rakena (Ngapuhi, 1858-1934). The photograph was taken at the Wesleyan Conference in Auckland in March 1921, which adopted (but did not implement) a proposal that Māori work should become a separate synod. (In *New Zealand Graphic*, 21 March 1908 p.32. Auckland Libraries Heritage Images Collection). [See p. 139]

Methodist Waiata Maori Choir, c. 1932. The choir performed in Māori traditional dress, and this postcard was signed by all the performers and sold to support the expenses.
Back row, from left to right: W. Nelson, Paikea Henare Toka (Ngāti Whatua, 1906-1974), Rima Perepe (also known as Rima Phillips), Te Aho-o-te-rangi Pihama (Tainui, 1874-1952), Hinerangi Hikuroa (possibly Hikuroa Te Maaha (1882-1941).
Front row, from left: Tarikura Bates, nee Bailey (1914-1976), Wanairangi Merepounamu Paihi (?Ngāti Maniapoto), Tuahine Tautari (Ngāpuhi, Ngāti Hine, Ngāti Kahu, 1910-1971).
(Alexander Turnbull Library, Wellington. PAColl-0240-01). [See p. 168]

MĀORI MISSION FIELD SPIRITUALITIES

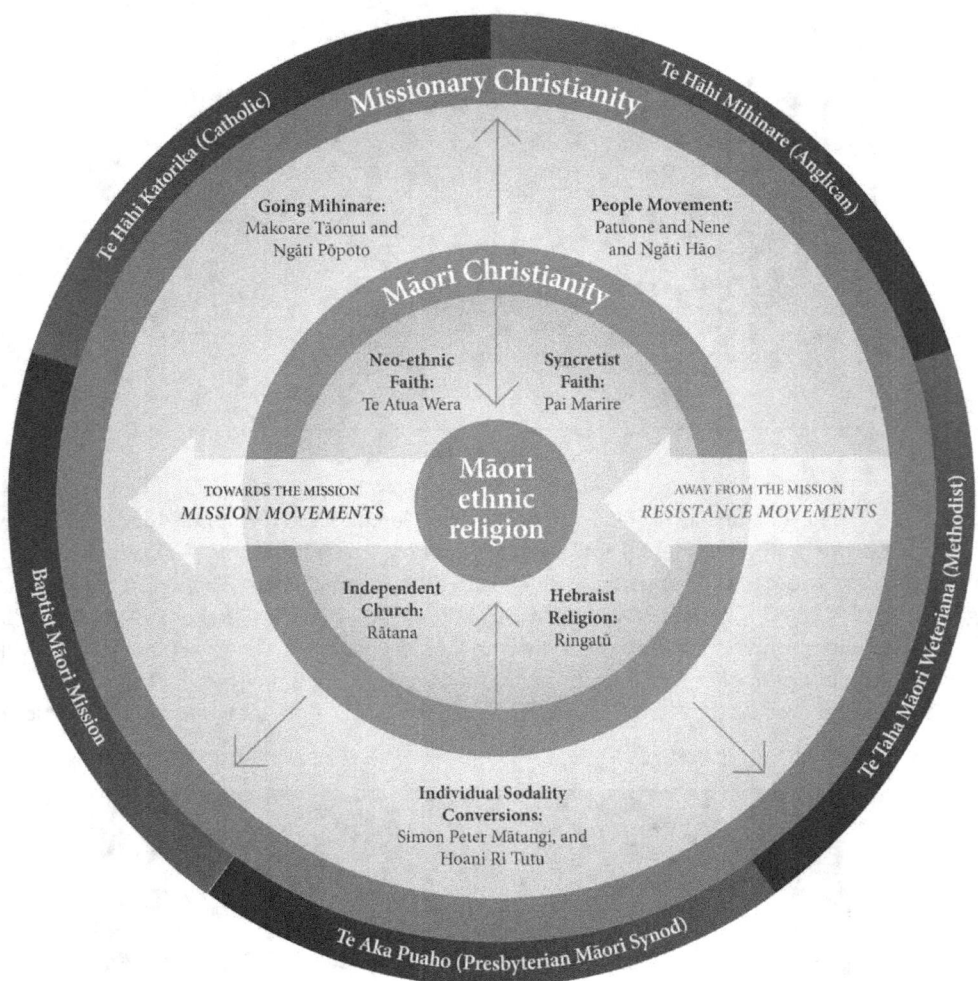

Māori Traditional Indigenous Ethnic Faith: (central Māori cultural/religious core)

Māori Resistance or Independent Movements: (movement back towards central core)

Neo-Ethnic Faith: Te Ātua Wera (1830s); **Syncretist Faith:** Ringatū (1870s);
Hebraist Faith: Pai Marire (1860s); **Independent Church:** Rātana (1920s).

Māori Christianities: (movement away from central core towards the missionaries)

Going Mihinare: Chief-led collective tribal associating with missionaries to obtain the missionaries'
cultural items & technology.

People Movement: Chief-led collective tribal embracing of aspects of Missionary Christian
worship and liturgy.

Sodality Conversion: Individual 'Mission Māori' & slaves residing within the Mission compound,
embrace aspects of the missionary lifestyle & religious beliefs & practices.

Present-day Churches: (outer circle). Autonomous Māori churches & partnerships within
Pākeha Christian denominations, e.g. Rātana, Te Taha Māori Weteriana, Te Hāhi Mihinare.

(Author © Gary Clover; Design © Andy Clover, Creative Director, Go Ahead Punk Ltd,
Richmond, Nelson) [See Chapter 3]

7 – Māori Methodism 1913-1960

Peter Lineham

Apology

I am writing as an outsider, not a Māori, not a Methodist. This chapter represents a shallow search of neglected material. There has been very little historical study of mission churches outside of the early era.[1] I am most grateful for the work of Donald Phillipps in recording the list of Māori clergy in the period.[2] I am grateful for the Methodist archivists for enabling me to take a brief dive into a rich and neglected part of their archives. There is much more scope for research using iwi and hapu resources, understanding the Māori community from within.

The European View

Knowledge of the values and circumstances of Māori Methodists was disguised from Pākehā Methodists. A major source of knowledge was the annual fundraising visit by the mission, and from 1930, by the Waiata choir. At these an image was carefully projected of the Māori world, and Methodists must have felt much better informed than most Pākehā, but the purpose of the visit limited the communication. The other major source, reports in the fortnightly Methodist magazine, focused largely on the work of the deaconesses, focusing particularly on children and health. Rarely were the Māori home missionaries and native ministers quoted, partly because they spoke primarily in te reo Māori, and so relied on Europeans for translation.[3] Certainly Methodist concerns over the Treaty of Waitangi and alcohol abuse were emphasised in a different way than in the general media.[4] But when Māori migrated in large numbers to the towns, Methodists often supported integration and assimilation as the only practical way to continue their ministry to Māori, but the lack of close and intimate contacts between Māori and Pākehā in the church soon showed in this failed strategy.[5]

The Home Mission Board sometimes scrutinised the Māori work, and occasionally issues were taken up at the annual church conference. The conclusions look flawed to 21st century readers. In 1917, a special committee declared that the long-term goal was the integration of the European and Māori work, and insisted that it must be under the control of a European. This was their justification for bringing Home Missions and Māori missions under a common committee.[6] Native ministers were entitled to attend conference, but they were not supposed to vote on European issues, and as a result very few attended.[7]

Despite all these limitations, the church found a way to operate in the interim, which was relatively effective. Those close to the local communities knew that the task was large and complex. In 1922, the church received a report from the Home Mission Department which spelt out the need:

> … publication of census returns show encouragement in native education and industry – but religious and ethical not so. It is not keeping pace and this is a grave concern. The New Zealand church can never have full blessing until it faces the Maori problem and deal adequately with it. Almost all Europeans go to one extreme of other in view of Maori. Either assume that this generation can reach English standards, or say Maori cannot be lifted out of superstition and non-morality. The Maori is one of the highest types of primitive people, and a potential equal, but he has not yet attained, and in the very nature of things, cannot yet attain. But in the future he may, if we render him the assistance that is his due as our child in the Christian faith. We have before us, in the Maori mission, an intensely interesting test of our ability as a Church to grapple successfully with one of the world's most difficult mission problems. Our church in responsible before God and man, for the Christian development of the 12000 descendants of the tribes that God gave our pioneer missionaries. We must prepare ourselves for a stern and protracted struggle. We cannot fail. We dare not fail.[8]

The words were probably penned by A.J. Seamer, and they pose for modern readers a standard against which the achievements of the next forty years may be measured. The results were reasonably impressive.

Statistically Speaking

Māori religious statistics were first gathered in the 1926 census. Thy showed that Mihinare (Anglican or Church of England Mission) was the largest Māori religious affiliation, attracting 40% of all Māori, while Rātana, founded just a few years earlier, was in second position with 18.2%, while Catholic (Katorika) was third with 13.4%, Ringatū fourth with 7.1% and Methodist or Weteriana fifth with 6.3%. In the 1936 census (which probably provided more reliable statistics) Rātana had climbed a little to 19.9% (its highest ever level), yet Methodist numbers had grown somewhat, (whereas Anglican affiliation steadily declined until 1986). Methodist growth peaked in the 1945 census at 7.63% of Māori (although there was a late high result of 7.89% in 1966). This growth is largely because they recovered remarkably in the Waikato and the King Country.

Actual numbers of adherents peaked at 17,325 in 1976. Meanwhile Presbyterians, who were late in the field, grew slowly and steadily, peaking at 5.59% in 1986. Ringatū like Rātana peaked in 1936, and today sit at around 1.5%, while Methodist sit at 8442 people or 1.09%. A key factor after 1945 was the failure of Methodism to retain its young people, given that the Maori population was very young. The median age of Māori Methodists is today very elderly. 7.2% of Māori aged 55-59 years old are Methodist, but just 1.86% of the under 5 year olds identify with the denomination.

As for the church membership and attendance statistics, these were always regarded as somewhat approximate given that most services were held on marae, but in 1903 the official statistics recorded 1196 members and 8000 attendees,[9] and in the year of Methodist

Union, 1913, there were some 2052 members and 8270 attendees.[10] These figures are approximate, since Waikato attendees were stated as exactly 4000. In 1932, the last year that Methodists collected attendance figures, there were 7120 attendees. Membership figures showed a modest growth, from 2523 in 1920, 3661 when next reported in 1931; 3821 in 1936 (when the census reported Māori Methodist adherents at 5743). From 1937 the figures were gathered by the senior Maori minister, and that year's report distinguished junior membership (2143 in that year) and senior (2762).[11] By 1946 these figures had reached 3975 senior and 5986 junior members (while the census reported 7535 Māori Methodists), and in 1950 there were 4069 senior and 5018 junior members and a Sunday school roll of 5194. In 1951, the year of the next census, the figures were 4094 and 5068, while the census recorded 8529, suggesting that the children's membership may have been inflated by counting everyone who attended Sunday school. The General Superintendent took care in collecting membership numbers, since the budget was based on this and he reminded people to call themselves Methodist in the census.[12]

The Alienation of Māori from the Church

Methodism suffered more acutely than any other denomination from the "falling away" of Māori as a result of the land wars from the 1860s. Taranaki, the Waikato and especially the King Country were largely lost to Methodism in this period. Reports to the conference emphasised that in these areas throughout the first half of the twentieth century, there was significant hostility to the church within Maori communities. Northland was not exempt from such feelings, but they were less intense there. The most prominent Maori Methodist minister, R.T. Haddon, was well aware of the churches that had been burned down during the land wars, and he cited his own ancestor, Titokowaru who had "folded up his religion" and put it aside, because of the confiscation of lands. Māori viewed missionaries as part of the cause.[13] In the King Country there was a massive abandonment of Christianity. The Methodist commentary was that: "Through events over which our devoted Missioners had no control, the tribes deliberately turned their back upon European civilisation, and, though they struggled nobly for a time to retain their Christian religion, they eventually turned aside and adopted frightful superstitions that beggar description."[14]

The Methodist missionaries encountered a good deal of hostility in their work. They spoke of "semi-heathenism", which they put down to pernicious superstition, fanaticism and witchcraft.[15] The Kīngitanga regions were particularly hostile to Christianity and to Europeans in general.[16] They worried that Maori communities were often "ignorant, superstitious and immoral".[17] In an interesting metaphor, Methodist audiences were told how:

> In the field of the Maori mind, Europeans, - sailors, travellers, traders, missionaries, and others – had destroyed a lot of the virgin bush, including much that had its own peculiar beauty and value and was indeed essential to the welfare of the race until supplanted by something better. The Missionaries supplied the "something better" and a garden full of promise in beauty and utility was established. But when disruption came and vicious superstitions replaced religion, and the garden was neglected, rank growths quickly took possession

and very soon it was covered with a veritable riot of noxious weeds. When the gardeners returned, it was almost impossible to get even a foothold in the garden.[18]

They also noted a tendency to turn back to old pre-Christian beliefs.[19] Fanaticism and witchcraft were also blamed. Methodists could not see any good in Ringatū, Pai Mārire and the Parihaka movements.[20] They also observed with alarm the growth of Mormons and other sects.[21]

The Last European Missionaries

In the early twentieth century very few European ministers felt attracted to the Māori mission. William Gittos (1829-1916) and Thomas Hammond (1846-1926) were the last. Gittos was 10 years old when his family came to New Zealand, and was ordained in 1856, the first year when the mission was handed over to the Australasian church, while Hammond, who was born in Richmond, Nelson, was called by the first New Zealand conference in 1874. Gittos had been raised in the Hokianga, and married Marianne Hobbs, daughter of John Hobbs, and served in Buller's station on the Kaipara for twenty years. In 1890 he was given responsibility for the Waikato Wesleyan missions, and gained the confidence of Kīngitanga.[22] He was at the great age of 86 when he laid aside leadership of the Māori Mission in 1916. Hammond served initially in the Hokianga, but from 1887 to 1917 he was based in Pātea in South Taranaki, and responsible for all the West Coast missions of the North Island south of Auckland. Hammond took Gittos's place as General Superintendent of the missions in 1916, but retired in 1920.[23] There was little support from the Pākehā church, but the small group of loyal Maori Methodists held them in high esteem. Hammond became a guardian of Taranaki Maori traditions, and wrote about them in his retirement.[24]

That, however, was the limit of European control of the Mission. There had been by this time generations of faithful Māori Methodists, and the story needs to focus on the heritage of faith within the Māori world. Oral traditions would doubtless enhance this story. For example, Mohi Tāwhai, the first Wesleyan convert was from Waimā in the Hokianga.[25] Mohi Tāwhai's son was the M.P. for Northern Māori 1879-1884, and his grandson, Graham, had distinguished himself as a student of the law and of the temperance cause before his untimely death in 1885.[26] A series of later descendants served the church, including Davis Pou Wilcox (Werekake), who served as a native minister, and Atawhai Wilcox, who was a deaconess. Such genealogical links reflect the deep loyalty of Māori Wesleyan commitment. On the other hand, many Wesleyans were drawn into Rātana in its early days. These two strands are central in this account.

The Significance of Seamer

From the European perspective, the story enters a new stage with the appointment of A.J. Seamer as superintendent. His predecessor, T.G. Brooke, had been head of the Home Mission Department, but had no responsibility for Māori missions. When Brooke retired, A.J. Seamer was nominated to take the role. Seamer's background as a Salvation Army officer sent from Australia to evangelise Māori in Taranaki and Taupo, meant that he was fluent in *te reo*. He had left the Salvation Army in discontent at their leadership, was employed by the Home Mission Department of the Wesleyan Methodist Church, from which he was ordained to the Wesleyan ministry. He served as a soldier and then as a military chaplain on the Western Front.[27]

Seamer was appointed as superintendent of both the Home and Māori missions when there was no-one else to take the Māori role – a merger which troubled some.[28] He presided over a staff of fifty European home missionaries and eighteen native staff. The Methodist Conference insisted that Pākehā must lead the Māori mission. Seamer's significant responsibility for other aspects of the Home Mission Department meant that he needed help from his Māori assistants.[29] He quickly became an eloquent exponent of the need to give Māori more responsibility within the church. In well-argued reports, in public addresses and in his leadership of the Home Mission Board, he drew attention to change within Māori communities, insisting that Māori would need to lead the way.[30] He proposed a partnership of Māori and European, taking a positive view of inter-marriage, and hoped that a Māori church would emerge.[31] He was complementary about the work of the Presbyterian Church among their Māori, which was developing on similar lines.[32] One scholar describes him as "converted" to a Māori identity as "Te Hiima".[33] E.T. Olds served alongside him as Assistant General Secretary of the Home Mission 1925-28 and also took a generous attitude to Māori development.[34] George Laurenson subsequently took that role (albeit in a part-time role 1933-35 as a cost saving measure). Laurenson acted for Seamer when he was away with the Waiata choir in Australia (April-October 1935) and in Australia and England, (March 1937-May 1938). Laurenson succeeded from Seamer in 1939, and proved more willing to share authority with Maori.

It is something of an insult to men like Hauraki Paul and Wiremu Patene to frame the story around Seamer, but actually he preferred to keep firm control. The correspondence between Seamer and his Māori staff indicates that in actuality Seamer retained his Salvationist military approach to leadership, and expected obedience from his Māori staff, who knew that they depended on his favour for their livelihood. He shaped the Mission strategically, insisting to R.D. Rakena in 1934 that:

> to a very great extent the appointments of ministers and the allocation of finance will be in proportion to the number of people that we have under our care in the different districts. For instance, it is useless our spending much time and effort and money in areas where the people desire, as they turn to Christianity, some other Church to guide them. We must spend our strength where the people desire to be guided by us.[35]

There are no hints in the official correspondence as to how his imperious voice was interpreted by the Māori ministers, but some degree of irritation was probably inevitable. The money and therefore the power was held by the European church, for Māori Methodists struggled to raise funds for the Mission, since they were essentially landless and not organised into modern economic units. All this neatly illustrates the thesis of postcolonial theorists of the role of the subaltern in the colonial world. Seamer had a very different and warmer relationship with the deaconesses, and at the end of his life, two deaconesses were diverted from their prime responsibilities to care for him.[36] These deaconesses were mostly Europeans.

Responding to Rātana

A critical moment in Māori spirituality occurred with the rise of Rātana after the First World War.[37] The existing Māori missions were puzzled as to how to respond to Rātana when its aspirations impinged on their territory.[38] Rātana accounts curiously cite A.J. Seamer's comment about the era: "to Maori, the air was full of thought storms, and semi-heathen superstitions developed alarmingly ... feverish religious and at times fanatical activity dominated whole districts ... a critical and markedly transitional period."[39] The research of Garth Cant has explained Methodism's creative response to Rātana. A number of Māori Methodists had very close links with T.P. Rātana. A.J. Seamer was positive about the movement as a spiritual renewal movement among Māori, although this approach faced a crisis in 1925 with the formation of a separate denomination. Even after this, Methodist leaders continued to be sympathetic to Rātana, exercising discretion rather than opposition.[40] The formation of the system of home missionary agents responded to Rātana's impact. In 1925 many Rātana sympathisers had to decide between rival loyalties. Anglicans determined to excommunicate those who linked with Ratana, despite valiant attempts by Arthur Williams and W.G. Williams to defend it. Seamer called a special meeting of the Home and Māori Mission Board on 16 June 1925 to gain endorsement for a very different strategy:

> He stressed the strong desire of leading men in that movement to form a separate Native Church. He expressed a fear that such a step would react most injuriously upon the Christian position among the Maoris. Mr Seamer said that after many long and earnest consultations with Ratana, he considered the wisest course to take in the very delicate situation which had arisen would be for the Board to give him authority at once to appoint Maori agents to take up work amongst any Maoris who were at present without church oversight because of their loyalty to the Ratana movement. Mr Seamer informed the Board that these agents would be supported by the Movement, but that, if the church paid to each of them £10 annually it would strengthen our control. He did not claim this as an ideal development but as a compromise that might save the situation for our own church and practically also for the other mission churches.[41]

So in appointing new part-time home missionary agents, Seamer was seeking to welcome back those whose loyalties had wavered.

This policy was not kept secret, but was explained to Methodists across the dominion.[42] Seamer persuaded the Home Mission Board that Rātana remained a positive forces of change in the Māori community, for its central focus was an attack on prevailing anti-religious superstitions.[43] Seamer was clear that "Rātana saved hundreds of lives by his campaign against tohungaism, as a result of which many of the worst tohungas in certain districts will never again have any influence."[44] He sharply contrasted Rātana with the traditions of Ringatū and Rua Kēnana. Rātana was related to the leading Māori Methodist minister, Robert Haddon, and so Methodism was welcomed to establish a school at Rātana pā, at a time when the Rātana community was suspicious of state education.[45] Rātana sent a telegram and two representatives to the opening of the centennial memorial cairn in Kaeo in 1922, and identified Methodism as within the movement that embraced the light.[46] Seamer instructed his Taranaki minister in 1934:

> I don't want you to worry any of the Ratana people. I am quite satisfied that those who are with the Ratana Church should stay there for the present. Tell them that we recognise them as belonging to us in a general way and that you know they look to me as their "father," so tell them that they do not necessarily come into this scheme. Of course, if they have broken with Ratana, then there is nothing to prevent you taking their names, but in that case I want you to let me know at once so that I can arrange accordingly. If you offend the Ratana people to get a few members now, you will lose hundreds who would come to you naturally in the next few years.[47]

In 1938 the new senior Methodist Māori minister, Eruera Te Tuhi, when visiting Rātana Pā, was invited to conduct their morning service.[48]

Several significant Māori had feet in both camps, among them Robert Haddon. John Tenetahi Harris, a home missionary in Matakana and then in Pākiri (his own village) from 1939 to 1959, was married to Robert Haddon's daughter, and was involved in Rātana, prior to returning to Methodism. Hoani Hākaraia Te Uawiri who had been on probation as a native minister in Paea from 1921-26 was then appointed an apostle in Rātana. After expressing concern at Rātana's inadequate view of Christ, he and his wife returned to the Methodist church in 1930.[49] He was a home missionary in Kai Iwi 1932-1947, but he was then involved in the Te Māramatanga movement as a gazetted marriage celebrant.[50] Wiremu Hēnare Toka was an early home missionary at Waimarino 1922-24 who thereafter supported Ratana.[51] Paikea Henare Toka, son of Wiremu, went on Rātana's world tour in 1924, but was later a performer in the Waiata Choir, and then became a Methodist home missionary from 1932 to 1957. He then resigned from his role with Methodist Māori in Auckland to become a leader in Rātana.[52] Another was Hapeta Rari Rēnata who served at Kaeo as a native minister for a long time, but in 1926 retired from Methodism as he was recognised as an *āpotoro* of Rātana, leaving the Methodists to support his deserted wife.[53] Hone Taotahi (1874-1938), a rangatira of Ngāti Kura, who had been tried in court for seeking to cause an abortion to his wife in 1909, had been awakened to faith in the early mission of Rātana. He then (at the suggestion of Ratana) connected with Methodism, and was sent as a native home missionary at Pipiriki 1924-1927, and then at Kāwhia in 1930-1931.[54]

It is reasonable to ask whether the strategy of accommodating Rātana was successful. Overall Māori Methodism lost ground to Rātana, and in a number of places of former strength, for example in the Kaipara, Methodism lost most of its supporters to Rātana in the period. But perhaps the losses would have been greater without these concessions. Certainly by the 1950s, Rātana was declining and Laurenson was of the view that many Ratana people were ready to return to Methodism.[55]

Māramatanga was a group that grew out of Methodism and Rātana. Ngāpiki Hākaraia, wife of Hoani (mentioned above) began a healing movement that became Māramatanga.[56] Her husband was gazetted as a minister of Te Māramatanga in 1949 but died in the same year.[57]

Reshaping Methodist Structures

Māori Methodism from the late nineteenth century had little to do with other Methodist institutions, but it remained very Methodist in its values. Under Seamer it was organised into three circuits, each of which held quarterly meetings, and maintained a preaching plan for its various congregations with laity and ministers scheduled to preach at regular intervals. Membership was highly important, and when the church introduced a junior membership, Māori were expected to follow. By the early 1940s there were annual meetings of staff, and the first signs of independent thinking came from these gatherings, recommending ministerial candidates.[58] The mission was entitled to be represented at the Methodist Conference but there was always a struggle to find delegates, since so little was relevant to them. Ministers and home missionaries itinerated between the congregation and the stationing committee of Conference finalised their circuits (although the Home and Māori Mission Superintendent made most of the decisions). Seamer disapproved of local congregations trying to choose their minister, grumbling that "… the Conference has usually not told Maori Ministers that they were to shift until just a week or so before the move took place because in nearly every case, when longer notice was given, the opportunity was taken to get up petitions and other nonsense like that so that the work has been considerably upset".[59] These practices were quite different from Te Hāhi Mihinare, where the emphasis fell on the ordination of ministers who often served in the same place for long period, but in both denominations ministers were sometimes moved away from their iwi bases by Pākehā.

The Home Mission Department and the Māori Mission Department had been amalgamated because Seamer was well suited to lead both. There were, however, few links between the two (despite occasional attempts to join up Māori and European circuits). The Home Mission Committee, based in Auckland, met rarely, and Māori mission matters were not often a priority.[60] The two missions reported separately to the Conference.

Seamer and Laurenson introduced the position of Senior Māori Minister, responsible for the visitation of staff, since the Pākehā superintendent had no time to complete this. Laurenson relied on the judgement of Eruera Te Tuhi and showed more alertness to the needs than Seamer had shown to Haddon. The role seemed to trouble some Methodist leaders. After a debate at the 1943 conference, Laurenson sought to safeguard the position of Senior Māori Superintendent, as he had come to term Te Tuhi. The Conference approved a proposal to appoint a European minister as an assistant superintendent in 1944 but found no-one to fill the position.[61] A year later Rev. Harold Darvill was appointed as an itinerant minister to Māori, but he never became superintendent despite the Conference's preference, serving as an equal to the senior Māori minister, not as his supervisor.[62] He seems to have been careful not to try to take over leadership of the ministry.[63] A critical moment towards equality came when Te Tuhi, on the eve of his retirement in 1950, was recognised as a full minister, not just a native minister. This was an awkward milestone on the road to equality.

The Work of the Deaconesses

The most obvious change in the mission strategy in the twentieth century in the eyes of Pākehā Methodists was the use of deaconesses in the Māori work. In 1907 the Wesleyan conference approved the establishment of the order of deaconesses and the appointment of two deaconesses to labour among Māori.[64] The rules of the order required that the deaconesses be supervised directly by the General Superintendent of Home Missions, rather than by Māori ministers or the Quarterly Meetings.[65] The first deaconesses sent to Māori communities were Helen Elizabeth Thomson Hayes (Sister Nellie) who had migrated from the Isle of Man in 1892, and had been the first President of the Wellington YWBCU, along with Julia Benjamin, although the latter moved on to overseas ministry within two years. Nellie served at Okaiawa in Taranaki until 1916, and then moved to Hawera but she resigned in 1920.[66] Her achievements included a successful campaign for the registration of Māori births, deaths and marriages, and setting up an emergency hospital in Hawera during the influenza epidemic of 1918.[67]

Then in 1921, Eleanor Dobby was sent to Tāheke in the Hokianga, while Sister Waiata Nicholls was sent back to Te Kūiti where her Pākehā family's work among Māori was already well established.[68] Deaconesses from that point played a significant role among Māori, and were recognised by Seamer as key instrument in awakening Maori communities to the value of the church.[69] A high proportion of Methodist deaconesses served among Māori, in contrast to the use made of deaconesses by the Presbyterian church. Their role including holding services (mostly attended by women and children), conducting Sunday Schools, visiting homes, and attending to health needs.[70] The role called for considerable physical stamina.[71]

The deaconesses were acute observers of their communities. They were very aware of poverty and lack of hygiene, and much of their work was focused on addressing these aspects of life, especially seeking to protect the children.[72] The Methodist Women's Missionary Union financed most of the deaconesses, and as a result there are many records of speeches given by them at MWMU meetings. Sister Nicholls' report for 1935 after she moved to Hamilton provided an illuminating insight into needs of Māori in the region.[73] Margaret Tennant has movingly described the agonies that Eleanor Dobby faced in the Hokianga.[74] Dobby was like a pioneer with her long horse rides to visit Māori communities scattered around the Hokianga.[75] Heeni Wharemaru told her own story in a remarkable biography.[76] So also did Sister Dorothy Pointon.[77]

Waiata Nicholls' calling owed much to her father, John Nicholls. Nicholls had been a Salvation Army officer, serving alongside A.J. Seamer in the Māori work of the Salvation Army. In 1895 he had led a Māori party on an evangelistic tour in New South Wales and Australia. Then in 1900, disagreements with the new leader of the Salvation Army Māori work led both Seamer and Nicholls to resign.[78] When Margaret was born in 1894, her parents had given her a middle name, "Waiata" at the suggestion of Māori and they subsequently dedicated her to serve the Māori people.[79] Moving to Te Kūiti, John Nicholls and his wife continued their Christian work on independent lines. When Seamer opened a Methodist mission to Te Kūiti, he reached out to them, and their daughter Margaret Waiata began assisting in the Te Kūiti "hospital", subsequently enrolling as a deaconess for the area.[80]

Most of the deaconesses to the Māori seem to have felt a specific call to Māori ministry. Sister Olive Bott was drawn to volunteer because she saw Eleanor Dobby at Tāheke, where her father (Ernest Lovell Bott) was a grocer and farmer.[81] Netta Gittos was the niece of William Gittos, and although she did not know the Māori language, she certainly shared her uncle's devotion to the Māori community. After initial service alongside Waiata Nicholls in Te Kūiti, she was placed at Rātana pā.[82] Fanny Irene Hobbs (Sister Arini) was a great grand-daughter of John Hobbs, and her Hamilton Methodist family had links to the Nicholls family. She served in several places in the Waikato and Taranaki, with long stints at Rātana Pā and at Hamilton.[83] Some of the European deaconesses operating in the Māori world were warmly received and became part of the community, but there was often a period of initial suspicion, especially as the focus was often on changing Māori approaches to childcare, health and education.

There were also deaconesses who were Māori. They may have been inspired by the Catholic, Ākenehi Hei, who in 1901 trained as a nurse to support her people and teach healthy living.[84] Huia Tuatini from Pipiriki was the first Māori deaconess, serving from 1911 until 1913. Her daughter Rūmātiki Ruth Wright (nee Gray) was a prominent Māori welfare worker. Whaitiri Tapito from Raetihi was placed at Pipiriki in 1916 but within a year had returned to her own people. Bella Cassidy was also sent out briefly as a probationer, but returned to her people at Waimā after Sister Nellie retired in 1920. Another woman also inspired by Sister Nellie, Tere Tūpaea, had to be sent home from training to attend to family needs.[85] Evidently Māori society was more critical when one of their own people being called into ministry, but they had little say in the calling of Europeans. A new group of Māori entered the ministry in the 1930s, including Atawhai Wilcox (niece of the home missionary Davis Wilcox, whose nephew also became a home missionary), Miriama Kirkwood (daughter of Hori Kirkwood/Kakuere), Rangi-Marie Ellison, Taka Ropata, Marama Muriwai and Heeni Wharemaru. Another was Marama Kawaiti, who withdrew from training in 1941.[86] Family support was a factor in their calling. Once they had overcome family resistance, these women proved to have significant advantages over Pākehā deaconesses, not just their knowledge of *te reo*, but also a natural welcome from their home iwi. Unfortunately pressing needs and available funding sometimes led to awkward placements in different iwi. Even Pākehā deaconesses sometimes found that they were cautiously received by iwi that had suffered severe land losses.[87] Māori deaconesses had great advantages so long as the local community respected them.[88]

It was remarkable that women were able to negotiate a leadership role in very traditional Māori communities.[89] Lachy Paterson has noted how in the Presbyterian church the position of deaconesses was challenged and undermined after the Second World War by ordained Māori men.[90] This did not happen to the same degree in the Methodist church, for Māori ministers and home missionaries were active much earlier in Methodism. On the whole these deaconesses were a kind of district nurse rather than a pastor, and usually they were not authorised to preach. The General Superintendent was careful to protect the sisters, who were his direct responsibility.[91]

The Ordained Māori Ministry

Māori Methodism since the 1870s had Māori leaders at the local level. Methodism had ordained native clergy from the outset, with less of the baggage that surrounded Anglican ordination of Māori. They were, however, placed in a separate class of ministry, as "native ministers". Each followed the usual Methodist pattern of a probationary period, usually five years, prior to being ordained into "full connexion" if that is the correct term, since they were not eligible for appointment to Pākehā congregations. (Full connexion meant that they were authorised to conduct communion services and could attend the Conference, although it is far from clear how common communion services were among Māori congregations.)

The list of nineteenth century Māori ministers is short. Piripi Hana was ordained in 1856, while Hone Eketone was appointed as an assistant in 1857 and never got beyond that level. Wiremu Te Koti Te Rato was ordained in 1863, Wiremu Pātene in 1859, while Hōhepa Ōtene was made an assistant in 1857. Hoani Waiti was ordained in 1864, Hāmiora Ngaropi in 1861, Heteraka Warihi in 1865, and Wiremu Pātene in 1871, while Karawini Waiti was appointed an assistant in 1878. Wiremu Pewa was ordained in 1879, Hōri Te Kuri in 1879, Matena Waiti in 1885, Hauraki Paul in 1882, Rameka Waikerepuru in 1885, Piripi Rakena in 1886 (the beginning of a ministerial dynasty), and Hāmiora Kingi in 1898. This was a modest group of native ministers, and many of them served for relatively short terms. Yet they expressed the ethos of the Māori church.

A few new ministers were ordained in the early twentieth century, including Te Tuhi Heretini (father of Eruera Te Tuhi) in 1900, Robert Tahupōtiki Haddon and Hapeta Renata in 1904, Hone Hare in 1907, Nemo Hemi (Koroneho) Papakakura in 1908, Hori Kakuere (Kirkwood) in 1915, who had served for five years as a home missionary before his ordination. Others included Davis Pou Werekake (Wilcox) in 1915, Eruera Te Tuhi in 1915, Rakena Piripi Rakena in 1918, Paraire Paikea in 1920, and Matarae Tauroa in 1924.

Ordinations slowed after this. Hoani Te Uawiri became an assistant in 1921 but was never fully ordained although he later became a native home missionary. Oriwa Haddon was given probationary ordination in 1926 but soon left the church and followed other interests. Mātene Keepa, who had been an Anglican (Mihinare) minister from 1908 to 1920 served as a home missionary in Kāwhia 1924-28 before he was admitted into the Methodist native ministry. The next person to be ordained was Rangihoora Rogers in 1946, and he was initially excluded part-way through his training supposedly on health grounds.[92] At most there were twelve ordained "native ministers" who worked for the Methodist Maori mission. Some of these were very notable, but their work was somewhat restricted, and many had short periods in full connexion. This trend deserves reflection.

The dominant figures in the Māori Methodist ministry were multi-talented. Robert Tahupōtiki Haddon (father of Oriwa) was of great significance in the Methodist ministry, but also in Rātana and in temperance politics. He had been received by the Methodist conference as a student at Three Kings College in 1898 after Seamer befriended him while visiting Parihaka. He became a probationary preacher in 1900 and was received into full connexion in 1904. His father was a Scottish pioneer, but his mother was a high-born Maori of Ngāruahine who had ended up in the Hokianga where she had met Wesleyan missionaries, before her return to Taranaki. She was a descendant of Tītokowaru, whose reputation he defended. Haddon married Te Paenga Shelford, child of another bi-cultural marriage, and Haddon had come to feel an allegiance to Māori Christianity as the blend of the two cultures. His early ministry had been under the tutelage of Hammond in Pātea and Ōkaiawa and then in 1910 he was placed in Normanby, and after the retirement of Hammond, was given responsibility for the Taranaki Methodist circuit. It was in 1927 that he was appointed senior Māori Methodist superintendent.[93] Yet although he held this position, at the same time he was permitted to serve the New Zealand Alliance as a temperance speaker on a half-time basis, and informally acted as an adviser to Rātana. Then in 1930 he was moved to Ngāruawāhia, where he pioneered the Methodist – Kīngitanga alliance. Haddon's independence of action and heavy expenses seem to have troubled the board, but they valued his respected profile and his powerful presence as a preacher.[94]

Haddon was succeeded as senior minister after his death by Eruera Te Tuhi (1888-1976). He too was part of a dynasty. The Te Tuhi family of Ngāpuhi descent was based in Whirinaki. The father, Te Tuhi Heretini (1857-1933) was active as a local preacher as a young man, but was not admitted to Three Kings College until 1894, and was viewed with some caution because of his poor English. After his five year probation, he became a native minister in his home village in 1900 and continued there until his death in 1933, building a chapel there.[95] His son, Eruera Te Tuhi was accepted as a home missionary in 1910 in the Hokianga, was received as a probationary minister in 1911 and was admitted into full connexion as a native minister in 1915. When appointed as Senior Māori Minister in 1937 after Haddon's death, he was a great contrast to his predecessor, fully engaged in organising Māori circuits and reporting to the General Superintendent. Laurenson respected him. It was Laurenson who campaigned that he be received into the general ranks of the ministry in 1950, even though this was just four years before his retirement.[96] He served mostly in the north, given his Ngāpuhi allegiance, although he had an initial placement at Ōtorohanga in 1917-1918 after his application to serve as a chaplain to the Pioneer Battalion had been declined by the Army because he was not an Anglican.[97] Most of his subsequent stations were in Northland, at Rewiti, Kawakawa, Waimā, apart from service at Tuakau 1931-34 and Kāwhia 1936-37. Finally he was sent to the city of Auckland in 1937 so that he could be close to Seamer in the administration of the Mission.[98] In this role he struggled financially, commenting to the General Superintendent that:

> our monthly cheque does not meet our monthly local accounts and consequently some of the business folk are compelled to wait until the following month or a reasonable distribution of the cheque have to be made. I don't think that we can be classed as being extravagant. Mrs Te Tuhi is always careful with the food, clothing, etc, and our first consideration always is for the children with the increase cost of living and the possible extra taxation on our income the future does not look very bright for us without present stipend.[99]

Te Tuhi retired in 1954, but continued as honorary senior Māori minister after his retirement.[100]

The Home and Maori Mission had set up a simple pension scheme for native ministers, enabling them to erect a small cottage on tribal land when they retired. Once Te Tuhi was received into full connexion as the equal of other ministers, the whole existence of a separate Māori church was thrown into question, and the Māori Mission Report in 1959 wondered if there was now any need for a separate Māori ministry.[101] So in that year a separate Māori ministry ceased to exist. Rangi Rogers, now elevated to a full ministerial status, succeeded as Senior Māori Superintendent in 1962 until his death in 1971.[102]

There were dynasties of Methodist Māori ministers, as there were in Te Hāhi Mihinare. The Haddons and the Te Tuhis are examples. The Rakena family was a remarkable dynasty, including the father Rev Piripi Rakena (1858-1934) who ministered in various places in the Hokianga (as he was in part Ngāpuhi) and his son Rakena Piripi [Rakena] (1889-1956) who was born in Hawera and whose initial placement was with South Island Maori. After a brief placement in the Waikato in 1923 he was sent to South Taranaki, where he remained until 1936 when he transferred to Waimā in the north, back among his tribal roots. He had also married into the Rapaki Wesleyans of Lyttelton Harbour, and it was here he was buried.[103] Ruāwai David Rakena (1929-2019), who in 1973 became Tumuaki of the Church, was Piripi's son, and there was another home missionary in the family from 1942 until his death in 1950, Paoa Rakena of Mangamuka.

In the three circuits (Northland, Waikato and Taranaki-Waimarino) subsequently four, when Waikato was divided in two, a minister was supposed to be head of the circuit, with responsibility for preparing the preaching plan, monitoring the "native" home missionaries, and attending the conference.

The ministers had complex and conflicted identities, maintaining the new Christian code and seeking to impose it on their people, yet advocating and expressing it within the Māori context, although often not in their home iwi. They mimicked the European ministers, but were always somewhat ambivalent as to their role in the Māori world. Their ministries made them agents of Methodism, yet they were seen by Pākehā Methodists as not quite equal in knowledge or ability. They had limited scope to develop their own practices, for their authority lay in their role as agents of Methodism. When Te Tuhi was finally promoted into the general ministry, he gained a new status, but it was not immediately granted to other Māori ministers.

These "native" ministers were in fact a talented group. A number of them went on to other careers, including Paraire Paikea (who went to Rātana and became MP and Native Spokesman in parliament), Hapeta Renata (who went to serve in Rātana), Mate Rangiheua (who had previously been an Anglican deacon), Rameka Waikerepuru, Hone Hare and Oriwa Haddon. Koroneho Hemi Papakakura took a year off in 1919 to go on the Chautauqua Circuit of speakers in the USA along with a group of four other Māori (most if not all of them Methodists). He had been coached in English by Sir Peter Buck and also stood for the Northern Maori seat in 1914, and later left the ministry to become an entertainer.[104] Oriwa Haddon was part of the same group of Chautauqua performers, marrying the pianist, Ruihi Moringa while on tour. He trained as a pharmacist while in the USA but on return proposed becoming an overseas missionary, and his interest in the ministry may have waned when that proved impossible.[105] It is no surprise that these men found other careers, since they had bridges into two worlds, with some degree of English education. At the same time the outside historian must be careful in interpreting the lives of these Māori ministers, for it is difficult from outside to comprehend iwi pressures on these men.

Between Oriwa Haddon's ordination in 1926 and that of Rangi Rogers in 1947, just one man was sent for training. The training standard for Māori was set by the Conference and after Three Kings College closed, ministerial training was not easily organised. Wesley College was supposed to train Māori ministers, but it had evolved into a secondary school, and some blamed the College for the lack of potential candidates.[106] Maharia Winiata was the first Māori to be sent to the new Trinity College in 1935, where all general Methodist ministers trained. His success there was due to his fluency in English and academic ability. Few other Māori candidates could have succeeded in that rather academic context. The College suspended Rangi Rogers from his study supposedly on health grounds, to the intense annoyance of Māori workers.[107] Winiata decided that he would achieve more as a teacher than a minister, much to the disappointment of the senior Māori minister, Te Tuhi, who felt that this decision would have:

> a discouraging effect on church and those in authority and bad impression and stigma on Māori people generally ... To argue that teaching profession has the same opportunities and offers equal chances of work among the people, as that of the church, I agree only in a measure. The church or rather the minister, as I pointed out to Maha, is a highly authoritative person, due respect for him is not sought after and the chances for doing good work among the people is unlimited.[108]

This surely reflects the different values of two generations of Māori. After Winiata's probation as a minister, he went on to higher education, exercising a significantly wider influence than he could have had in the ministry. He remained an influential Māori Methodist, frequently preaching and assisting the ministers.[109] It may be significant that he was not from a traditionally Methodist region.[110] Winiata sensed that the age of the powerful Māori minister was coming to an end in the post-war years. Consequently, the post-war church was limited to a "pitifully insufficient staff" in the words of the 1944 Home Mission report.[111]

Employed Home Missionaries

While ministers were in short supply in the period, the number of home missionaries on annual contracts grew. Unordained staff had been widely used by all denominations in their missionary work, but they had gradually been converted to ministerial rank. The new policy, a kind of casualisation of labour, began around 1908, at the instigation of Hammond, who sought the appointment of four additional agents to assist the Mission.[112]

The new agents enabled the expansion of the mission with less budgetary implications, and perhaps that was the key difference from the role of ordained ministers.

Ironically, the first of the new native home missionaries, Hāmiora Kingi, was already ordained as a minister. He had served as a native minister at Whirinaki and in various places in the Hokianga and Waikato circuits but became a supernumerary in 1906, retiring to Raglan. He then served as a home missionary from 1908 until 1919 in the Waikato, in the Hokianga and in Taranaki, and then was re-appointed in 1934, serving at Waimate North until his death.[113] Perhaps his loyalty was a little suspect.

A significant proportion of these home missionaries came from Northland, but were sent to other regions. For example, Wi Kaitara was from the Bay of Islands, (and doubtless a descendant of his namesake who was signatory of the Treaty of Waitangi). Kaitara itinerated in the Taranaki and Raetihi region from 1913 to 1922 but he longed for the day when he could return home, and finally did so as a missionary from 1922 to 1926.[114] Hone Tamati was from Taumarere in the Bay of Islands but was sent as a home missionary in 1918 to Ōpārure (near Te Kūiti), returned home in 1926 for four years, and then was sent back to Te Kūiti, but after his retirement in 1933, he was kept on the list for Taumarere in an honorary role because of his reputation as a rangatira, even though he was no longer employed by the church.[115]

One might argue that the home missionaries sold their souls to the mission in return for modest salaries and motor vehicles. They were kept under a careful watch: "in most cases advancing travelling expenses in small quantities just when they are required and justified".[116] In post-colonial terms they had "hybrid" values; although significant in the Māori world, they were deeply committed to the mission's vision, and were willing to leave their home region to fulfil it. They might be described using post-colonial theory as subalterns, with limited independence of action. The home missionaries were approved by the Home and Māori Mission Board, and although regular supervision came from the Senior Māori minister, the General Superintendent had to approve their expenditure. So, for example, Te Āho o te Rangi Pihama was regularly lectured by Seamer for getting into debt, and Seamer in the end refused to honour his purchase of a car without permission. Finally in 1938 he was effectively suspended from his allowance:

> I often think you should be more grateful for the way in which the committee has assisted you during the past few difficult years, as well as allowing you to live in that house, and I think you made a very great mistake in complaining to the Quarterly meeting for it only makes all the others ask how much you get and why you had a house built for you. Of course I tell them that the house belongs to the church. "Well", they say, "if that is so he ought to be satisfied to have a free house and fenced paddocks" it is better not to complain. I trust that the services are being held regularly through your part of the district.[117]

Home missionaries could be employed and sent in at short notice, reflecting older Methodist traditions of a mobile ministry. Tapua Patuone was called in at short notice to provide supply ministry for Papakakura when his wife became seriously ill in 1922.[118]

In 1933, observing the tightness of the budget in depression times, the Mission reduced the number of full-time agents, and halved their stipend, rendering them part-time, in order to shave some £200 from the budget.[119] "What we are doing is quite sufficient so that you do a full day's reaching every Sunday and other general attention to people, especially sick and funerals," Pihama was told.[120] Subsequently the stationing list of the Māori mission included a significant proportion of stations that received only "supply" ministry by lay preachers.

Local Preachers and Honorary Home Missionaries

The changed policy which Seamer had urged in the wake of Rātana focused on the appointment of local agents to maintain Methodist services. His description of his strategy - "to appoint Maori agents to take up work amongst any Maoris who were at present without church oversight because of their loyalty to the Ratana movement" – implies that Seamer believed that the Rātana movement had reawakened their faith. Consequently, such men would be employed to recommence Methodist services which had lapsed. They were to be paid local preachers. Local preaching was the basis upon which Methodism had always maintained services, their quarterly preaching plans assigning local preachers and ministers to each location at regular intervals (usually but not always weekly). Effectively Seamer was proposing that leaders would be drawn back into Methodism by small payments to meet their travelling expenses. Figures of about £10 per year were proposed. Even before 1925 volunteer preachers had been paid to do "extension work" for the Mission.[121] Methodist leaders set out to recruit prominent Māori lay people to hold services on various marae and in churches with duties several times on Sunday. Confusingly, the term "home missionary" was from the 1920s used to refer not just to the employed home missionaries, but also to these local agents. The project was very successful and by 1929 there were many honorary workers in the King Country, where the footprint of Methodism had been almost erased. Later appointees were recruited even if they had no contact with Rātana.

This approach increasingly was also an economy measure, and in the Depression period provided most of the preaching.[122] In 1935 there was an appeal to provide them with appropriate used suits.[123] By 1944 there were just three full-time paid home missionaries and four native ministers and one probationer - a "pitifully insufficient staff" for the work, but there were 28 honorary home missionaries.[124] Some of these men were retired itinerants, who continued to exercise a ministry in their local district. Others were prominent members of the community, who were effectively chosen by the local community. Others gained status in their communities through the title. For example, a deaconess identified a man at Parihaka, whom she thought suitable as a local preacher, commenting that "He is concerned no proper service for funerals there. He wants to lead his own people in a Christian way of living. He is not very popular among his neighbours because he will not go their way in drinking & gambling, and it is in his house the Sunday School is held." Te Tuhi was to make inquiries through the local home missionary with the aim of recognising him as a local preacher and then once his credentials were clear, as an honorary home missionary.[125] Sometimes meetings of Māori staff produced suggestions of new candidates. Occasionally the privilege was withdrawn when the person's moral life was in question.[126]

These home missionaries were typically kept on until death. The title of home missionary was sometimes inherited. Te Urunga Wetere passed his role at Frankton on to his son Tita Taui Wetere in 1951. In the Pihama family the role passed from father to first one and then all three sons. In some ways this meant that little changed in the religious tone of the Māori villages until well into the 1960s. The Herangi family from Te Kopua was another such family.

These agents who were generally leaders on their marae, who were concerned to guide the spirituality of their community. Their story can often be traced in Māori records. There were still a few unpaid local preachers some of whom were very distinguished, for example Waata Roore Erueti, who was spokesperson for Kīngitanga in the early postwar years.[127] This local marae-based Methodism no doubt shaped the aspirations and concerns of Māori communities. For these people the small payment and the limited supervision possible meant that they had significant freedom to express and shape religiosity in local terms.

Church Buildings and Places of Worship

In 1917 there were 49 worship locations in Northland, 35 in the Waikato and 50 in the Taranaki region.[128] Some were mission churches on land with insecure title deeds, including those on marae. About eighteen churches were Methodist property. Church officials frequently expressed concern about securing property under appropriate trust deeds, and about maintaining buildings, some of which were rather rundown.[129] Some churches had been burned down during the war period, and at least two (at Orouaiti and at Nukumaru) seems to have fallen into Rātana hands, provoking efforts to recover them.[130] There were only two Methodist buildings in the Taranaki-Waimarino circuit.[131] A memorial church was erected at Kāwhia in 1934-35, reflecting the revival of Methodist ministry in the district.[132] The church built at Ōtākou on the Otago Peninsula in 1940 was erected primarily by Methodists.

There were just four parsonages in 1916, including one in Whangaroa, one in the Hokianga, one at Te Kopua in Raglan, which was subsequently sold, and one in Pātea, which Hammond had occupied.[133] A new policy developed from 1940 onwards with the creation of Maori centres in which the work of the deaconesses were focused, along with facilities for services. Such buildings were erected in Dargaville, Te Kūiti, Hawera and later in Auckland. They gradually reshaped Māori Methodism and were a recognition of the refocusing of Methodism as Māori urbanisation developed.

South Island Māori

In the twentieth century, ministry to the South Island Methodists was curtailed. Although there were 22 preaching places there according to reports before 1921, they were scattered. In 1900 an undenominational South Island Mission chose Koroneho Hemi Papakakura as their agent while he was a student at Three Kings College.[134] He later became a probationer Methodist minister, and the Mission came under the Home Mission Department. After ordination he served at Ōraka near Riverton from 1904 to 1914, and at Tihaka (Southland) in 1921-22 Rakena Piripi Rakena had pioneered the Tihaka placement in 1915-16, then moved to Temuka 1916-17, and Rāpaki on the banks of the Lyttelton Harbour, serving there until 1921, marrying into the Couch family in 1920. When he died, he was buried at Rāpaki and at his tangi he was fondly remembered by folks from all over the South Island.[135] Matarae Tauroa served as a probationer at Temuka from 1921 to 1923 and was described as a travelling agent. All of these locations were among Ngāi Tahu and Methodism had introduced Christianity to the iwi. But there were just 95 members in the whole South Island Mission by 1913, and 132 in 1930, so there was a growing sense that responsibility needed to be handed over to the adjoining Pākehā circuits.[136] All three preachers were from Northland, and so had few local contacts. Oriwa (Oliver) Tahupōtiki Haddon served as a colporteur across the South Island in 1925-26, and in 1931 he toured the South Island, visiting Methodist families and communities.[137] There was some potential in Marlborough, but the opportunities were largely left to Pākehā circuits.[138]

For a period Sister Atawhai Wilcox (while based in Taranaki) was made responsible for corresponding with scattered Maori Methodists including those in the South Island. When Māori ministers attended Methodist conferences in South Island, they were often sent on tour (at the expense of the Conference). Te Tuhi made tours in 1939, in 1943 and in 1946.[139] Sister Eleanor Dobby on her retirement in 1940 was stationed in Christchurch and given responsibility for South Island Methodist families. Until her death in 1974, she visited some communities (notably Rapaki and Temuka), also writing and sending Sunday school lessons to some 380 homes.[140] The Couch family from Rapaki was one of the significant families Era Valentine Couch was appointed Honorary Home missionary to the South Island by the 1954 conference, and after his death Arthur Couch his brother took his place, but the role was necessarily restricted by the lack of funding, and the Māori Methodist community in the South Island had few opportunities to gather together.

There were two South Island church buildings. The Kotahitanga Church at Moeraki (HPT 9437 Category 1) is the oldest surviving mission church in the South Island. Then in 1940 Methodists played a key role in the erection of a church on the site of the first Christian service in the South Island at Ōtākou on the Otago peninsula, (HPT 5177 category 1) but there were struggles to supply Methodist preachers for the church and today it is mostly used by Presbyterians.[141] The matter was raised at the 1949 Conference at the initiative of Rev W.A. Chambers, and awakened a new generation of Pākehā to the need.[142]

The Hokianga and Kaipara Districts

The main strength of Methodism at the beginning of the twentieth century was in Northland. In 1913, conference statistics claimed that there were 303 members in the Whangaroa district, with 700 attending services, 594 in the Hokianga district with 1430 attending and 255 in the Kaipara district, with 640 attending. The numbers drifted down in later years. In the 1926 census, 20.5% of the Māori population of the Hokianga County was nominally Methodist, but Catholics (39%) and Mihinare (21.9%) were stronger groups. In the other counties of Northland, Rātana attracted well over a third of all Maori. By 1945 these figures had not changed much. In the north, Methodism attracted 19% of Hokianga Maori, while in 1956 allegiance in the county had fallen slightly to 16.4%.

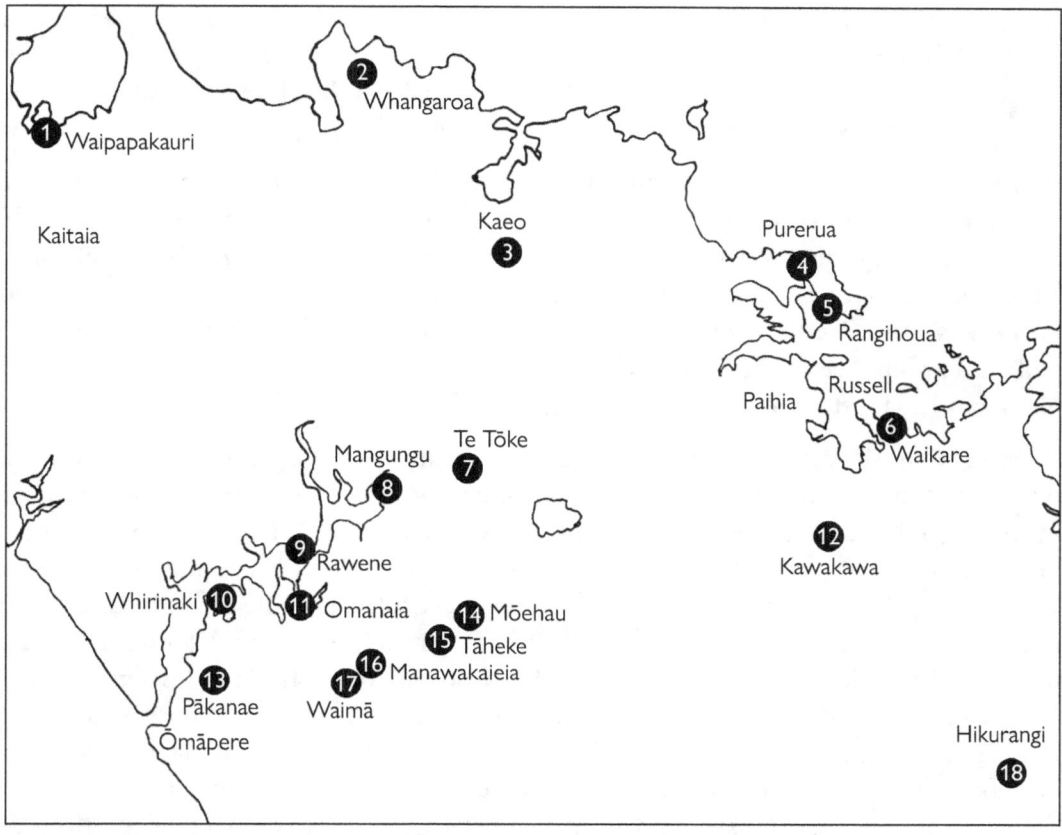

Northland preaching places, churches & mission stations

1. Waipapakauri: preaching place
2. Whangaroa church
3. 'Wesleydale', Kaeo: mission station
4. Purerua: preaching place
5. Rangihoua: mission station
6. Waikare: Methodist church
7. Te Tōke: mission station
8. Mangungu: mission station
9. Rawene church
10. Whirinaki Church

11. Omanaia Church
12. Kawakawa: preaching place
13. 'Newark', Pākanae: mission station
14. Waimā at Te Poinga, Mōehau: mission station
15. Tāheke church
16. Waimā at Manawakaieia: mission station
17. Waimā church
18. Hikurangi

Throughout the county, there were an abundance of marae where Methodists held services. In 1917 the Mission reported it had 16 preaching places in Whangaroa and 22 in the Hokianga. There were only a small number of churches – in 1913 there was one in Whangaroa and four in the Hokianga which had been built in the missionary era. There was a very old Wesleyan church at Ōmanaia.[143] The Ōmanaia church, was built in 1885 (HPT 429). The Whirinaki Church in the Hokianga was built in 1907 (HPT 431). A Methodist church was built at Maraeroa and opened in February 1930.[144] There was a church at Tāheke in Hokianga 1930. A church was finished in Waimā later that year and a

147

parsonage site was donated at this time.[145] That little church at Te Poinga in Lower Waimā (HPT 3883) remains in use, and was often used by a European congregation as well.[146] There was also a small church being built at Whananaki in the Hokianga in 1953.[147] The Rawene church (HPT 430 category 2) is no longer used for religious purposes.

The Hokianga remains a Methodist location. Its centre was in Māngungu in the inner harbour of the Hokianga, along with Whirinaki closer to the sea on the southern side of the Hokianga, the location of the second mission opened in 1828 while Catholics largely occupied the northern side. In the 1890s there was a significant schism among the Wesleyans, when Hōne Riiwi Tōia rejected the ministrations of Gittos and Piripi Rakena and led a group meeting at Tāheke, Ōmanaia and Waimā that seemed to adopt the values of Papahurihia, listening the whistling (whiowhio) of the spirits.[148]

In 1914 consideration was given to distributing the preaching places into two circuits, one on the northern side, based at Kohukohu, while a second home missionary or minister could be stationed at Rawene on the southern side.[149] The policy of honorary home missionaries suited the area, and by 1930 there were home missionaries at Pureria, Whangaroa, Waiōmio, Kawakawa; Whananāki and Utukura.[150] The most notable of the missionaries was Kirihi Te Riri Maihi Kawiti of Ngāti Hine, who was appointed home missionary at Waiōmio in 1927, retiring in 1943 when he was replaced by his son Te Tāwai Kawiti Kawiti at the urging of the Quarterly meeting.[151] He remained in this role until 1949. Te Riri, the father, was a leading iwi leader, grandson of the great Ngāpuhi warrior, Te Ruki Kawiti, and he was notable for his focus on Maori land claims, and served on the Waitangi National Trust Board, playing a key role in the Centenary celebrations of 1940. For this he was honoured with an O.B.E. He remained associated with Methodism in his old age.[152]

From 1917 a deaconess (Edith Goodall), was based at Waimā near Rawene, where Hammond had been based many years earlier. Subsequent deaconesses were based in various locations in the Hokianga, especially Tāheke and Kohukohu.[153] Eleanor Dobby lived in Tāheke in Hokianga from 1921 to 1939, using horseback, launch and walking to visit isolated Māori communities. Olive Bott was based here from 1933-36 and then on and off until her retirement in 1956, near her parents, and her horse Dick supposedly had carried her for 4000 miles! The area was extremely poor, and many Maori were landless. Sister Dobby's reports from Tāheke in Northland are shocking reading. During the depression she appealed for Methodists to send her sugar bags and flour bags so that local Maori could make dresses, sheets and petticoats.[154]

It was important to have clergy in the Hokianga. Whirinaki in the south Hokianga was where Te Tuhi Heretini was born and served his ministry from 1896 until his death in 1933. The area was contested between the Anglicans and Methodists, and some congregations seceded from Methodism in 1902.[155] When Florence Harsant held temperance meetings at Otaua, she tactfully welcomed contributions by Catholics, Anglicans and Mormons as well as Wesleyans.[156] Another native minister, Matarae Tauroa, was based here from 1927 until 1934. Occasionally laymen represented the area at Auckland synods and conferences, for example Hauraki Te Moti, Henare Hemara (a future home missionary) and Wiremu Pekikuru.[157]

There were congregations around the top of the Island around the Rangaunu Harbour north of Kaitaia, and at one time thought was given to a home missionary at Paparore (north of Kaitaia) to reach these people.[158] For several years Henare Hemara served as home missionary in the Mangonui/Aupouri region based at Waipapakauri, but he died early in 1918, and was not replaced.[159]

Kaeo and the Whangaroa Harbour had unhappy memories for Wesleyans as the site of the original mission, but in 1915 it was reoccupied when Paraire Paikea was placed there.[160] Tapua Patuone (perhaps a descendent of the celebrated rangatira, Eruera Maihi Patuone, whose father's name was Tapua) was recognised as a home missionary at Whangaroa 1922-23. A church was built at Patunga near Whangaroa in 1930. From 1934 Hone Taotahi was moved a few kilometres north from Purerua at the north of the Bay of islands to his home at Matauri Bay, where he continued in retirement until his death in 1938. Rangi Rogers served at Matauri Bay in 1940-41 as a home missionary before his ordination, moving in 1942 to Punakitere near Waimā, but thereafter the position was left vacant and preachers came from Kaeo to conduct services. Later, a series of honorary home missionaries were stationed at Kaeo, including Robert Hukaati Taka (Tucker) from 1961 to 1973 and more recently Te Uru Hone Heta from 1982 to 2006.

There were also congregations on the southern side of the Bay of Islands, not easily reached from Kaeo, and in 1915 a further grouping of congregations with a native minister based at Waikare, on the road south of Russell. The Waikare church (HPT 9280 Category 2) near the Bay of Islands, built in 1913 is the site where Sister Atawhai Wilcox, Henare Te Hemara and Pou Werekake conducted their ministries. Davis Wilcox based his ministry from 1918 to 1921 at Opua (where the Russell car ferry leave from today). In 1917 there were ten churches in the Bay of Islands. The Purerua Peninsula at the north of the Bay was Hone Taotahi's base 1930-1934. In 1939 Olive Bott was moved from the Hokianga to Paihia for four years, and subsequently worked part time in Paihia in the late 1950s.[161] There was significant religious competition in the north as Anglicans, Ratana and Mormons grew in strength in one-time Methodist strongholds.[162]

Around the Kaipara Harbour there were many Maori congregations, and at one time almost all Maori there saw themselves as Methodist.[163] The location was linked to the Te Taoū people in the Ngāti Whatua tribal confederation. There were five churches in the Kaipara in 1913, survivors of early missionary work. Gittos had been stationed for many years in Ōtamatea county, and in 1917 there were eleven Methodist churches in the district. Hauraki Paul was stationed at Reweti on the road from Auckland to Helensville from 1888 to 1910. He preached as far north as Mangakāhia, about 30 km north of the harbour, and he was often sent into the Waikato as well.[164] He was succeeded by Eruera Te Tuhi, but many of the young minister's flock went over to Ratana, while in 1917 the little village of Batley was used by Paraire Paikea as a base for visits to other congregations around the harbour. Rātana visited the area in the early 1920s and his followers became very numerous in the area, largely at the expense of Methodism.[165] In 1926 Methodism had 25.1% of Rodney County's Māori. Paikea Toka was based there 1934-36, although in subsequent years there was no home missionary available. There were deaconesses here briefly in 1936-1939. In Dargaville and in the Wairoa, there were other preaching places

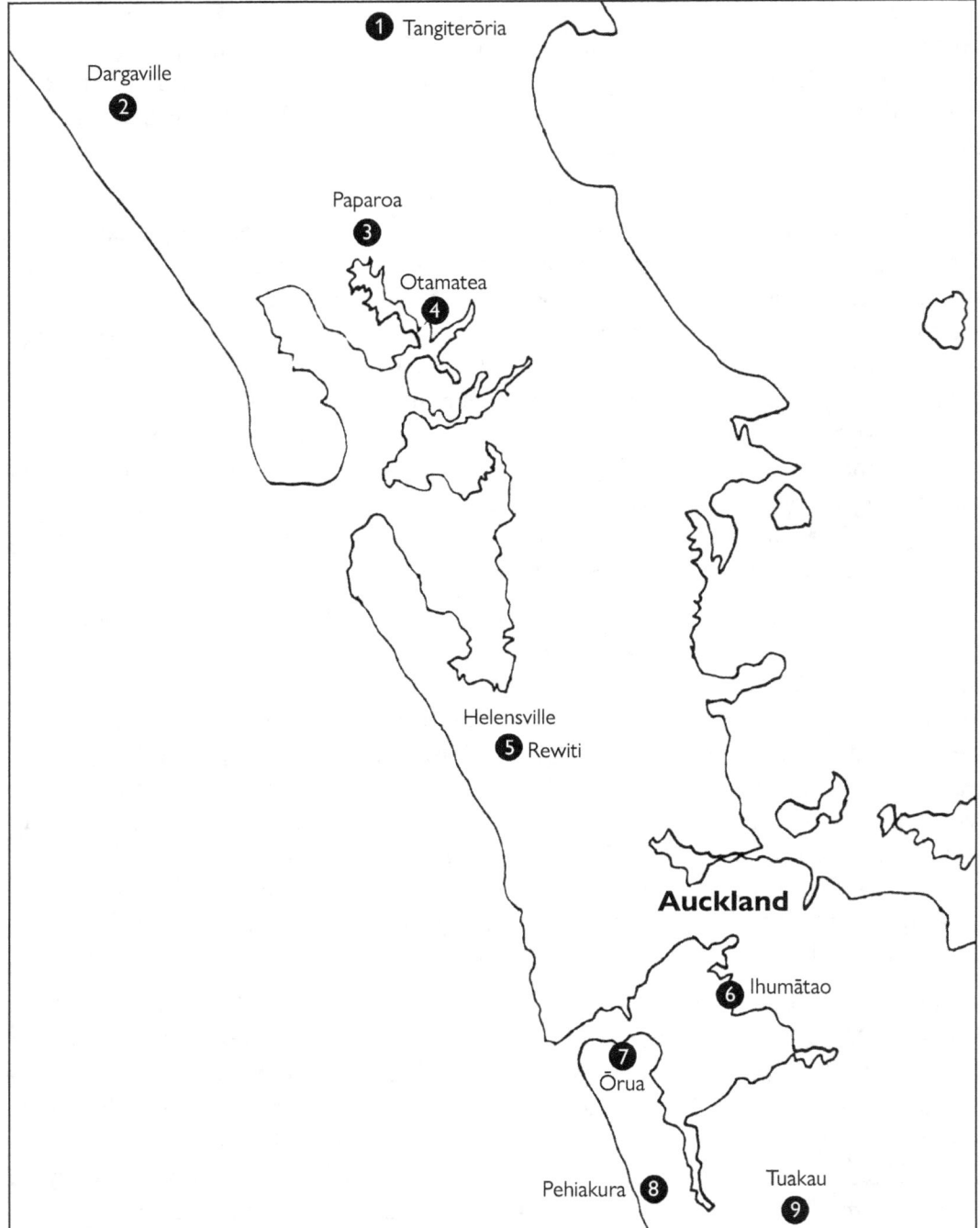

Auckland preaching places, deaconess locations and mission stations

1. Tangiterōria: mission station

2. Dargaville: deaconess centre and location of Māori minister

3. Paparoa: church for settlers and Maori

4. Otamatea marae: location of Gittos's Kakaraea Church home of Gittos

5. Rewiti: preaching place

6. Ihumātao: mission station

7. Ōrua, South Manukau Heads: mission station

8. Pehiakura: mission station

9. Tuakau: mission base

including Te Kopuru, and in 1930 Eruera Te Tuhi who had local family connections was placed here. There were deaconesses and a Māori centre in Dargaville from 1947 to 1974.[166] In Helensville Methodists were 20% of a small Māori population, but Rātana was nearly double this.

The Kakaraea Church at the Ōtamatea Marae in Tanoa, built in 1874 at the urging of William Gittos was seen as his cathedral and is a category 2 HPT listing, but it had largely become a Rātana gathering place after the district converted to Rātana in the 1920s.[167] Nearby on the Ōtametea river sits the Gittos house built in 1866, with the same HPT status. Some of the dedicated Methodist buildings were run down, and two were renovated in the 1920s.[168] There was a church at Poutu at the Kaipara Heads, rebuilt in 1953. The Paparoa Methodist church, built in 1878, served both the settler and Māori congregations. (HPT 3910 Category 2).

There was a huge decline in the population of the Northland counties in the post-war years, as many young people sought employment in Whangārei and Auckland, where Methodism was weak. Methodist proportions were still relatively high in their old centres of strength, but the actual numbers made the maintenance of worship difficult. By 1976 Rawene had 32 Methodists (a quarter of the village's population) and Hokianga County 290. Hikurangi had 53. Between 2001 and 2018 Methodism in the far north declined from 5% to 2.5% of the Māori population.

In Auckland city in 1945 Methodists were not particularly strong, and primarily clustered at Manukau where they formed 21% of the Māori population – presumably many of them from the Raglan district. In 1956 In Manukau and Franklin counties they were 15% of Māori. Between 2001 and 2018 In Mangere-Otahuhu it dropped from 5.8% to 3.0%.

Taranaki-Waimarino

Southern and central Taranaki was the other great base for missionary work in the nineteenth century, under Skevington, Woon, Stannard and Whiteley, but there was great bitterness among Māori for the way that Whiteley had encouraged them to sell their lands. T.G. Hammond was one of the very few New Zealand born Methodists in the nineteenth century to feel called to work among Māori, and he led West Coast Mission, as it was called, from 1887 until his retirement in 1917 from a base at Patea. His retirement forced the restructuring of the mission. Taranaki Māori seemed little interested in European religions, and Methodist preachers were horrified at the lack of spirituality shown in some of the pā.[169] Methodism was the strongest religion among Māori in the Province of Taranaki in 1926 at 21%, ahead of Rātana (18%), which struggled to surmount tribal barriers. The Taranaki-Waimarino Circuit was created in the 1920s with a base in southern Taranaki, but it had an inland presence in the Waimarino plain on which Raetihi was found. There was a European home mission station as well as a Māori outpost in this isolated region, but there were just 16 Methodist Māori in Waimarino County in 1926, while 56% of the Māori were Rātana. Anglicans and Catholics both were active along the Wanganui River valley, stemming back to competition in the early days of Christianity

Taranaki / Whanganui preaching places, deaconess locations and mission stations

1. Ngāmotu: mission station

2. Rahotu: home mission base – Papakakura's base

3. Raetihi: home mission base

4. Ōhinemutu/Te Āo Marama: mission station

5. Okaiawa: deaconess base

6. Normanby: Methodist Māori minister R.T. Haddon's base

7. Heretoa/Waimate: mission station

8. Patea: mission station, T.G. Hammond's home

9. Waitōtara: home mission base

10. Kai iwi: home mission base

there.[170] Methodism had Māori home missionaries at Rāhotu, Pātea, Waitotara, Kai Iwi, Pipiriki, Raetihi, and Rangitīkei in 1930.

Methodism was strongest in the southern coastal counties, and in 1926, 59% of Hawera Māori, 40% of Pātea Māori and 33% of Waimate West Māori were Methodists. Mihinare and Catholic numbers were low, except in Pātea, while an unusual numbers "objected" to specify a religion. By 1936 there were more Catholics than Methodists among Māori in the province, and Rātana had also greatly strengthened. The exception was in the boroughs of Eltham, Waimate and in Hawera county. Methodists were 24% of Taranaki Māori in 1945, and at Hawera they were just under 50%. In Normanby, Haddon's old town, they were also strong. Subsequently the numbers gradually declined, but south Taranaki still had a reservoir of Methodists.

Primitive Methodism had been founded in Taranaki, and there was a Pākehā Wesleyan circuit at Hawera from 1887. Ōkaiawa was important for Methodists, with a deaconess, Helen Hayes (Sister Nellie) based here from 1908. Then from 1915 Neho Papakakura led the West Coast Mission, based at Rāhotu in 1915 and again in 1918-19 and at Ōpunake in 1916. Normanby, inland from Hawera was Robert Haddon's base as superintendent in 1920, with a native home missionary at Ōpunake, another at Pariroa Pā just out of Pātea and another inland at Raetihi. There was a native deaconess at Pipiriki, inland on the Wanganui River (the home base of Ngāti Kura, of the Ngāti Ruanui peoples, among whom most of this Methodist work was based). An Ōkaiawa Hall was opened in 1931 as a base for deaconess work.[171] From the 1930s South Taranaki seemed to be slowly declining, with Catholicism recruiting among Methodist Māori, although the base in Hawera helped Methodism. There were other home missionaries appointed, among them Rangiiri Tumahuki at Whenuakua Pā near Patea, and Puna Hamiora at Waipapa Pā, both of whom died in 1947.[172]

Hori Kakuere was placed as a home missionary in Raetihi in 1910. While placed there, he erected a church, which was opened in a huge hui at Easter in 1912. (It is curious that Anglicans, Ringatū and Brethren assisted in the service, and Father Vibaud provided mass for the Catholic contingent).[173] Wi Kaitara took over from Kakuere in 1915 but also had duties in Waimarino, Toanui and served for a period at Rāhotu, near Opunake. (He may possibly be identified with the Ratana minister, Wi Kaitara Mangakahi.) Thereafter there was no resident missionary in the area, and Raetihi, Ohura and Taihape were described as almost hopeless causes in 1933.[174]

On the southern edge of the district, preaching stations were re-established in Rangitīkei, and in Wanganui, despite the strength of the Anglican and Rātana presence in these districts, but there were never honorary missionaries or staff in the area.

In 1926 exactly one Māori Methodist was reported by the census in New Plymouth, and 12 in Taranaki County on the northern side of the province. There was an attempt to build a presence there. A chapel was opened at Moturoa, New Plymouth on the occasion of the centennial of the mission.[175] Deaconesses and the girls boarding school were part of the plan to grow Methodism, and especially to cater for Māori attracted to work in the town.

Waikato

Methodism in the Waikato had developed from the coastal mission stations at Port Waikato, Raglan, and Kāwhia. The significance of Wesleyan contribution to the region has been largely ignored by historians.[176] These places declined during the nineteenth century, while the inland towns of Tuakau, Te Kūiti and Ōtorohanga became significant, especially once the Main Trunk Line was opened. This region had been almost totally disrupted by the land wars, and many Māori had dropped their Methodist links, but this was where the greatest recovery occurred in the twentieth century. In 1936 the circuit was divided in two: Waikato in the North and King Country in the south, in view of the significant growth of the work. This reflected the old boundary defined by Kingi Tāwhaio as Te Rohe Pōtae. Methodists sometimes called the area the Maniapoto Circuit. There is no natural geographical boundary, but the King Country/Maniapoto circuit encompassed the counties of Ōtorohanga, Waitomo and Ruapehu, while the Waikato circuit was essentially the area in Western Waikato confiscated by the Crown in 1864 from Raglan in the south to Port Waikato and Tūākau in the north. In 1914 the Mission Department considered transferring the northern Waikato work to the Auckland superintendent, and Tūākau was often placed in the Auckland district. In retirement 1930-1938 Hori Kakuere returned to Pukekohe, perhaps his family's home marae, since his daughter, Piu Ngatiai Kakaure (who later became Sister Miriama Kirkwood) was born here in 1908, but his own place of birth was Terekanauku near Te Ākau between Raglan and Port Waikato.[177]

Overall Methodist official statistics in 1913 suggested there were 605 members 431 junior members and 4000 attendees in the Waikato-King Country district, with the "guesstimates" rising in the 1930s to 632 members, 450 juniors and (once again) 4000 attendees. Census figures in 1926 show that Methodism was very strong. Methodists were the second largest group in Raglan at 23%, while 32% of the Māori population were Anglicans. Methodists were 22% in Waipā and here Anglicans were just ahead of them. By 1936 Methodism claimed the allegiance of 32% of Waipa County Māori. In 1945, Methodism had fallen back to 24% of Waipā Māori, and it remained stable with this figure until a large jump to 39% in 1976. In Raglan County in 1945 Methodism had double the allegiance of Anglicanism, at 37% of the Māori population, and the figures remained in this vicinity until 1976 when the proportion fell back to 31%. The towns of the Waikato were more varied. By 1956 Methodism claimed the allegiance of a high proportion of Waiuku, Tuakau, Huntly and Cambridge Māori. Between 2001 and 2018 Methodism in the Waikato declined greatly to just 2% of Māori.

Particular note should be taken of Hamilton, one of the earliest places to experience urbanisation of the Māori population, and in Ngāruawāhia, as the King Movement warmed to Methodism. In 1936 there were 70 Methodist Māori in Hamilton and 23% in Ngāruawāhia. By 1956 Methodists were 25% of a much-increased Hamilton Māori population. These figures remained strong for the next 40 years. Since Māori in this area were essentially landless, poverty was very evident. In the opinion of the deaconesses, the districts of the Waikato were very poor.[178] In Tuakau, Sister Ivy Jones reported that many Māori had to resort to work in Chinese gardens preparing food for urban markets.[179]

Waikato preaching places, churches and mission stations

1. Ngāruawāhia: Kingitanga centre and Methodist mission

2. Te Hōrea: mission station

3. Hamilton: Te Rahui hostel

4. Nihinihi, Raglan: mission station founded by James & Mary Ann Wallis

5. Whatawhata: Mission base for Te Aho-o-te-Rangi Pihama

6. 'Beechamdale', mission station

7. Papakarewa, Kawhia: mission station of Whiteley and Schnackenberg. Location of memorial church, opened in 1935

8. Te Kōpua: marae & mission station founded by Thomas Buddle

9. Te Ahuahu/Te Waitere ('Lemon Point'): mission station

10. Kinohaku: home mission base for Aihe Huirama

11. Ōtorohanga: home mission base

12. Marokopa: home mission base for Kawhia

13. Hangatiki: home mission base for Wetini Hotu

14. Opurare: marae and base for Hone Tamati

15. Te Kūiti Methodist hospital & deaconess base and home of Nicholls family

16. Wakatumutumu/Arapae: mission station

17. Mokau: most southern home mission station for Maniatoto Māori circuit

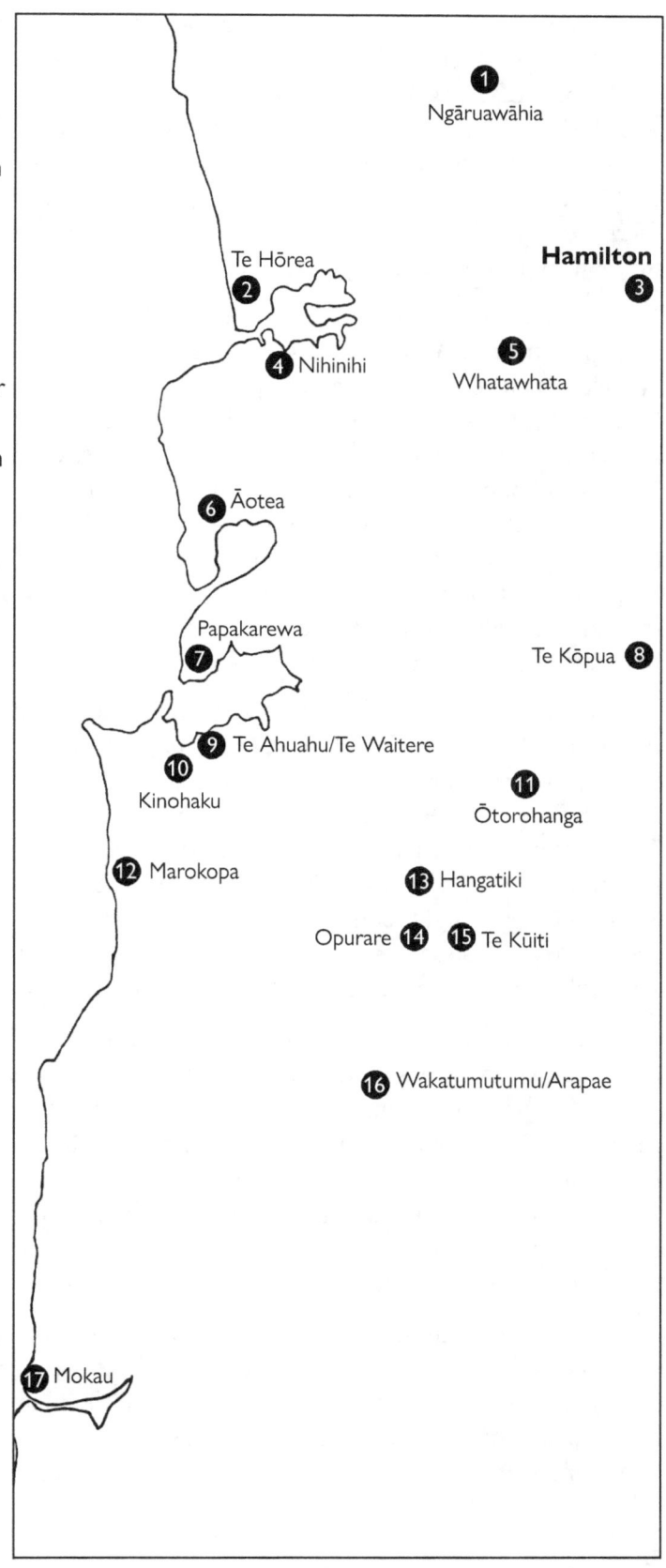

Raglan was a historic station, going back to the pioneering work of James and Mary Ann Wallis in 1839. Raglan was seen as an important centre, with many marae open to Methodist preaching, but it was important to have a native minister there. Piripi Rakena was stationed here in 1913, Rev Hapeta Renata in 1915-16, while Te Hira Ratete was based here as an honorary home missionary in 1925, Davis Wilcox from 1928 and then Te Āho-o-te Rangi Pihama, who in 1929 gifted the mission a site for a parsonage. In 1930 there were home missionaries at Raglan and Cambridge. From 1926 a minister or home missionary was based at Ngāruawāhia.

The Raglan group of outposts included at various times Ohiapokoko (just south of Raglan), where Te Āho o te Rangi Pihama was stationed from 1933 to 1947. When Davis Wilcox was moved from Raglan in 1930 there was significant resentment from the people.[180] Several home missionaries were employed here, until Honehone Kereopa from Te Kōpua (the father of Eva Rickard and a prominent member of Tainui) was named from 1935 to 1949 as an honorary home missionary at Whāingaroa.[181] In 1941 an additional missionary was stationed at "Raglan Rural" with Tuteao Manihera placed there presumably visiting outposts there which Kereopa may have been too old to visit, for when he retired in 1949, Manihera took over the Raglan station, remaining on the list until 1965 when he moved to Hamilton. He too was very distinguished as a guardian of Māori traditions and was the recipient of an O.B.E. in 1977. His wife was a Pihama.[182]

The old mission house at Te Kōpua marae was established in 1841 by Rev. Thomas Buddle and located off the Ōtorohanga/Pirongia road. Hāmiora Kingi from the Hokianga was based here from 1895.[183] Later occupants of the mission house included Kirkwood (Hori Kakuere) in 1913-15, and Rev. Hone Hare in 1916-17, Rev. Piripi Rakena in 1918-20, and then home missionaries including Hone Tamati (1922) and Te Āho-o-te-Rangi Pihama in 1924-25. In 1924, however, the property was sold to the Herangi family.[184] Some of the Herangi (Searle) family, who were closely related to Princess Te Puea, were staunch Methodists, and several served as honorary home missionaries, including Tahuna Herangi from Te Kopua, from 1937 until his untimely death in 1939.

Whatawhata also had a missionary station from 1922. Te Āho-o-te-Rangi Pihama was a home missionary based here from 1920 to 1924 and again 1927-1930. Hoani Ahi Ahi was an honorary missionary here in 1933-34. Te Poo Kingi, another very distinguished Maori and descendent of Hoturoa, captain of the Tainui canoe, was honorary missionary here from 1934 until his death in 1954.[185] The tradition of honorary home missionaries has continued here with Ngerungeru Materori Tame Pihama (son of Te Ako) as honorary missionary, 1954 to 1974. Hoera Whakaari Hakopa was an honorary missionary here from 1959 to 1973.[186] Mātengaro Te Rutu (Sam) Grace was a minita-a-iwi here from 1995.

In Hamilton, the first Māori hostel, Te Rāhui, for girls working in the city, was constructed in 1944, and in his retirement A.J. Seamer managed it and served as circuit superintendent. It also served as a centre for their deaconesses and ministers in the circuit, and was later converted into a boys hostel which was lovingly described by Sister Heeni Wharemaru.[187]

In the southern part of the circuit, bitterness against Europeans was strong, and there were few Europeans. From the Kāwhia Harbour inland the work of European Methodist missionaries had at one time had a great influence until Kīngitanga had insisted on the removal of Pākehā from the area. During the period after 1880, a key influence was Hone Omipi (John Ormsby), who opposed the separatism of Kīngitanga and Ngāti Maniapoto, helped to organise the Kāwhia Native Committee in 1883, permitting the lease of land to Pakeha, and established the town of Ōtorohanga.[188] Ormsby was an active Anglican lay reader, who held services in Maori in the region.[189] Ormsby died in 1927, and it may be significant that Methodist influence grew largely after his death, but he was a key figure in the King Country Proclamation banning alcohol, so had friends among the Wesleyans.[190]

This was an area where Maori significantly outnumbered Europeans. Standards of health and medical care were drastically lacking, and travel by horseback remained standard through the 1930s. The poverty and poor health of the Māori of the King Country was widely recognised. Sister Frances Hayman wrote a harrowing narrative in 1932 about the poor housing, the illness of children, the lack of access to basic medical and social resources in the district.[191]

In the 1926 census up to 32% of Māori objected to state their religion in the Waikato King Country counties, reflecting the lack of church activities in the region and Kīngitanga's take on religion at that time. Among the King Country counties, the strongest Methodist presence in 1926 was Ōtorohanga at 32% followed by Kāwhia at 29%, and in both of these it was the strongest religion. Through the King Country the only strong Rātana area was Waitomo County. In 1936 Methodism rose to above 30% in Ōtorohanga county, and in Kāwhia it dramatically grew to 50% of the Maori population. In 1945 25% of Waitomo Māori and 48% of Kāwhia were Methodist and there were high levels in Te Kūiti and Ōtorohanga townships. By 1943 George Laurenson, the General Superintendent, took some pride in noting that the Methodist Church had more Māori ministers, deaconesses and lay agents in the King Country than at any time since the land wars.[192] Numbers declined somewhat between 1945 and 1956 but in 1966 46% of Ōtorohanga Māori were Methodist, and also a significant number at Waitomo, and these figures remained high for the next twenty years. From 2001 to 2018 Methodism's remaining strength was in the Ōtorohanga district at 15% but by 2018 even it Waitomo it was below 4%.

The regrowth of Methodism began in Te Kūiti, which became the centre of a very active ministry. There was also a European circuit based here from 1916. A Methodist native minister was based in Te Kūiti in earlier years. In 1921, a deaconess was stationed there, and a small Methodist hospital was set up, and after the state hospital was opened, the Methodist building served briefly as a school. John Nicholls, the former Salvationist, ran the local shop, and his family, who were accomplished in *te reo*, threw their energies into Māori Methodism. His daughter Margaret (Sister Waiata) was a deaconess there from 1921 to 1925, and he was persuaded to serve as an honorary home missionary here from 1934 to 1950. Te Kūiti was used as a base for the mission, with John Nicholls providing a perspective Pākehā eye over the Māori staff (with an interesting correspondence with his old friend, Seamer). Mate Rangiheuea was here as a home missionary, and when ordained in 1928 he remained here but ceased to be recognised in 1931. Hone Tamati who was at nearby Opārure 1919-22 and returned to Te Kūiti 1929-1934. Ngapaka Kukutai was based here 1941-54 after his ordination, as the minister superintendent of the circuit. He was succeeded by Kukutai Moke 1954-56. There was also a home missionary for rural Te Kūiti, Tame Ponui 1945-49 and he continued till 1962 based in Kōpaki/Waimā. Taniora Tokoroa was here from 1944 to 1949. In 1930 there were home missionaries (most of them honorary) surrounding Te Kūiti, to the north at Ōtorohanga.

Ōpārure (the location of the Te Waipatoto Marae), a Methodist stronghold, was 7 km north east of Te Kūiti, and in 1918 a home missionary was stationed there for the first time.[193] At Hangatiki (the crossroads between the road from Ōtorohanga and Te Kūiti and the Waitomo Caves Road), there was strong support for Methodism from Hotutaua Pakuhatu (c1838-1934) a leader in Ngāti Maniapoto, and in Kīngitanga, and A.J. Seamer presided at his funeral.[194] Wetini Hotu (1892-1951) served from 1930 until a year before his death as honorary home missionary at Hangatiki.[195]

At Aotearoa marae, at Wharepapa South, south-east of Te Awamutu, the Mission stationed Te Āho-o-te-rangi Pihama 1925-27, followed by Haotu Hapimana, 1927-1930, and in response the hapū set aside ten acres to build a church in 1924.[196] The missionaries placed in the other main King Country town of Ōtorohanga were Paraire Paikea and then Eruera Te Tuhi. Subsequent missionaries were moved to nearby Te Kawa.

At Kāwhia Harbour the Ahuahu mission station had been founded by John Whiteley and occupied by various missionaries, until Cort Schnackenberg was evacuated from it in 1863. There were no regular Christian services in the district thereafter for a lengthy period. A very significant change took place in 1921 when a Māori home missionary, Aihe Huirama was stationed here. Remaining until 1937 and on his retirement became an honorary missionary nearby at Kinohaku, until 1942. The base from 1921 was the little village of Marokopa south of the harbour. In 1924 a Māori minister, Mātene Keepa, was sent to minister in the area. This led to the breakthrough which is so apparent in the census figures. A profound sign of the recovery in Methodism was the building of a memorial church and parsonage in Kāwhia to celebrate the centenary of Methodism in the district.[197] By 1934 the church claimed more than half of the Māori in the area among its members.[198] It was deeply symbolic when Māori presented the church with its bell, which they had hidden for many years, and the Māori king rang the bell for the first service.[199] The church was also supposed to serve as a European site, but European clergy proved hard to find.[200] Wene Herangi (part of a very loyal family) who was based at Te Manaia at Rakaunui in the Kāwhia area from 1941 to 1952 was one of the honorary home missionaries in the area.[201] There were a number of other preaching places in Kāwhia harbour, including Te Waitere which was an early mission site of Whiteley. From 1940 until 1947 this was the site of a home missionary, Te Paki Kinita.[202]

Kīngitanga Links

The Waikato story was profoundly affected by the growing sympathy for Methodism within the King Movement. Kīngitanga had become more willing to embrace traditional Christianity in the 1890s, when King Mahuta showed willingness to observe the Sabbath

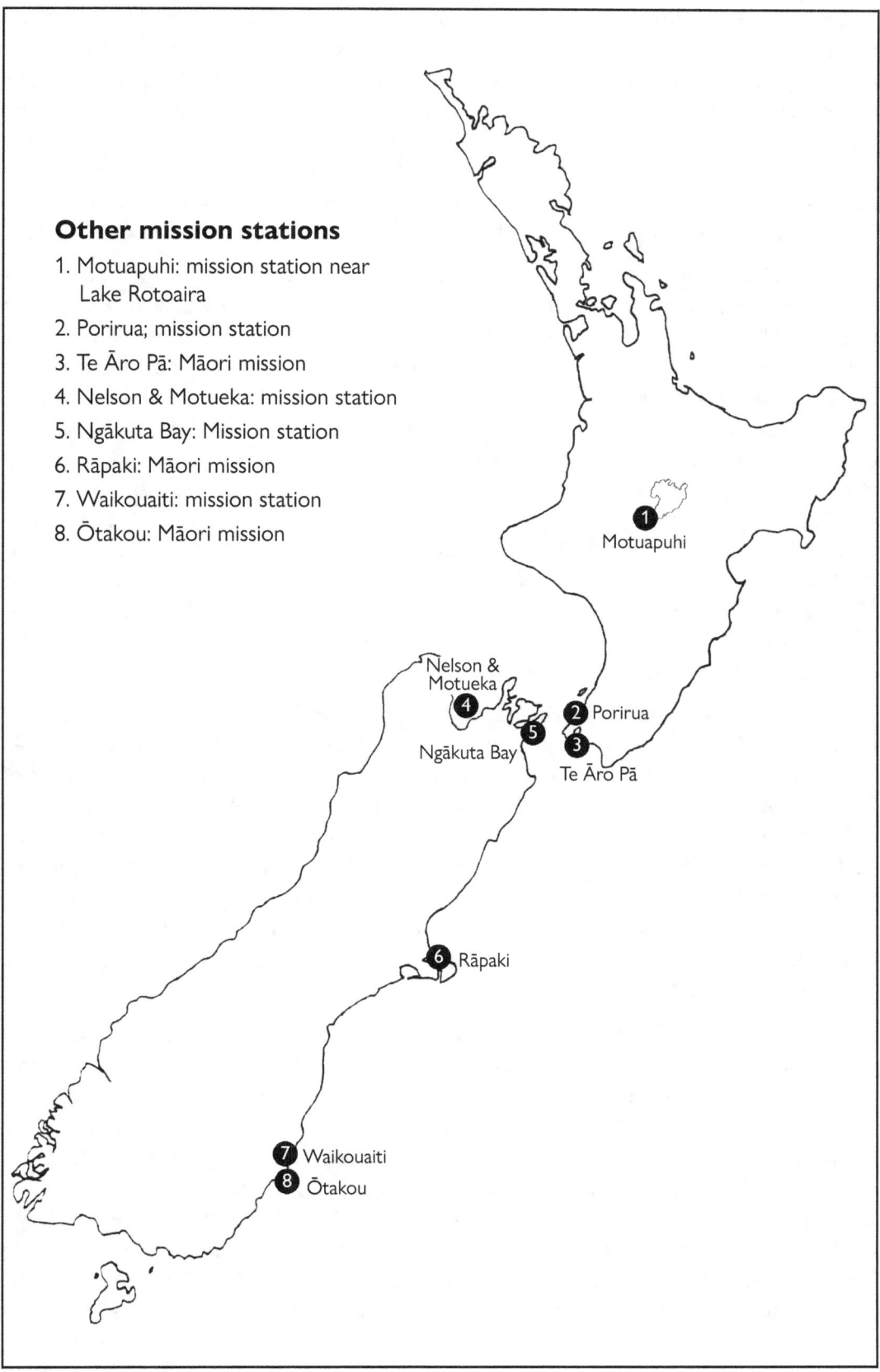

Other mission stations

1. Motuapuhi: mission station near Lake Rotoaira
2. Porirua; mission station
3. Te Āro Pā: Māori mission
4. Nelson & Motueka: mission station
5. Ngākuta Bay: Mission station
6. Rāpaki: Māori mission
7. Waikouaiti: mission station
8. Ōtakou: Māori mission

and encouraged children to attend Christian schools.[203] A.J. Seamer was encouraged by the Maori ministers to seek links with Kīngitanga and accepted an invitation from the king to spend a weekend of conference at his kāinga in 1921.[204] Thus his policy towards Ratana had in effect been preceded by the links with Kīngitanga. Methodist leaders were initially cautious, conscious that they were a small movement, with limited resources to supply when opportunities provided to them. Nevertheless, they were impressed by the advantages the Presbyterian Māori Movement had gained from cooperation with Ringatū. The relationship with the King movement soon became close.

Perhaps the boldest of the home missionaries was Te Āho o te Rangi Pihama. His namesake who died in 1905 is well known from a Goldie portrait. He was direct descendent through of Wiremu Neera Te Awaitaia of Ngāti Mahanga (1796-1866), the notable friend of the British in the years of the formation of the Kīngitanga, whom Methodists remembered as the friend and sponsor of the missionaries James and Mary Wallis.[205] He was a close relation of King Mahuta, entrusted with one of the taiaha of the king, and a direct descendant through the male line of Hoturoa who navigated the Tainui canoe, and was not frightened to criticise the government.[206] He served several times on the Māori Mission Party and stands out in photographs of that group.[207] He enhanced his mana when he used eloquent oratory (often criticising government policies) on the mission tours, raising money for the Maori mission. His ministry was based at Aotearoa marae south of Te Awamutu from 1925 to 1927, at Rāhotu in Taranaki 1928-1931, and then at Ohiapopoko, just south of the Raglan Harbour 1930-1947. He then moved closer to Hamilton to serve at Whatawhata. He was honoured to be buried in the Kīngitanga sacred land at Taupiri.[208]

Another significant figure in Kīngitanga was Rev. Erueti Matete-Kukutai who was based at Tuakau and was related to King Korokī. He was buried in the presence of King Korokī and Princess Te Puea at Taupiri, and Methodists were honoured guests at the unveiling of Kukutai's monument a year later.[209] Remi H. Kukutai succeeded him, and was appointed as home missionary at Te Kohanga marae, although in the Mission's view he was "not a perfect Christian, nor minister but far above his predecessor and some others who have worn the white collar".[210] Ngatete Kerei Kukutai had the same pedigree and in all his roles maintained the link between Methodism and Kīngitanga until he died in 1966.[211] Two other missionaries, Wene Wiremu Herangi (Serancke) and Paddy Tumanako Serancke were closely related to Te Puea.[212]

Cooperation with Kīngitanga was fostered by a careful selection of home missionaries at Ngāruawāhia. Hori Kakuere was placed here in 1923 remaining until 1930 and was much involved with the establishment of Tūrangawaewae marae – a very natural choice since he was a cousin of Te Puea.[213] Kakuere was from Te Ākau north of Raglan on the coast and he was raised in Pukekohe but had travelled extensively including Australia and involved in politics in the Western Māori electorate, before marrying a Hokianga woman. Converted at Kaikohe, he then settled in the Bay of Islands area. He began as a home missionary but was admitted as a native minister in 1915 and moved to Raglan. He then was placed at Ngāruawāhia from 1923 until his retirement in 1930. At this point he returned home to Pukekohe.[214] His daughter became a prominent deaconess.

In 1931 the senior Maori Superintendent, Robert Haddon, was moved to Ngāruawāhia, to maintain the Methodist influence.[215] A year later, Seamer and Haddon who had the respect of the King, conducted most of King Te Rata's funeral at the instigation of Princess Te Puea.[216] Haddon preached the sermon at the coronation of Korokī.[217] Subsequently Mātene Keepa, a descendent of a paramount chief from Rotoiti and a former Anglican minister, held this critical role until his death in 1941, and as virtually the royal chaplain, he was accorded burial at the sacred mountain, Taupiri.[218] Hotutaua Pakuhatu, chief of Ngāti Maniapoto who died at the age of 93 in 1934, was another deeply Methodist Kīngitanga figure, who had served as ambassador for the movement from the time of Tawhiao.[219] Cervin notes that Seamer tolerated the revival of Pai Mārire prayers in the Waikato circuit, which was standard Kīngitanga practice.[220]

A significant patronage of the mission was accorded by Te Puea, as she reinvigorated Kīngitanga, and special delegations were sent to her marae.[221] She was taken to visit Wesley College in 1938, and this inspired her vision for Māori agriculture.[222] She in return invited Methodists to special events in Ngaruawahia.[223] She also agreed that Methodist ministers could hold a conference on the marae.[224] Heeni Wharemaru, the Māori Methodist deaconess, was in effect trained up to serve at Te Puea's lady in waiting.[225] When Tonga royalty visited Ngāruawāhia in 1936, there were Methodist connections everywhere in evidence.[226] A letter was sent to Princess Te Puea in 1942, and in 1947 Methodist representatives (Eruera Te Tuhi and Heeni Wharemaru) were chosen by Kīngitanga to accompany Te Puea to the royal wedding in Tonga.[227] Michael King's biography of Te Puea acknowledges Seamer's influence on Te Puea.[228] In 1946 the deaconesses were encouraged to use Tūrangawaewae for their work.[229] In post-war years the church struggled to find suitable missionaries or a minister for the location, but Roi Moke was based there 1942-1951 and Heemi Rihimona, counsellor for Te Puea and King Korokī and a welcoming elder at Tūrangawaewae, was based there and in Hamilton from 1949.[230] Ngatete Kerei Kukutai acted as assistant to Princess To Puea in her meetings.[231] When Princess Te Puea died, Methodists formally lamented.[232] Te Poo Kingi was a descendant of the captain of the Tainui canoe and a great kingite.[233] The tradition of a strong Methodist presence in Ngāruawāhia continued with Te Orahi O Raukawa Pumipi who served here in an honorary capacity from 1961 to 1984. A factor that undoubtedly helped this reception was the very public statement by leaders of the mission that the confiscation of land after the wars of the 1860s was unjustified (reflecting the finding of the Royal Commission of 1926) and that Māori deserved compensation.[234]

Links with other Denominations

A number of former Mihinare (Anglican) Māori clergy sought acceptance into the Methodist ministry in the year 1923. Presumably one recruit led to another. Mate Rewiti Wharehuia Rangiheua (sometimes called McDavis) from Ngāti Manawa, born in 1883, trained at Te Rau, deaconed in 1916 by the Bishop of Waiapu and serving at Nūhaka, in 1923 began serving at Te Kūiti with the Methodist church, and in 1928 was admitted to the native ministry but resigned in 1931 and became a farmer at Murupara until his death in 1967.[235] His links with both denominations remained; he went on the 1936 Waiata choir tour, and his foster son, the future great All Black, Sid Mead, attended St Stephen's and Te Aute Colleges.

Wharehuia (McDavis) was related to Mātene Keepa (1884-1941) of the Ngāti Pikiao hapu, who had been a Mihinare (Anglican) minister at Tokomaru, Tūranga, Motea and Nūhaka, but in 1920 resigned from the Anglican ministry, presumably because his wife had deserted him within a month of their 1919 marriage. In 1926 he divorced this wife.[236] Keepa was very well-regarded in Methodist circles, and was received as a native minister at the 1928 conference. In 1929 was remarried to Kepa Rangitaka. He frequently spoke at fund raising events for the mission, wearing a rangatira's cloak.[237] Like Rangiheua, his service continued until the end of his life, and he ended up as the minister in charge of the Waikato native circuit, based at Ngāruawāhia.[238] He was undoubtedly the most useful of these recruits. His advice persuaded the church not to accept the offer of another Anglican minister, Tamiora Tokoroa Poihipi, who was evidently out of favour with the Bishop of Auckland.[239]

Another recruit in 1923 was Waata Tuahangata Fraser (1876-1963), also of Te Arawa, who had served at Rotorua, Waipawa, Moteo and Tūranga, and as a military chaplain in a local training camp, who was suspended "on a serious charge" by Bishop Sedgwick in 1922, left the Anglican church, and was admitted by the Methodist Conference as a native minister on probation at Te Kūiti. He stayed just one year, was drawn into Rātana, and can be traced in Rātana, Apostolic and Presbyterian records before he tried to cajole his way back as an Anglican military chaplain after the Second World War![240]

While not previously a minister, Eruera Matete had been a lay reader in the Anglican Church and attended St Stephen's College, and was highly connected, but in 1934 he became an honorary Māori Home Missionary at Tuakau.[241]

A possible factor in these transfers was resentment of Bishop Cherrington, whose tactlessness was legendary and who was inclined to regard Waikato Māori as in a heathen state. The Methodist Maori synod was very critical of his statements, and of his opposition to the King Country Accord.[242] In general, Methodist Māori were a little suspicious of Anglicanism and Presbyterianism, particularly in the South Island. There was also bitterness when Anglicans exploited their political links to retain control of the military chaplaincies in the Second World War.[243] Still on the whole these resentments were more common in the offices of the Mission Department than among the home missionaries, who were much more likely to lament "the lack of interest and lukewarmness of the local spiritual leaders".[244]

Relationships improved from the late 1940s particularly as the National Council of Churches Māori section brought together the leaders of the main Protestant missions.[245] This cooperation facilitated a Bible Society project to prepare a new edition of the Māori Bible. Eruera Te Tuhi served as the Methodist on the committee, and greatly enjoyed the co-operation within the NCC. On a visit to Gisborne for a translation meeting, he was stunned by the economic and religious base of Te Hāhi Mihinare in the East Coast. As he wrote,

The Lord has given me a wonderful chance to see the East Coast and its people. No doubt they are well off as far as lands are concerned and the wealth from their extensive holdings make it easy for them to support anything that concerns the people. The mission too (Anglican) is strong and healthy and the various parishes is strongly back to the people.[246]

Other religions were not viewed so benignly. There was concern about the growth of theosophy and spiritualism, the teachings of which were spread by literature as well as by itinerant preachers.[247] There was a great deal of concern about incursions by the Catholic Church, particularly in Taranaki, partly reflecting the decline in Methodist pastoral involvement in the region.[248] There was also some concern in the late 1950s when a Pentecostal preacher held a mission in Waiomio.[249]

The Tone of Māori Methodism

The ministry remained relatively small-scale. The number of communicants was tiny – just 150 in 1946.[250] By and large services were held on marae, with the largest congregations at tangihanga, and only some attendees would have thought of themselves as Methodists. More Methodist meetings were being held by the 1930s, but they were small, comparable to cottage meetings.[251] Methodist Sunday schools, in contrast, were large. Te Hāhi Weteriana slowly became better known.[252] As Rakena observed, the denominational and paternalist tone of the Pākehā church world and its definitions of valid Christianity left many Māori uncomfortable.[253] Māori Methodism flourished partly because it was rather separate from the Pākehā church. Laurenson, Seamer's successor, looked forward to the ultimate blending of Maori with Pākehā, but he knew that his vision had little appeal to Māori.[254]

The Methodist missions were located in some of the most deprived and damaged parts of the Māori community. The Waikato confiscations, the Taranaki land seizures and the lack of incomes in the north all meant that the Methodist Māori community faced acute problems.[255] They had little of the stature that Ngāti Porou felt or of the new economic activity of the Bay of Plenty and the Wairarapa. The work might be seen as profoundly colonialist in its orientation. Rua Rakena later noted the lack of distinctive Māori hymns from the Methodist world, and of those, only one had Māori tune.[256]

Presbyterian Māori work, although smaller than that of Methodists, showed greater coherence because it was tightly grouped in the central North Island, and better resourced by a larger denomination. The two churches were not in competition, and shared in discussions about church union. Methodism had its own magazine, *Te Kotuku Kai Whakaata*, edited by Mātene Keepa from 1933 to 1941, but they then combined with Presbyterians in *Te Waka Karaitiana* which Laughton had begun in 1932. Later *Te Kotuku* was revived with Tita Taui Wetere (1949-1950) as editor.[257]

One aspect that often bothered the European church was that many of the distinctives of Methodism, its systematic use of leaders meetings, quarterly meetings, synods and conference with stationing at the conference were circumvented by the Māori traditions and by the Mission Department. The staff conferences carried much of the leadership of the movement. Methodists had a limited consciousness of church membership since it was largely integrated within the life of the village and the iwi.[258] It was the annual meetings of the staff which debated issues of critical concern. On these occasions, the Māori staff were not afraid to express their opinions.[259] Deaconesses also met annually and used these occasions to speak out on matters of concern.[260]

The demography was against Māori Methodism. The drift, particularly to the towns of Whangārei and Auckland presented the Maori church with an impossible conundrum. In these places, all separate Māori churches struggled. The 1956 review noted grimly that the tiny group of Māori staff were almost all in rural areas, and although five of the honorary home missionaries were in Auckland, there was a massive lack of resources to meet the needs of the relocated people. But it was surely a tragedy that Māori Methodists were not allowed to open their own churches. The policy of integration essentially failed. Pasifika people, arriving in the cities ten years later, opted for separate language services or schismatic affiliations to the island churches. This was never an option for the Māori church at that time.

Politics and Faith

In the newly energetic Māori section of the Home Mission Department, politics were not off limit. In the aftermath of the land wars, the Protestant churches' reputation with Māori had been smeared on account of the way they had encouraged Māori to sign the Treaty.[261] One reason for the Methodist struggles was the frequent accusations that missionaries were implicated in land confiscations.[262] The change of tone was striking. The Methodist Māori preachers were vocal in their concern that the Treaty of Waitangi had not been honoured.[263] The issue was raised in successive Māori Mission reports to the conference.[264] Neglect of the Treaty was raised in speeches given to Methodist audiences by the 1928 Mission party for example.[265] A.J. Seamer's view was that the land had been illegally seized by the settlers, and the confiscations of 1864 of so much of the "Methodist region" surely justified this.[266] In the 1940 centennial events the church (in line with Rātana) called on the government to ratify the Treaty of Waitangi.[267]

The Methodist leaders blamed the bad reputation of the churches on government misdemeanours. Seamer told attendees of the 1929 fundraising tour that Māori should have blamed the government rather than the churches, because it was the government that had betrayed them.[268] The church was rather defensive about accusations from Māori that it had retained their lands illegally.[269] A Methodist report in 1930 commented that the work of the deaconesses was "a slight return for the occupation of their country and the introduction of European life".[270] The Māori Mission leaders were aware of the underlying issues of justice, and did not limit themselves to evangelism. This is very evident in the priorities of the deaconesses. It also explains the Methodist defence of the alcohol ban in the King Country. Methodists, led by deaconess Helen Hayes, initiated the campaign for the registrations of Māori births, deaths and marriages, a campaign, with the Conference backing this call in 1912.[271] In a very real way, this was a holistic approach to mission.

Impoverishment and Community Decline

Methodist Māori leaders were acutely aware of the desperate needs of their communities. So much land in these areas had been taken in confiscations and purchases, and so much remaining land had been transferred to individual titles that village life was undermined, meaning that few could eke out a satisfactory existence on their small plots.[272] Frequently menfolk were absent, itinerating in search of work, so the ministry was largely conducted among women and children who had little or no money. Shortage of money sometimes led women to stay away from meetings.[273]

The poverty of the communities affected the ministry. There was rarely money available for participants to use to cover the costs of schooling or health needs. The deaconesses generally had to seek support from the Pākehā churches, and in explaining the need, they sometimes presented an unfavourable picture of their Māori communities.

Māori "irresponsibility" irritated Pākehā Methodists. At the 1943 conference, there were sharp attacks on Māori morals from a number of Pākehā ministers, based on reports of the bad behaviour of Māori girls in Auckland, but also controversies about Māori behaviour in the country districts. For example, Rev J.R. Nelson of Paeroa claimed that the church had lost influence with Maori who had moved away from their home areas in search of work, while Rev Gabriel Elliott of Te Kūiti said the church was "slipping very badly" in the King Country.[274]

Advancing Māori health and well-being

The Mission placed high value on raising the health and wellbeing of Māori. The standards of hygiene and customs on the marae particularly troubled the deaconesses. They saw these as spiritual threats to the Christian message.[275] Most, if not all the deaconesses practised some basic nursing particularly for young children. In 1923 a small hospital was established in Te Kūiti at the centre of the King Country, to address Māori health needs in the vicinity.[276] It was staffed by a skilled deaconess. After a state hospital was established in 1928, the hospital served briefly as a school.[277] Methodists naturally associated cleanliness and godliness. Seamer urged the government to attend to Māori health and well-being in an address in 1936.[278]

One very Methodist concern was alarm at the ravages of alcohol, and at the way it led to poverty. Methodist Māori were ardently committed to the temperance cause. Hori Kakuere was described as a "well-known and powerful exponent of temperance" at his ordination in 1915.[279] and R.T. Haddon was given leave for several years to work for the New Zealand Alliance. Hemi Papakakura often joined him on the platform as a solo singer who would attract the crowds. Methodists continued to work closely with the New Zealand Alliance for many years, issuing a Māori language leaflet in 1940.[280] Methodist Maori within the King country were strong defenders of the pact with the government to keep alcohol sales from the area.[281] Kīngitanga leaders embraced the liquor ban as a way to preserve their people from Pākehā vices.[282] The Maniatoto Methodist Circuit, along with the Methodist Conference was a significance voice in favour of the alcohol ban.[283] The Methodist Conference also joined in supporting the ban.[284]

There were Pākehā in the King Country who disliked the strong influence of the Methodist Church on the Māori King.[285] The tone of the Methodist campaign was perhaps somewhat patronising. Some offence was created when Matarae Tauroa's words at Conference about the alcohol abuse he had seen in Taranaki were read by his Taranaki flock.[286] Similarly when Eruera Te Tuhi gave evidence to the Royal Commission in Licensing in 1945, he was quoted as saying "Liquor has always been a problem among the Maoris — a problem in connection with their livelihood, in connection with their moral life, and in connection with their social welfare."[287] On this subject their concerns were echoed by the whole church, and they felt betrayed by the liquor poll of 1953 and the rejection by a government report of the legitimacy of the pact.[288] Methodism lost influence when the ban was removed in 1953.

Sunday Schools and Other Schools

Sunday schools had the potential to touch a very significant proportion of young Māori. Deaconesses placed a high priority on holding Sunday Schools in as many communities as possible. Their sheer dedication ensured that they attracted most of the Māori children in their areas to the schools. In 1950 there were 5194 on their Sunday School rolls.[289] Deaconesses also used these contacts to connect with the students' whanau. They recorded the birth date and family details of these pupils. Since families were very large, the relief they offered for mothers must have been significant. In the review in 1956, the scale of the work was detailed. The deaconesses held these schools weekly, fortnightly, monthly and even quarterly (sometimes not on a Sunday).[290] It seems that almost all the children in these districts attended, and this activity explains the rapid rise in Methodist Māori in the census from 1936 to 1966, even if few progressed into church attendance or membership.

Wesleyan education for Māori in the 19th century focused on the Native Institution at Three Kings, which was closed in 1869, and then reopened for a second phase in 1876-1923, as a place of training for Pākehā and Māori ministry candidates, while Prince Albert College functioned as a secondary school from 1895. In 1912 land was purchased at Paerata and Wesley College moved there in 1922 as a secondary school. A number of the Māori Methodist leaders attended the school, but it was unsuitable as a training place for ministers.[291] Some thought was given in 1918 to amalgamating the role of principal of Wesley College with that of the superintendent of Māori Missions, but instead the decision was made to amalgamate the Home and Māori mission departments.[292]

Methodist belief in the value of education was not confined to Wesley College. The need for a girls school was placed before the Māori and Home Mission Board in 1929.[293] A school for girls was opened at Te Kūiti in October 1929 to make use of the vacant hospital building. It could only accommodate a few students, so in 1931 it was moved to Onehunga as the Kurahuna Training Home. It was a school of domestic science, curiously described by Heeni Whakarau as having "the primary goal of teaching students how to conduct themselves in such a manner that they'd become ladies".[294] European approaches to eating hygiene and learning were encouraged. In 1932 Netta Gittos, (niece of William Gittos, deaconess and previously teacher at the Methodist school at Rātana Pā) was appointed principal, and she was succeeded by Madeline Holland who was there 1942-45 and 1949-

1968.[295] As a centennial project, a Māori girls school, Rangiātea, was planned for New Plymouth, with funding assistance from the Wellington Charitable and Educational Trust. This was to be a girls college matching the Presbyterian Māori Girls College at Turakina, but the board struggled to raise enough money to build and equip a school, and few Māori could afford to send girls to a boarding school.[296] So it became a hostel for the local state schools, and served as a base for the work of Sister Evelyn Marriott with local Māori.[297]

The number of girls and boys attending such institutions was small, and the schools were dependent on grants. Wesley College enrolled about 20 Māori boys, but needed about 50 European students. Kurahuna claimed to be popular but it enrolled just twelve girls a year.[298] The cost of operating it was inevitably high – some £702 in 1936.[299] Schooling had been a priority of missions since the earliest years, and boarders were thought to be more likely to benefit from learning, but the rapid rise in the Māori population rendered the strategy rather exclusive. Rua Rakena, Rangi Rogers, Lane and Edward Tauroa and a number of Pasifika leaders were educated here, but financial factors made it beyond the reach of most lay Māori.[300]

Financing the Māori Mission

The Home and Maori Mission was a fundamental aspect of church extension work, but there was never enough money to support the work. The Māori budget was within the Home Mission budget, and in 1912 that stood at £2176 (plus a secretary, who was paid £500). The estimate for 1913 was £1943.[301] By 1956 the total Home and Māori Mission budget was £25,220 of which £15,220 was spent on Māori work.[302] Aspects of the work were sponsored by various Methodist groups, notably the Women's Missionary Union, which supported most of the deaconesses, but Sunday school children supported one, the Young Women's Bible Class Union another, and the Wellington Methodist Charitable & Educational Trust two others.[303] Funding was controlled from the Auckland Office of the Mission. Consequently, the General Superintendent was both patron and paymaster of the Māori staff through his control of their pay and allowances. The Mission frequently struggled to break even, and the high cost of providing and repairing vehicles caused regular crises.

Ministers' annual stipends had been just £30 in 1900. By 1921 payments had increased somewhat. Seamer was paid £206, Haddon as senior Māori minister, £195; the native ministers between £95 and £157, and the home missionaries between £50 and £125 (including allowances).[304] Stipends of ministers were raised to £200 in 1929, but during the Depression a 17% cut was imposed on the Mission's income, so just five ministers and two home missionaries remained on the staff, with others only paid expenses.[305] Ministers' allowances stood at £180 in 1935 and then rose to £225 in 1947, and £390 (including allowances) in 1953. This was not a lot of money, especially for those living far from their home marae. In 1913 native ministers were paid £100 plus travelling expenses and rent. Probationers were paid £70 and native home missionaries £50. Te Tuhi commented, "the whole trouble is the fact that our Māori ministers do not get sufficient money to live on. The sum of £15-0-0 a month is not enough to make ends meet and the Māori minister is carrying a heavy burden apart from the weight of his mission work."[306] Nevertheless, this pay was higher than what Māori Anglican clergy in the diocese of Waiapu received paid - just £100-150 a year before World War Two and £260 from 1945. (No wonder Anglican ministers aspired to join the Methodist church!) It was also much higher than the Methodist Māori home missionaries received -£50-£100 in 1935, while deaconesses (mostly European women) were paid £125 in that year.[307]

The Mission was under pressure to raise income from Māori and from other sources. Congregations were constantly urged to contribute to the work of the mission, but little money came from this source. Local Maori communities were poor, and the expenses involved in tangi and other communal events fell heavily upon them. Moreover it was not possible to take up a collection at a service on a marae, given the rules around providing a koha towards marae expenses. Where the church had its own buildings, collections were possible but rarely amounted to much.[308] In 1921 a total of £154 was raised across the whole mission, compared to expenses of £2865. A 1940 circular informed congregations that just £36 had been received from Māori donations, and this was described by Te Tuhi as "a lamentable state of affairs and demands an inquiry to our individual heart and consciences whether we are really and truly holding up this important phase of the Lord before our people".[309] £1380 came from rental of land owned by the mission.

Other support came from donations from the Wellington Charitable and Educational Trust, and support for the deaconesses from the Young Women's Bible Class Union and the Women's Missionary Union. In 1938, for example, these three sources raised £1390 towards expenses for the Māori mission. This was never enough. A.J. Seamer therefore decided to raise funds directly from the Pākehā circuits, taking advantage of a growing sense of interest in the Māori world. This proved the key to funding a significant expansion of the mission.

The Waiata Choir

Seamer was from the outset expected to go on deputation to raise this support. In 1924 he formed two teams, called the Home Mission Parties, to perform anniversary rallies held up and down the country. From the first, a Māori speaker and Māori performances were included.[310] The teams toured for some eight months, and were massively popular with audiences, often drawing in people who were not regular church-goers. One team went to the South Island and another to the North Island.[311] In 1925 Seamer, who was himself a keen singer, decided to hold concerts which featured Māori singing and culture. Mātene Keepa was a member of the first choir in 1925. The choirs that Seamer organised soon became well known.[312] Members were selected from Methodist Māori congregations. Deaconess Margaret Nicholls took a major role in organising it 1930-1935, and from 1934, it was renamed the Waiata Choir, and some efforts we made to reduce the organisational burden of taking the choir on tour.[313] Some choir members became famous in their own right, notably the opera singer Īnia Te Wīata. There are a number of posed portraits of the choir in various archives, all clad in native costumes including Seamer draped with a cloak over his suit and Sister Nicholls with a flax cape.[314] Deaconess Sister Rangimarie (Mori Ellison) served on the party 1935-38 including its overseas tours.[315] The choir went on to tour Australia three times and Great Britain in 1937-38, even singing before the King and Queen. On their return they were given the high honour of a reception at Ngāruawāhia.[316]

The choir was successful in raising significant income and removing pressures from the Māori mission. The overseas trips also brought in significant income, some £1700 for the 1935 Australian visit.[317] There were other consequences, mostly beneficial. Many of the mission members grew close to each other through participation in the choir. Contacts with the Pākehā who provided hospitality meant that Maori Mission leaders became better known, notably Te Āho-o-te-Rangi Pihama.[318] The choir and its speakers took the opportunity to enlighten New Zealand audiences about Māori grievances, including treaty issues and land loss. But on the other hand, it stereotyped Māori culture, paying no attention to iwi differences and ignoring the deep issues caused by impoverishment and urbanisation.

Responding to Urbanisation

There was evidence even in the 1920s of the drift to the towns or to new regions by families in search of work. Communities were evidently struggling to have the resources to survive. The home mission staff were very aware of the move to towns, given that Methodists were in the poorest parts of the Māori world. As early as 1928 a Māori Girls Club was established in Auckland by Sister Ivy Jones in associations with the Methodist Social Services Mission.[319] A small welfare centre was opened in Airedale Street beside the Mission in 1943, focusing on Māori welfare services.[320] Sister Heeni described Jones as "pretty well in charge of all the Auckland Māori people".[321]

After the Second World War the drift to Whangārei, Auckland, Hamilton and New Plymouth had a major effect on Māori Methodism.[322] The rise in tensions between Maori and Pākehā caused concern, and in the face of racism in Pukekohe, a home missionary, George Bennett, was placed there for a year.[323] The Mission had long recognised the problem of keeping in touch with urban Māori.[324] They tried to station deaconesses or home missionaries in towns like Hawera, Te Awamutu, Dargaville and Kaitaia and at large public works sites like Karāpiro. They explored a strategy of opening Methodist centres in Northland, Waikato and Taranaki towns. In the 1950s these were opened in Dargaville, Hawera and Te Kūiti, taking advantage of subsidies made available by the new National Government. These were also used as a base for deaconesses and home missionaries.[325] Auckland was a particular problem. There was a loss of momentum when Ivy Jones moved from Māori work to the Auckland orphanage in 1946, but several deaconesses and home missionaries were transferred into the city in the next few years.[326]

There was particular concern for young Māori moving to work in the towns, ill-equipped to deal with urban pressures. Like other denominations, they began to establish hostels. The first hostel was established in Hamilton in 1944, with Sister Heeni Wharemaru as matron.[327] Others followed in Auckland, Christchurch and New Plymouth.[328] In these hostels great care was taken to protect the young people (including Te Arikinui Dame Te Atairangikaahu the future Māori Queen) from the evils of Pākehā culture.[329]

The Post-War Crisis in Direction

The approach by the Mission was not applauded by all Methodists. A resolution from the floor in 1954 insisted that the policy of the church was that the Māori Mission should not expand out of its existing areas, or into the cities.[330] In 1955, commenting of the Annual Report of the Mission, and its warnings of racial tensions ahead, Rangi Rogers accused the Conference of excluding Māori from decision-making: "For years they have wholly adhered to top-level instructions, and I feel that now they should be given equal status with the Pakeha."[331] As a result conference ordered a special review for widespread discussion throughout the church and at the 1956 conference.[332] In this report, the policy was clarified, including this statement on urban Māori:

> That except in predominantly Maori areas, the Maori people be urged to link their family life with the nearest Pakeha Church for all their regular Church worship and Sunday School and Youth activities, in between these Maori visits. In suggesting this, it is recognised that there will be many difficulties to be overcome. There will be need for great patience and Christian grace on all sides. Groups of Maori folk, young or old, are more likely to feel reasonably at ease with pakehas, rather than one lonely individual. Hence it will be necessary to try to arrange gatherings where the Maori workers may bring and introduce the Maori folk to the combined gatherings. The aim is not making a Pakeha Church with Maoris in it, but a Christian Church with both races sharing and both races contributing to the content of the worship.[333]

These comments and the whole issue of how separate the Mission should be, awoke extensive debate in local synod meetings, many of which were alarmed at the funding issue.[334] By 1958 the Department was firmly committed to the integration of Māori in the towns into European circuits.[335] The Home and Māori Mission Department surveyed Māori Methodists in 1964. It found that 1253 families were identifiable, of which just 151 families lived outside of the Māori mission circuits. 598 Māori worshipped alongside Pākehā but most of these were in the mission districts where Pākehā and Māori numbers were similar. But only 128 Māori families were Methodist members in Pākehā circuits, and just 380 persons attended regularly. There were stronger results in Sunday School with 598 children enrolled.[336] This should have been a warning to the Church that the policy of integration had failed, but the alternative of creating Māori circuits in the towns was unpalatable.

The implications of this urbanisation were to undermine the impact of the mission. In the towns there was much weaker agency of the Māori home missionaries on the lives of the migrants, except where they remained resident in hostels. Out in the suburbs, the missionaries had limited access to the Māori diaspora, and the weakening of iwi loyalties there meant that the mission had little to offer to what had in effect become a Māori working class. The support provided by the mission proved of little value. Māori were forced to seek a new identity, in the face of a huge decline of identity.

Explaining this era

The achievements of the Home Mission Department in the inter-war years were impressive, given the lack of resources. Methodist Māori work survived and even grew significantly, especially in the King Country. As early as 1909 the conference noted "the indications of an upward movement amongst the Maoris" and urged all ministers within reach to hold services for them.[337] We cannot attribute the growth to Seamer alone. Certainly, Seamer's strategic sense was important, for he called for "a definite progressive policy".[338] The deaconesses also contributed significantly, by identifying Māori ministry as one of their main priorities.[339] The revival of this home mission paralleled the launch of a new foreign mission after Methodist union in 1913.

The state also changed its attitude to Māori in this era. The increase in Māori population is evident in the censuses of 1926 and 1936 (helped by the success of Sister Nellie's campaign that Māori births, deaths and marriages be registered).[340] Once it was established that Māori were not in decline, state interest was rekindled.

Methodism took advantage of the new movements in the Māori world after the First World War. These movements are evident in the religious world. Rātana is only one part of the renewed interest to Christianity. Piripi Rakena and Hapeta Renata described conversions in the Home Missions Report in 1919.[341] In the 1923 report to the conference, an account was given of the Spirit moving in "semi-heathen" districts, 47 adults baptised in one settlement, and 127 people who enlisted as catechumens on the path to church membership.[342] There was a proposal (which Seamer rejected) to send Val Trigge, an Australian employed as connexional evangelist to hold a mission among Māori.[343] Special evangelistic services were held in the three districts in 1922, leading many to Christian conversion.[344] These moves were separate from, although parallel to Rātana's ministry.

But in the end, the greatest contribution came from the activities of the home missionaries and native ministers. Almost invariably the honorary home missionaries are described in obituaries as rangatira or kaumātua within their local community, and they are often described as possessing knowledge of traditions and history (which would normally be the special interest of tohunga). The church regained respect, largely on account of the status of its local representatives. For example, Mātene Keepa was welcomed into the council of chiefs of Taihui, even though he was of Te Arawa descent.[345] Another case is Hori Kakuere "well versed in Maori lore and custom" according to his obituary.[346]

Robert Takapōtiki Haddon certainly helped. "Standing over 6 ft tall, erect as a spear, with flashing grey eyes set in a rugged yet kindly countenance, active and virile in every movement despite advancing years, Robert Haddon is a noble specimen of Maori manhood. He comes from a long line of chieftains which we understand can trace its descent back for over a millennium. [He] is himself a chief of high rank."[347] But I am profoundly impressed by the diligence and convictions of the cluster of home missionaries like Eruera Te Tuhi and the Rakenas, by Keepa and Kakuere, by Pihama and Tauroa. These men made a very distinctive mark on their communities.

The Influence of Māori Methodism

The collapse of the policy and the direction of Māori Methodism after World War Two is very evident, but prior to this, Māori Methodism had the potential of becoming an indigenous movement. In its open and unsectarian style, it enabled Māori of this era to make some sort of accommodation with Pākehā. Among its prominent leaders were men of the calibre of Maharia Winiata, and among its "by-products" were Paraire Paikea, who later served as representative of the Native Race in the First Labour Government, and Edward Oriwa Taupotiki Haddon, son of R.T. Haddon, who developed a name as educator, broadcaster, politician and artist.[348] He wrote eloquently in the Methodist newspaper about Māori aspirations, and the need to encourage their agricultural and industrial ventures.[349]

This story calls for more research. Especially in the Waikato and Maniatoto (King Country) circuits, Methodism found new and striking ways of ministering in its community. There is much more to learn of these people who were at once truly Māori and truly Methodist.

Notes

1 George Laurenson's *Te Hahi Weteriana: Three Half Centuries of the Methodist Māori Missions, 1822-1972*, WHS (NZ) Proceedings, 27, nos. 1-2, 1972; one of the 150th anniversary volumes published by the WHS (NZ), provides a chronological narrative with many personal asides, but it has no references and inevitably it has an internal perspective.

2 Donald Phillipps, Te Taha Maori Register of Home Missionaries, Honorary Home Missionaries and Minita-a Iwi [unpublished paper, c 2014]. This complements Phillipps, 'A Register of Ministers of the Methodist Church of New Zealand' (Methodist Church of New Zealand website, 2020) https://www.methodist.org.nz/assets/Whakapapa/Archives/4-Methodist-history/Methodist-Biography-A-Z-29-March-2021-with-introduction-corrected.pdf

3 See for example *Waipa Post*, 18 October 1924, 4 (Pihama translated by Seamer); *NZMT*, 26 July 1930, 7. (concerning Haddon).

4 For example, Te Āho o te Rangi Pihama at Stratford, *Stratford Evening Post*, 14 September 1928, 2.

5 Rua Rakena, *The Māori Response to the Gospel*, WHS (NZ) Proceedings, 25, nos. 1-4 1971, 2; citing J.G. Laughton, Māori and Pākehā: Race Relations in New Zealand, which has not been traced.

6 MAC, 1917, 95.

7 MAC, 1919, 100.

8 MAC, 1922, 135-36.

9 *New Zealand Herald*, 11 December 1903, 6.

10 MAC, 1913, appendix, lxiv.

11 MAC, 1937, 198.

12 Laurenson to Rakena, 29 March 1951; Box 22A; Seamer to Te Tuhi, 3 December 1938, Box XX; circular letter, (all in MCNZA).

13 Haddon explained this in *NZMT*, 26 July 1930, 7.

14 *NZMT*, 24 November 1934, 4.

15 MAC, 1923, 129.

16 MAC, 1933, 131.

17 MAC, 1922, 136.

18 *NZMT*, 24 November 1934, 4.

19 MAC, 1935. 128.

20 MAC, 1926, 114.

21 MAC, 1929, 121.

22 See Seamer to the Editor, *Te Awamutu Courier*, 4 March 1949, 5.

23 MAC, 1920, 17; MAC, 1927, 17-18.

24 Thomas Hammond, *'In the Beginning': the History of a Mission*, 1 ed. 1915; 2 ed., Auckland Methodist Literature & Colporteur Society, 1940.

25 Laurenson, *Te Hahi Weteriana*, 26, 50; MAC, 1937, 20.

26 *Auckland Star*, 8 December 1885, 2.

27 Ruawai D. Rakena. 'Seamer, Arthur John', DNZB, first published in 1998. Te Ara - the Encyclopedia of New Zealand, https://teara.govt.nz/en/biographies/4s18/seamer-arthur-john (accessed 17 January 2023).

28 *Waikato Times*, 5 March 1923, 2.

29 Ruawai D. Rakena. 'Seamer, Arthur John', DNZB.

30 See for example his talk to Matamata Methodist Church, *Matamata Record*, 3 December 1925, 4.

31 *Waikato Times*, 17 July 1923, 9.

32 *Taranaki Daily News*, 1 November 1932, 11.

33 Georgia Rae Cervin, 'Te Hiima: Reverend A. J. Seamer and His Māori Mission.' B.A. Honours, University of Otago, 2011, 41.

34 *Taranaki Daily News*, 6 December 1927, 11.

35 Seamer to R.D. Rakena, 5 December 1934, Box 22A [C101570]. (MCNZA).

36 Heeni Wharemaru and Mary Katherine Duffie, *Heeni, a Tainui Elder remembers*, Auckland: HarperCollins, 1997, 184-85.

37 MAC, 1926, 114.

38 Te Tuhi to Laurenson, 14 January 1938, MCNZA.

39 Henderson, *Ratana*, p. 16. (Henderson's reference 'Rev. A.J. Seamer, Minutes of Conference of the Australasian Methodist Churches 1921-25' is incorrect (for the church was the New Zealand Methodist Church by then) and is probably a reference to MAC, 1922, 137.

40 MAC, 1926, 114. See Garth Cant, *The Methodist Response to the Formation of the Ratana Church in 1924-1925*. WHS (NZ) Proceedings, 104, 2018 and Garth Cant, 'The Methodist and Ratana Connection.' *WHS (NZ) Journal*, 100 (2015): 31-42

41 MB 1925-1935, 8 (MCNZA).

42 For Dunedin, see *Waikato Times*, 7 June 1927, 11.

43 See MAC, 1925, p.115. See also H. L. J. Halliday, 'The Reverend A.J. Seamer and the Attitudes of the Methodists to the Ratana Movement.' Research Essay, University of Auckland, 1966.

44 *Waikato Times*, 7 June 1927, 11

45 See Henderson, J. M. *Ratana: The Man, the Church, the Political Movement*. Polynesian Society Memoir. 2 ed. Wellington: A.H. & A.W. Reed and the Polynesian Society, 1963, 34-35; 50-54. The school was in a small house, subsequently staffed by a deaconess., See Maoe and Māori Mission Board MB 1925-1935, 9 in 9312 folder 2 (MCNZA).

46 *New Zealand Herald*, 23 March 1922, 7.

47 Seamer to Rakena, 5 December 1934 (MCNZA).

48 Te Tuhi to Seamer, 31 October 1938 (MCNZA).

49 See Henderson, 51-52.

50 Angela Ballara. 'Hākaraia, Ngāpiki - Hakaraia, Ngāpiki', DNZB, first published in 1998. Te Ara - the Encyclopedia of New Zealand, https://teara.govt.nz/en/biographies/4h3/hakaraia-ngapiki (accessed 6 January 2023).

51 MAC, 1923, 128, 158.

52 MAC, 1958, 147. NLMZ photography collection: Tesla Studies 1/1-017026-F (1924) [Ratana World Tour group]; and Turnbull PAColl-0240-01: Nichols, James Keith, 1909-1972: Photographs and postcards: Waiata Choir.

53 Phillipps, Methodist list. MB 1925-1935, 27, 9 February 1926 and ibid, 56, 25 February 1927. (MCNZA).

54 See his obituary in MAC 1939, 18. See also Seamer to R. Eru and Te Tuhi, 29 August 1938, (MCNZA). Also *New Zealand Herald*, 3 September 1938, 14. For the abortion case see *Auckland Star*, 22 September 1909, 3; *New Zealand Herald*, 29 November 1909, 7.

55 Laurenson to Rakena, 29 March 1951 (MCNZA).

56 Angela Ballara. 'Hākaraia, Ngāpiki - Hakaraia, Ngāpiki', DNZB. Curiously there is no reference to Methodism or to Hakaraia in Karen Sinclair, *Prophetic Histories: the People of the Māramatanga*. Wellington: Bridget Williams Books, 2002.

57 Phillipps, Maori list.

58 Two typed up resolutions concerning Rangi Rogers and Methodists on the Chaplaincy were issued in 1940 (probably with the strong support of Laurenson, the new General superintendent). Te Tuhi papers 1935-1949, (MCNZA).

59 Seamer to Rakena, 1 December 1936. Rakena Files, Box 22A, (MCNZA).

60 See Board Minute book, 24 July 1929, p. 124 section D (MCNZA).

61 Laurenson to Te Tuhi, 21 October 1943; Supplementary Report to 1944 Conference in 1944 Emergency Committee, pp. 135-36. See Laurenson, *Te Hahi Weteriana*, 238.

62 I have not had opportunity to consult his papers (MS-1187 in MCNZA). But see [Darvill] to Te Tuhi, 13 August 1957 (Te Tuhi files, MCNZA) for an indication of his approach.

63 MAC, 1945, 128; MAC, 1946, 143.

64 Margaret Tennant, 'Pakeha Deaconesses and the New Zealand Methodist Mission to Maori, 1893-1940.' *JRH*, 23, no. 3 (October 1999): 309-26.

65 See Section 7 of 'Maori Work', MB 1925-35, Report to Board, 25 June 1934. (MCNZA).

66 Marcia Baker, *For Others with Love: A Story of Early Sisters and Methodist Deaconesses*. Christchurch: Baker Family Trust, 2007, 62-67.

67 Wesley Chambers, *Not Self - but Others: The Story of the Methodist Deaconess Order Together with an Index of All Those Who Have Served in It*. WHS (NZ) Proceedings, 48, 1987, 87.

68 MAC, 1923, 132.

69 Annual Report (Draft in MB, 1926, pasted into pp. 41-42); see also MAC, 1927, 131.

70 *NZMT*, 23 May 1925, 3 has a description of Sister Nicholls' work. *NZMT*, 22 March 1930, 3 has an account of another deaconess's daily routines.

71 See Sister Nicholls' account in *NZMT*, 28 August 1926, 3.

72 MAC, 1934, 137.

73 *NZMT*, 26 October 1935, 4.

74 Margaret Tennant, '"Sometimes When My Heart Was Sad with Snubs and Coldness ..." Narrative of Maori Mission Work.' *History Now: Te Pae Tawhito o te Wa* 7, no. 3 (August 2001), 14-18.

75 See M. Baker, *For Others with Love*, 121-124.

76 *Heeni: A Tainui Elder Remembers*, 1997.

77 *Memoirs of D. M. Pointon (Sister Dorothy) including her Work among the Maori People 1939-1953.* Auckland: The author, 1993.

78 *Te Ope Whakeora: the army that brings life*, ed. Harold Hill, Flag Publications, 2007, 39, 41, 72.

79 Chambers, *Not Self*, 51.

80 See M. Baker, *For Others with Love*, 106-116.

81 See Methodist list; Chambers, *Not Self*, 65-66; M. Baker, *For Others with Love*, 164-65.

82 See M. Baker, *For Others with Love*, 137-139.

83 See the obituary in MAC, 1992, 404.

84 Patricia A. Sargison. 'Hei, Ākenehi', DNZB, first published in 1996. Te Ara - the Encyclopedia of New Zealand, https://teara.govt.nz/en/biographies/3h13/hei-akenehi (accessed 15 March 2023)

85 M. Baker, *For Others with Love*, 64.

86 Chambers, *Not Self*, 145.

87 See Ruth Fry, *Out of the Silence: Methodist Women of Aotearoa 1822-1985*, Christchurch: Methodist Publishing, 1987, 108-109.

88 See the comments in 'E. Te Tuhi's Northern Tour' [1940] in E Te Tuhi files (MCNZA).

89 Margaret Tennant, 'Sisterly Ministrations: the Social Work of Protestant Deaconesses in New Zealand.' *NZJH*, 32, no. 1 (April 1998): 3-22.

90 Lachy Paterson, 'The Rise and Fall of Women Field Workers within the Presbyterian Maori Mission, 1907-1970.' Chap. 9 In *Mana Maori and Christianity*, edited by Hugh Morrison, Lachy Paterson, Brett Knowles and Murray Rae, Wellington: Huia Books, 2012, 179-204.

91 For example, see Seamer to Nicholls, 10 January 1939 (Nicholls files, MCNZA). In the preaching plans, a few deaconesses are listed to preach in Auckland and Hamilton and latterly in New Plymouth, including Sister Ivy, Sister Rita [Snowden] and Sister Marara Kawiti, Heeni Wharemaru. They are not listed to preach on marae. (See the 1939 and 1940 plans in the Te Tuhi files, MCNZA).

92 Report [from Māori Workers Meeting, January 1941] in Box D25 Te Tuhi 1936-1945. (MCNZA).

93 Angela Ballara. 'Haddon, Robert Tahupōtiki', DNZB, first published in 1996, updated June 2015. Te Ara - the Encyclopedia of New Zealand, https://teara.govt.nz/en/biographies/3h1/haddon-robert-tahupotiki (accessed 16 January 2023). See Annual Report of Māori Mission, in MAC 1927, 130.

94 MB 1925-1935, p. 192 (Meeting of 15 August 1932); Seamer to Rakena, 5 December 1934, Box 22A; also Nicholls to Seamer, 23 April 1934. (Nicholls files) (MCNZA).

95 MAC, 1934, 18.

96 MAC, 1953, 22; MAC, 1976, 40. Laurenson to [Fiebig] Connexional Secretary, 13 March 1950; Fiebig to Laurenson, 17 October 1950 (MCNZA).

97 E. Te Tuhi (Rewiti, Auckland) to Defence Minister, 19 July 1915 R22434278, Archives New Zealand.

98 MAC, 1976, 40.

99 Te Tuhi to Seamer [or Laurenson] 6 December 1938, Te Tuhi 1936-1945 Box D25 (MCNZA).

100 See Laurenson to Te Tuhi, 14 August 1957 (MCNZA).

101 MAC, 1959, 155-156.

102 H. A. H. Insull, *The Wesley College Register 1844-1974*. Auckland: Wesley College Old Boys Association, 1974, 133.

103 MAC, 1956, 24.

104 Phillipps, Methodist list. See *Taranaki Daily News*, 7 May 1918, 4; *Wanganui Herald*, 22 May 1918, 8; *Feilding Star*, 4 October 1919, 2.

105 Peter J. Lineham. 'Haddon, Ōriwa Tahupōtiki', DNZB, first published in 1998. Te Ara - the Encyclopedia of New Zealand, https://teara.govt.nz/en/biographies/4h2/haddon-oriwa-tahupotiki (accessed 20 January 2023).

106 *New Zealand Herald*, 27 February 1943, 8.

107 Report of Māori Workers, c 1940 (handwritten and typed) in Te Tuhi papers (MCNZA).

108 Te Tuhi to Laurenson, 12 September 1941. See also Te Tuhi to Laurenson, 2 September 1941, Both in Te Tuhi 1935-44 files (MCNZA).

109 There is a delightful description in *Heeni, A Tainui Elder remembers*, 100-103.

110 Frances Winiata and Piripi Winiata. 'Winiata, Maharaia', DNZB, first published in 2000. Te Ara - the Encyclopedia of New Zealand, https://teara.govt.nz/en/biographies/5w41/winiata-maharaia (accessed 6 January 2023).

111 MAC, 1944, 132.

112 I place the origins of home missionaries earlier than Phillipps does in his list of Māori home missionaries (see his introduction, unnumbered) since the terminology is in use in MAC, 1913, 62.

113 *Auckland Star*, 17 April 1920, 18. See MAC, 1939, 18 for his obituary, and for a draft, see Seamer to E. Te Tuhi, 29/8/1938 (MCNZA).

114 See Phillipps' list for a discussion of this case. MAC, 1923, 128.

115 See MAC, 1946, 20.

116 'Māori Work' position paper, no. 6, report, 25 June 1934, enclosed in MB, 1925-1935, (MCNZA).

117 Seamer to Pihama 1 September 1938. See also Seamer to Pihama, 24 March 1934, (Box D22 MCNZA).

118 MAC, 1922, 139.

119 MAC 1933, 112; MB 1925-1935, 296 (Meeting of 26 September 1933) (MCNZA).

120 MAC, 1929, 122; Seamer to Pihama, 24 March 1934, (Pihama files, Box D22 MCNZA).

121 MAC, 1923, p. 127.

122 MAC, 1932, p. 111.

123 *NZMT*, 2 March 1935, 4.

124 MAC, 1944, 132.

125 Laurenson to Te Tuhi, 4 September 1942 (MCNZA).

126 For example, Te Urupa Wetere, Laurenson to Te Tuhi, 21 January 1959 (MCNZA).

127 MAC, 1952, 126.

128 MAC, 1917, Appendix, 24.

129 For example, Te Tuhi to Laurenson, 14 March 1938; Te Tuhi to Laurenson, 22 March 1938; Te Tuhi to Seamer, 27 June 1938; Te Tuhi to Laurenson, 29 May 1941; Te Tuhi to Laurenson, 28 March 1944. (MCNZA)

130 Te Tuhi to Laurenson, 4 February 1938; Te Tuhi to Seamer, 31 October 1938 (MCNZA).

131 MAC, 1929, 122.

132 *King Country Chronicle*, 27 November 1934, 5; *NZMT*, 24 November 1934, 4.

133 *NZMT*, 2 September 1933, 5.

134 *Otago Witness*, 5 April 1900, 19.

135 Memorial note [1956], in Rakena files, Box D22A (MCNZA).

136 MAC, 1913, 66; MAC, 1922, 137; MAC, 1930, 51.

137 MAC, 1929, 123. 'The Māori Work', *NZMT*, 24 January 1931, supplement, 4.

138 MAC, 1931, 132; MAC, 1936, 130; MAC, 1946, 144.

139 Seamer to Te Tuhi, 3 December 1938; Te Tuhi to Laurenson, 10 March 1943; Te Tuhi to Laurenson, 16 November 1945. (MCNZA)

140 M. Baker, *To Others with Love*, 125-126. See Chambers, *Not Self*, 44.

141 MAC, 1940, 176-77; MAC, 1941, 146.

142 MAC, 1949, 123. MAC, 1950, 125.

143 https://northlandhistory.blogspot.com/2018/11/omanaia-historical-church.html

144 *Northern Advocate*, 11 February 1930, 4.

145 *NZMT*, 24 January 1931, 8; *NZMT*, 2 May 1931, 3.

146 *NZMT*, 2 May 1931, 3.

147 MAC, 1952, 128.

148 See Angela Ballara. 'Tōia, Hōne Riiwi', DNZB, first published in 1993. Te Ara - the Encyclopedia of New Zealand, https://teara.govt.nz/en/biographies/2t45/toia-hone-riiwi (accessed 15 March 2023). Also see Judy Ward, The Invention of Papahurihia, PhD thesis, Massey University, 2015, 313-327.

149 MAC, 1914, 32.

150 MAC, 1930, p. 15.

151 Te Tuhi to Laurensons, 11 June 1942.

152 Kene Hine Te Uira Martin. 'Kawiti, Kirihi Te Riri Maihi', DNZB, first published in 1998. Te Ara - the Encyclopedia of New Zealand, https://teara.govt.nz/en/biographies/4k4/kawiti-kirihi-te-riri-maihi/sources (accessed 10 April 2023). General Superintendent to Te Tuhi, 3 April 1956 (MCNZA).

153 Chambers, *Not Self*, 123.

154 *NZMT*, 26 November 1932, 16.

155 *Advocate*, 5 November 1901, 263.

156 Florence Harsant, *They called me Te Maari*, Christchurch: Whitcoulls, 1979, 107-108.

157 *New Zealand Herald*, 11 December 1903, 6.

158 MAC, 1915, 36.

159 MAC, 1915, 46; MAC, 1916, 46; MAC, 1917, 45. MAC, 1918, 80. (The latter reference is puzzling, as it implies he is in the King Country.)

160 *Lyttelton Times*, 8 March 1915, 11.

161 Chambers, *Not Self*, 123.

162 See Te Tuhi to Laurenson, 14 January 1938 (MCNZA).

163 *Waikato Independent*, 25 November 1924, 5.

164 *Advocate*, 5 November 1901, 262.

165 See Harsant, *They called me Te Maari*, 82-83.

166 Chambers, *Not Self*, p. 123.

167 https://www.heritage.org.nz/list-details/460/Listing.

168 MAC, 1924, 20.

169 *Taranaki Daily News*, 3 October 1917, 8.

170 See T.G. Hammond, *"In the Beginning"*, 41.

171 *Hawera Star*, 24 March 1931, 8.

172 Rakena to Laurenson, 6 July 1947 (MCNZA).

173 *Hawera & Normanby Star*, 12 April 1912, 7.

174 MB, Report to Board, 25 June 1934, 'Assistant Superintendent' (MCNZA).

175 *NZMT*, 30 December 1939, 13.

176 There are only passing references to Wesleyans in H.E.R.L. Wiley, *South Auckland*, Pukekohe: Franklin Printing & Publishing Co, 1939, 223, 246-47, and a brief reference in *Pukekawa Profile 1839-1970: a Tribute to our Pioneers* Pukekohe, [Alpine Printers] 1970, unpaginated.

177 *Northern Advocate*, 23 August 1938, 6.

178 MAC, 1937, 100.

179 *NZMT*, 26 November 1932, 16.

180 MAC, 1931, 132.

181 Angeline Greensill and Hineitimoana Greensill. 'Rickard, Tuaiwa Hautai Kereopa (Eva)', DNZB, first published in 2018. Te Ara - the Encyclopedia of New Zealand, https://teara.govt.nz/en/biographies/6r4/rickard-tuaiwa-hautai-kereopa (accessed 5 August 2024).

182 See his brief contribution 'Learning and Tapu' in *Te Ao Hurihuri: Aspects of Māoritanga*. Edited by Michael King, Wellington: Hicks Smith & Methuen NZ, 1975, and reprint, Wellington: Reed, 1992, 9.

183 *Advocate*, 5 November 1901, 263. For details, see Robin Astridge, *A Brief Outline of Wesleyan Mission Stations in the Waikato, New Zealand*, https://barretthoneyfield.com/wp-content/uploads/2015/08/waikato-wesleyan-missions1.pdf, 2013, 9-10.

184 See *Te Awamutu Courier*, 15 January 1937, 7 which commemorates the Te Kopua Native school, but has many references to the continuing Methodist presence.

185 MAC, 1954, 20.

186 He was registered as a minister in *New Zealand Gazette* no. 25, 1961, 560.

187 MAC, 1945, 125. *Heeni: a Tainui Elder remembers*, 119-141, 157-191.

188 M. J. Ormsby. 'Ormsby, John', *Dictionary of New Zealand Biography*, first published in 1993, updated November 2001. Te Ara - the Encyclopedia of New Zealand, https://teara.govt.nz/en/biographies/2o8/ormsby-john (accessed 15 March 2023).

189 See Alexandra: St Saviour's. *Church Gazette*, March 1875, 29.

190 See his obituary in *Kawhia Settler and Raglan Advertiser*, 17 June 1927, 2. See also *King Country Chronicle*, 21 June 1927, 5.

191 *NZMT*, 26 November 1932, 16.

192 Laurenson to John Nicholls, 3 March 1943, Nicholls file, Box D21, (MCNZA).

193 MAC, 1918, 80; MAC, 1919, 94.

194 *King Country Chronicle*, 27 November 1934, 5.

195 MAC, 1951, 20.

196 *Waipa Post*, 21 October 1924, 5.

197 See Alan Leadley, *A Brief History of the Kawhia Methodist Mission, 1834-1994*. Hamilton: Waikato-Bay of Plenty Bicultural Working Group, 1994.

198 *NZMT*, 19 November 1934, 11; ibid, 24 November 1934, 4.

199 *NZMT*, 22 December 1934, 2.

200 Te Tuhi to Seamer, 17 June 1938 (MCNZA).

201 MAC, 1952, 20.

202 See MAC, 1948, p. 19; Astridge, *Wesleyan Mission Stations*, 11-12.

203 *Auckland Star*, 14 December 1895. 2.

204 *New Zealand Herald*, 27 February 1922, 8.

205 Gary Scott. 'Te Awa-i-taia, Wiremu Nēra', DNZB, first published in 1990. Te Ara - the Encyclopedia of New Zealand, https://teara.govt.nz/en/biographies/1t26/te-awa-i-taia-wiremu-nera (accessed 16 January 2023).

206 *Stratford Evening Post*, 14 September 1928, 2; *Evening Post*, 10 September 1928, 8.

207 See https://ancestors.familysearch.org/en/KZQT-LDV/te-ahooterangi-pihama-1874-1952

208 MAC, 1952, 19; For Pihama in full flight of oratory, see *Taranaki Daily News*, 1 November 1932, 11.

209 *Franklin Times*, 4 September 1936, 4; *Franklin Times*, 14 April 1937, 4; *NZMT*, 22 May 1937, 4; *New Zealand Herald*, 1 September 1936, 12.

210 John Nicholls (Te Kuiti) to Seamer, 25 May 1936, Nicholls Correspondence, Box D21 (MCNZA).

211 MAC, 1966, 21.

212 See MAC,1986, 414; Laurenson, *Te Hahi Weteriana*, 233.

213 See Phillipps, Methodist ministers list.

214 Phillipps, Methodist ministers list; MAC, 1930, 38; MAC, 1934, 178; *Northern Advocate*, 23 August 1938, 6.

215 MAC, 1931, 132.

216 *New Zealand Herald*, 22 September 1927, 13; *NZMT*, 28 October 1933, 7.

217 *New Zealand Herald*, 9 October 1933, 10.

218 See Phillipps Maori Ministers List, The Blain biographical directory of Anglican clergy in the South Pacific (online at Project Canterbury); MAC 1942, 18. *Waikato Times*, 20 June 1941, 6.

219 *King Country Chronicle*, 27 November 1934, 5.

220 Cervin, 'Te Hiima', 46.

221 *NZMT*, 22 July 1933, 3.

222 Te Tuhi to Seamer, 19 December 1938 (MCNZA).

223 Laurenson to Te Tuhi, 2 March 1938, and Te Tuhi to Laurenson, 5 March 1938 in Te Tuhi files (MCNZA).

224 Te Tuhi to Laurenson, 10 April 1938 (MCNZA).

225 *Heeni, A Tainui Elder remembers*, 119-120, 130-134.

226 *New Zealand Herald*, 5 October 1936, 10.

227 MAC, 1942, 141; MAC, 1948, 136; *NZMT*, 27 September 1947, 4; Laurenson to Te Tuhi, 28 April 1947 (MCNZA).

228 Michael King, *Te Puea*, Auckland: Hodder 7 Stoughton, 1987, 175-77; MAC, 1930, 38; *Sun* (Auckland), 19 September 1927, 17 has a photograph of him as 'one of Te Puea's stalwarts'.

229 MAC, 1946, 144.

230 See Phillipps Māori List. See also *Heeni: A Tainui Elder remembers*, 134.

231 MAC, 1953, 21.

232 MAC, 1952, 129.

233 MAC, 1954, 20.

234 *Waikato Independent*, 25 October 1928, 5.

235 See Blain and Phillipps lists.

236 *New Zealand Herald*, 4 September 1926, 14.

237 *Waihi Daily Telegraph*, 1 November 1925, 2. See the Blain and Phillipps biographical indices.

238 MAC, 1942, 18.

239 T.T. Poihipi to Te Tuhi, 10 February 1941 and Te Tuhi to Laurenson, 21 May 1941. (MCNZA)

240 He is listed in Blain's list, the Presbyterian Register, and for Ratana, see J.M. Henderson, *Ratana: the Man the Church, the Political Movement*, 80. In my report for the Waitangi Tribunal on the chaplains of the 28th Battalion I detail his eagerness in 1916 and his determination to enter the chaplaincy in 1946 from Army files.

241 *Franklin Times*, 4 September 1936, 4.

242 *New Zealand Herald*, 5 September 1935, 14; *Auckland Star*, 16 July 1936, 8; *New Zealand Herald*, 8 July 1939, 17.

243 See Te Tuhi to Laurenson, 1 December 1937; Te Tuhi to Laurenson, 15 October 1941.Te Tuhi to Laurenson, 28 February 1943 (MCNZA).

244 Te Tuhi to Laurenson, 4 February 1938 in Te Tuhi Files (MCNZA).

245 Laurenson to Te Tuhi, Seamer, et al, 9 October 1944; Laurenson to Te Tuhi, 13 November 1944 (all in Te Tuhi files, D25); Te Tuhi to Laurenson, 15 January 1954 in Te Tuhi files, D26 (MCNZA).

246 Te Tuhi to Laurenson, 12 June 1946 (MCNZA).

247 MAC, 1933, 131.

248 Laurenson to Rakena, 21 April 1944; Rakena to Laurenson, 4 July 1847; M.G. Milmine to Laurenson, 25 March 1947 (in Rakena files); Te Tuhi to Seamer, 21 October 1938 in Te Tuhi papers 1935-1945, D25; Te Tuhi to Laurenson, 28 May 1948, Te Tuhi files D26 (all in MCNZA).

249 Riri Kawiti to Laurenson [n.d.] and Laurenson to Kawiti, 7 December 1959. In Te Tuhi Files, 1955-1966, in D26. See Brett Knowles, *The History of a New Zealand Pentecostal Movement: the New Life Churches of New Zealand from 1946 to 1979*. Lewistown: Edwin Mellen Press, 57, 298-99.

250 MAC, 1946, 210-211.

251 MAC, 1932, 111.

252 See for example *New Zealand Herald*, 23 March 1922, 7 and some Māori usage for example *Hawera Star*, 23 February 1929, 11. The term 'Te Hahi Metoriti' was occasionally used. See the comments about Ratana in MAC, 1926, 115.

253 Rakena, *The Māori Response*, 5.

254 *Northern Advocate*, 20 July 1944, 2.

255 See the Māori Mission Report in MAC, 1923, 136-37.

256 Rakena, *The Māori response*, v.

257 No copies of the earlier title seem to be held by public libraries. The latter is held by Auckland War Memorial Museum and NLNZ.

258 MAC 1956, 140-141.

259 For example, *Auckland Star*, 14 July 1936, 10 and their statement critical of the Bishop of Waikato, *Auckland Star*, 16 July 1936, 8.

260 *Te Awamutu Courier*, 31 July 1936, 7.

261 *New Zealand Herald*, 27 February 1922, 8.

262 See *New Zealand Herald*, 27 February 1922, 8.

263 For example, *Stratford Evening Post*, 14 September 1928, 2.

264 MAC, 1922, 137

265 *Waikato Independent*, 25 October 1928, 5.

266 *Waikato Times*, 22 October 1928, 6.

267 MAC 1941, 124. See also MAC, 1944, 131.

268 *Waipa Post*, 28 May 1929, 3.

269 MAC, 1956, 145 (1).

270 *NZMT*, 22 March 1930, 3.

271 Auckland Star, 11 March 1912, 2. Chambers, *Not Self*, 87.

272 MAC, 1938, 135.

273 *NZMT*, 21 January 1933, 3.

274 *Auckland Star*, 27 February 1934, 3.

275 See Sister Frances Hayman's report from Kawhia, *NZMT*, 26 November 1932, 16.

276 *King Country Chronicle*, 12 November 1923, 5.

277 *King Country Chronicle*, 7 December 1929, 4.

278 *Auckland Star*, 31 July 1936, 8.

279 *Lyttelton Times*, 8 March 1915, 11.

280 Laurenson to Te Tuhi, 8 August 1940; Laurenson to Te Tuhi, 16 August 1940. (MCNZA).

281 MAC, 1923, 129

282 See the letters in *Te Awamutu Courier*, 4 March 1949, 5.

283 *NZMT*, 31 July 1926, 16; *ibid*, 28 August 1926, 9.

284 See MAC, 1923, 129.

285 *New Zealand Herald*, 9 November 1934, 10.

286 Te Tuhi to Laurenson, 21 May 1941. (MCNZA).

287 *Auckland Star*, 12 June 1945, 6.

288 *Press*, 17 December 1952, 9; ibid, 16 November 1953, 11.

289 MAC 1950, appendix..

290 MAC,1956, 140-145.

291 H. A. H. Insull, 'The Three Kings Native Institution.' *Journal Auckland & Waikato Historical Societies*, no. 25 (October 1974): 32-36.

292 MAC, 1918, 86.

293 MB, 1925-1935 p. 128 (Meeting of 24 July 1929). (MCNZA).

294 *Heeni: a Tainui Elder remembers*, 87.

295 MAC, 1932, 100. See MAC, 1934, 145; *Taranaki Daily News*, 9 March 1931, 9.

296 MAC, 1922, 138.

297 Chambers, *Not Self*, 48.

298 *Auckland Star*, 21 September 1937, 13. *NZMT*, 30 December 1939, 2.

299 MAC, 1936, 249.

300 Insull, *The Wesley College Register 1844-1974* is an invaluable source.

301 MAC, 1913, appendix.

302 MAC, 1956, 145.

303 *New Zealand Methodist Times*, 25 April 1936, 4, has details.

304 MAC, 1921, appendix.

305 MAC, 1933, 131.

306 Te Tuhi to Laurenson, 27 October 1943. (MCNZA)

307 *Auckland Star*, 28 September 1929, 31; MAC, 1935, appendix (Home Mission financial statements and estimates were always appended at the back of the Conference reports.) Chrystall to Rakena, 2 March 1953. (D22A) (MCNZA).

308 See MAC, 1956, 145 and the conference resolution, ibid, 148.

309 Circular (in Māori and in English) 1940 in Te Tuhi correspondence, 1935-1949. (MCNZA)

310 For example, *Waipa Post*, 18 October 1924, 4.

311 See Spencer Ratcliffe, 'The average minister's greatest problem', *NZMT*, 3 July 1926, 6. Michelle Willyams, 'Singing Faith: A History of the Waiata Maori Choir, 1924-1938.' Master of Arts thesis, University of Otago, 2012, 38-49.

312 See Michelle Walker, 'The Methodist Home Mission Party, on Stage in New Zealand, 1924–1934.' *Journal of New Zealand Studies*, no. 15 (2013): 77-89.

313 M. Baker, *For others with love*, p. 113. See 'Assistant Superintendent', report to Board, 25 June 1934, in MB (MCNZA).

314 See Cervin, 'Te Hiima', 38.

315 Chambers, *Not Self*, 77.

316 *Waikato Times*, 14 May 1938, 9.

317 *NZMT*, 23 November 1935, 3. See MB 5 November 1935, 364. (MCNZA).

318 MAC, 1952, 19.

319 *New Zealand Herald*, 10 October 1928, 9; *ibid*, 12 December 1931, 21.

320 *Auckland Star*, 15 January 1943, 5.

321 *Heeni: a Tainui Elder remembers*, 99.

322 MAC, 1948, 137-38.

323 MAC,1951, 131.

324 MAC, 1942, 139-140; MAC, 1948, 137-138.

325 MAC, 1944, 132.

326 Chambers, *Not Self*, 47.

327 *Waikato Times*, 19 October 1944, 4.

328 Claire Kaahu White, *Te Pou Herenga Waka O Rehua: The Story of Rehua Hostel and Marae - the First Fifty Years*. Christchurch: Te Whatumanawa, Maoritanga O Rehua Trust Board, 2021.

329 See *Heeni: a Tainui Elder remembers*, 122-125.

330 MAC, 1954, 129, resolution 5. For context see *Press*, 10 November 1954, 12.

331 Press, 10 November 1955, 15.

332 MAC, 1955, 132.

333 MAC, 1956, 146.

334 MAC, 1956, supplementary report (in response to the synods which preceded the conference), 147-149; *Press*, 30 August 1956, 6.

335 MAC, 1958, 147.

336 MAC, 1965, 193, with additional comments in Rakena, *The Maori Response*, 4.

337 *New Zealand Herald*, 3 March 1909, 8.

338 *New Zealand Herald*, 25 November 1921, 5.

339 *Taranaki Daily News*, 7 March 1914, 3.

340 See for example *New Zealand Herald*, 9 September 1921, 5 (which cited Seamer).

341 MAC, 1919, 94.

342 MAC, 1923, 127.

343 MAC, 1921, 56.

344 MAC, 1922, 131.

345 MAC, 1942. 18.

346 MAC, 1939, 18.

347 *NZMT*, 28 September 1935, 169.

348 Peter J. Lineham. 'Haddon, Ōriwa Tahupōtiki', DNZB, first published in 1998. Te Ara - the Encyclopedia of New Zealand, https://teara.govt.nz/en/biographies/4h2/haddon-oriwa-tahupotiki (accessed 4 September 2024).

349 Oliver Haddon, "A Maori Review", *NZMT*, 24 January 1931, 9-10.

Appendices

Appendix 1 – Alphabetical Record of Wesleyan Missionaries to 1855

Gary Clover

A bibliography is attached for each named person. For details of clergy, consult Donald Phillipps A Register of Ministers of The Methodist Church of New Zealand, online at the Methodist Church website. This is an expansion of Donald Phillipps, *Companion to William Morley's History of Methodism in New Zealand: A Guide to Nineteenth Century New Zealand Methodism*. Auckland: Wesley Historical Society, 2006. At the end of this list, the names of employed agents and Māori catechists and ministers are listed with some biographical data.

Missionaries

Aldred, John: Born 1818. Arrived on the Triton 7 May 1840, with Buddle, Buttle, Smales, Turton. Served Te Āro Pā 1840-1843. Thereafter European stations including Nelson, Hutt, Christchurch. Ordained 1844. Married Mary Lawry, 1849. Died Christchurch 1894.

McClintock, A.H., ed, *An Encyclopedia of NZ,* Vol.1 (1966), 30-31, also online.

Morley, 82-4, 88, 331-32, 376.

Pratt, M.A. Rugby, *Nelson Methodist Centenary,* 'The Story of the Methodist Church', 8-9.

Roberts, John H., 'The Wesleyan Maori Mission at Te Aro', *WHS (NZ) Journal,* 95 (1990): 14-49.

Scholefield, G.H. ed., *DNZB.* 1940, I. 9.

Buddle, Thomas: Born Durham, 1812, Ordained 1839. Arrived with Aldred, Buttle, Smales, Turton on the Triton, 7 May 1840. Hokianga, Te Kōpua (1840-45), Auckland. Grafton Institution (1845-1849), Oversight of Māori missions 1849-1854. Later European circuits. Retired 1882. Married Sarah Dixon 1839. Died Auckland 1883.

Glen. Frank, 'Buddle, Thomas', *DNZB*, 1990, also available online.

McLintock, A.H, *An Encyclopedia of New Zealand*, I.268-9.

Morley, 83, 86-92, 96, 201-203.

Rev. Thomas and Mrs Buddle, Pioneer Missionaries to New Zealand 1840-1884: A Tribute to their Memory by their Descendants, by a 'Grandaughter', Methodist Literature and Colporteur Society, 7 May 1940. (available online)

Scholefield, G.H. ed, *DNZB.* 1940, I. 115-16.

Buller, James: Born 6 December 1812 at Helston, Cornwall; father a Baptist deacon; converted at 20; pre-missionary occupation teacher; married Jane Tonkin Martin, 1835; arr. NZ 27 April 1836, aged 24; served as lay missionary tutor; received into full connexion October 1837; served at Māngungu, & Tangiteroria; left mission 1854; thereafter worked among Europeans; died 6 November 1884, aged 72.

Gadd, Bernard, *The Rev James Buller 1812-1884* WHS (NZ) Proceedings, 23, nos. 1-2, 1966.

Morley, 74-75.

Scholefield, G.H. ed., *DNZB*. 1940, I. 118.

Bumby, John Hewgill: Born 17 November 1808 at Thirsk, Yorkshire; parents in Wesleyan ministry; converted at 15; educated at an Academy in Leeds; ordained 1834; arr. NZ 18 March 1839, aged 31 on *James*; Chairman at Māngungu; toured North Island 1839; drowned 26 June 1840 in the Hauraki Gulf, aged 32.

Barrett, Alfred, *The Life of The Rev John Hewgill Bumby: With a Brief History of the Commencement and Progress of the Wesleyan Mission in New Zealand*. London, John Mason, 1852.

Morley, 75-76, 78, 85-86.

Scholefield, G.H. ed., *DNZB*. 1940, I. 119.

Whyle, Ivan, 'By a Mysterious Providence', WHS (NZ) Proceedings, 56, 1990, 65-73

Buttle, George: Born Yorkshire 1810, arrived with Aldred, Buddle, Smales, Turton on the Triton on 7 May 1840 as a probationer. Ordained 1843. Served Kāwhia & Mōkau, 1840-1845, then Waipa, Te Kauri 1845-57. Returned to England, returned to New Zealand 1862. Wife Jane Newman died 1857; remarried her sister Mehetabel Newman 1865. Died Mangere, 1874.

Buttle, Richard N., *Te Kopua: the story of George and Jane Buttle*. Auckland: R. N. Buttle, 2007.

Elliott, Gabriel, *Miller of Wakatumutumu: Sowing the Seed in Pioneer New Zealand*, WHS (NZ) Proceedings, 16, no.5, 1959.

Morley, 83-84 & 88.

Creed, Charles: Born 8 October 1812, at Hembridge Farm, Somerset; parents COE; converted at 18; pre-missionary occupation farmer; educated Hoxton Theological Institution, ordained 1837; arr. NZ 18 March 1839, aged 27, on the *James*; served in Hokianga, Kaipara, New Plymouth, & Waikouaiti (North Otago); left NZ mission 1852; served in Australia; retired 1867; died February 1879, aged 67. Married Eliza Harris.

Morley, 75-76, 86, 97.

McClintock, A.H., ed, *An Encyclopedia of New Zealand*, 1 (1966), 407, 'Creed, Charles (1812-79); &, https://teara.govt.nz/en/1966/aldred-john.

Paine, Frank, 'Charles Creed: Intrepid Traveller', in *WHS (NZ) Journal* (2005): 30-37.

Scholefield, G.H. ed., *DNZB*. 1940, I. 182-83.

Fletcher, Joseph Horner: Born West Indies, 1823. Probationer, 1848. Arrived 1849. Headmaster, Wesley College 1850-1855. New Plymouth, then Australian circuits and high positions. Died Sydney, 1890. Married Kathrine Green, 1848.

> Morley, 203-4, 276-7.
>
> Australian Dictionary of Biography, IV.189.

Hobbs, John: Born 22 February 1800 at Isle of Thanet, Kent; father an agricultural implement maker & Wesleyan local preacher; converted at 16; local preacher; little formal education; pre-missionary occupation carpenter, joiner & blacksmith; arr NZ 3 August 1823, aged 23; ordained 1827; married Jane Brogreff, 1827; arr. NZ 3 August 1823, aged 23; served at Whāngaroa & Māngungu; left NZ mission for Tonga May 1833; returned February 1838; retired 1856; died Auckland, 24 June 1883, aged 83.

> McLintock, A. H., *An Encyclopaedia of New Zealand*. II.88-9.
>
> Morley, 35-41;
>
> Spooner, T.G.M., *Brother John: The Life and Times of the Rev John Hobbs*. WHS (NZ) Proceedings, 13, nos. 2-4, 1955.
>
> Scholefield, G.H. ed, *DNZB*, I. 393-4.
>
> Williment, Tola M. I., 'Hobbs, John', *DNZB*, 1990, I.195 and online.
>
> Williment, Tola M.L., *John Hobbs 1800–1883: Wesleyan Missionary* Wellington: Government Printer, 1985.

Hosking, James Alfred: Born Penzance, 1831 Probationer, 1857, to New Zealand 1857, stationed as home Missionary, Māngonui, 1857- but may not have served. Printer and publisher, home missionary in European circuits, 1871-1888. Died 1888. Married Ellen Davey, 1859.

> Clover, Gary, 'Hokianga Māori after Māngungu …' (unpublished typescript, 2016).
>
> Laurenson, *Te Hahi Weteriana*. 1972, 159.
>
> Morley, 399.

Ironside, Samuel: Born 1814, Sheffield, Arrived on the James with Bumby & Creed, 19 March 1839. Initially at Māngungu 1839-1840. Cloudy Bay 1840-1843. Wellington and European circuits from 1843. Moved to Australia 1858. Died Tasmania, 1897. Married Sarah Eades 1838.

> Chambers, W.A., 'Ironside, Samuel', *DNZB,* 1990, 1. 209-10 and online.
>
> Chambers, Wesley A., 'Samuel Ironside in Church and Community', in *WHS (NZ) Journal* 1985.
>
> Chambers, Wesley A., *Samuel Ironside in New Zealand, 1839–1858*. Auckland: Ray Richards & WHS (NZ), 1982.
>
> McClintock, A.H., ed, *An Encyclopedia of NZ*, I.407.
>
> Morley, 76.

Scholefield, G.H. ed., *DNZB*. 1940, I. 427-29.

Smith, F.W., 'Samuel Ironside and the Cloudy Bay mission' WHS (NZ) Proceedings, 11, no.1, 1952.

Kirk, William: Born Lincolnshire 1825; a local preacher; probationer 1846, arr. NZ on *John Wesley* April 1847; ordained 1850m served at Auckland 1847-1848, then Pakanae 1847–1848 where marr. Emma Hobbs, Upper Whanganui 1848–1853, Waikouaiti 1853–1857, Kai Iwi 1857–1860, Whāngaroa 1860–1863, then European ministry until retired after 1885. Died 1915.

Morley, 105-6. 117

Scholefield, G.H. ed., *DNZB*. 1940, I. 470.

Lawry, Henry Hassell: Born Sydney, 1821 (Father Walter Lawry). To New Zealand with parents, 1844. Probationary minister 1844. Ordained 1848. Ihumatao 1848-49, Kaipara 1854-56, Manawakaieia, Waimā (upper Waimā Valley) 1856-1862. Principal Three Kings College, 1862-64. Retired and served BFBS. Married Hephzibah Forsaith 1849. Died Auckland, 1906.

Hames, Eric W., *Walter Lawry and the Wesleyan Mission in the South Seas*, WHS (NZ) Proceedings, 23, no.4, 1967.

Morley, 100.

'Rev. Henry H. Lawry', in, *The Cyclopedia of New Zealand* [*Auckland District*].

Scholefield, G.H. ed., *DNZB*. 1940, I. 488.

Lawry, Walter: Born Cornwall, 1793, Probationer 1817, to New South Wales 1818. Ordained 1821. Served in Tonga. Returned to Britain. Appointed to New Zealand 1844. Chairman, 1844-1854, based in Auckland. Married Mary Hassall, 1819; Eliza White 1829. Retired 1854 aged 61. To Sydney. Died Sydney 1859.

Hames, Eric W., *Walter Lawry and the Wesleyan Mission in the South Seas*, WHS (NZ) Proceedings, 23, no.4 1967.

Morley, 93.

Scholefield G.H. ed. *DNZB*. 1940, I. 489-490.

Leigh, Samuel: Born 1 September 1785 at Milton, Staffordshire; Congregationalist, converted at about 15; pre-missionary occupation student; educated at Dr Bogue's Congregational Seminary, Gosport; Wesleyan Probationer, ordained 30 September 1814; arr. NZ , 5 May 1819, stayed 1 month; the 2d arr. 22 February 1822; age on arrival in NZ 34; served with CMS Bay of Islands, & at Whāngaroa; left NZ mission 14 November 1823; married Catherine Clewes 1831, (2) Elizabeth Kaye (1842); later served in Australia & England; retired 1845; died 2 May 1852 aged 66.

Bawden, Patricia, *The Years Before Waitangi: a story of early Maori-European contact in New Zealand* Auckland: The Author, 1990.

Chambers. Wesley A., 'Leigh, Samuel', *DNZB*, I, 1990 and online.

de Reland, Elizabeth, Keith Hamilton, et al Parramatta Mission Heritage Committee, *Samuel Leigh: First Wesleyan Missionary to Australia & New Zealand*, Sydney: Parramatta Mission, 2019.

Jones, Pauline, *Milton's Missionary: The Life and Work of Rev. Samuel Leigh 1785-1852, First Missionary to Australia and New Zealand*, Stoke-on-Trent: P. Jones, 1986.

Laws, Charles H., *The Methodist Mission to New Zealand: Toil and Adversity at Whangaroa.* WHS (NZ) Proceedings, 1-2, 1944.

McLintock, A. H., *An Encyclopaedia of New Zealand.* Wellington: Government Printer, 1966. I.88-89.

Morley, 'Maori Missions', 26-28.

O'Brien, Glen, '"Not Radically a Dissenter": Samuel Leigh in the Colony of New South Wales.' *Wesley and Methodist Studies* 4 (2012): 51-69. See also O'Brien's chapter in this volume.

Owens, John Morley Roberts, *Prophets in the Wilderness: The Wesleyan Mission to New Zealand 1819–1827.* Auckland: Auckland & Oxford University Presses, 1974.

Scholefield, G.H. ed, *DNZB.* Wellington: Government Printer, 1940, I. 492-3.

Sharp, Andrew, *The World, the Flesh & the Devil: The Life and Opinions of Samuel Marsden in England and the Antipodes, 1765-1838.* Auckland: Auckland University Press, 2016.

Reid, Alexander: Born Edinburgh, 1821. Taught at Methodist school, came to New Zealand 1849 with Fletcher, ordained 1853. Principal Grafton Institution 1849-1858. Waipa 1858-1864; European circuits 1864-1885; Principal, Wesley College, 1885-1891. Married Georgina Darby 1848, who died 1864; married Sarah Kingcome, 1866. Died Auckland, 1891.

Morley, 114-15, 176.

Scholefield, G.H. ed., *DNZB.* 1940, II. 217-18.

Riemenschneider, Johannes Friedrich: Born Bremen, 1817. Studied at North German Mission House, 1837-42. Came to New Zealand 1843. Served in Methodist mission stations, first at Wakatumutumu 1844-1845, Wārea 1846-1863, Otakou 1862-1866. In 1863 became a Presbyterian minister. Married Catherine Woon 9 Oct 1849. Died 24 June 1866.

Greenwood, William, *Riemenschneider of Warea.* Wellington: A.H. & A.W. Reed, 1967.

Oettli, Peter H., *God's Messenger: J.F. Riemenschneider and Racial Conflict in 19th Century New Zealand.* Wellington: Huia Publishers, 2008.

Scholefield, G.H. ed., *DNZB.* 1940, II. 243

Schnackenberg, Cort Henry: Born Hanover, 1812. Becomes Methodist 1835. To Sydney 1838, New Zealand 1839. Catechist based at Mōkau: Te Māhoe 1844-1858. Ordained 2 Jan 1858, based at Lemon Point Kawhia, 1858-1863, Auckland 1863-64, Kawhia 1864-65; Raglan, 1865-80. Wife Annie Allen (married 1843). Died at sea 1880.

Hammer, G.E.J, *A Pioneer Missionary, Raglan to Mokau, 1844-1880: Cort Henry Schnackenberg.* WHS (NZ) Proceedings, 57, 1991.

Morley, 107, 138.

Scholefield, G.H. ed., *DNZB.* 1940, II. 276-7.

Skevington, John: Born Nottingham, 1815. probationer 1839, Tasmania mission, 1840. To New Zealand 1842 on *Triton.* Stationed Heretoa/Waimate, Taranaki, 1842-45; Ordained 1843. 1842-1845. Died 1845 in High St Chapel, Auckland. Married Jane Etchells, 1839.

Chappell, A.B., *Early Mission Days in South Taranaki* WHS (NZ) Proceedings, 1, no.4, 1942.

'Memento Mori - John Skevington - 1814-1845.' WHS (NZ) *Journal '89,* (1989): 50-52.

Clover, Gary A., '150th Anniversary "Heretoa" Wesleyan Maori Mission Station Waimate South, May 30th 1992', *WHS (NZ) Journal 1991-92,* (1992): 61-65.

Clover, Gary A., 'Rescuing from Obscurity: A Life of The Reverend John Skevington, 1815-1845', 22-43, in *WHS (NZ) Journal,* 89 (2009): 22-43.

Skinner, Thomas: Born Sussex, 1821. School teacher & Catechist. To New Zealand 1840. At Grey Institution, Heretoa, 1848, then Pātea, 1848, to Motuapuhi, Taupō; Aotea (Beechamdale) 1858-1863, Waimā, Patea, 1863. Died 30 Oct 1866. Wife Hannah Taylor (married 6 May 1851). 8 children.

Laurenson, *Te Hahi Weteriana.* 1972, 137.

McKay, Veda & Verna Mossong, 'Thomas Skinner: Catechist', *WHS (NZ) Journal,* 67 (1998): 50-54.

Morley, 106-107, 116.

Rossiter, Trish, 'Finding Thomas: The search for my great-great grandfather', in, *WHS (NZ) Journal,* 105 (2018): 12-23.

Scholefield, G.H. ed., *DNZB.* 1940, I. 488.

Smales, Gideon: Born 1818 at Whitby, Yorkshire; parents shipping magnates; pre-missionary occupation printer; ordained 1839; arr. NZ 7 May 1840 aged 22, on the *Triton*; served at Māngungu & Pākanae until 7 February 1843, then transferred to the Southern District, ministered at Porirua 1843-44, Beechamdale, Āotea 1844-1857; 1856 left the Mission to farm 300 acres at East Tamaki, Auckland; died 5 October 1894, aged 76. Wives: Mary Ann Bumby in 1840, died 1862; Mary Ann Baxter in 1864 died 1869; Elizabeth Tayler in 1873.

Morley, 83.

Roberts, David, 'A Man and His Church', in *WHS (NZ) Journal '85* (1985): 50-57.

Scholefield, G.H. ed, *DNZB.* 1940, II. 308-9.

Steele, John, *Smales' Trail: Gideon Smales, his extraordinary story.* [Auckland], J. Steele, 2011.

Stack James: Born 1 September 1801 at Portsmouth; parents Catholic & Anglican; pre-missionary occupation naval service in England & NSW; arr. NZ February 1823, aged 22; probationer 1825; served at Whāngaroa & Māngungu; left NZ mission 2 August 1832; married Mary West, 1833; transferred to CMS; returned to NZ until 1847; returned to England; died 18 April 1883 aged 82.

Morley, 40, 43, 45-52.

Scholefield, G.H. ed, *DNZB*. 1940, II.318).

Stannard, George: Born Ireland 1803. Local preacher. arr. NZ on Sophia Pate 1841; Oct 1843 appointed Assistant Missionary to Waima, then Pākanae 1843-48, Ihupuku & Kai Iwi 1848-1857. Ordained 1854. Briefly to Beechamdale (Raglan) 1857, then to Waikouaiti 1857-59, Mangonui 1859-60, Three Kings College 1860-62, Raglan 1863-65; retired 1865. Died 1888. Wives: Christina Woods; Anne.

Barrett, Tom, 'George Stannard', in, 'Family Explorer': Whanganui Historical Society *Historical Record*, 19, no.2 (1988) 17-21. (available online).

Morley, 99-101, 292.

Turner, Nathaniel: Born 1793 at Wynbury, Cheshire; father a farmer; member COE; converted at 18; pre-missionary occupation farming?; home missionary in Cheshire; ordained 23 January 1822; married Anne Sargent, 1822; arr in NZ 3 August 1823, aged 30; served at Whāngaroa & Māngungu; left NZ mission 24 August 1839; later served in Australia; retired 1850; died 5 September 1864, aged 71.

Clover, *Collision, Compromise and Conversion during the Wesleyan Hokianga Mission*. Nelson: The Author, 2018, esp, chapt 13, 'The Turner Years, 1836-1839'.

Morley, 59-64;

Mossong, Verna, 'The Story of the Rev Nathaniel Turner, a Missionary at Kaeo', in, *WHS (NZ) Journal*, (1998): 55-60.

Scholefield, G.H. ed., *DNZB*. 1940, I. 405-6.

Turner, J.G., *The Pioneer Missionary: Life of the Rev Nathaniel Turner, Missionary in New Zealand, Tonga, and Australia*. Melbourne: Geo Robertson & Wesleyan Book Depots, 1872.

Turton, Henry Hanson: Born Bradford, Yorkshire, 5 July 1818; father a Wesleyan circuit preacher; 1839 received 'on trial' to minister at Waimā; arrived New Zealand 7 May 1840 aged 22, on the *Triton*; appointed to the Kāwhia Circuit at Āotea 1840-February 1844, New Plymouth 1844-56; at Pehiakura, 1858-1859. 1859 resigned from the Mission; later worked as a Government Agent and Native Interpreter; 1863-64, briefly MP for New Plymouth; died 18 September 1887 in Wellington. Wife Susannah Linsley Kirk died 21 Oct 1849; 2nd wife Maery Emily Walsall, 10 Apr 1851.

Brown, David O., 'H. Hanson Turton: Missionary, Magistrate, Man of Many Parts', Revised ed, 21 November 2021. (A descendant's unpublished DVD biography from letters, with family notes.)

Brown, David O., "Methodist Biography: Henry Hanson Turton", 40p (Unpublished notes – copy held by the author.

Brown, D. O., 'H. Hanson Turton: Missionary, Magistrate, …', Rev. ed., 21 November 2021, 220-21.

Brown, David O, 'Methodist Biography: Henry Hanson Turton', Printed ed in 2 vols., Nelson: Copy Press, 2024. (Collated letters, documents & family notes.)

Buttle, Nora, *The Voyage of the Triton*, WHS (NZ) Proceedings, 22, nos.1 & 2, 1965.

Laurenson, *Te Hahi Weteriana*. 1972, 60-64, 158-9.

Morley, 82-3, 86, 116, 374.

Scholefield, G.H. ed., *DNZB*. 1940, II. 409.

Turton, Rev H. Hanson, 'Tritonia: or Memoranda of the First Voyage of the Wesleyan Missionary Ship "Triton" from England to New Zealand in 1839-40' by a 'New Zealand Missionary', Ms in Archives Hub, GB 102 MMS/17/02/10/06 (School of Oriental and African Studies (SOAS) Archives, University of London, 1846, and online.

Wade, Luke: Born 1795; NSW whaler, waged mission 'servant'; with James Stack arr. NZ February 1823; December 1824 Luke returned to England (returning October 1826), for wife Sarah (who April 1826 arrived NZ independently); both retired from Māngungu 19 September 1829; in Sydney, Sarah died October 1829, & Luke died 1868 aged 73.

Clover, Gary A.M., *Collision, Compromise and Conversion during the Wesleyan Hokianga Mission, 1827–1855: a critical study of Hokianga Maori, missionary, and kauri merchant interactions*. Nelson: Copy Press, 2018.

Morley, 40, 45—46, 512.

Phillipps, Donald, 'The Handyman and the Idealists: Luke Wade 1795-1868', 'Unsung Methodists' series: *Touchstone*, March 2023, 16.

Wallis, James: Born 18 April 1809 at Blackwall, near London; parents Wesleyan; pre-missionary occupation cabinet maker; local preacher, then minister at Ely; ordained 1 April 1834; married Mary Ann Riddick, 1834; arr. NZ 1 December 1834, aged 25; served at Māngungu, Whaingaroa, Tangiteroria; left NZ mission 1863; thereafter worked amongst Europeans in Auckland; retired 1868; died Auckland 5 July 1895, aged 86.

Luxton, C.T.J., *The Rev James Wallis of the Wesleyan Missionary Society*. WHS (NZ) Proceedings, 21, Nos. 1 & 2, 1965.

Morley, 61, 67-9.

Scholefield, G.H. ed. *DNZB*. 1940, II. 498-99.

Warren, John: Born 1814 in Norfolk; father a farmer; converted at 17; pre-missionary occupation tailor; local preacher, probationer 2 years, ordained 14 September 1838?; arr. NZ January 1840 from Tasmania, aged 26; served at Waimā to Dec 1855; then 15 years in European ministry, Wellington, Nelson & Auckland; retired 1869; died November 1883, aged 76. Wife Sarah Smith.

Clover, *Collision, Compromise and Conversion*.

Morley, 76.

Scholefield, G.H. ed., *DNZB*. 1940, II. 465.

Warren, John, *The Christian Mission to the Aborigines of New Zealand, its connection with the Colonization of the Country and the results which have followed*. Lecture. Auckland, 1863.

Watkin, James: Born Manchester, 1805, Probationer, 1830, Served in Tonga, 1830-1837. Ordained, 1834. To New Zealand 1840. Served at Waikouaiti 1840-44, then Wellington; then NSW conference. Died NSW 1886. Married Annah Entwisle 1830.

Belmer, Roy, *James Watkin, Pioneer Missionary*, WHS (NZ) Proceedings, 33, 1979.

McClintock, ed., *An Encyclopedia of New Zealand*. III. 591.

Morley, 88, 136-7, 473.

White, William: Born 1792 at Durham; parents Wesleyan?; pre-missionary occupation cabinet maker?; ordained 23 January 1822; arr. NZ 15 May 1823; age on arr. 31; married Eliza Leigh, 1829; served at Whāngaroa & Māngungu; left NZ mission April 1836; later occupation, kauri trade in Hokianga & Kaipara; died Auckland, 25 November 1875, aged 83.

Gittos, Murray B., *Mana at Mangungu: A Biography of William White, 1794–1875, Wesleyan Missionary at Whangaroa and Hokianga*. Auckland: M.B. Gittos, 1982.

Gittos, M.B., 'White, William 1794-1875', *DNZB*, 1 (1990), 589-90 and online.

Morley, 42-3.

Scholefield, G.H. ed., *DNZB*. 1940, II. 497.

Whiteley, John: Born 26 July 1806 at Kneesall, Nottinghamshire; of pious parents, Independents; pre-missionary occupation miller & baker; four years local preacher; Ordained 27 September 1832; married Mary Ann Cooke, 1832; arr. NZ 21 May 1833; served at Kāwhia, Pākanae & Taranaki; killed by Hau Hau at Pukearuhe 13 February 1869, aged 63.

Brazendale, Graham. 'Whiteley, John', DNZB, 1990, 590-91 and online.

Brazendale, Graham, *John Whiteley: Land, Sovereignty and the Land Wars of the 19th Century* (Wesley Historical Society (NZ) Publication 64, 1996). Based on his 1970 MA thesis.

Greenslade, William H. W., *John Whiteley 1806-1869*. WHS (NZ) Proceedings, 24, nos.2 & 3, 1968.

McLintock, A. H., *An Encyclopaedia of NZ*, III.655.

Morley, 59, 166-8;

Scholefield, G.H., ed., *DNZB*. 1940, II. 498-9.

Woon, William: Born 16 December 1803 at Truro, Cornwall; parents opposed; pre-missionary occupation printer; 7 years a Wesleyan member, 4 years a local preacher; served in Tonga April 1831-October 1833; visited NZ January 1831, arr NZ 21 January 1834, aged 33; served as lay missionary, received into full connexion at 1837 Centenary Conference; served at Māngungu, Kāwhia; Manukau, Pākanae, & South Taranaki; retired 31 October 1853; died Whānganui 22 September 1858, aged 54. Wife Jane.

> Bruce, Audrey, *In the Trail of the Missionary: 163 Years of Methodism in West Franklin*. Waiuku: The Author [1999].

> Clover, Gary A.M., William Woon 1803-1858: Wesleyan Printer in Tonga and New Zealand. WHS (NZ) Proceedings, 97, 2014.

> Clover, Gary A.M., William Woon: Wesleyan Printer in Tonga and New Zealand; The Other Missionary Printer Beau Bassin, Mauritius: Scholars Press, 2018.

> Morley, 60, 76, 84.

> Scholefield, G.H., ed. *DNZB*. 1940, II. 532.

Incomplete List of Employed Staff of the Mission

Day, Dr Richard: Employed at Hokianga mission.

> Clover, *Collision, Compromise and Conversion*, 315-16, 333, 339, 343.

> Scholefield, G.H. ed., *DNZB*. 1940, I. 197.

> Morley, 99-100.

Hough, William: Born Yorkshire, 1806. To New Zealand 1842. Employed as lay catechist, Pātea, 1844-1848. Retired to Nelson. Died Nelson, 1885. Married Ann Hepworth 1831 died 1839; married Ann Ellerker, 1839.

> Barker, Mary Troup, *Seeker of Souls and Gold: William Hough, Pioneer Preacher and Prospector*. Christchurch: M.T. Barker, 1985.

> Morley, 107, 376-77.

> Mossong, Verna, 'William Hough, Catechist and Lay Preacher: A New Zealand Pioneer', in *WHS (NZ) Journal*, 68 (1999): 29-35.

> Pratt, M.A. Rugby, *Nelson Methodist Centenary*. WHS (NZ) Proceedings, 2, no. 1, 1942.

Jenkins, William: Born Shropshire, 1813. Came to New Zealand 1842, cabinet maker and lay preacher in Wellington succeeded Ironside at Cloudy Bay as employed catechist, 1843-1848, teacher at Motueka 1848-1850. Died Wanganui, 1883. Married Catherine Mewis, 1839.

> Morley, 107, 152, 331.

Miller, Frederick: Born Co Londonderry, 1818. Moravian, sent by LMS to Australia. Arrived New Zealand 1843. Employed as lay 'Catechist' at Māngungu from 1841 and at Whatumutumu 1843-47. Married Susannah Thomas nee Napier, 1841. Died Dec 1847.

Elliott, Gabriel., *Sowing the Seed in Pioneer NZ, Frederick Miller of Wakatumtumu.* WHS (NZ) Proceedings, 16, no.5, 1959.

Morley, 332.

Weeks, Jill, 'Susannah Napier: Her Story', *WHS (NZ) Journal*, 61 (1994): 54-56.

Meurant, William Edward: Born 1803 Paid catechist at Papakārewa, Ngāmotu (North Taranaki) Died 1851.

Gittos, Murray B., *Mana at Mangungu: A Biography of William White ...* (1982), 113-15.

Luttrell, Julie, *The Governors Interpreter* ([Auckland?] Ron H. Mortensen, 2019.

Stephenson, George. Born Bridlington, 1807. To New Zealand 1835. Employed as carpenter at Hokianga mission. Home missionary Coromandel, 1878-1882. Died Whangaroa, 1898. Married Eleanor Baker, 1842.

Clover, *Collision, Compromise and Conversion during the Wesleyan Hokianga Mission...* (2018), esp, Appendix Three, 'George Stephenson', 451.

Morley, 77.

White, Francis: Born 1801, To New Zealand 1835. Served at Hokianga as paid worker.

Clover, *Collision, Compromise and Conversion during the Wesleyan Hokianga Mission...* (2018), Appendix Three, 'Francis White, born ca.1801', 451-2.

Scholefield, G.H. ed., *DNZB.* 1940, II. 495.

Early Māori Catechists and Native Ministers

(Partial list, based on Appendix 2 and Phillipps, Register.)

Eketone, Hoani or **Honi** (John Egglestone): Born Raglan, 1828. Māori minister, Kawhia, 1857-58; Mōkau (Te Māhoe) 1858-1862. Died Mokau, 1862. Married Heramahina Karipa c1848.

Laurenson, *Te Hahi Weteriana.* 1972, 160, 168.

Morley, 96, 135.

Phillipps, Register of Ministers, 150.

Mātangi, Haimona Pita (Simon Peter): Māngungu chief; baptised by William White, 23 December 1833. Translator and class leader and exhorter for Woon at Papakārewa 1834-1835. Died 1839. Obituary by Woon in the *Colonist*, 13 April 1839.

Clover, *Collision, Compromise and Conversion*, 199.

Nene, Tamati Wāka (Thomas Walker): Born in the 1780s, Ngāti Hao. Friend of Wesleyans at Māngungu baptised 1839 taking name of CMS leader. Died 4 August 1871.

Ballara, Angela, 'Tāmati Wāka Nene, Biography', *New Zealand History*, in, https://nzhistory.govt.nz/people/tamati-waka-nene; also, *DNZB*, I, 1990, 306-8.

Morley, 66.

Ngāropi, Hāmiora (Samuel Honeybee): Born Waingaroa c1809. Māori probationer, Ihumatoa, 1855-57; Te Kōpua 1858-1861. Ordained 1861. Native Minister, Whatawhata 1862-1870; New Plymouth 1870-1872, Whatawhata, 1872-1887. Died Whatawhata 1887.

Laurenson, *Te Hahi Weteriana.* 1972, 168-9.

Phillipps, Register of Ministers, 336.

Ōtene, Hōhepa (Joseph Orton): Born Hokianga, c1780. Rangatira in Mangamuka valley. Māori Assistant Minister, Conf apptd 1857-9. Assistant minister at Pehiakura, 1857-1859 at Ihumātao, at Mangatawhiri (Manukau) 1861-64. Died Matauri Bay, 1874. Married Rihi Poroa.

Belich, James *'I Shall Not Die': Titokowaru's War, New Zealand, 1868-1869*, Wellington: Bridget Williams Books, 1993.

Clover, *Collision, Compromise and Conversion*, 258, 280, 311-12, 360.

Laurenson, *Te Hahi Weteriana.* 1972, 42, 101, 118.

Morley, 104, 159.

Phillipps, Register of Ministers, 349.

Pātene, Wiremu (William Barton): Born Whaingaroa, c1810. Educated at Three Kings, 1844. Catechist on Waipa River 1850s. Appointed Native Assistant, 1859. Probation at Whaingaroa 1859-1863; Received as Native Assistant Minister, 1864. At Whaingaroa, 1863-1872. Ordained 1871. At Te Kopua 1872-1884 as Māori Assistant Minister, at Waipā. Died Karakariki, 1884.

Laurenson, *Te Hahi Weteriana.* 1972, 168, 172.

Phillipps, Register of Ministers, 361.

Patuone, Eruera Maihi (Edward Marsh). Protected the missionaries fleeing from Whangaroa and sponsored them in Hokianga.

Ballara, Angela, 'Patuone, Eruera Maihi', DNZB, 1990, I.338-40; and online.

Davis, Charles Oliver, *The Life and Times of Patuone: The Celebrated Ngapuhi Chief.* Auckland: J.H. Field, 1876.

Morley, 40, 45, 66.

Pohio, Horomona: Born 1815 at Wainoni, Baptised 18 June 1843 by James Watkin at Waikouaiti. Assistant pastor at Waikouiti and Moeraki, 1840s and 1850s. Later followed Te Maiharoa, Died 1880.

Dacker, Bill, *Te Mamae me te Aroha*, 1994, 16-18.

Tau, Te Maire, 'Pōhio, Horomona' DNZB I, 1990, also online.

Pura, Hōhepa Te Ōtene [This is Ōtene, Hohepa – see above]

Ri, Hoani (John Leigh): Ngāmotu (North Taranaki). Young Hokianga teacher, Left in charge of Ōrua station, South Manukau Heads, 1836. Stationed at Ngāmotu 1841-1844 as Native Assistant Missy.

Laurenson, *Te Hahi Weteriana.* 1972, 72-3.

Tāwhai, Hone Mohi (John Moses): Born 1827, Ngāpuhi leader at Waimā Baptised by mission in Hokianga and supported it. Died 1894.

Walker, Ranganui, 'Mohi Tāwhai', DNZB II 1993 and online.

Morley, 77, 105, 172.

Te Awa-i-taia, Wiremu Nēra: leader of Ngāti Māhanga, converted in 1833-34, influenced by William White, protected Kāwhia station. Ngāti Māhanga chief, left in charge of Te Hōrea mission, Raglan, during vacancy 1836.

Scott, Gary, 'Te Awa-i-taia, Wiremu Nēra', *DNZB*, I (1990) and online.

Te Rangi-hatu-ake, Minarapa: At Port Nicholson as Wesleyan preacher 1839-1842.

Clover, Gary, 'More Heroes of the Faith: Minarapa Te Rangihatuake' in, *WHS (NZ) Journal*, 95 (2012): 31-52.

Roberts, John H. 'Rangihatuake, Minarapa', DNZB I, 1990, and online.

Roberts, John H., 'The Wesleyan Maori Mission at Te Aro', WHS (NZ) *Journal '90*, 56 (1990): 14-49.

Te Rangitaahua Ngamuka/Epiha Putini (Jabez Bunting): Māori Assistant Minister to H.H. Lawry. Then in 1849 assistant minister at Pehiakura.

Laurenson, George, *Te Hahi Weteriana*. 1972, 42, 118.

Morley, 95, 98, 103-4, 159.

Scholefield, G.H. ed., *DNZB*. 1940, II. 195.

Te Rātou [Rato], Wiremu Te Kote: Born Wairarapa c 1820, Ngāti Kahungunu; Captured by Ngati Toa, converted at Porirua, baptised by Ironside. Native assistant, Chatham Island, 1859-1862. Native Minister Christchurch 1862-65. Ordained 1863. Native minister at Rapaki 1865-1891. Died 1895.

Laurenson, *Te Hahi Weteriana*. 1972, 84, 160, 168.

Morley, 103, 135, 204.

Phillipps, Donald, Register of Ministers, 457.

Roberts John H., 'Te Rato, Wiremu Te Koti', DNZB, II (1993) 523-24 and online.

Tītokowaru, Riwha (a.k.a. Hōhepa Ōtene): Baptised by Skevington at Heretoa, 1842. After 1854 abandoned Methodist links. Leader in Pai Mārire and led war against Pākehā, late 1860s. Died 1888.

Belich, James, Titokowaru, Riwhi, *DNZB* I (1990). Available online

Belich, James *'I Shall Not Die': Titokowaru's War, New Zealand, 1868-1869*, Wellington: Bridget Williams Books, 1993.

Waiti, Hoani. Born Kaipara, 1820, Died Otamatea, Kaipara, 1879. James Buller calls him Hoani Hikitanga. Converted 1843 Native Institution, Grafton, 1844-1850; Catechist, Kaipara, 1850-1860, Native Assistant, 1860-1867. Ordained 1864. Native minister Hokianga, 1867-1868; Otamatea, 1868-1879.

Phillipps, Register of Ministers, 482.

Appendix 2 – New Zealand Wesleyan Mission Stations 1819-1860

Gary Clover

Introduction

By the end of the eighteenth century the evangelical revival in Great Britain, of which Wesleyan Methodism was a growing part, began to spawn a number of Protestant missionary societies outside of the Church of England. First off the mark in 1792 was the Baptist Missionary Society which sent William Carey to India. This was followed by the interdenominational London Missionary Society (LMS) in 1795 and the nominally Anglican Church Missionary Society (CMS) in 1799 which sent missionaries to the West Indies, West Africa, India, and to Tahiti. Meanwhile local Wesleyan missionary societies began to raise funds to likewise send Wesleyan missionaries to these areas. By 1814 these local missionary efforts began combining organisationally into what in 1818 became the Wesleyan Missionary Society (WMS).[1] Also in 1814 the Rev Samuel Marsden, the second chaplain to the New South Wales (NSW) convict settlement, visited Rangihoua in the Bay of Islands at the invitation of its Māori chief, Ruatara, who had previously spent some months at Marsden's Parramatta estate. While at Parramatta Ruatara recognised much congruence between Marsden's evangelical gospel of the good news of the coming of the 'King of Kings' who would bring the blessings of peace amidst warring tribes and gain them entrance into the encroaching world of European technology and trade goods, and the ancient spiritual significance of Rangihoua (entry to heaven), his home pā and the waka landing site of his tipuna (ancestors), who atop Rangihoua mountain met 'Mataroa' of 'flaming eyes', the God of eternity.[2]

Early in 1819 the new WMS-appointed missionary, the Rev Samuel Leigh, arrived in NSW. He and Marsden shared many similar doctrinal, ecclesiastical and missiological ambitions, became firm friends, and worked closely together to evangelise NSW convicts, free settlers, and neighbouring Aborigines. Both men soon turned their gaze across the Tasman, seeking to bring their evangelical gospel to the indigenous Māori. In May 1819 Leigh accompanied Marsden to Rangihoua and stayed for nearly two months. Leigh was unsuccessful in converting any Māori 'natives', and soon fell so ill he had to be hurriedly returned to Sydney. But he developed a passion to set up a Wesleyan mission in pre-Waitangi Āotearoa to work alongside the CMS mission. Returning to England, and without the financial or organisational support of the Wesleyan Methodist Conference, Leigh stumped up and down England, raised funds and a considerable supply of trade goods, and in January 1822, with his new wife, Catherine, returned to Rangihoua to start a Wesleyan mission. Over the next eighteen months five ordained and waged lay missionaries arrived in the Bay of Islands to join Leigh. These included the Revs William

White, and Nathaniel Turner with his wife, Ann, and the waged servant, Luke Wade with his wife Sarah Wade, and the unmarried lay assistant missionaries, James Stack and John Hobbs. On 6 June 1823, the New Zealand Wesleyan mission began in earnest when the Leighs, White, Stack, & the Wades, with the assistance of CMS missionaries, were landed among the Ngāti Uru iwi (tribe) near today's Kaeo at the head of the Whāngaroa Harbour. They called their new mission station 'Wesleydale'.

However, the cultural and religious environment in which these early missionaries found themselves was initially hardly conducive to evangelical conversion. The Māori people were proud, warlike, and immensely confident in the validity of their customs and spirituality, and content with their religious beliefs and forms. Many received the missionaries into their midst for reasons which were far from what the English missionaries thought was occurring. More than the missionaries' strange teachings, what their Māori hosts first wanted from them, in secular terms, was their European trade goods and technology, especially the muskets the missionaries were forbad from selling to them. Also the mana (authority, prestige) which accrued to each tribe from having a 'mihinare' (missionary) under their oversight as an interpreter of this new world and a source of its material riches.

Early missionary endeavour in pre-colonial New Zealand was not for the faint hearted. The English missionaries at first were entirely at the mercy and sufferance of their hosts. They often depended on them for their food, their safety, and their lives. If the missionaries inadvertently crossed any traditional customary cultural or spiritual lines they were liable to be punished with significant sanctions, including robbery of their supplies and physical harm. Māori rules applied. And if their privations were not hard enough, these earliest missionaries found their cherished religion and beliefs mocked and often rejected out of hand. It was only very gradually, over time, after coming perilously close to losing their lives on not a few occasions, and after the missionaries had begun to become familiar with the customs, language, and norms of their hosts culture and society, that the tide began to turn. Especially crucial for opening the way to Māori conversions, was for the missionaries to become sufficiently fluent in te reo Māori (the Māori language) for them to begin to teach their Māori neighbours to read and write, and for copies of the New Testament in te reo to be able to be printed and distributed. This enabled Māori to read for themselves in their own tongue the Christian stories and message. Then, the really early effective missionaries were largely, young chiefly Māori converts who, in turn, through the length and breadth of New Zealand, taught their fellow tribesmen and women a unique "Māorified" indigenous Christianity which sometimes left the English missionaries perplexed.

The motives for much of Maori turning to Christianity were very mixed and, at first, often more secular and cultural or economic than spiritual. But remarkably for a highly collectivised tribal society, and in a vastly different cultural and religious environment, many Maori did also experience individual evangelical conversion experiences similar to those which the missionaries themselves had experienced back in Europe. But despite all the terror and privation of early missionary life, their deaths by drowning and disease, and high infant mortality rates, by the mid-1800s many Wesleyan missionaries achieved an honoured status and position in colonial society which they could not have aspired to in their home countries, as land holders, government interpreters, civil servants, and high ecclesiastical officeholders.[3]

The following list of missionary appointments and personnel arose from the author's own need to list the appointments and movements of the earliest Wesleyan European and Māori missionaries, ordained, lay, and waged, in early colonial New Zealand. For their movements are complex and they moved often. The list covers forty New Zealand Wesleyan Mission stations, each arranged geographically by region from north to south. Mission personnel are then arranged within each region, station by station, chronologically then alphabetically from the dates of their arrival or appointments, most with additional identifying information and the names of their wives.

I remain much indebted to Jo Smith, the New Zealand Methodist Connexional Archivist, for helpful suggestions to include a Glossary and Sources, and to the Rev Dr Terry Wall for his encouragement.

Glossary

arr	arrived
appovd	approved
appt/d	appointment/ted
assist	assistant
Assist.Min	Assistant Minister
chapt/s	chapt/ers
Crct	Circuit
comp	compiler
dep	departed
d	died
D.Mtg	District Meeting (NZ Wesleyan)
D.Phillipps	Rev Donald Phillipps
Eng	England
empl	employed
fl	flourished
Gen.Supt.Sth Pac	General Superintendent of the South Pacific
Govr	Governor
incl	included
Indep. Cong.	Independent Congregational
Institn	Institution
jnctn	junction
marr	married
Mssn. Stn	Mission Station

Missy	Missionary
Nat.Institn	Native Institution
NZ Chair	New Zealand Wesleyan Mission Chairman
Nth.Dist.Mtg	Northern District Meeting (NZ Wesleyan)
poss	possibly
R	River
recomd	recommended
restart	restarted
rcd	received
retd	retired
Rev	Reverend
Sch	School
startd	started
stn	station
UK	United Kingdom
Wes	Wesleyan
Wgtn	Wellington
yrs	years

Bay of Islands: Rangihoua & Paihia, 1819-1823

1819 May 5-17 June	Rev Samuel Leigh	arr. with Rev Samuel Marsden
1822 Jan 22	Samuel & Catherine Leigh	arr to start NZ WMS Mission
1823 Feb	James Stack	Arr 'Assistant Missionary on trial'
1823 Feb	Luke & Sarah Wade	Arr as lay, waged servant
1823 May 15	Rev William White	arr: Bay of Islands as ordained missy

Whāngaroa: Wesleydale, Kaeo, 5 June 1823-10 January 1827

1823 June 5	Leigh. White, Stack, Wade	start 'Wesleydale' Mission
1823 Aug 6	Nathaniel & Anne Turner	Arr Bay of islands w Marsden
1923 Aug 6	John Hobbs	Arr as lay waged mechanic
1823 Aug 7	Samuel & Catherine Leigh	Return to NSW
1824 Dec	Luke Wade	Dep to UK for a wife; ret: 6 April 1826
1824 Dec?	John Hobbs	Apptd Assistant missy
1825 July	James Stack	Appointed assistant missionary
1826 Jan 1?	William White	dep: UK for wife; ret: 17 Feb 1830

1827 Jan 10	Turner, Hobbs, Wade, Stack & wives	Flee to Paihia, then Sydney
1827 Aug 14	John Hobbs	marr: Jane Broggref in Sydney
1827 Oct 8	John Hobbs	at Sydney D.Mtg: ordained
1827 Oct 8	Nathaniel Turner & family	Depart to Tonga

References:

Clover, G. *Collision, Compromise and Conversion during the Wesleyan Hokianga Mission, 1827–1855: A Critical Study of Hokianga Māori, Missionary, and Kauri Merchant Interactions*, Nelson: The Author, 2018, c. 4, 'Beginnings at Whāngaroa, 1823-1827'.

Laws, Charles H., *The Methodist Mission to New Zealand; First Years at Hokianga, 1827–1836*, WHS (NZ) Proceedings, 4, nos.2 & 3, 1945, reprinted 1977.

Morley, 'Maori Missions', 26-41.

Mossong Verna (comp), 'Celebration in Kaeo', *WHS (NZ) Journal*, 67 (1998): 37-44.

Owens, John M.R. *Prophets in the Wilderness*. Auckland: Auckland & Oxford University Press, 1974.

Owens, 'John M.R. Religious Disputation at Whangaroa 1823-7', *Journal of the Polynesian Society*, 79, No.3 (September 1970) 288–304

Sherrin, R.A.A., *From Earliest Times to 1840*, in, *Brett's Historical Series: Early History of New Zealand*, c. XXVII.

Hokianga

1827	Eruera Maihi Patuone	protected Wesleyan Mission's restart
1827 Sep 20	James Stack	Returned to Bay of Islands
1827 Oct 31	Hobbs, Wade, & wives	Arr. Hokianga by *Gov Macquarie*
1827 Oct 31	Kezia Bedford	Arr Hokianga, intended as missy wife
1827 Oct 31	Augustus Earle	visited

Te Tōke: 14 December 1827-20 March 1828

1827 Nov 11	Hobbs & Henry Williams	First H.C. service
1827 Dec 14	Hobbs, Stack, Wade	'buy' Te Tōke

Māngungu: 20 March 1828-[December?] 1855

1828 Jan 29	Hobbs	begins building Māngungu
1828 Mar 20	J & J Hobbs, Stack, Wade	start Māngungu Mission
1829 Sept 19	Luke & Mrs Wade	retd to Sydney; Mrs W dies
1830 Feb 17	William & Eliza White	returned to Māngungu
1831 Jan 16	Hika Tawa	1st Māori baptised at Māngungu, witnessed by William Woon, Peter Turner. James Watkin & wives
1831 Aug 4	Mr & Mrs Parker	empl. 2 yrs as doctor trainee, preacher
1831 Sep 17	James Stack	departed for Eng; joins CMS
1833 May 21	John & Mary Ann Whiteley	arr: at Paihia; & to Māngungu
1833 May 30	John Hobbs & family	Depart for Tonga
1833 June 7-Jul 17	Joseph Orton	NSW superintendent visits
1834 Jan 28	William & Jane Woon	lay printer, arr from Tonga
1834 Feb 18-Mar	Edward Markham	Tourist visits
1834 Nov 16	William & Jane Woon & family	Leave to start Kāwhia Mission, Papakārewa
1834 Nov	Hōhepa Ōtene Pura	fl. 1834-41; baptised; bro. of Mohi Tāwhai
1834 Dec 1	James & Mary Ann Wallis	arr Māngungu
1835	Tāmati Wāka (Thomas Walker) Nene	Wesleyan 'mihinare' chief, bapt. 1839
1835	Ryan	empl. to supervise 'Mihinare' Māori
1835 Apr 29	John Whiteley & family	Leave to start Waiharakeke Mission, Kāwhia
1835 Apr 29	James Wallis & family	Leave to start Whaingaroa Mission, Te Hōrea
1835 Nov 13	Francis White & family	Arr w printing press
1835 Nov 13	Rev Dartnell & Miss Payne	(arr: Indep. Cong. Preacher, dies Dec 1835
1836 Jan 28	George Stephenson	empl: lay preacher, mission helper
1836 Apr 18	Nathaniel & Ann Turner	arr: Māngungu as 'Superintendent'
1836 Apr 18	James Buller	arr: Māngungu, as lay 'tutor'

1836 Apr 28	Wallis & Whiteley families	recalled: from Waikato mission stns
1836 Apr	Whiteley family	start: 'Newark' mission at Pākanae
1836 Jun	Wallis family	start: Tangiteroria mission
1836 Jun 21	William White	dismissed: as 'Superintendent'
1836 Jul 28	William & Eliza White	Depart for England
1836 Aug	George Hawke	marooned visitor; helper for 13 months
1837 Oct 12	James Buller marries Jane Tonkin	D.Mtg. recomd: to trial as 'Missy'
1837 Oct 12	Whiteley & Walllis	D.Mtg. recomd: 'Full Connexion'
1837-1838	James Buller	on 'Probation': at Māngungu
1838 Feb 19	John & James Hobbs & family	arr: from Tonga en route to Eng
1838 Aug 18	Māngungu fire	Mission House (Turner's residence) burnt
1838 Dec	Dr Richard Day	arr: lay mission tutor, Irish coloniser
1839 Feb	William & Jane Woon & family	apptd: to 'Newark', Pākanae
1839 Mar 6	James & Mary Ann Wallis	restarts at Nihinihi, Whaingaroa
1839 Mar 19	John Bumby & sister Mary Ann & Revs Creed, Ironside, Waterhouse	Arr on. *James.* (Waterhouse was newly appointed General Superintendent South Pacific)
1839 Mar 19	John Whiteley & family	restarts: at Te Ahuahu, Kāwhia
1839 Aug 24	Nathaniel Turner & family	departed to Sydney
1839-1840	John Hewgill Bumby	apptd: NZ Chair; d. 26 June 1840
1839-1840	Charles & Eliza Creed	1st appt: Māngungu
1839-1840	Samuel & Sarah Ironside	1st appt: Māngungu
1839-1840	Hone Mohi (John Moses) Tāwhai	Wesleyan 'mihinare' chief of Waimā
1840 Jan	John & Sarah Warren	arr: at Māngungu, from Sydney
1840-1855 Mar	Warren family	begin: at Te Poinga, Waimā
1840 May 7	Buddle, Turton families and Aldred, Buttle, Smales	Arrive on *Triton*
1840 May	William Woon	installed: as a 'Full Missionary'

1840 May	John Hobbs & family	apptd: to 'Newark', Pākanae
1840 Jun 26	John Bumby	drowned in Hauraki Gulf
1840 Jul	John Hobbs	'Interim Chair Nth.Dist.Mtg'
1840 Dec 29	Gideon Smales & Mary Ann Bumby	Married by Rev J. Waterhouse
1840-1843	John Aldred & Mary Lawry married	1st appt: Port Nicholson
1840-1842	George & Jane Buttle	1st appt: Kāwhia & Mōkau
1840-1845	Thomas & Sarah Buddle	1st appt: Te Kōpua
1840-1855 Dec	John Hobbs & family	apptd: back to Māngungu
1841 Jan	Hobbs family	Arrive
1841 Jan	Smales	moved: to 'Newark', Pākanae
1841-1842	Frederick & Susannah Miller	lay 'Catechist' at Māngungu
1841 May	H. H. & Susannah Turton	1st appt: Kāwhia with Whiteley
1842 Mar 30	Rev John Waterhouse	d: Gen. Superintendent, in Hobart
1843	George Stannard	accepted: as 'Assistant Missionary'
1847 Apr-1848	William Kirk	arr: on *John Wesley*
1855 Dec	Hobbs family	retired: to Onehunga; Govr., Native Institn

'Newark', Pākanae: 1836-1848

1836 Apr 28-1838	Whiteley family	established: Pākanae mission
1838-1839	James Buller	'Probationary Missionary'
1839-1840	William Woon & family	apptd + Moetara; died Dec. 1838)
1839-1841	John Hobbs	'Acting Chair' aft Bumby drowned
1841-1843	Gideon & Mary Ann Smales	apptd in place of John Hobbs
1843 Feb 7	Gideon Smales & family	departed 'Newark', for Porirua
1845 Oct	George Stannard	apptd as Assist.Missy'
1848-1849 Jan	William Kirk	apptd to Newark; marr: Emma Hobbs

Waimā at Te Poinga, Mōehau: 1840-1855 (= near junction Waimā & Punakitere rivers)

1840 Mar	John & Sarah Warren	moved to & started Te Poinga stn
1855 Dec	Warren family	departed for Nelson

References

Clover, Gary A.M., *Collision, Compromise and Conversion* 2018, cc 5-16.

Laws, Charles H., *The Methodist Mission to New Zealand; First Years at Hokianga, 1827–1836*, WHS (NZ) Proceedings, 4, nos.2 & 3, 1945, reprinted 1977.

Morley, 'Maori Missions', cc. 2-9.

Sherrin, R.A.A., *From Earliest Times to 1840*, in, *Early History of New Zealand Brett's Historical Series: Early History of New Zealand*, c. XXXV.

Hokianga Circuit

Sarah Warren planted Waimā Oak ca. March 1840

Waimā at Manawakaieia: 1856-1858 (= Māori village in upper Waimā River valley)

1856-1862	Henry Hassell & Hephzibah Lawry	Stationed there
1863 Dec 12	Thomas Skinner	Appointed
1866 Oct 30	Skinner dies	Hannah and 8 children widowed.

Māngonui:

1857-1858	James Hosking	Appointed Home Missy. possibly 'didn't take up appt'

Northern Wairoa

Tangiterōria: 1836-1853

1836 Jun-1838	James & Mary Ann Wallis	established: Nthn Wairoa Mission
1838-1853	James & Jane Buller	Appointed here. 12 Oct 1837 recommd: Full Connexion
1841-1842	George Stannard	Lay assistant to Buller
1843	George Stannard	Accepted as Assistant missionary

References

Byrne, Brian, *The Unknown Kaipara: Five Aspects of Its History, 1250-1875*. T.B. Byrne, 2002, 81–96, 121–9.

Ryburn, Wayne, *Tall Spars, Steamers & Gum: A History of the Kaipara from Early European Settlement*. Kaipara Publications, 1999. 9.

Stallworthy, John, Early Northern Wairoa Dargaville, Wairoa Bell & Northern Advertiser print, 1916; Facsim. ed, Whāngarei: Dargaville Maritime Museum, 2016.

Auckland

High Street Chapel: 1843-1854

1843-1845	George & Jane Buttle	1st minister, Auckland
1844 Mar 17	Walter & Mary Lawry	arr: to start as NZ Chairman
1845-1855	Thomas Buddle	Assistant minister to Lawry
1847 Apr		*John Wesley* mission ship arrives
1847-1848	William and Emma Kirk	Assist Buddle in Māori ministry
1848	George Stannard	2nd appoint to Auckland
1854	Walter Lawry	Retires

References

Chappell, A. B. *Across a hundred years, 1841–1941: a brief story of the beginning and early progress of Methodism in Auckland, N.Z.* Auckland: Auckland Centenary Committee, 1941.

Glen, Frank G., *Methodism in Auckland during the Maori Wars, 1860-1864* WHS (NZ) Proceedings, 16, nos. 1 & 2, 1957.

Grafton Institution: 1844-1848

1844-1845	Thomas Buddle	1st principal
1844-1847	Henry H Lawry	Assistant teacher

References

Hames, Eric, *Wesley College: A Centenary Survey 1844-1944* WHS (NZ) Proceedings, 3, no.4 & 4, no.1, 1945.

Hames, Eric W., *From Grafton to Three Kings to Paerata: Wesley College, 1844-1982*, WHS (NZ) Proceedings, 39, 1982.

Thompson, Susan J., *Knowledge & Vital Piety: Education for Methodist ministry in New Zealand from the 1940s* WHS (NZ) Proceedings, 90 & 91, 2010.

Three Kings Wesleyan Native Institution: 1849-1869 (Foundtn Stone, 5 April 1848)

1849 Apr 17-1858	Alexander Reid	First principal
1850-1855 and 1857	Joseph Fletcher	arr:1849, 1st Head Wesley Coll

Manukau Circuit

Ōrua, South Manukau Heads: 1835-1836

1835 Jan 23-Mar	William Woon & family	Stationed
1836?	Hoani Ri (John Leigh)	young Hokianga Māori teacher, left in charge

Pehiakura: 1846-1859

1847 Mar-1854	Walter Lawry	Superintendent
1847	Epiha Putini (Jabez Bunting)	Māori 'Assist. Minister'
1857-1859	Hōhepa Ōtene (Riwha Titokowaru)	Māori Assist. Minister & South Taranaki colonial war general
1858-1859	Hanson Turton & family	Superintendent, till resignation from Mission

Ihumātao: 1847-1863?

1847-1854	Henry H Lawry	Māori station: of Manukau Circuit
1847-1863?	Epiha Putini = Te Rangitaahua, Ngamuka	Māori Assist. Minister

References

Hames, Eric W., *Walter Lawry and the Wesleyan Mission in the South Seas*, WHS (NZ) Proceedings, 23, No.4, 1967.

Luxton, C.T.J., *Methodist Beginnings in the Manukau: The story of the Pehiakura Mission 1834–1862*. WHS (NZ) Proceedings, 17, No.4, 1960.

Waikato Coast

Whaingaroa: Te Hōrea: 1835-1836 (north side Raglan Harbour)

1835 April 29	James & Mary Ann Wallis	start Te Hōrea Mission
1836 Jun 1	James & Mary Ann Wallis	recalled from 'Waingaroa' Mission Station
1836 Jun 1	Wiremu Nera Te Awaitaia	Ngāti Māhanga chief, left in charge during vacancy

Nihinihi: 1839-1866 (south side Raglan Harbour)

1839 Mar 6-1863	James Wallis & family	re-start of Whaingaroa mission
1840 May-1840 Dec	Thomas Buddle	assistant at Whaingaroa
1859-1884	Wiremu Pātene (William Barton)	Māori Assistant Minister, at Waipā
1863 Apr 24	Wallis family	Retire to Onehunga, Auckland

Āotea: 'Beechamdale': 1840-1866

1840 Jul?-1844 Feb	Henry & Susannah Turton	Stationed. Turton named Āotea 'Beechamdale'
1844 Jan 28	Gideon Smales & family	arr: landed at Rauraukauere
1856 Nov 27	Smales family	retired to East Tamaki farm estate
1857 Sept	George Stannard	lay missionary, 1 yr apt?)
1858-1863	Thomas Skinner & family	catechist, lay missionary; then to Waimā

References

Astridge, Robin, comp, *Waikato Wesleyan Missions, A brief insight into the work of the early Wesleyan Missionaries in the Waikato of New Zealand: A brief outline of Wesleyan Mission Stations in the Waikato, New Zealand, established early 1800s.* The Author, November 2013. [online]

Cooper, Barbara, *The Remotest Interior: a history of Taupo.* Tauranga: Moana Press, 1989.

Houston, John, *Maori Life n Old Taranaki.* Wellington: A.H. & A.W. Reed, 1965.

Leadley, Alan, *A Pilgrimage to Kawhia: The Heart of West Coast Methodism* (Saturday, 9 November 2013), https://docslib.org/doc/3223969/a-pilgrimage-to-kawhia-the-heart-of-west-coast-methodism

Kāwhia

Papakarewa: 1835-1836

1834 Nov 26	William Woon & family	Arrived with William White
1834-1835	Simon Peter Mātangi	Māngungu chief; translator for Woon
1836 Apr 28	Whiteley family	recalled: to 'Newark' at Pākanae

Te Ahuahu & Te Waitere ('Lemon Point'): 1839-1866

1839 Mar 19	Whiteley family	restarted at Te Ahuahu
1839 Apr?	Whiteley family	moved: to Te Waitere/Lemon Pt.
1840 May 29	Hanson & Susannah Turton	arr: Kāwhia; assist to Whiteley
1841 Nov 17	George Buttle	apptd: to Mōkau, Te Kōpua
1854	John Whiteley	Moved to Auckland as chair
1856	Whiteley family	Appointed to New Plymouth
1857-1859	H. Hanson Turton	Served then 1859 resigns from Mission
1858 May 7-1863	Cort Schnackenberg	German; Catechist.

Reference

Francis, Andrew, *The Rohe Potae Commercial Economy in the Mid-Nineteenth Century, c.1830-1886: A Report commissioned by the Waitangi Tribunal*, February 2011 (Wai 8987, # A 26).

Waipā River

Te Kōpua: 1841-1864 ('The Deep Pool'; on Waipā River)

1841 May-1844	Thomas & Sarah Buddle	began Te Kōpua on mid-Waipā R.
1845-1858	George & Jane Buttle	appt: Kāwhia Circuit; Jane d. 1857
1858-1864	Alexander Reid	Appointed. forced to leave by Waikato War
1858-1861	Hāmiora Ngāropi (Samuel Honeybee)	recd. as Māori Probationer

Mōkau: Te Kauri: 1841 (at Mōkau River mouth)

1841 Apr 27-1841 Nov 17	George Buttle	Circuit incl: Motukaramu, Te Kōpua

Mōkau: Te Māhoe: 1844-1858 (2kms up Mōkau River)

1844 Apr 27-1858	Cort Schackenberg	lay Catechist
1858 Jan 2	Cort Schnackenberg	Ordained to Wesleyan ministry
1858 June-1862	Hoani Eketone (Rev John Egglestone)	Māori minister

Wakatumutumu or Arapae: 1844-1848 (at upper Mōkau above '8 Mile Junction')

1844-1845	Johannes Riemenschneider	Lutheran, Nth German Mission
1844-1847	Frederick & Susannah Miller	lay Catechist; Miller died Dec.1847

Taupo

Motuapuhi: 1848-1849

1848 Oct-1849 Dec	Thomas Skinner	mission stationed near Lake Rotoaira

North Taranaki

Ngāmotu: 1840-1869

1840 Jan 13	William White & Edward Meurant	tapu'd Taranaki mission sites
1841 Jan 14-1844 Mar 4	Charles & Eliza Creed	arr on *Triton*, via Pātea
1841 Jan 14-1844	Hoani Ri (John Leigh)	Māori Assist. Missy
1844 Mar 7-1856 Mar 31	H.H. Turton	Founded Grey Institution, 1845
1856 Mar 31	H.H. Turton	furlough in England; 1857 moved briefly to Kāwhia
1856 Mar 31-1869 Feb	John Whiteley	killed: 28 Feb 1869 at Pukeāruhe

Grey Institution: 1843-1856 (at Ngāmotu)

1844-1856	H.H. Turton	founded 1844 as a 'Native School'
1850 Jan 5-1856	Thomas Skinner	Assistant to Turton

Wārea: 1845-1863 (North German Mission, Lutheran)

1846-1863	J.C. Riemenschneider	station

Reference

Morley, 116.

South Taranaki

Heretoa/Waimate: 1842-1853

1842 May 30- 1845 Sep 17	John & Jane Skevington	Stationed. Died 17/9/1845 in Auckland
1846 May 27- 1853 Oct 31	William Woon & family	Woons moved on retirement to Whānganui
1848 Jan 31- 1848 Oct 29	Thomas Skinner	lay 'Catechist': to Motuapuhi, Taupō

Pātea: 1844-1848

1844 Apr 14-1848 Feb 4	Willian & Anne Hough	lay 'Catechist': retired to Nelson
1848 Jan 21- 1848 Oct 29	Thomas Skinner & family	lay 'Catechist': to Taupō

Waitotara & 'Kai Iwi Native Farm School': Oct 1848-1857

1849 Jan	George & Ann Stannard	arr: Te Ihupuku pā, Waitotara
1853	George & Anne Stannard	Moved to Kai Iwi
1853 Jan	William Kirk & family	moved Ōtakou Māori mission
1857 Sep	George Stannard & family	apptd Ōtakou Māori mission
1857-1860	William & Emma Kirk	at: Kai Iwi 'Native Farm Sch'

Reference

Church, Ian, *Heartland of Aotea: Maori and European in South Taranaki Before the Taranaki Wars*. Hawera: Hawera Historical Society, 1992.

Upper Whānganui River

Ōhinemutu/Te Āo Marama: 1848-1853

1848-1853 Dec	William & Emma Kirk	Stationed. chief Ngapara 'converted'
1853 Jan	Kirk family	moved: to Ōtakou Māori mission

References

Clover, Gary, 'Te Putakarua, Te Awaroa, Te Matoe and Te Hau Maringi: Why Methodists should know and commemorate them', in *WHS (NZ) Journal*, 92 (2010): 6-19.

Downes, T.W., *Old Whanganui*. Hawera: W.A. Parkinson, 1915.

Port Nicholson

Te Āro Pā: 1839-1843

1839 Jun 7-1842	Minarapa Te Rangihatuake	Wesleyan preacher left in charge
1840 Dec 23- 1843 Feb 24	John & Mary Aldred	1st missionary to Te Āro
1842-1843	George & Jane Buttle	1st Wes. Minister, Wellington

Porirua: 1843-1845

1843 Feb 7-1845	Gideon Smales & family	departed: for Āotea

References

Fildes, H.E.M., *Advent of the Church: a contribution to the founding of Methodism.* Wellington: Blundell Bros print, 1921.

Roberts, John H., 'The Wesleyan Maori Mission at Te Aro', *WHS (NZ) Journal 95*, 56 (1990), pp.14-49.

Port Underwood

Ngakuta Bay ('Pisgah Vale', Port Underwood): 1848-1848 (Mission ruined by Wairau Affray)

1840 Dec 20	Samuel & Sarah Ironside	
1844 Jan 29	Ironside family	Abandoned. to Nelson; Paramena left in charge
1845 Sep-1848	William Jenkins	lay 'Catechist', + at Motueka

References

Clover, Gary, 'Another Hero of the Faith: Taawao, first missionary to Banks Peninsula', in *WHS (NZ) Journal*, 96 (2013): 23-35.

Mitchell, Hilary & John, *Te Tau Ihu o Te Waka: A History of Māori of Nelson and Marlborough*, Vol. II, *Te Ara Hou: The New Society.* Wellington: Huia Books, 2007.

Nelson & Canterbury

Nelson & Motueka: 1843-1849

1843 Feb 24- 1849 Feb	John & Mary Aldred	1st missionary in Nelson

Rāpaki, Lyttelton Harbour: 1853-1859

1853	Kirk, Aldred, Buller	Held services at Rāpaki
1854 Jan-1859	John & Mary Aldred	1st missy appointed Christchurch
1865-1892	Te Kōte Te Rātou	Māori Probationer; apptd to Rāpaki

References

Chambers, Wesley A., *Our Yesteryears: Being a short history of Methodism in Canterbury, New Zealand*. Christchurch: Willis & Aiken print, 1950.

Mitchell, Hilary & John, 'Christianity's major impact among Maori': 'Stories from The Prow', in, *The Nelson Mail*, Saturday, 9 October 2010, 17.

Mitchell, Hilary & John, *Te Tau Ihu o Te Waka*, II Wellington: Huia Press, 2007.

Pratt, M.A. Rugby, 'The Story of the Methodist Church', in, *Nelson Methodist Centenary: Souvenir 1842-1942*. Nelson: [Centennial Committee], 1942.

Williment, Tola M.L. *John Hobbs* (Wellington: Government Print, 1985.

Otago

Waikouaiti: 1840-1844

1840 May 15-1844 Apr	James & Hannah Watkin	in 'purgatory', at Waikouaiti
1843	Horomona Pohio	Watkin's '1st pastor' to Ruapuke & Rakiura Islands

Ōtakou: 1844-1866

1844 Apr1853	Charles & Eliza Creed	dep: to Wgtn-Hutt, 1853-1856
1854 Jan 3-1857 Oct	William & Emma Kirk	dep: to Kai Iwi Inst.,1857-1860
1857 Nov 14-1860	George & Anne Stannard	dep: to be Govr. Three Kings Instn
1862 June-1866	Riemenschneider	

References

Clover, Gary, 'Another Hero of the Faith: Taawao, first missionary to Banks Peninsula', in *WHS (NZ) Journal*, 96 (2013): 23-35.

Dacker, Bill, *Te Mamae me te Aroha, The Pain and the Love : a history of Kai Tahu Whanui in Otago 1844-1994*. Dunedin: University of Otago Press & Dunedin City Council,1994.

Fairclough, Paul Wynyard, *Early History of Missions in Otago.* Dunedin: New Zealand Bible, Tract and Book Society, 1902.

McNab, Robert, *Old Whaling Days: A History of Southern New Zealand from1830 to 1840.* Christchurch: Whitcombe & Tombs, 1913.

Pybus, T. Arthur, *Maori and Missionary: Early Christian Missions in The South Island of New Zealand.* Wellington: A.H. & A.W. Reed, 1954.

Taylor, W.A., *Lore and History of the South Island Māori.* Christchurch: Bascands Ltd, [1951].

Sources: Printed & Digital

Basic Sources

Fact Sheet: Internet sites for researching New Zealand Methodist history. https://www.methodist.org.nz/public/assets/Whakapapa/Archives/3-How-to-use-the-archives/Fact-sheets/Internet-Sites-for-NZ-Methodist-Research.pdf

Laurenson, George I., *Te Hahi Weteriana: Three Half Centuries of the Methodist Maori Missions 1822- 1972* WHS (NZ) Proceedings, 27, Nos. 1 & 2, 1972.

McLintock, A. H., *An Encyclopaedia of New Zealand.* Wellington: Govt Print, 1966.

Morley.

Owens, John Morley Roberts, 'The Wesleyan Mission to New Zealand 1819-1840', PhD thesis in History, Victoria University of Wellington, 1969.

Phillipps, Donald, *Companion To William Morley's History of Methodism In New Zealand: A Guide To Nineteenth Century New Zealand Methodism* WHS (NZ), 2006. An alphabetical index of those named in Morley's *History of Methodism in New Zealand.*

Phillipps, Donald J. 'A Register of Ministers of the Methodist Church of New Zealand' (Methodist Church of New Zealand website, 2020) https://www.methodist.org.nz/assets/Whakapapa/Archives/4-Methodist-history/Methodist-Biography-A-Z-29-March-2021-with-introduction-corrected.pdf

Scholefield, G.H. ed, *DNZB.* Two Volumes Wellington: Department of Internal Affairs, 1940. Contains short biographies of nearly all early Wesleyan missionaries.

Sherrin, R.A.A., *From Earliest Times to 1840*, in, *Brett's Historical Series: Early History of New Zealand*, edited by Thomson W. Leys (Auckland: H. Brett publisher, 1890

Te Ara - the Encyclopedia of New Zealand, https://teara.govt.nz/en/biographies (Online biographies from *DNZB*, 5 vols, 1990-2000.

The NZ Wesleyan Mission, Origins:

Davidson, Allan K., 'Early Protestant Missionary Beginnings in New Zealand Through Different Lenses', pp.32-51, in, *Te Rongopai 1814, 'Takoto te pai!': Bicentenary reflections on Christian beginnings and developments in Aotearoa New Zealand*, edited by Allan

K. Davidson, Stuart Lange, Peter Lineham & Adrienne Puckey Auckland: General Synod Office, 2014.

Findlay, G.G., & W.W. Holdsworth, *The History of the Wesleyan Methodist Missionary Society*, 3, London: Epworth Press, 1921.

Puckey, Adrienne, 'London, Church and Wesleyan Missionary Societies: Maritime and Pacific Connections, 1795-1835', pp.52-70, in, *Te Rongopai 1814, 'Takoto te pai!'...* Auckland: General Synod Office, 2014.

NZ Wesleyan Missionaries, Wives & Families:

Fry, Ruth, *Out of the Silence: Methodist Women of Aotearoa 1822-1985*. Christchurch: Methodist Publishing, 1987, esp, Part One, 'Early Years', pp.13-51.

Owens, John M.R, *The Wesleyan Missionaries to New Zealand Before 1840)*, *JRH*, 7, no.4, reprinted WHS (NZ) Proceedings, 38, 1973.

Snowden, Rita, *The Ladies of Wesleydale*, WHS (NZ) Proceedings, 15, nos.2 & 3, 1957.

Notes

1   Allan Davidson, 'Early Protestant Missionary Beginnings in New Zealand through Different Lenses", 32-51, in, *Te Rongopai 1814, 'Takoto te pai!': Bicentenary Reflections on Christian Beginnings and Developments in Aotearoa New Zealand*, ed, Allan Davidson, Stuart Lange, Peter Lineham & Adrienne Puckey. Auckland: General Synod Office, 2014.

2   J. Ruka, *Huia Come Home*, 6 March 2019, podcast, first episode, chat with Te Hurihanga Rihari about the arrival of the gospel into his rohe in 1814: https://soundcloud.com/user-227472867/what-went-down-at-waitangi-2019-te-hurihanga-rihari. See also: J. Ruka, *Huia Come Home*. Auckland: Oati publishers, 2017, passim.

3   G. Clover, *Collision, Compromise and Conversion during the Wesleyan Hokianga Mission, 1827–1855: A Critical Study of Hokianga Māori, Missionary, and Kauri Merchant Interactions*. Nelson: The Author, 2018, esp cc. 4 & 17.

Bibliography

Archival:

Alexander Turnbull Library, National Library of New Zealand, Wellington.

John H. Bumby and Smales Family Papers 1832-1860.

Newman-Buttle Family Papers 1831-85.

Archives New Zealand

Military Chaplains File, New Zealand Army, R22434378 and R22438911.

John Kinder Library, Auckland.

Eliza White diaries.

typescript of New Zealand Wesleyan Mission correspondence.

Methodist Church Archives, Christchurch.

Samuel Ironside Scrapbook and Journal.

Mary Aldred Scrapbook.

Lieutenant Governor William Hobson to John Hewgill Bumby, 29 May 1840.

Home and Māori Mission Minute book and letters.

Watkin Journal.

WMMS letters. typescript copy.

Mitchell Library, State Library of New South Wales.

Missionary papers, AL5.

Missionary Papers of the Bonwick Transcripts.

WMMS mission letters (microfilm).

Royal Bank of Scotland Archive.

Pole, Thornton, Free, Down & Scott Papers, PT/1/21.

School of Oriental and African Studies, London University.

Wesleyan Methodist Missionary Society archives, H-2720 – H-2721.

Books, Journal Articles and Theses

Abbott, Simon. 'How Governor George Grey failed to bring Peace, 1861–1863,' MA thesis in History, Massey University, 2020.

Abraham, William J. and James E. Kirby ed. *The Oxford Handbook of Methodist Studies*, Oxford: Oxford University Press, 2009.

Allier, Raoul. *La Psychologie de la Conversion ches les Peuples non-civilisées*, Paris: Payot, 1925

Allpress, Roshan. 'Making Philanthropists: Entrepreneurs, Evangelicals and the Growth of Philanthropy in the British World, 1756–1840', D.Phil. thesis, University of Oxford, 2015.

Anderson, Gerald H., ed. *Biographical Dictionary of Christian Missions*. New York: Macmillan Reference, 1998.

Arthur, Jennie. *Rev. Thomas and Mrs Buddle: Pioneer Missionaries to New Zealand 1840 to 1884: A Tribute to Their Memory by Their Descendants, 7th May 1940*. Auckland: Methodist Literature and Colporteur Society, 1940.

Astridge, Robin. *A Brief Outline of Wesleyan Mission Stations in the Waikato, New Zealand, Established Early 1800s*. New Zealand: The author, 2013. https://barretthoneyfield. com/wp-content/uploads/2015/08/waikato-wesleyan-missions1.pdf

Atkins, Gareth. *Converting Britannia: Evangelicals and British Public Life, 1770–1840*. Woodbridge: Boydell Press, 2019.

Baker, Marcia. *For Others with Love: A Story of Early Sisters and Methodist Deaconesses*. Christchurch: Baker Family Trust, 2007.

Baljit, Kaur, Helen May, Larry Prochner, and Claudia Nelson. *Empire, Education, and Indigenous Childhoods: Nineteenth-Century Missionary Infant Schools in Three British Colonies*. Ashgate Studies in Childhood, 1700 to the Present. Farnham, Surrey and Burlington, VT: Ashgate, 2014.

Ballantyne, Anthony. 'The Mission Station as "the Enchanter's Wand": Protestant Missionaries, Maori, and the Notion of the Household.' *Archaeological Review* 13, no. 2 (1996): 97-122.

Ballantyne, Tony. *Entanglements of Empire: Missionaries, Māori, and the Question of the Body*. Durham, NC: Duke University Press, 2014.

Barber, Lawrence, and J. Jensen. 'Henare Minita, a Neglected Missionary of the Second New Zealand War.' *Historical News*, no. 52 (May 1986): 6-12.

Barker, Mary Troup. *Seeker of Souls and Gold: William Hough, Pioneer Preacher and Prospector*. Christchurch: Concept Marketing, 1985.

Barnes, L. A. 'The Preparation of New Zealand for Settlement, with Special Reference to the Work and Influence of the Missionaries.' Master of Arts, Auckland University College, 1928.

Barnett, H.G. *Innovation: the Basis of Cultural Change*, New York: McGraw Hill, 1953.

Barrett, Alfred. *The Life of the Rev. John Hewgill Bumby: With a Brief History of the Commencement and Progress of the Wesleyan Mission in New Zealand*. 2 ed. London: J. Mason, 1853.

Barrett, Tom. '*Family Explorer*': 'George Stannard', *Whānganui Historical Record*, 19 no.2, (November 1988): 17-21.

Bawden, Patricia. *The Years before Waitangi: A Story of Early Maori/Pakeha Contact in New Zealand*. Auckland: Benton Ross, 1987.

Bawden, Patricia M. 'Christian Beginnings in New Zealand; the Historical Significance of the Ohi, Rangihoua, Te Puna Area.' Joint Board of Theological Studies S. Th. thesis, 1976.

Bawden, Patricia M. 'The Marsden Cross Heritage Centre and Chapel.' *WHS (NZ) Journal*, Proceedings, 85 (2007): 52-60.

Begg, Alison M. 'The Conversion to Christianity of the South Island Maori in the 1840s and 1850s.' *Historical and Political Studies Department of History University of Otago*, no. 3 (September 1972): 11-17.

Begg, Alison M. 'Early Maori Religious Movements: A Study of the Reactions of the Maoris to the Christian Gospel up until 1860.' Master of Arts, University of Otago, 1974.

Begg, Alison M. 'Elements in the Conversion to Christianity of the Kaitahu in the 1840s and 1850s.' Bachelor of Arts with Honours Dissertation, University of Otago, 1971.

Belich, James. *Making Peoples: A History of the New Zealanders from Polynesian Settlement to the End of the Nineteenth Century*. Auckland: Allan Lane, 1996.

Belich, James. *I Shall Not Die: Titokowaru's War, 1868–1869*. second edition, Wellington: Bridget Williams Books, 2015.

Belmer, F. Roy. *James Watkin - Pioneer Missionary*. WHS (NZ) Proceedings. 33, 1979.

Benfell, Neil. 'Christian Conflicts over Racial Policy in Early New Zealand.' *Christian Brethren Research Fellowship Journal*, no. 121 (April 1990): 7-17.

Bere, Thomas. *The controversy between Mrs Hannah More and the Curate of Blagdon relative to the Conduct of her Teacher of the Sunday School in that Parish*. London, 1801.

Binney, Judith C. 'Christianity and the Maoris to 1840: A Comment.' *New Zealand Journal of History* 3, no. 2 (October 1969): 143-65.

Binney, Judith C. 'The Expansion of Missions.' *New Zealand's Heritage* 1, no. 11 (1971): 281.

Binney, Judith C. 'Papahurihia: Some Thoughts on Interpretation.' *Journal of the Polynesian Society* 75 (September 1966): 321-31.

Birtwhistle, N Allen. 'Methodist Missions', in *A History of the Methodist Church in Great Britain* edited by R. Davies, A.R. George and G. Rupp, London: Epworth Press, 1983.

Blain, Michael. *Blain Biographical Directory of Anglican Clergy in the South Pacific* (online at Project Canterbury) The Blain Biographical Directory of Anglican Clergy in the Pacific (anglicanhistory.org)

Blake, Richard. *Evangelicals in the Royal Navy, 1775-1815: Blue Lights and Psalm-Singers*. Woodbridge: Boydell & Brewer, 2008.

Blight, Eva Margaret. 'The Work of the Reverend James Buller in the Methodist Church of New Zealand.' Master of Arts, University of New Zealand Canterbury University College, 1950. https://ir.canterbury.ac.nz/items/172ab4f0-3975-4568-87ed-ff73aa8b6a07.

Bogue David & James Bennett, *History of Dissenters from the Revolution in 1688, to the year 1808*, 4 vols., London: the Authors, 1812.

Bollen, J. D. 'A Time of Small Things: The Methodist Mission in New South Wales, 1815-1836.' *Journal of Religious History* 7 no. 3 (June 1973), 225-247.

Bolt Peter G. & Malcolm Falloon eds. *Freedom to Libel? Samuel Marsden v Philo Free: Australia's First Libel Case*. Epping: Bolt Publishing, 2017.

Bolt, Peter G., & David B. Pettett, eds. *Launching Marsden's Mission: The Beginnings of the Church Missionary Society in New Zealand, Viewed from New South Wales*. London: Latimer Trust, 2014.

Borgen, Peder. 'George Wolff (1736–1828)', *Methodist History* 40 no.1 (October 2001): 17–28.

Brazendale, Graham. 'John Whiteley and the Land Question.' *WHS (NZ) Journal 1991-92*. Proceedings, 83 (1992): 7-19.

Brazendale, Graham. *John Whiteley: Land, Sovereignty and the Land Wars of the 19th Century*. WHS (NZ) Proceedings, 64, 1996.

Broome, Richard. *Aboriginal Australians: Black Responses to White Dominance, 1788-2001*. Sydney: Allan and Unwin, 3 edition, 2002.

Broome, Richard. *Aboriginal Victorians: a History since 1800*. Sydney: Allen & Unwin, 2005.

Brownlie, Judith C. 'The Influence of Early Church Leaders and Missionaries on Maori-Pakeha Relations and Constitutional Development, 1839-1848.' Master of Arts, University of Otago, 1957.

Bruce, Audrey, *In the Trail of the Missionary: 163 Years of Methodism in West Franklin*. Waiuku: The Author [1999].

Buddle, Thomas. *The Maori King Movement in New Zealand, with a Full Report of the Native Meetings held at Waikato, April and May 1860*. Auckland: The New Zealander Office, 1860.

Buller, James. *Forty Years in New Zealand Including a Personal Narrative, an Account of Maoridom and of the Christianization and Colonization of the Country*. London: Hodder & Stoughton, 1878.

Burgess, William Pennington *Memoirs of the Rev. Joseph Burgess*, London: John Mason, 1842.

Buttle, Nora. *The Voyage of the Triton*. Proceedings. WHS (NZ) Proceedings, 22 nos. 1-2, 1965.

Buttle, Richard N. *Te Kopua: The Story of George and Jane Buttle* Auckland: R.N. Buttle, 2007.

Byrne, Brian, *The Unknown Kaipara: Five Aspects of Its History, 1250-1875*. Auckland: T.B. Byrne, 2002.

Cairns, N. 'The Missionaries as Ethnographers in the Bay of Islands.' Bachelor of Arts with Honours Research Exercise, University of Otago, 1997.

Campbell, Matthew, Simon Holdoway and Sarah Macready eds. *Finding Our Recent Past: Historical Archaeology in New Zealand*, Auckland: New Zealand Archaeological Association, 2013.

Cant, Garth. 'The Methodist and Ratana Connection.' *WHS (NZ) Journal* 100 (2015): 31-42.

Cant, Garth. *The Methodist Response to the Formation of the Ratana Church in 1924-1925*. WHS (NZ) Proceedings, 2018.

Cant, Garth. 'Te Rua Winiata and the World Council of Churches.' *WHS (NZ) Journal* Proceedings, 92 (2010): 36-49.

Cameron, Graham G. Bidois "That You Might Stand Here on the Roof of the Clouds.': The Development of Pirirākau Theology from Encounter to the End of Conflict, 1839-1881.' Master of Theology, University of Otago, 2016.

Carey, Hilary M. and John Gascoigne eds. *Church and State in Old and New Worlds*. Brill's Series in Church History, 233-59. Leiden: Brill, 2010.

Carpenter, Samuel D. 'The Reshaping of Political Communities in New Zealand: A Study of Intellectual and Imperial Texts in Context, C. 1814-1863.' Ph.D. thesis, Massey University, 2020.

Cervin, Georgia Rae. 'Te Hiima: Reverend A. J. Seamer and His Māori Mission.' B.A. Honours, University of Otago, 2011.

Chambers, Wesley A. 'Samuel Ironside in Church and Community.' *WHS (NZ) Journal* '85, Proceedings, 46 (1985): 18-31.

Chambers, Wesley A. 'Samuel Ironside in Church and Community.' *Journal N.Z. Federation of Historical Societies* 2, no. 3 (September 1985): 49-53.

Chambers, Wesley A. *Not Self - but Others: The Story of the Methodist Deaconess Order Together with an Index of All Those Who Have Served in It*. WHS (NZ) Proceedings, 48, 1987.

Chambers, Wesley A. *Our Yesteryears 1840-1950: Being a Short History of Methodism in Canterbury, New Zealand*. Christchurch: Willis & Aitken, 1950.

Chambers, Wesley A. 'A Psychological Analysis of Culture Contact: A Survey of Maori Relationships with the Wesleyan Methodist Missionaries, 1822-43.' Master of Arts, University of New Zealand Canterbury University College, 1953.

Chambers, Wesley A. 'Quiet Reminder at Mangungu.' *New Zealand Historic Places*, no. 29 (June 1990): 10-14.

Chambers, Wesley A. *Samuel Ironside in New Zealand, 1839-1858.* Auckland: Ray Richards & WHS (NZ), 1982.

Chambers, Wesley A. 'The Wesleyan Methodist Mission in New Zealand, 1819-1855.' *Christian Brethren Research Fellowship Journal*, no. 121 (April 1990): 19-27.

Chappell, Albert Bygrave. *Across a Hundred Years, 1841-1941; a Brief Story of the Beginning and Early Progress of Methodism in Auckland, N.Z.* WHS (NZ) Proceedings. 1 no. 1, 1941.

Chappell, Albert Bygrave. *Early Missionary Days in South Taranaki.* WHS (NZ) Proceedings, 1 no.4, 1942.

Chisholm, Robert F. *How the Bible Came to New Zealand and Goes Forth for All Men Everywhere.* Wellington: British and Foreign Bible Society (N.Z.), 1953.

Church, Ian. *Heartland of Aotea: Maori and European in South Taranaki Before the Taranaki Wars*, Hawera: The Author, 1992.

Clover, Gary A. M. 'Another Hero of the Faith: Taawao, First Missionary to Banks Peninsula.' *WHS (NZ) Journal* 96 (2013): 24-36.

Clover, Gary. 'Haimona Pita (Simon Peter) Matangi 1783?-1839.' *WHS (NZ) Journal*, 102 (2016): 39-43.

Clover, Gary A. M. 'More Heroes of the Faith: Minarapa Te Rangi-Hatu-Ake and Te Aro Pa, 1839-1841.' *WHS (NZ) Journal* 95 (2012): 27-50.

Clover, Gary A. M. 'Heroes of the Faith - Early Wesleyan Māori Teachers and Conversion.' *WHS (NZ) Journal* 99 (2014): 18-33.

Clover, Gary A.M. *William Woon: Wesleyan Printer in Tonga and New Zealand; The Other Missionary Printer.* Beau Bassin, Mauritius: Scholars Press, 2018.

Clover, Gary A. M. 'Te Putakarua, Te Awaroa, Te Matoe and Te Hau Maringi: Why Methodists Should Know and Commemorate Them.' *WHS (NZ) Journal* 92 (2010): 6-19.

Clover, Gary A. M. 'More Heroes of the Faith: The Two Methodist Maori Missionaries Martyred near Mangataipa in the Hokianga in 1837.' *WHS (NZ) Journal* 93 (2011): 5-12.

Clover, Gary A.M. 'Rescued from Obscurity: A Life of the Reverend John Skevington, 1815-1845.' *WHS (NZ) Journal* 89 (2009): 22-43.

Clover, Gary A.M. *The Wesleyan Colenso: The Missionary Career of William Woon 1830-1858.* Auckland: The Author, 2012.

Clover, Gary A.M. *William Woon 1803-1858: Wesleyan Printer in Tonga and New Zealand.* Proceedings. Auckland: WHS (NZ) Proceedings, 97, 2014.

Clover, Gary A. M. '150th Anniversary 'Heretoa' Wesleyan Maori Mission Station Waimate South, May 30th 1992.' In *WHS (NZ) Journal 1991-92*, (1992): 61-65.

Clover, Gary A. M. 'Another Hero of the Faith: Taawao, First Missionary to Banks Peninsula.' *WHS (NZ) Journal* 96 (2013): 24-36.

Clover, Gary A. M. 'Brethren and Rivals: Co-Operation and Conflict between Missionaries of the C M S and the W M S 1815-1870.' *Stimulus* 7, no. 2 (May 1999): 10-15.

Clover, Gary A. M. 'The Māngungu Treaty Signing, 12 February 1840, and Its Importance.' *WHS (NZ) Journal* 105 (2018): 24-49.

Clover, Gary A. M. 'More Heroes of the Faith: Minarapa Te Rangi-Hatu-Ake and Te Aro Pa, 1839-1841.' *WHS (NZ) Journal* 95 (2012): 27-50.

Clover, Gary A. M. "Going Mihinare', 'Experimental Religion', and Maori Embracing of Missionary Christianity.' *Christian Brethren Research Fellowship Journal*, no. 121 (April 1990): 41-55.

Clover, Gary A. M. 'Christianity among the South Taranaki Maoris, 1840-53: A Study of the Wesleyan Mission at Waimate South.' Master of Arts, University of Auckland, 1973.

Clover, Gary A. M. *Collision, Compromise and Conversion during the Wesleyan Hokianga Mission, 1827–1855: A Critical Study of Hokianga Maori, Missionary, and Kauri Merchant Interactions.* Nelson: The author, 2018.

Clover, Gary A. M. 'A Photographic Essay of Methodism's 1927 Centenary of Commemoration at Mangungu.' *WHS (NZ) Journal*, 107 (2019): 40-54.

Coke, Thomas. *A Plan of the Society for the Establishment of Missions among the Heathens*, [no publication details] 1784.

Colwell, James. *A Century in the Pacific. Scientific, Sociological, Historical, Missionary, General.* London: Charles H. Kelly, 1914.

Colwell, James. *The Illustrated History of Methodism. Australia: 1812 to 1855. New South Wales and Polynesia: 1856 to 1902; with Special Chapters on the Discovery and Settlement of Australia, the Missions to the South Sea Islands, New Zealand and the Aborigines, and a Review of the Movement Leading up to Methodist Union; Compiled from Official Records and Other Sources.* Sydney: William Brooks and Co., 1904.

Coney, Sandra. 'Man with a Mission.' *Southern Skies* (March 1991): 24-29.

Cooke, Raymond C. 'Two Aspects of Philanthropy: The Aborigines Protection Society and the New Zealand Company.' *Journal of Religious History* 5 (1968): 31-44.

Cooper, Barbara, *The Remotest Interior: a History of Taupo.* Tauranga: Moana Press, 1989.

Cordery, Carolyn J. 'Hallowed Treasures: Sacred, Secular and the Wesleyan Methodists in New Zealand 1819-1840.' Working Paper No. 39. *Accounting History* 11, no. 2 (2006): 199-220.

Curnow, Jenifer/Hopa and Ngapare/McRae, Jane eds. *Rere Atu, Taku Manu! Discovering History, Language and Politics in the Maori-Language Newspapers*, Auckland: Auckland University Press, 2002.

Dacker, Bill. *Te Mamae me Te Aroha, the Pain and the Love: A History of Kai Tahu Whanui in Otago, 1844- 1944*. Dunedin: University of Otago Press & Dunedin City Council, 1994.

Dakin, Jim, Jack Shallcrass and Anne Ferguson eds. *Honest to Goodness*, Wellington: Humanist Society of New Zealand, 1992.

Daniels, W. H. *The Illustrated History of Methodism in Great Britain, America, and Australia.* Sydney and Melbourne: George Coffey, 1879.

Davidson, Allan K., Stuart Lange, Peter Lineham and Adrienne Puckey, eds. *Te Rongopai 1814 'Takoto Te Pai!': Bicentenary Reflections on Christian Beginnings and Developments in Aotearoa New Zealand*, Auckland: General Synod office of Anglican Church in Aotearoa New Zealand, 2014.

Davidson, Allan K. 'New Zealand Missions and Emigration.' In *Dictionary of Scottish Church History & Theology*, edited by Nigel M de Cameron, David F Wright, David C. Lachman and Donald E. Meek. Edinburgh: T. & T. Clark, 1993.

Davidson, Allan K. 'The Interaction of Missionary and Colonial Christianity in Nineteenth Century New Zealand.' *Studies in World Christianity* 2, no. 2 (1996): 145-66.

Davidson, Allan K. 'Religious Studies in Dialogue with Missionaries.' In *Religious Studies in Dialogue: Essays in Honour of Albert C. Moore*, edited by M. Andrew, P. Matheson and S. Rae, 115-24. Dunedin: Faculty of Theology University of Otago, 1991.

Davidson, Allan K. *Aotearoa New Zealand: Defining Moments in the Gospel-Culture Encounter.* Geneva: WCC Publications, 1996.

Davison, Graeme, John Hirst, & Stuart Macintyre eds. *The Oxford Companion to Australian History*, Melbourne: Oxford University Press, 2001.

Dawson. J. B. ed. *Wesley's South Seas Heritage*, WHS (NZ) Proceedings, 50, 1987.

de Reland, Elizabeth, Keith Hamilton, et al, Parramatta Mission Heritage Committee, *Samuel Leigh: First Wesleyan Missionary to Australia & New Zealand*, Sydney: Parramatta Mission, 2019.

Dictionary of New Zealand Biography, vol 1, *1769-1869* ed. W.H. Oliver. Wellington: Department of Internal Affairs and Allen & Unwin, 1990. Vol. 2: *1870-1900*, ed. Claudia Orange. Wellington: Bridget Williams Books, 1993; vol. 3, *1901-1920*, ed. Claudia Orange, Auckland: Auckland University Press, 1996; vol. 4 1921-1940 ed. Claudia Orange, Auckland: Auckland University Press. Also available online at Te Ara – the Encyclopedia of New Zealand.

Downes, T.W. *Old Whanganui*, Hawera: W.A. Parkinson, 1915.

Duffy, Mervyn. 'The Perils of Published Missionary Letters.' *International Bulletin of Mission Research* 42, no. 3 (2018): 251-61.

Edwards, Maldwyn. *After Wesley: A Study of the Social and Political Influence of Methodism in the Middle Period (1791–1849)*. London: Epworth Press, 1935.

Eketone, Anaru. 'Wetere Te Rerenga and the Murder of Rev. John Whiteley.' Chap. 4 In *Aftermaths: Colonialism, Violence and Memory in Australia, New Zealand and the Pacific*, edited by Angela Wanhalla, Lyndall Ryan and Camilla Nurka, 59-68. Dunedin: Otago University Press, 2023.

Elliott, Gabriel. *Miller of Wakatumutumu: Sowing the Seed in Pioneer New Zealand*. WHS (NZ) Proceedings, 16, no.5, 1959.

Ellis, Malcolm H. *Lachlan Macquarie: His Life, Adventures and Times*. Sydney: Dymock's, 1947.

Elsmore, Bronwyn. 'According to the Scriptures: The Influence of the Publication of the Christian Scriptures in Maori on Maori Religious Movements.' Ph.D. thesis, Victoria University of Wellington, 1986.

Elsmore, Bronwyn. *Like them that Dream: the Maori and the Old Testament*. Tauranga: Moana Press, 1985.

Fairclough, Paul Wynyard. *The Early History of Missions in Otago*. Dunedin: New Zealand Bible & Tract Society, 1902.

Fairclough, Paul Wynyard. *The Mother Church of Otago Methodism: Souvenir of 75th Anniversary 1862:1937*. Dunedin: Otago Daily Times Print, 1937.

Falloon, Malcolm. 'The Maori Conversion and Four Early Converts.' Ph.D. thesis, University of Otago, 2020.

Fildes, H.E.M., *Advent of the Church: a Contribution to the Founding of Methodism*. Wellington: Blundell Bros., 1921.

Findlay, G.G., & W.W. Holdsworth, *The History of the Wesleyan Methodist Missionary Society*, 3, London: Epworth Press, 1921.

Fitzgerald, Tanya. 'Cartographies of Friendship: Mapping Missionary Women's Educational Networks in Aotearoa/New Zealand 1823-40.' *History of Education* 32, no. 5 (September 2003): 513-28.

Fitzgerald, Tanya. 'Fences, Boundaries and Imagined Communities: Re-Thinking the Construction of Early Mission Schools and Communities in New Zealand 1823-1830.' *History of Education Review* 30, no. 2 (2001): 14-25.

Fitzgerald, Tanya. 'Jumping the Fences: Policy, Practice and Maori Women's Resistance to Schooling in Northern New Zealand 1823-1835.' *Paedagogica Historica: International Journal of the History of Education* 37, no. 1 (2001): 175-92.

———. 'Missionary Women as Educators: The C M S Schools in New Zealand 1823-1835.' *History of Education Review* 23, no. 3 (1994): 139-49.

Fletcher, C. Brunsdon. *The Black Knight of the Pacific*. Sydney: Australasian Publishing Co, 1944.

Fordyce, Stephen. *Tangiteroria: Crucible of the Kaipara 1836-54 Missionary Impulse & Impact.* Ruawai: Charford Press, 2009.

Francis, Andrew, *The Rohe Potae Commercial Economy in the Mid-Nineteenth Century, c.1830-1886: A Report commissioned by the Waitangi Tribunal*, February 2011 (Wai 8987, # A 26).

Frost, Alan. *Botany Bay and the First Fleet: The Real Story*, Melbourne: Black, 2019.

Fry, Ruth. *Out of the Silence: Methodist Women of Aotearoa 1822-1985.* Christchurch: Methodist Publishing, 1987.

Gadd, D. Bernard H. *The Rev. James Buller, 1812-1884.* WHS (NZ) Proceedings. 23 nos. 1-2, 1966.

Garthwaite, Justine. 'The Anglican and Methodist Reaction to the Ratana Movement 1919-1929.' Bachelor of Arts with Honours, University of Otago, 1991.

Gittos, Murray B. 'Two Methodist Missionaries of the North: The Maverick and the Model [1].' *Auckland & Waikato Historical Journal*, no. 40 (April 1982): 1-4.

Gittos, Murray B. 'Two Methodist Missionaries of the North: The Maverick and the Model [2].' *Auckland & Waikato Historical Journal*, no. 41 (September 1982): 19-23.

Gittos, Murray B. *Mana at Mangungu: A Biography of William White 1794-1875, Wesleyan Missionary at Whangaroa and Hokianga 1823-36.* Auckland: The Author, 1982.

Glen, Frank G. *Methodism in Auckland during the Maori Wars 1860-1864.* WHS (NZ) Proceedings, 16 nos. 1-2, 1957.

Glen, Robert, ed. *Mission and Moko: Aspects of the Work of the Church Missionary Society in New Zealand, 1814-1882.* Christchurch, N.Z.: Latimer Fellowship of New Zealand, 1992.

Goldsbury, Sheryl Jacqueline. 'Behind the Picket Fence: The Lives of Missionary Wives in Pre-Colonial New Zealand.' Master of Arts, University of Auckland, 1986.

Great Britain, House of Commons. *Report of the Parliamentary Select Committee on Aboriginal Tribes*, London: House of Commons, 1837.

Great Britain, House of Commons. *Report from the Select Committee on Aborigines (British Settlements) Together with the Minutes of Evidence, Appendix and Index.* London: House of Commons, 1836

Greenslade, William W. H. *John Whiteley, 1806-1869.* WHS (NZ) Proceedings. 24 nos. 3-4, 1968.

Grimshaw Patricia and Andrew May, eds. *Missions, Indigenous Peoples and Cultural Exchange.* Eastbourne: Sussex Academic Press, 2010.

Gunson, W. Niel. 'Evangelical Missionaries in the South Seas.' Ph.D., Australian National University, 1959.

Gunson, Walter Niel. *Messengers of Grace: Evangelical Missionaries in the South Seas 1797-1860*. Melbourne: Oxford University Press, 1978.

Halliday, H. L. J. 'The Reverend A.J. Seamer and the Attitudes of the Methodists to the Ratana Movement.' Research Essay, University of Auckland, 1966.

Haltaway, F. G. 'History of Missionary Labours in the Bay of Islands, Whangaroa, and Hokianga Districts, and the Influence of Missionary Work.' Master of Arts, University of New Zealand Auckland University College, 1931.

Hames, E. W. *From Grafton to Three Kings to Paerata: A History of Wesley College Auckland, New Zealand, from 1842 to 1982*. WHS (NZ) Proceedings, 39, 1982.

Hames, E. W. *The Origins and Fortunes of the Prince Albert College Trust: A Footnote to New Zealand Methodist History*. WHS (NZ) Proceedings, 34, 1979.

Hames, E. W. *Out of the Common Way: The European Church in the Colonial Era 1840-1913*. WHS (NZ) Proceedings, 27, nos. 3-4, 1972.

Hames, E. W. *Walter Lawry and the Wesleyan Mission in the South Seas*. WHS (NZ) Proceedings. 23 no 4, 1967.

Hames, E. W. *Wesley College: A Centenary Survey, 1844-1944*. WHS (NZ) Proceedings, 3 no 4, 1944.

Hamilton, Lila. 'The Introduction of Christianity.' *New Zealand's Heritage* 1, no. 8 (1971): 203-07.

Hammer, George Edward Johnston. 'Cort Henry Schnackenberg, Pioneer Missionary, 1812-1880.' Master of Literature, University of Auckland, 1990.

Hammer, G. E. J. *A Pioneer Missionary, Raglan to Mokau 1844-1880: Cort Henry Schnackenberg*. WHS (NZ) Proceedings, 57, 1991.

Hammond, T. G. *In the Beginning: The History of a Mission*. 2 ed. Auckland: Methodist Literature & Colporteur Society, 1940. Hawera: W.A. Parkinson, 1915.

Harsant, Florence. *They Called Me Te Maari*. Christchurch: Whitcoulls, 1979.

Hempton, David. *The Church in the Long Eighteenth Century*. London: IB Tauris, 2011

Hempton, David. *Methodism and Politics in British Society 1750–1850*. London: Hutchinson, 1984.

Henare, Manuka, Anne Salmond, Billie Lythberg, and Amber Nicholson. *He Whenua Rangatira: A Mana Maori History of the Early-Mid-Nineteenth Century*. Research in Anthropology & Linguistics. Auckland: University of Auckland Department of Anthropology, 2021.

Henderson, J. M. *Ratana: The Man, the Church, the Political Movement*. Polynesian Society Memoir. 2 ed. 36, Wellington: A.H. & A.W. Reed and the Polynesian Society, 1963.

Hiatt, R. Jeffrey. 'John Wesley's Approach to Mission', *The Asbury Journal*, 68 no.1 (2013): 108–124.

Hight, James ed. *New Zealand*, Cambridge History of the British Empire, 47-59. Cambridge: Cambridge University Press, 1933.

Hill, Harold, ed. *Te Ope Whakaora the Army That Brings Life*. Wellington: Flag Publications, 2007.

Hobbs, Richard. *Wesleyan Native Institution; Established in 1844 by W. Lawry and Thos. Buddle*. Auckland: Brett Printing Co., 1906.

Hogan, Michael. *The Sectarian Strand: Religion in Australian History*. Melbourne: Penguin, 1987.

Hohepa, Pat. 'My Musket, My Missionary, and My Mana.' In *Voyages and Beaches: Pacific Encounters 1769-1840*, edited by Alex Calder, Jonathon Lamb and Bridget Orr, 156-79. Honolulu: University of Hawaii Press, 1999.

Houston, John, *Maori Life in Old Taranaki*. Wellington: A.H. & A.W. Reed, 1965.

Howe, K.R. 'The Maori Response to Christianity in the Thames-Waikato Area, 1833-1840.' *New Zealand Journal of History* 7, no. 1 (1973): 28-46.

Hunt, C. G. *Some Notes on the Wesleyan Mission at Aotearoa*. WHS (NZ), 1965.

Hunwick, E. C. 'Missioner Shouldered Cross at a Wilderness Station.' *Footprints in History* 3 (October 1989): 49-51.

Hutchings, Jessica and Jenny Lee-Morgan eds. *Decolonisation in Aotearoa: Education, Research and Practice*, Wellington: NZCER Press, 2016.

Hylson-Smith, Kenneth. *Evangelicals in the Church of England, 1734-1984*. Edinburgh: T&T Clark, 1988.

Insull, H. A. H. 'The Three Kings Native Institution.' *Journal Auckland & Waikato Historical Societies*, no. 25 (October 1974): 32-36.

Insull, H. A. H. *The Wesley College Register 1844-1974*. Auckland: Wesley College Old Boys Association, 1974.

Irvine, Jean. *Northland Pilgrimage, 1972*. Kaikohe: Anniversary Committee, Methodist Church of New Zealand, 1972.

Irvine, Jean. *Historic Hokianga: An Introductory Guide*. Rāwene: The Author, 1965.

Irwin, James. *An Introduction to Maori Religion: Its Character before European Contact and Its Survival in Contemporary Maori and New Zealand Culture*. Special Studies in Religion. 4: Australian Association for the Study of Religion, 1984.

Jenkins, Kuni E. H. K. , and Alison Jones. *Words between Us: First Māori-Pākehā Conversations on Paper = He Kōrero*. Wellington: Huia, 2011.

Jenkins, Kuni E. H. K. 'Haere Tahi Taua.' Ph.D. thesis, University of Auckland, 2000.

Jensen, J. H., and Lawrence H. Barber. 'The Schnackenberg Family Papers.' *Auckland & Waikato Historical Journal*, no. 51 (September 1987): 24-27.

Jones, Alison, and Kuni E.H. Jenkins. 'Invitation and Refusal: A Reading of the Beginnings of Schooling in Aotearoa New Zealand.' *History of Education* 37, no. 2 (2008): 187-206.

Jones, Barry, and Arepara Ngaha. 'All Things New: The Bicultural Journey of the Methodist Church of New Zealand - Te Hahi Weteriana O Aotearoa.' Chap. 5 In *Listening to the People of the Land: Christianity, Colonisation & the Path to Redemption*, edited by J. F. Healy, 113-38. Auckland: Pax Christi, 2019.

Jones, Pauline, *Milton's Missionary: The Life and Work of Rev. Samuel Leigh 1785-1852, First Missionary to Australia and New Zealand*, Stoke-on-Trent: P. Jones, 1986.

Keeling, Annie E. *What He Did for the Convicts and Cannibals: Some Account of the Life and Work of the Rev. Samuel Leigh.* London: Charles H. Kelly, 1896.

Kempthorne, Renatus. *Maori Christianity in Te Waipounamu: A History.* Christchurch: Te Hui Amorangi o Te Waipounamu, 2000.

King, Christopher Paul. 'Stranger and Other: Evangelical Missionaries.' Master of Social Sciences, University of Waikato, 1992.

King, G. S. R. 'Maori Denominational Boarding Schools.' Master of Arts, Victoria University of Wellington, 1980.

King, Joseph. *Ten Decades: The Australian Centenary Story of the London Missionary Society.* London: London Missionary Society, 1900.

King, Michael. *The Penguin History of New Zealand.* Auckland: Penguin, 2003.

King, Michael, ed. *Te Ao Hurihuri: Aspects of Māoritanga.* Wellington: Hicks Smith & Methuen NZ, 1975, reprint, Wellington: Reed, 1992.

King, Michael. *Te Puea*, Auckland: Hodder & Stoughton, 1987.

Kirk, Athol. 'Christian Martyrs Recalled.' *Historical Record Whanganui Historical Society* 17, no. 2 (November 1986): 8-10.

Klein, Milton M. *An Amazing Grace: John Thornton and the Clapham Sect.* New Orleans: University Press of the South, 2004.

Knowles, Brett. *The History of a New Zealand Pentecostal Movement: The New Life Churches of New Zealand from 1946 to 1979.* Studies in Religion and Society. 45, Lewistown: Edwin Mellen Press, 2000.

Lang, John Dunmore. *New Zealand in 1839, or, Four Letters to the Rt. Hon. Earl Durham, Governor of the New Zealand Land Company .. On the Colonization of That Island and on the Present Condition and Prospects of Its Native Inhabitants.* London: Smith, Elder and Co., 1839.

Lange, Raeburn. 'Ordained Ministry in Maori Christianity, 1853-1900.' *Journal of Religious History* 27, no. 1 (2003): 47-66.

Lange, Raeburn. 'Indigenous Agents of Religious Change in New Zealand, 1830-1860.' *Journal of Religious History* 24, no. 3 (October 2000): 277-95.

Lange, Raeburn, *Island Ministers: Indigenous Leadership in Nineteenth Century Pacific Islands Christianity*. Christchurch: Macmillan Brown Centre for Pacific Studies, University of Canterbury and Canberra: Pandanus Books, Research School of Pacific and Asian Studies, Australian National University, 2005.

Laurenson, George I. *Methodist-Maori Missions Yesterday and Today*. WHS (NZ) Proceedings. 5 no. 2, Auckland: Methodist Literature and Colporteur Society N.Z., 1946.

Laurenson, George I. *Te Hahi Weteriana: Three Half Centuries of the Methodist Maori Mission 1822-1972*. WHS (NZ) Proceedings, 27 no. 1-2, 1972.

Lawry, Walter. 'A Missionary Marries: Walter Lawry Seeks and Obtains a Wife.' *WHS (NZ) Journal '86*, Proceedings, 49 (1986): 53-55.

Laws, Charles H. *The Methodist Mission in New Zealand: Toil and Adversity at Whangaroa*. WHS (NZ) Proceedings, 3 nos. 1-2, 1944.

Laws, Charles H. *The Methodist Mission to New Zealand: First Years at Hokianga 1827-1836*. WHS (NZ) Proceedings, 4 nos. 2-3, 1945.

Leadley, Alan. *A Brief History of the Kawhia Methodist Mission, 1834-1994*. Hamilton: Waikato-Bay of Plenty Bicultural Working Group, 1994.

Leadley, Alan, *A Pilgrimage to Kawhia: The Heart of West Coast Methodism* (Saturday, 9 November 2013), https://docslib.org/doc/3223969/a-pilgrimage-to-kawhia-the-heart-of-west-coast-methodism

Lee, Jack. *An Unholy Trinity: Three Hokianga Characters*, Russell: Northland Historical Society Publications Society, 1990.

Lewis, Donald M. (ed.) *Dictionary of Evangelical Biography, 1730–1860*, 2 v., Oxford: Blackwell, 1995.

Lewis, Miles. 'Heavenly Groundings: Missionary Architectural Practice in Nineteenth-Century New Zealand.' In *Shifting Views: Selected Essays on the Architectural History of Australia and New Zealand*, edited by Andrew Leach, Antony Moulis and Nicole Sully. St Lucia, Queensland: University of Queensland Press, 2008.

Lineham, Peter J. ed. *Weaving the Unfinished Mats: Wesley's Legacy: Conflict, Confusion and Challenge in the South Pacific*, WHS (NZ) Proceedings, 83-84, 2007.

Lineham, Peter J. *New Zealanders and the Methodist Evangel: An Interpretation of the Policies and Performance of the Methodist Church of New Zealand*. WHS (NZ) Proceedings, 42, 1983.

Lovegrove, Deryck W. *Established Church, Sectarian People: Itinerancy and the Transformation of English Dissent, 1780–1830*, Cambridge: Cambridge University Press, 1988.

Luttrell, Julie, *The Governors Interpreter* ([Auckland]: Ron H. Mortensen, 2019.

Luxton, Clarence T. J. *The Rev. James Wallis of the Wesleyan Missionary Society*. WHS (NZ) Proceedings, 21, nos, 1-2, 1965.

Luxton, Clarence T. J. *Methodist Beginnings in the Manukau: The Story of Pehiakura Mission 1834-1862*. WHS (NZ) Proceedings, 17, no. 4, 1960.

Macdonald, Charlotte, Merimeri Penfold, and Bridget Williams, eds. *The Book of New Zealand Women: Ko Kui Ma Te Kaupapa*. Wellington: Bridget Williams Books, 1991.

MacDonald, E. 'The Methodist and Catholic Missions in the Waikato.' *Historical Journal Auckland & Waikato History Societies*, no. 22 (April 1973): 27-28.

Major, Margaret E. 'Christian Missions in the South Island in the 1840s.' Master of Arts, University of Canterbury, 1964. http://hdl.handle.net/10092/7831.

Mandeno, J. F. 'Wesleyan Missions on the West Coast and Inland.' *Footprints of history* 1, no. 1 (October 1988): 15-18.

Maning, Frederick Edward. *Old New Zealand: Being Incidents of Native Customs and Character in the Old Times by A Pakeha Māori*. London: Smith, Elder and Co., 1863.

Markham, Edward. *New Zealand or Recollections of it*, ed. E.H. McCormick, Wellington: Government Printer, 1963.

Marshall, Lucy C. *Walter Lawry, Cornwall, Australia, Tonga, New Zealand*. Occasional Publications 12. Cornwall: Cornwall Methodist Historical Society, 1967.

Martin, Kate and Brad Mercer, eds. *The French Place in the Bay of Islands: Te Urunga Mai O Te Iwi Wiwi: Essays from Pompallier's Printery*, Kororareka Russell: Matou Matauwhi with Rim Books, 2011.

Maskell, W. 'Early Missionary Enterprise in New Zealand.' Master of Arts, University of New Zealand, 1924.

Maxwell, Alexander, and Evan Roberts. 'The Whangaroa Incident, 16 July 1824: A European–Māori Encounter and Its Many Incarnations.' *Journal of Pacific History* 49, no. 1 (2014): 50-75.

McHaig, I. S. 'The Acquisition of Lands by the Whalers and Missionaries.' *Historical Review Whakatane Historical Society* 18 (1970): 20-28.

McKay, Veda, and Verna Mossong. 'Thomas Skinner, Catechist.' In *WHS (NZ) Journal 1998*, Proceedings, 67 (1998): 50-54.

McKenzie, D. F. *Oral Culture, Literacy and Print in Early New Zealand - the Treaty of Waitangi*. Wellington: Victoria University Press & Alexander Turnbull Library, 1985.

McLintock, A. H., *An Encyclopaedia of New Zealand*. 3 v., Wellington: Govt Print, 1966. [Also available online at Te Ara.]

McNab, Robert, *Old Whaling Days: A History of Southern New Zealand from 1830 to 1840*. Christchurch: Whitcombe & Tombs, 1913.

Mein Smith, Philippa, Peter Hempenstall & Shaun Goldfinch, *Remaking the Tasman World*. Christchurch: Canterbury University Press, 2008.

Melbourne, Te Waaka. 'Te Wairua Kōmingomingo O Te Māori = the Spiritual Whirlwind of the Māori.' Ph.D. thesis, Massey University, 2011.

Mellor, E. J. 'Church Missionary Society and Wesleyan Schools in the Waikato Area 1834-1865.' Master of Education, University of Waikato, 1974.

'Memento Mori - John Skevington - 1814-1845.' *WHS (NZ) Journal '89*, Proceedings, 52 (1989): 50-52.

Middleditch, Anne. *Mary Bumby: The First Person to Take Honey Bees to New Zealand.* United Kingdom: Northern Bee Books, 2018.

Middleton, Angela. *Pēhairangi: Bay of Islands Mission and Maori 1814 to 1845.* Dunedin: Otago University Press, 2014.

Mikaere, Buddy. 'God's Leaf: Wiremu Te Kooti Te Rato.' *Te Karanga* 3, no. 2 (August 1987): 5-11.

Miller, Harold. *The Maori and the Missionary.* Wellington: School Publications Branch, Dept. of Education, 1954.

Miller, John Owen. *Early Victorian New Zealand, a Study of Racial Tensions and Social Attitudes, 1839-1852.* London: Oxford University Press, 1958.

Mitchell, Hilary & John, *Te Tau Ihu o Te Waka: A History of Māori of Nelson and Marlborough*, II, *Te Ara Hou: The New Society.* Wellington: Huia Books, 2007.

Moon, Paul. 'Wesleyan Wives: The Role of Women in the Wesleyan Mission to New Zealand in the 1820s.' *Stimulus* 22, no. 2 (July 2015): 22-29.

Morley, William. *The History of Methodism in New Zealand.* Wellington: McKee, 1900.

Morrison, Hugh, Lachy Paterson, Brett Knowles, & Murray Rae, eds. *Mana Maori and Christianity.* Wellington: Huia Books, 2012.

Morris, Henry. *The Life of Charles Grant.* London: John Murray, 1904.

Mossong, Verna. 'Celebration in Kaeo; the Story of Wesleydale; Rev. Nathaniel Turner; President's Introduction to a Cemetery Series; Eliza White's Autograph Album.' In WHS (NZ) *Journal 1998*, Proceedings, 67 (1998): 37-49, 50-62.

New Zealand Correspondence between the Wesleyan Missionary Committee and the Right Honourable Earl Grey, Her Majesty's Principal Secretary of State for the Colonial Department, on the Apprehended Infringement of the Treaty of Waitangi. London: Wesleyan Missionary Society, 1848.

Newman, Keith. *Beyond Betrayal: Trouble in the Promised Land - Restoring the Mission to Maori.* Auckland: Penguin, 2013.

Newman, Keith. *Bible & Treaty: Missionaries among the Maori - a New Perspective.* Auckland: Penguin Books, 2010.

Nichol, Chris and James Veitch. *Religion in New Zealand*, Wellington: Tertiary Christian Studies Programme, 1983.

Nobbs, K. J. 'William & Dinah Hall and the First Wesleyan Missionaries 1819-1825.' *WHS (NZ) Journal '88*, Proceedings, 51 (1988): 46-56.

Nottingham, Isla M. 'The Coming of the Missionaries: A Study of Evangelical Beliefs and Maori Understandings: 1814-1822.' Master of Arts, University of Waikato, 1980.

O'Brien, Glen. "Not Radically a Dissenter': Samuel Leigh in the Colony of New South Wales.' *Wesley and Methodist Studies* 4 (2012): 51-69.

O'Brien, Glen. & Hilary Carey (eds.), *Methodism in Australia: A History.* Farnham, Surrey and Burlington, Vermont: Ashgate, 2015.

O'Malley, Vincent. *The Meeting Place: Māori and Pākehā Encounters, 1642-1840.* Auckland: Auckland University Press, 2012.

O'Malley, Vincent. *The New Zealand Wars | Ngā Pakanga o Aotearoa.* Wellington: Bridget Williams Books, 2019.

Oettli, Peter. *God's Messenger: J.F. Riemenschneider and Racial Conflict in 19th Century New Zealand.* Wellington: Huia, 2008.

Olsson, Arthur L. 'A Lonely Road.' *Stockade* 15, no. 20 (November 1987): 2-3.

Olsson, Arthur L. *Methodism in Wellington: Methodism in Wellington 1839 to 1989: A Chronological Outline of the Growth and Development of the Methodist Church in the Wellington District.* Wellington: Wellington District Synod of the Methodist Church of New Zealand, 1989.

Our Land Story and Guidelines for taking Action on Land and responding to the Waitangi Tribunal, Bricks and Mortar, 1991.

Owens, J. M. R. *Prophets in the Wilderness: The Wesleyan Mission to New Zealand 1819-1827.* Auckland: Auckland University Press & Oxford University Press, 1974.

Owens, J. M. R. 'Religious Disputation at Whangaroa 1823-1827.' *Journal of the Polynesian Society* 79, no. 3 (1970): 288-304.

Owens, J. M. R. *The Unexpected Impact: Wesleyan Missionaries and Maoris in the Early 19th Century.* WHS (NZ) Proceedings, 27 no 6, 1973.

Owens, J. M. R. 'The Wesleyan Mission to New Zealand, 1819-1840.' Ph.D. thesis, Victoria University of Wellington, 1969.

Owens, J. M. R. 'The Wesleyan Missionaries to New Zealand before 1840.' *Journal of Religious History* 7, no. 4 (1973): 324-341. Also published in WHS (NZ) Proceedings, 38, 1982.

Owens, J. M. R. 'William White and the Wesleyans.' *New Zealand's Heritage* 1 (1968): 292.

Owens, J. M. R. 'Christianity and the Maoris to 1840.' *New Zealand Journal of History* 2, no. 1 (April 1968): 18-40.

Owens, J. M. R. 'Missionary Medicine and Maori Health: The Record of the Wesleyan Mission to New Zealand before 1840.' *Journal of the Polynesian Society* 81 (December 1972): 418-36.

Oxford History of New Zealand, Second Edition, ed. Geoffrey W. Rice, Auckland: Oxford University Press, 1992.

Parr, C. J. 'A Missionary Library: Printed Attempts to Instruct the Maori 1815-1845.' *Journal of the Polynesian Society* 70, no. 4 (1961 1961): 429-50.

Parsonson, G. S. *The Conversion of Polynesia*. Hocken Lecture. Dunedin: Hocken Library University of Otago, 1984.

Paterson, Lachy. 'Ngā Ritenga Pai: Māori and Modernity in the 1850s.' *Journal of New Zealand Studies* new series 35 (2023) 22-35.

Paul VI, Pope. *Evangelization of the World*, Encyclical, Vatican City, 1976.

Petrie, Hazel. *Chiefs of Industry: Maori Tribal Enterprise in Early Colonial New Zealand*. Auckland: Auckland University Press, 2006.

Petrie, Hazel. 'The Sanctity of Bread: Missionaries and the Promotion of Wheat Growing among the New Zealand Māori.' In *Food and Faith in Christian Culture*, edited by K Albala and T Eden, 125-46. New York: Columbia University Press, 2011.

Phillipps, Donald J. *Companion to William Morley's History of Methodism In New Zealand: A Guide To Nineteenth Century New Zealand Methodism*. WHS (NZ), 2006.

Phillipps, Donald J. Māori and Methodism: A Perspective: The Wesleyan Mission in Aotearoa/New Zealand 1822-1855. 2010. Trinity Methodist College, Auckland.

Phillipps, Donald J. 'Methodism's Debt to Marsden.' *WHS (NZ) Journal*, Proceedings, 99 (2014): 34-48.

Phillipps, Donald J. 'The Handyman and the Idealists.' *Touchstone*, March 2023, 16.

Phillipps, Donald J. Te Taha Maori Register of Home Missionaries, Honorary Home Missionaries and Minita-a Iwi [unpublished paper, c 2014, available from Methodist Church Māori Division].

Phillipps, Donald J. 'A Register of Ministers of the Methodist Church of New Zealand' (Methodist Church of New Zealand website, 2020) https://www.methodist.org.nz/assets/Whakapapa/Archives/4-Methodist-history/Methodist-Biography-A-Z-29-March-2021-with-introduction-corrected.pdf

Phillipson, G. A. 'The Thirteenth Apostle, Bishop Selwyn and the Transplantation of Anglicanism in New Zealand, 1841-1868.' Ph. D. thesis, University of Otago, 1992.

Pinfold, James T. *Fifty Years in Maoriland*. London: The Epworth Press, 1930.

Pointon, D. M. *Memoirs of D. M. Pointon (Sister Dorothy) Including Her Work among the Maori People 1939-1953*. Auckland: The author, 1993.

Pratt, M. A. Rugby. *The Pioneering Days of Southern Maoriland*. London: Epworth Press, 1932.

Pratt, M. A. Rugby. *Rev. J. H. Bumby and the New Zealand Mission*. WHS (NZ) Proceedings, 4 no. 2, 1933.

Pratt, M. A. Rugby. *The Treaty of Waitangi. Governor Hobson Thanks Wesleyan Missionaries*. WHS (NZ) Proceedings. 4 no. 1, 1933.

Pratt, M. A. Rugby. *Nelson Methodist Centenary Souvenir 1842-1942*. WHS (NZ) Proceedings, 2 no. 1, Nelson: R.W. Stiles, 1942.

Prestidge, Paul. 'The Choices of Mary Anna Bumby.' *Historic Places in New Zealand*, no. 16 (March 1987): 20-21.

Prochner, Larry, Helen May, and Baljit Kaur. "The Blessings of Civilisation': Nineteenth-Century Missionary Infant Schools for Young Native Children in Three Colonial Settings--India, Canada and New Zealand 1820s-1840s.' *Paedagogica Historica: International Journal of the History of Education* 45, no. 1-2 (2009): 83-102.

Pukekawa Profile 1839-1970: a Tribute to our Pioneers Pukekohe: [Alpine Printers] 1970.

Punnett, Graham. 'The Maori and the Missionary: An Exploratory Study.' Master of Arts Research Exercise, Massey University, 2005.

Pybus, T. A. *Otakou and the First Christian Mission: A Brief Statement. Centenary Commemoration South Island*. Dunedin: O.D.T. Print, 1940.

Pybus, T. A. *Otakou: A Story for Far-Off Days*. WHS (NZ) Proceedings, 1, no. 2, 1941.

Pybus, T. A., and A.W. Reed. *Maori and Missionary: Early Christian Missions in the South Island of New Zealand*. Wellington: A.H. & A.W. Reed, 1954.

Rakena, Ruawai D. *The Maori Response to the Gospel: A Study of Maori-Pakeha Relations in the Methodist Maori Mission from Its Beginnings to the Present Day*. WHS (NZ) Proceedings, 25 nos. 1-4, 1971.

Ramsden, Eric. *Marsden and the Missions: Prelude to Waitangi*. Sydney: Angus & Roberston, 1936.

Reed, A. W. *The Fish-Hook Man (Samuel Leigh)*. Endeavour Books. Christchurch: Presbyterian Bookroom, 1942.

Reeson, Margaret. *Currency Lass*. Sutherland, NSW: Albatross, 1985.

Reeson, Margaret. *A Singular Woman*. Adelaide: OpenBook, 1999.

Reilly, Michael and Jane Thomson ed. '"When the Wave Rolled in Upon Us": Essays on Nineteenth Century Maori History*, edited by. Dunedin: University of Otago Press, 1998.

Reynolds, Henry. *This Whispering in Our Hearts*. St. Leonards NSW: Allan and Unwin, 1998.

Ritchie, John. *Lachlan Macquarie*. Melbourne: Melbourne University Press, 1986.

Ritchie, Samuel Gordon Gardiner. "'[T]he Sound of the Bell Amidst the Wilds": Evangelical Perceptions of Northern Aotearoa/New Zealand Maori and the Aboriginal Peoples of Port Phillip, Australia, C.1820s-1840s.' Master of Arts, Victoria University of Wellington, 2009.

Roberts, Dave. 'The Beechamdale Mission "a Day Well Spent".' *WHS (NZ) Journal 1991-92, Proceedings*, 58 (1992): 35-38.

Roberts, John H. 'Alternative Tourism with a Bicultural Slant: Canterbury Methodists Journey into Their Past.' *WHS (NZ) Journal '86, Proceedings*, 49 (1986): 11-16.

Roberts, John H. 'Nga Tupuna Maori O Te Hahi Weteriana I Te Waipounamu: Maori Ancestors of the Methodist Church in the South Island.' *Te Karanga* 5, no. 3 (November 1989): 7-17.

Roberts, John H. 'The Wesleyan Maori Mission at Te Aro.' *WHS (NZ) Journal '90, Proceedings*, 56 (1990): 14-49.

Roberts, John *H. The Wesleyan Maori Mission in Te Upoko O Te Ika Wellington District 1839-1885.* Christchurch: Methodist Publishing, 1992.

Roberts, John H., and Diana Roberts. 'Mary Bumby's Hive of Story: Review Article of Tanya Batt's Storytelling Performance.' *WHS (NZ) Journal, Proceedings*, 108 (2020): 28-32.

Rogers, Lawrence M., ed. *Early Journals of Henry Williams, Senior Missionary.* Christchurch: Pegasus, 1961.

Ross, Cathy. *Women with a Mission: Rediscovering Missionary Wives in Early New Zealand.* Auckland: Penguin, 2006.

Rossiter, Trish. 'Finding Thomas - the Search for My Great-Great-Grandfather.' *WHS (NZ) Journal*, 105 (2018): 12-23.

Rountree, Kathryn. 'Remaking the Maori Female Body: Marianne Williams's Mission in the Bay of Islands.' *Journal of Pacific History* 35, no. 1 (June 2000): 49-66.

Ruka, Jay. *Huia Come Home.* Oati, 2018.

Ryburn, Wayne, *Tall Spars, Steamers & Gum: a History of the Kaipara from Early European Settlement, 1854-1947.* Auckland: Kaipara Publications, 1999.

Salmond, Anne. *Between Worlds: Early Exchanges Between Maori and Europeans 1773-1815.* Auckland: Viking/Penguin Books, 1997.

Scholefield, Guy H. ed. *The Richmond-Atkinson Papers*, 2 v., Wellington: R. E. Owen, Government Printer, 1960.

Scholefield, G.H. ed. *Dictionary of New Zealand Biography*. 2.v., Wellington: Department of Internal Affairs, 1940.

Scott, Eleanor. 'James Buller's Journey to Wellington in 1839.' *Auckland & Waikato Historical Journal*, no. 13 (October 1968): 24-26.

Scott, Eleanor. 'Missionary Home-Making.' *Auckland & Waikato Historical Journal*, no. 10 (May 1967): 32-33.

Sharp, Andrew & Paul McHugh eds, *Histories, Power, and Loss*, Wellington: Bridget Williams Books, 2001.

Shawcross, Kathleen. 'The Maoris of the Bay of Islands 1769-1840: A Study of Changing Maori Responses to European Contact.' Master of Arts, University of Auckland, 1967.

Sherrin, R.A.A., J.H. Wallace, T.W. Leys. *From Earliest Times to 1840*, in, *Brett's Historical Series: Early History of New Zealand*, Auckland: H. Brett, 1890.

Silson, J. H. 'Early Missionary Journeys in the North Island of New Zealand.' Master of Arts, University of New Zealand Auckland University College, 1931.

Simmonds, E.R. *Pompallier: Prince of Bishops*. Auckland: CPC Publishing, 1984.

Sinclair, Karen. *Prophetic Histories: The People of the Maramatanga*. Wellington: Bridget Williams Books, 2002.

Sinclair, Keith. *A History of New Zealand*. Harmondsworth: Penguin Books, 1959; rev. ed., 1969, new impression, Auckland: Penguin 2000.

Sinclair, Sophia, ed. *Our Story: Aotearoa: The Story of Mission in Aotearoa through the Lens of the New Zealand Church Missionary Society*. Christchurch: New Zealand Church Missionary Society, 2014.

Smith, Bryan T. 'The Wesleyan Mission in the Waikato 1834-1841.' Master of Arts, University of New Zealand Auckland University College, 1948.

Smith, F. W. *Samuel Ironside and the Cloudy Bay Mission*. WHS (NZ) Proceedings, 10 no. 4 & 11 no. 1, 1953.

Snowden, Rita F. *The Ladies of Wesleydale*. WHS (NZ) Proceedings, 15 no. 2, 1956.

Sorrenson, M. P. K. 'How to Civilize Savages: Some "Answers" from Nineteenth-Century New Zealand.' *New Zealand Journal of History* 9, no. 2 (October 1975): 97-110.

Spooner, T. G. M. 'Missionary Enterprise in New Zealand before 1870.' Master of Arts, University of New Zealand Auckland University College, 1934.

Spooner, Thomas G. M. *Brother John; the Life of the Rev. John Hobbs*. WHS (NZ) Proceedings, 13 nos. 2-4, 1955.

Stack, James West, and A. H. Reed. *Early Maoriland Adventures of J. W. Stack*. Dunedin and Wellington: Reed, 1933.

Stack, James West. *Further Maoriland Adventures of J. W. Stack*. Dunedin and Wellington: Reed, 1938.

Stallworthy, John, *Early Northern Wairoa*. Dargaville, Wairoa Bell & Northern Advertiser print, 1916.

Stenhouse, John, and Jane Thomson. *Building God's Own Country: Historical Essays on Religions in New Zealand*. Dunedin: University of Otago Press, 2004.

Stenhouse, John & G.A Wood eds., *Christianity, Modernity and Culture: New Perspectives on New Zealand History*. ATF Series 15. Adelaide: ATF Press, 2005.

Stott, Anne. 'Hannah More and the Blagdon Controversy, 1799–1802', *Journal of Ecclesiastical History*, 51 no.2 (2000): 319–346.

Strachan, Alexander. *Remarkable Incidents in the Life of the Rev. Samuel Leigh Missionary to the Settlers and Savages of Australia and New Zealand: With a Succinct History of the Origin and Progress of the Missions in Those Colonies*. London: Hamilton, Adams, 1853.

Sutherland, Yvonne. 'Te Reo O Te Perehi: Messages to Maori in the Wesleyan Newspaper, Te Haeata, 1859-1862.' Master of Arts, University of Auckland, 1999.

Taylor, W.A. *Lore and History of the South Island Maori*, Christchurch: Bascands Ltd, [1951, 1952].

Tennant, Margaret. 'Pakeha Deaconesses and the New Zealand Methodist Mission to Maori, 1893-1940.' *Journal of Religious History* 23, no. 3 (October 1999): 309-26.

Tennant, Margaret. '"Sometimes When My Heart Was Sad with Snubs and Coldness..." Narrative of Maori Mission Work.' *History Now: Te Pae Tawhito o te Wa* 7, no. 3 (August 2001): 14-18.

Tennant, Margaret. 'Sisterly Ministrations: The Social Work of Protestant Deaconesses in New Zealand.' *New Zealand Journal of History* 32, no. 1 (April 1998): 3-22.

'The Methodist Mission House from Hokianga.' *Auckland & Waikato Historical Journal*, no. 19 (September 1971): 2-3.

Thompson, Susan J. 'Knowledge and Vital Piety: Methodist Ministry Education in New Zealand from the 1840s to 1988.' Ph.D., University of Auckland, 2002.

Thompson, Susan J. *Knowledge & Vital Piety: Education for Methodist Ministry in New Zealand from the 1840s*. WHS (NZ) Proceedings, 90 & 91, 2010.

Thompson, L., and J. B. W. Roberton. 'Te Kopua.' *Journal Te Awamutu Historical Society*, no. 7 (December 1972): 40-66.

Thomson, Arthur S. *The Story of New Zealand: Past and Present, Savage and Civilized*. London: John Murray, 1859; reprinted, New York, Praeger Scholarly Reprint, 1970.

Troughton, Geoffrey, ed. *Pacifying Missions: Christianity, Violence, and Empire in the Nineteenth Century*. Leiden: Brill, 2023.

Troughton, Geoffrey, and Philip Fountain, eds. *Pursuing Peace in Godzone: Christianity and the Peace Tradition in New Zealand*. Wellington: Victoria University Press, 2018.

Troughton, Geoffrey. 'Scripture, Piety and the Practice of Peace in Nineteenth-Century New Zealand Missions.' *Studies in World Christianity* 25, no. 2 (2019): 128-44.

Troughton Geoffrey and Stuart Lange eds. *Sacred Histories in Secular New Zealand*, Wellington: Victoria University Press, 2016.

Troughton, Geoffrey and Hugh Morrison eds. *The Spirit of the Past: Essays on Christianity in New Zealand History*, Wellington: Victoria University Press, 2011.

Tuato'o, D. "'Te Tahi O Pipiri': Literacy and Missionary Pedagogy as Mechanism in Change: The Reactions of Three Rangatira from the Bay of Islands, 1814-1834." Master of Arts, University of Otago, 1999.

Turley, C. B. 'The Claim of Maori Identity on the Cultural Structure of Church and Society in New Zealand.' D.Min thesis, Claremont University, 1977.

Turner, Harold. 'The Gospel's Mission to Culture in New Zealand', [1992], https://www.latimer.org.nz/wp-content/uploads/Harold-Turner-The-Gospels-Mission-to-Culture-in-New-Zealand.pdf.

Turner, John Munsey. *Conflict and Reconciliation: Studies in Methodism and Ecumenism in England, 1740-1982.* London: Epworth, 1985.

Turner, Josiah G. *The Pioneer Missionary: Life of the Rev. Nathaniel Turner, Missionary in New Zealand, Tonga and Australia.* Melbourne: Robertson & Wesleyan Bookroom, 1872.

Twells, Alison. *The Civilizing Mission and the English Middle Class, 1792-1850: The 'Heathen' at Home and Overseas.* Basingstoke: Palgrave Macmillan, 2009.

Twyman, Erin. 'Worthy Helpmeets: Mission Wives of Early New Zealand.' Post-graduate Diploma, University of Otago, 1991.

Udy, Gloster S. *Spark of Grace: The Story of the Methodist Church in Parramatta and the Surrounding Region.* Parramatta: Epworth Press, 1977.

Udy, James S. and Eric G. Clancy eds. *Dig or Die*, Sydney: World Methodist Historical Society, 1981.

Vyle, H. R. *A Hundred Years of Methodist Witness in Hamilton: St. Paul's Church London Street.* WHS (NZ) Proceedings, 20 no. 4, 1964.

Waitangi Tribunal. *He Whakaputanga me te Tiriti | The Declaration and the Treaty: The Report on Stage 1 of the Te Paparahi o te Raki Inquiry (WAI 1040).* Lower Hutt: Waitangi Tribunal, 2014.

Waitangi Tribunal. Muriwhenua Land Report (Wai 45), Lower Hutt: Waitangi Tribunal, 1997.

Walker, Michelle. 'The Methodist Home Mission Party, on Stage in New Zealand, 1924–1934.' *Journal of New Zealand Studies*, no. 15 (2013): 77-89.

Walker, R. B. 'The Growth and Typology of the Wesleyan Methodist Church in New South Wales, 1812-1901.' *Journal of Religious History*, 6 no. 4 (December 1971): 331-347.

Wallace, Ritane. 'Kotahi Anō Te Tupuna O Te Tangata Māori, Ko Ranginui E Tū Nei, Ko Papatūānuku E Takato Nei. Colonisation through Christianity.' Master of Māori and Pacific Development, University of Waikato, 2021.

Wanhalla, Angela. 'The 'Bickerings' of the 'Mangungu Brethren': Talk, Tales and Rumour in Early New Zealand.' *Journal of New Zealand Studies*, no. 12 (2011): 13-28.

Wanhalla, Angela. *Matters of the Heart: A History of Interracial Marriage in New Zealand*. Auckland: Auckland University Press, 2013.

Ward, Alan. *A Show of Justice: Racial 'Amalgamation' in Nineteenth Century New Zealand*. Canberra: Australian National University Press, 'Corrected edn.', Auckland: Auckland & Oxford University Presses, 1995.

Ward, Judith. 'The Invention of Papahurihia.' Ph.D., Massey University, 2016.

Ward, Robert. *Life among the Maories of New Zealand: Being a Description of Missionary, Colonial and Military Achievements*. Edited by Thomas Lowe and William Whitby. London: G. Lamb, 1872.

Ward, W.R. *Religion and Society in England, 1790-1850*, London: B.T. Batsford, 1972

Ward, W.R. *The Early Correspondence of Jabez Bunting 1820–1829*. London: Royal Historical Society, 1972.

Ward, W.R., *The Early Correspondence of Jabez Bunting 1830–1858*, Oxford: Oxford University Press, 1976.

Wesleyan Methodist Missionary Society. *The First Report of the General Wesleyan Methodist Missionary Society*, London, 1818/

'Wesleyan Missionary Farm School, Kaiiwi.' Whanganui Historical Society *Historical Record* 19, no. 1 (May 1988): 11-12.

Wharemaru, Heeni, and Mary Katherine Duffie. *Heeni: A Tainui Elder Remembers*. Auckland: HarperCollins, 1997.

White, Claire Kaahu. *Te Pou Herenga Waka O Rehua: The Story of Rehua Hostel and Marae - the First Fifty Years*. Christchurch: Te Whatumanawa, Maoritanga O Rehua Trust Board, 2021.

Whyle, Ivan. 'By a Mysterious Providence.' *WHS (NZ) Journal '90*, Proceedings, 56 (1990): 65-73.

Whyle, Ivan. *Rev. John Bumby Sesquicentennial Commemoration June 26 1990*. Auckland: Author for Methodist Church of Aotearoa New Zealand, 1990.

Wiley, H.E.R.L. *South Auckland*, Pukekohe: Franklin Printing & Publishing Co, 1939.

Williams, William James. *Centenary Sketches of New Zealand Methodism*. Christchurch: Lyttelton Times Co., 1922.

Williamson, L. A. D. 'The Relations between the Various Missions in New Zealand up to the Hauhau Outbreak 1814-1864.' Master of Arts, University of New Zealand, 1934.

Williment, Tolla M. I. *John Hobbs 1800-1883: Wesleyan Missionary to the Ngapuhi Tribe of Northern New Zealand*. Wellington: Government Printer, 1985.

Willing, Len. *'Ready, Willing and Able-': One Man's Bicultural Journey*. Red Beach: Colcom Press, 1996.

Willyams, Michelle. 'A Brief History of the Waiata Maori Choir, 1924-1938.' *WHS (NZ) Journal*, Proceedings, 95 (2012): 19-26.

Willyams, Michelle. 'Singing Faith: A History of the Waiata Maori Choir, 1924-1938.' Master of Arts, University of Otago, 2012.

Wohlers, Johann F. H. *On the Conversion and Civilization of the Maoris in the South Island of New Zealand.* Transactions of the New Zealand Institute. Wellington: New Zealand Institute, 1881.

Woodburn, Susan. 'Making Books for God: Mission Printing in the Pacific Islands and Australia.' *Bulletin (Bibliographical Society of Australia and New Zealand)* 27, no. 3-4 (2003): 91-106.

Woodfield, Mary-Anne. 'Sowing the Gospel of Peace: Missionary James Watkin at Karitāne and Wellington, 1840-1855.' Master of Arts, Victoria University of Wellington, 2016.

Woods, S. E. 'The Translation of the Bible into Maori.' *Journal Tauranga Historical Society*, no. 51 (August 1974): 10-15.

Wright Don & Eric G. Clancy. *The Methodists: A History of Methodism in New South Wales.* Sydney: Allen and Unwin, 1993.

Wright, Harrison M. *New Zealand 1769-1840: Early Years of Western Contact.* Cambridge, Mass.: Harvard University Press, 1959.

Yarwood, A. T. *Samuel Marsden: The Great Survivor.* Wellington: A.H. & A.W. Reed, 1977. 1996.

Yates, Timothy. *The Conversion of the Maori: Years of Religious and Social Change, 1814-1842.* Studies in the History of Christian Missions. Grand Rapids: Eerdmans, 2013.

About the Contributors

Roshan Allpress has since 2017 been the National Principal and CEO of Laidlaw College. He holds degrees in History from Canterbury and Oxford, with research interests in the history of social and cultural reform, evangelicalism and religious reform, the origins of philanthropy and humanitarianism, and intersections of theology and political economic thought. He is a fellow of the Royal Historical Society. He is the author of *British Philanthropy in the Globalizing World: Entrepreneurs and Evangelicals, 1756-1840*, published by Oxford University Press in 2023.

Gary Clover completed a thesis on the Wesleyans' South Taranaki Mission to graduate from Auckland University with an MA Honours degree majoring in early New Zealand's colonial history under Professors Judith Binney and Keith Sorrenson, in 1973. During short stints at the Alexander Turnbull Library and the Canterbury Public Library, followed by thirty years as a Methodist parish presbyter, and on into retirement, he continued exploring and writing about how it was that Māori embraced Christianity in Āotearoa-New Zealand. His publications include a biography of the Wesleyans' missionary printer William Woon (WHS Proceedings, 97, 2014), and *Collision, Compromise and Conversion* (2018) a critical study of the Wesleyans' Hokianga mission at Māngungu; also numerous journal articles.

Peter Lineham is Professor Emeritus of History at Massey University, and in retirement continues to research widely on New Zealand's religious history. He was awarded membership of the Order of New Zealand in 2019 for services to religious history and for community service. His books include *There we found Brethren* (1977), *No Ordinary Union* (1980), *Bible and Society* (1996), *Destiny* (2013), *Sunday Best* (2017), and *Agency of Hope* (2020), and he co-edited the standard text on New Zealand's religious history, *Transplanted Christianity*. He is also well-known as a commentator in the media on religious trends in New Zealand. He has contributed to the WHS previously in Proceedings 42 on Methodist Evangelism, Proceedings 98 on North Shore churches and edited Proceedings 83-84 on Wesley's South Seas Heritage.

Glen O'Brien is Professor of Christian History and Thought in the University of Divinity, Melbourne, where he serves as Research Coordinator at Eva Burrows College, one of the twelve colleges of the University. A Uniting Church in Australia minister, he is a member of the Methodist Roman Catholic International Commission and of the Board of IAMSCU (International Association of Methodist-Related Schools, Colleges and Universities). He is widely published in the field of Wesleyan and Methodist studies, including *Methodism in Australia: A History*, edited with Hilary Carey (Ashgate/Routledge 2015), *Wesleyan-Holiness Churches in Australia* (Routledge, 2018), and *John Wesley's Political World* (Routledge, 2023). His co-edited book with Arseny Ermakov, '*A Curious Machine': Wesleyan Reflections on the Post-Human Future* (Wipf and Stock, 2023) was shortlisted for the 2024 Australian Christian Book of the Year.

Rowan Tautari (Te Whakapiko o Ngāti Manaia, Ngāti Kahu o Torongare, Ngātihine) is a historian who crafts stories that reflect Māori values and lived experience. She lives at a coastal papakāinga (ancestral settlement) in Northland, Aotearoa/New Zealand, and her work is inspired by the land and the sea.

Susan Thompson is a Methodist minister currently working as Chaplain at the Tamahere Eventide Home and Village in the Waikato. Born in Christchurch, she completed postgraduate studies at the University of Canterbury, trained for ministry at Trinity College, Auckland and undertook doctoral studies at the University of Auckland. Susan's main research interests are New Zealand Methodist Church history. Her 2002 PhD thesis was published by the Wesley Historical Society in 2010 as *Knowledge & Vital Piety: Education for Methodist Ministry in New Zealand from the 1840s*. She has also been an active member of the WHS committee and has contributed to several of its journals.

Geoffrey Troughton is Associate Professor in the Study of Religion at Victoria University of Wellington. His research addresses issues in New Zealand religious history, modern Christianity, and contemporary religious change. Major publications include *New Zealand Jesus* (2011), and numerous edited volumes including *Saints and Stirrers* (2017), *Pursuing Peace in Godzone* (2018), and *Pacifying Missions* (2023).

www.ingramcontent.com/pod-product-compliance
Lightning Source LLC
Chambersburg PA
CBHW080954120626
46546CB00010B/2889